Arab Spring-Arab Fall

Arab Spring-Arab Fall

Divergent Transitions in post-2011 Tunisia and Egypt

Ayfer Erdogan

LEXINGTON BOOKS
Lanham • Boulder • New York • London

Published by Lexington Books
An imprint of The Rowman & Littlefield Publishing Group, Inc.
4501 Forbes Boulevard, Suite 200, Lanham, Maryland 20706
www.rowman.com

6 Tinworth Street, London SE11 5AL, United Kingdom

Copyright © 2021 by The Rowman and Littlefield Publishing Group, Inc.

All rights reserved. No part of this book may be reproduced in any form or by any electronic or mechanical means, including information storage and retrieval systems, without written permission from the publisher, except by a reviewer who may quote passages a review.

British Library Cataloguing in Publication Information Available

Library of Congress Cataloging-in-Publication Data
Library of Congress Control Number: 2020949432
ISBN 978-1-7936-1067-6 (cloth)
ISBN 978-1-7936-1069-0 (pbk)
ISBN 978-1-7936-1068-3 (electronic)

*To All Those Who Fought Relentlessly and Died
for Dignity, Justice, and Freedom . . .*

Contents

List of Illustrations	ix
Preface	xi
Acknowledgments	xiii
List of Abbreviations	xv
Introduction	1
1 On Democracy and Democratic Transitions	9
2 Democratization in the Arab Middle East Context	27
3 The Tunisian Revolution	35
4 Egypt's Failed Revolution	83
5 Democratic Divergence between Egypt and Tunisia in the Post-Arab Spring Context	155
Conclusion	215
Bibliography	223
Index	245
About the Author	255

List of Illustrations

FIGURES

5.1	Lipset's Modernization Theory	164
5.2	Models of Transitions in Tunisia and Egypt	169

TABLES

3.1	Timeline of the Key Events during the Tunisian Revolution	51
4.1	Timeline of the Key Events during the Egyptian Revolution	105

Preface

The idea to write a book emerged during the course of my research for dissertation entitled *Transitions from Authoritarian Rule: A Comparative Analysis between Tunisia and Egypt Post-Arab Spring* (2018). Transitions from authoritarian rule sought to explain the divergent transition experiences of Tunisia and Egypt post-2011.

Following the recent wave of uprisings that shook the Arab world to its very foundations in 2011, I was astonished by the remarkable differences in the transitional outcomes of the post-Arab Spring states. While the wave of popular protests ousted the long-entrenched autocrats in Tunisia and Egypt in few weeks, it led to protracted civil wars in most of the region swept by the popular protests. Surprisingly enough, the political system in some states witnessed superficial changes and it remained almost intact in others. These different transitional paths prompted me to investigate the factors that led to such divergent outcomes. To this end, I chose two cases—Tunisia and Egypt—two geographically proximate countries that share various similarities both prior and following the uprisings as a starting point. Various books have been published on what happened in post-Arab Spring states such as Egypt, Tunisia, or Libya or why the course of transition ended up in conflict or chaos. Yet, how and why transition experiences have indicated such divergence in post-2011 remained underexplored.

Investigating the divergent outcomes of the transitions in Tunisia and Egypt, I analyzed the impact of structure versus agent. While arguing that agent lies central to determining the outcome of any regime change from authoritarianism, from the outset, I sensed that the impact of agents cannot be analyzed in isolation from structural factors, in other words, historical, institutional, and political structures in which transitions took place. Therefore, this work goes beyond a clear-cut theoretical framework.

The book provides a brief analysis of the concepts and theories in democratization literature and the historical background of the regime changes in Tunisia and Egypt. Then, it compares the two countries in terms of democratic outcome in post-2011 and analyzes the factors that have impacted the trajectory of their political transitions. The book also incorporates the literature accumulated during the former regime changes in democracy's third wave to the transitional outcomes of the post-Arab Spring Egypt and Tunisia.

Writing on the political developments in the Middle East is almost like trying to catch up with something that is in a constant state of flux. By the time you have done your research and published your article, it might become obsolete. The hypotheses that seem valid and strong once could become irrelevant. This simple fact makes us to face the limits of studying an ever-shifting region. It also forces us to be more humble in the claims we put forward and avoid big-bounded generalizations. In that regard, this book must be seen as a point of departure for further research investigating the Arab Middle East and the question of democratization.

Acknowledgments

This book would not have come out without the invaluable support I received from many people. I would like to express my sincere gratitude to Prof. Ozden Zeynep Oktav who supervised this work in its original form as a doctoral dissertation submitted to the Department of Political Science at Yıldız Technical University (Turkey). Her valuable contributions enabled to develop this work combining empirical developments with theoretical framework. I am greatly indebted to Prof. Omer Caha who was my former supervisor and continued to provide me with insightful and constructive comment even after his change of workplace. I would also like to thank Joseph Parry and Alison Keefner, the senior acquisitions editor and the assistant editor of Lexington Books, for their tremendous support from the initial phase of the manuscript preparation to the final publication. Their assistance and encouragement were key to achieving this mission. Last but not the least, I would like to express my heartfelt gratitude to my mother Aysel Erdogan for her relentless support, patience, and encouragement during the writing of this book in particular, and in life in general. My most sincere thanks are dedicated to my beloved grandmother, Mahture Kayser, who didn't live up to see the publication of this book. She will be forever missed and remembered with a smile on our faces. May she rest in peace!

List of Abbreviations

ARP: The Assembly of the Representatives of the People
AST: Ansar Al-Sharia Tunisia
ASU: Arab Socialist Union
CGT: Confédération Générale du Travail (General Confederation of Labour)
CPR: Congrès pour la République (Congress for the Republic)
CSO: Civil Society Organization
ETUF: The Egyptian Trade Union Federation
EU: The European Union
FJP: Freedom and Justice Party
GDP: Gross Domestic Product
ICER: Independent Commission for Election Review
IMF: International Monetary Fund
ISIE: Instance Supérieure Indépendante pour les Elections (Independent High Authority for Elections)
ISIS: Islamic State of Iraq and Syria
FPTP: First-Past-the-Post
LTDH: Ligue Tunisienne de Droits de l'Homme (Tunisian Human Rights League)
MB: Muslim Brotherhood
MCC: Millennium Challenge Corporation
MENA: Middle East and North Africa
MEPI: Middle East Partnership Initiative
MERF: Middle East Response Fund
MOU: Memorandum of Understanding
MP: Member of Parliament

MTI:	Mouvement de la Tendance Islamique (Islamic Tendency Movement)
NAC:	National Association for Change
NCA:	National Constituent Assembly
NDP:	National Democratic Party
NGO:	Nongovernmental Organization
NSF:	National Salvation Front
ODA:	Official Development Assistance
OECD:	Organization for Economic Cooperation and Development
ONAT:	Ordre National des Avocats de Tunisie (Tunisian Bar Association)
OPIC:	Overseas Private Investment Corporation
PDP:	Progressive Democratic Party
PR:	Proportional Representation
PSD:	Parti Socialiste Destourien (Socialist Destourien Party)
RCC:	Revolutionary Command Council
RCD:	Rassemblement Constitutionnel Démocratique (Constitutional Democratic Rally)
SAC:	Supreme Administrative Court
SAP:	Structural Adjustment Program
SCAF:	Supreme Court of the Armed Forces
SCC:	Supreme Constitutional Court
SPEC:	Supreme Presidential Electoral Commission
TAF:	Tunisian Armed Forces
UAE:	United Arab Emirates
UGTT:	Union Générale Tunisienne du Travail (Tunisian General Labour Union)
UPL:	Union Patriotique Libre (Free Patriotic Union)
US:	United States
USAID:	United States Agency for International Development
UTICA:	l'Union Tunisienne de l'Industrie, du Commerce et de l'Artisanat (Tunisian Union of Industry, Commerce and Handicrafts)

Introduction

A global wave of democratization originated from 1970s onward with the fall of dictatorships in Southern Europe and the militaries handing over power to civilian governments in Latin America. In 1989, the disintegration of the Soviet Union and the collapse of communism paved the way for stunning transformations in the former communist regimes in Central and Eastern Europe, most of which have become consolidated democracies over the last few decades. Finally, democratic transitions swept through Sub-Saharan Africa in the mid-1990s and occurred in some parts of Asia. This global democratization trend since the mid-1970s was termed as "Third Wave of Democratization" by Samuel Huntington.[1] To some political scientists, the end of the Cold War meant that there isn't any respectable alternative to democracy any longer and democracy has advanced both normatively and practically while the rise of liberal democracy would be the final form of human government and the endpoint of mankind's ideological evolution, widely known as "The End of History."[2] Surprisingly enough, the democratic wave that swept many regions of the world from Southern Europe to Latin America, and from Eastern Europe to Asia Pacific countries in the second half of the twentieth century bypassed the Middle East and North Africa (MENA). Whereas many countries of the developing world progressed toward some form of democracy, if not fully fledged one, the Arab world saw a trend that was totally opposite to the global trend. The data provided by the Freedom House indicated that no Arab country in the region was considered free before 2011. Given the long history of autocratic rule in the Middle East, the mainstream scholarship on Arab politics centered on "Arab exceptionalism"; in other words, scholars sought to come up with explanations for the lack of democratic governance in the region while investigating the means, tools, and tactics used by the autocrats to maintain power. For those scholars, historical background, the rise of ethnic and sectarian tensions bringing forth the problem of a unified nation-state, political economy, institutional legacy, the incompatibility of Islam with democracy are assumed to account for the democracy deficit and the failure to set up an accountable political system in the region.

The outbreak of the popular protests in December 2010, following the self-immolation of the street vendor Mohammed Bouazizi in Sidi Bouzid, in Tunisia, marked a critical turning point in the Arab political history. The popular protests, or the uprisings, were labeled by many regional and international observers as the "Arab Spring." The self-immolation of Bouazizi was an act of protest against the police and municipal officials who seized his wares and mistreated him, but more importantly it was a protest to the long-standing injustice and oppression under Ben Ali regime. The protests demanding the fall of the Ben Ali regime in Sidi Bouzid ignited the wick spreading to neighboring cities in Tunisia and the wider Arab world. The overthrow of Ben Ali was a breakthrough for the Arab publics since they saw that the long-entrenched authoritarian regimes were not as tough and robust as they were once believed to be, and change was not impossible.

Only eleven days after the toppling of Ben Ali regime, thousands of protestors gathered in Tahrir Square demanding the resignation of the president of Egypt, Hosni Mubarak. After two weeks of protests and bloodshed, on February 11, Mubarak had to step down and hand over his powers to the Supreme Council of the Armed Forces. Encouraged by protestors' success in bringing down the dictators in Tunisia and Egypt, popular protests broke out in Syria, Libya, Yemen, and Bahrain; however, in these countries, the outpourings of popular discontent culminated in protracted civil wars between either competing political forces or opposition groups and ruling regimes. Protests also arose in Oman, Morocco, Jordan, and Algeria, yet they didn't lead to a breakdown of the authoritarian regimes. The Arab uprisings left virtually no country unaffected in the region while generating divergent outcomes across the region.

Following the wave of popular protests that shook several Arab states to their very foundations, it was only Tunisia and Egypt where their authoritarian leaders were ousted rather in short period of time and with relatively little violence witnessed. The two countries successfully moved toward a democratic form of government with free and fair elections held in the year that followed the overthrow of the dictators. On the other hand, democratic transition prospects were soon overthrown by a military coup in Egypt in 2013; the uprisings in Libya and Syria were succeeded by protracted civil war among rival factions seeking control over territory; the protests movements were suppressed to consolidate a minority-led regime in Bahrain with a military intervention by neighboring Gulf Arab states; and internal conflict emerged in Yemen in 2015 as two factions—Houthi forces supported by Iran and the Yemeni government supported by the United Arab Emirates (UAE) and Saudi Arabia—claimed to constitute the Yemeni government along with their supporters and allies. In the Arab states affected by revolutionary protests, political and economic instability has taken root and violence has become normalized and no progress has been witnessed as to democratic reforms and freedoms; in other words, the Arab Spring movements gave way to the long-standing Arab winter.

The popular protests in early 2011 reflected at least the aspirations of Arab publics for democratic governance and accountability and their quest for freedom, dignity, and justice. Bread, freedom, and social justice were the rallying cries of the Arab uprisings which revealed long-standing demands that were neither acknowledged nor addressed by their respective rulers. Through street protests and strikes that lasted for several days, Arab citizens sought not only to push for a more just, accountable, and equitable system of governance but also to redefine the relationship between the ruler and the ruled. However, almost a decade after the uprisings, it became evident that those demands remained unfulfilled and worse still, the region is now plagued by political instability, violence, growing threat of terrorism, economic crisis which forced millions of refugees to look for a host country to lead their lives in more humane conditions. The gloomy political scene and security atmosphere accompanied by economic challenges in the region led many observers including me to rename this recent wave of uprisings and the transition that followed as the "Arab winter."

In the initial phase of the Arab Spring movements, Tunisia and Egypt were the two countries that raised hopes for democratic change. The two countries didn't fall victim to ethnic, sectarian, and tribal tensions that have paralyzed other states in the region. They largely enjoyed national unity and strong popular sentiments for a nation-state. After liberation from Western colonialism, Tunisia and Egypt went through similar political and economic developments including state-led economic policies followed by stagnation in the 1960s and opening up their markets with the adoption of economic liberalization from 1980s onwards. In terms of their political systems, both countries were ruled by liberal autocrats who sought to create a democratic facade while in reality employing various strategies to maintain their power. To this end, both autocrats at times opened the way for political liberalization and limited space for opposition groups and civil society, followed by a period of political deliberalization in which political dissent were suppressed cruelly and space for opposition was largely closed.

Moreover, the initial period of the Arab Spring movements in Tunisia and Egypt bears remarkable similarities. In both countries, a year after the deposition of autocrats, free and fair elections were held leading to the electoral victory of the moderate Islamist groups, the Muslim Brotherhood, and Ennahda. In both political settings, the initial transition period was volatile and marked by growing polarization between the two camps; the Islamists who have long aspired to become a part of the political game, and the seculars who viewed the rise of Islamists as a threat for their country's future political development.

Nine years in retrospect, the hopes raised for a democratic change in Egypt were largely dashed in only two years following the uprisings, whereas Tunisia became the only beacon of hope glittering out of the Arab Spring. Tunisia achieved several milestones in its transition to democracy by having political power peacefully transferred from one political force to another twice and took important steps toward consolidating its democracy with the most progressive constitution in the region adopted in 2014 and made substantial headway in civil and political liberties. Despite several challenges and limitations lying ahead, Tunisia remains as the only success story of the Arab Spring movements. Egypt, in contrast, saw its first freely elected president and the Muslim Brotherhood government thrown out by the army in a coup d'état, surprisingly with much popular support, yet the coup resulted in a regime that is no less authoritarian than Mubarak's. Since the coup in 2013, Egypt's political landscape gradually reverted to the *ancient* regime with the return of abusive practices under the state's robust security apparatus and the arbitrary application of law to suppress political dissent.

On the other hand, Tunisia was able to get out of the political gridlock through a transition guided by negotiation and compromise in stark contrast to Egypt which was stuck in the early phase of the transition by the failure or reluctance of political actors to negotiate a mutual solution to the long-standing ideological divisions. Despite numerous similarities in their historical background and the way how political developments in the initial period of their transitions unfolded, Tunisia and Egypt took very divergent paths in their democratic development, which presented scholars in the field of comparative politics and specifically transition studies with an important question: "Under what conditions does a democratic transition occur?"

There is a rich scholarly literature that investigates conditions or drivers that make democracy a likely outcome or hinder prospects for democratization in the aftermath of a regime change based on the former democratic transition experiences observed in different regions of the world. The former transition experiences have indicated that not all regime changes end up in a democratic outcome just as there is no single universally acceptable route to democratization. Recent history regarding regime changes has shown that among dozens of transition experiences succeeded by popular protests only some ended up in becoming fully fledged democracies; in some other countries, democratic transition reversed generating a new form of authoritarianism or a hybrid regime which combines some notable aspects of democracy with authoritarian rule, while some countries became fully entrenched autocracies with no progress in civil and political rights.

The variations in the democratic outcome following regime breakdown prompted scholars in the field of democratization to come up with different theoretical approaches that have offered a wide range of analytical frameworks accounting for causal links between a set of variables and democratic transition. To some scholars in this field, democracy is most likely to come out in a country that enjoys high level of socioeconomic development, GDP per capita incomes, literacy levels, and industrialization to a considerable extent, which are assumed to equip a society with necessary attributes to create a democratic system. For some other scholars, democracy can't be simply correlated with the indices of economic development. Instead, democratic transition is driven by consensus and commitment to democracy by elites. According to those scholars, when authoritarian regime falls down, it is a set of actors which seek to define or redefine the rules of the new system based on mutual guarantees to serve the shared interests of those engaged in democratic crafting process. Still, there are other political scientists who view variations in democratic outcome of transitions as a result of the relationship between economy and politics. They argue that it is the economic crisis that is most likely to bring about regime change or the transformation of the authoritarian regime while failure to handle economic challenges effectively would obstruct chances for democratic consolidation.

In the light of the existing literature on comparative study of democratic transitions, this book provides a detailed analysis into the political, economic, and constitutional developments in Tunisia and Egypt following the fall of the authoritarian regimes and compares the two countries in terms of the divergence in their democratic outcomes since the fall of the authoritarian regimes up to the present. The book mainly centers its focus on the role of the political actors in designing the transition and explores the transitional period with respect to the interactions among the political elite and their cost–benefit assumptions, ideological interests as well as their commitments to democratic processes. However, various structural factors also come to fore when political actors engage in negotiations, bargain over key issues and make decisions that lie at the heart of the transitional process. In other words, political and historical structures are closely linked to agents' choices and decision-making at critical points as they make agents more or less compromising depending on the context. Hence, structural factors could not be totally isolated from the study of democratic transitions, instead, they should be analyzed in relation to their influence on pushing certain actors to compromise or discouraging them from coming to terms with their opponents on the key issues central to a transition. Eventually, this book seeks to answer why Egypt's path to democratization has been eroded by several transitional actors, whereas Tunisian political elite managed to address critical challenges during the transition and enabled the country to transition to democracy by acting within the boundaries of democratic game. Last but not the least, by combining historical background with contemporary politics, this study will be a launching pad for further studies on this topic and contribute to the existing literature on the Middle East and North African politics.

This book is divided into mainly five chapters. Chapter I offers a discussion of the key concepts and approaches that will be used in this study and provides an overview into the two theories of democratization—the transition and the modernization theory—with their prospects and pitfalls in explaining the complex nature of a transitional period. Chapter II follows with a discussion of democratization in the Arab Middle East context and investigates the reasons why the Middle East has been resilient to the global democratic waves in the light of the scholarly literature accumulated so far.

Chapters III and IV are organized similarly. First, they present the political and economic developments that led up to the popular protests in Tunisia and Egypt; in other words, the causes of the popular protests that are rooted in people's long-standing political and economic grievances. Second, they offer an in-depth analysis into the transition process that succeeded the fall of Ben Ali and Hosni Mubarak, respectively, and continued up to present. In these sections, key political developments are highlighted such as elections, the establishment of the interim governments, the disputes surrounding the constitutional drafting and political crises in the two countries, as well as the National Dialogue and political developments that followed in Tunisia and the coup and its aftermath in Egypt. Finally, these chapters analyze the peculiar characteristics and the historical evolution of key political actors and the critical role played by them during the popular protests and the transition.

Chapter V is the core of this book where the bulk of analysis and theoretical contributions are made. The chapter first compares the structuralist and agency-centered approaches in their explanatory power to analyze the variations in democratic outcome of transitions in Tunisia and Egypt in the post-Arab Spring context. Subsequently, the chapter mainly propounds six variables to account for the democratic divergence between the two countries. Among these variables, the degree to which elite consensus took place, strategic choices during the transition and the leadership styles of political Islamist movements largely determined the outcome of the transitional processes in two countries. However, political actors were motivated or constrained by a set of a structural factors that influenced their calculations, compromising or noncompromising attitudes and decision-making processes. In this regard, this chapter explores the role of the military, civil society, external actors, and the power equilibrium among divergent political forces as critical factors that had significant impact on the cost–benefit analyses of political decision-makers. A thorough comparative analysis between the two countries on the basis of those factors largely explains why Tunisia was able to successfully transition to democracy, but not Egypt.

NOTES

1. The first wave included establishment and strengthening of the Western democracies (United States, United Kingdom, France, and North European countries) during the era between the French Revolution and the World War I. The second wave of democratization took place following the World War II with the democratization of Germany, Italy, Japan, and some postcolonial countries. Finally, the third began in the mid-1970s in Southern Europe, and more than sixty to seventy countries throughout Europe, Latin America, Asia. and Africa underwent some form of democratic transition.

2. Francis Fukuyama, *The End of History and the Last Man* (New York: The Free Press, 1992).

Chapter 1

On Democracy and Democratic Transitions

Since democracy became the subject of political philosophy and political theory, there has been considerable debate on how to define and use the term "democracy." The terminology is derived from the Greek words *demos* meaning people and *kratos*, meaning power or rule, thus, *demokratia* means "rule by the people." John Keane defines democracy as the "self-government of equals."[1] However, this simple definition brings some fundamental questions, such as "who are these equals?" and "how does self-governing take place?" In theory, democracy is an egalitarian form of government in which all citizens determine public policy, laws, and the policies of the state together, nonetheless, in practice, it is the extent to which a given system approximates this ideal and a political system is uttered as democracy as long as it allows certain approximation to ideal democracy.

The term "democracy" has no clear core meaning that is universally applicable and essentially objective. A classical definition of democracy has been given by Abraham Lincoln as "the rule of the people, by the people, for the people." However, democracy as the rule of the people doesn't mean much for contemporary democracy today. Giovanni Sartori defines democracy by explaining what it is not: "democracy is a system in which no one can choose himself, no one can invest himself with the power to rule and, therefore, no one can abrogate to himself unconditional and unlimited power."[2] In his prominent work, Huntington defines a twentieth-century political system as democratic "to the extent that its most powerful collective decision makers are selected through fair, honest and periodic elections in which candidates freely compete for votes, and in which virtually all the adult population is eligible to vote."[3] From this definition, two dimensions are critical to the realization of democracy: contestation and participation, similarly, it also implies that in a democratic system, the existence of civil and political freedoms such as freedom of speech, publication, assembly, and organization, the conduct of electoral campaigns are inevitable.

Guillermo O'Donnell and Philippe Schmitter add a further dimension to this definition and they emphasize "citizenship" as democracy's guiding principle. To this end, democracy involves the right to be treated by fellow human beings as equal with respect to making collective choices and the obligation of those implementing such choices to be equally accountable and accessible to all members of the polity. Democratization, thus, refers to "the processes whereby rulers and procedures of citizenship are either applied to political institutions previously governed by other principles (e.g., coercive control, social tradition, expert judgment or administrative practice), or expanded to include persons not previously enjoying such rights and obligations, or extended to cover issues and institutions nor previously subject to citizen participation (e.g., state agencies, military establishments, partisan organizations, interest associations, productive enterprises, educational institutions, etc.)."[4]

One major divide in transition studies is between the formal or procedural conception of democracy and the substantive conception of democracy, which is fundamental to democratization studies as it affects terminology and definitions regarding the regime change process. *Formal* or *procedural* democracy, in Schumpeter's terminology, involves "institutional arrangement for arriving at political decisions in which individuals acquire the power to decide by means of a competitive struggle for the people's vote."[5] One of the most influential presentation of this "procedural" or "formal" notion of democracy was revisited by Robert Dahl in his famous concept "polyarchy," which not only highlighted political competition and participation but also placed a particular emphasis on different forms of freedom and pluralism that enable expression of political preferences.[6] On procedural democracy, Kaldor and Vejvoda have comprised their own list of formal criteria adapting a set of *procedural minimal* conditions, originally drawn up by Dahl. According to them, these procedural minimal conditions are as follows[7]:

1. *Inclusive citizenship*: exclusion from citizenship purely on the basis of race, ethnicity or gender is not permissible
2. *Rule of law*: the government is legally constituted and the different branches of government must respect the law, with individuals and minorities protected from the "tyranny of the majority."
3. *Separation of powers*: the three branches of government—legislature, executive, and judiciary—must be separate, with an independent judiciary capable of upholding the constitution.
4. *Elected power-holders*: power-holders, that is, members of the legislature and those who control the executive, must be elected.

5. *Free and fair elections:* elected power-holders are chosen in frequent and fairly conducted elections, in which coercion is comparatively uncommon, and in which practically all adults have the right to vote and to run for elective office.
6. *Freedom of expression and alternative sources of information*: citizens have a right to express themselves without the danger of severe punishment on political matters, broadly defined, and a right to seek alternative sources of information; moreover, alternative sources of information exist and are protected by law.
7. *Associational autonomy:* citizens also have the right to form relatively independent associations or organizations, including independent political parties and interest groups.
8. *Civilian control over the security forces*: the armed forces and police are politically neutral and independent of political pressures and are under the control of civilian authorities.

A democracy must meet three basic procedural criteria. Competitive elections must be the principal route to political office, which means that fraud and coercion should not determine the outcome of democratic elections. In addition, there must be broad adult citizenship meaning nearly universal citizenship recently. Some exclusions such as criminals, the insane, military personnel, and the illiterate are tolerated in many democracies, though. Lastly, democracies necessarily provide guarantees of traditional civic liberties for all and minority rights must be protected within this context.[8]

Substantive democracy, on the other hand, is considered as a process that has to be continually reproduced, as way of regulating power relations in such a way as to maximize the opportunities for individuals to influence the conditions in which they live, to participate in and influence debates about the key decisions that affect society.[9] Substantive democracy in no way clashes with formal democracy, instead it claims that formal procedures are essential but not sufficient for achieving democracy. Similarly, to Tocqueville, democracy has essentially two meanings: One is a political regime defined by the rule of people with all institutional and procedural mechanisms that were specified by earlier theorists of democracy. The other is a condition of society characterized by its tendency toward equality and this social or societal democratic condition meant that democracy could not be reduced to its formal, institutional aspects.[10] Thus, whereas formal democracy is about the rules and procedures of democracy including a full adult suffrage, regular elections, freedom of association and media, substantive democracy is concerned about political equality. Substantive democracy goes beyond formal democracy in that it is about our ability to have a say on the decisions that affect our lives and it is about democratic culture, "the habits of the heart" as Tocqueville puts it. Formal democracy could be seen as the initial step in regime transition and when constitutional settlement and other procedural rules are achieved, the next step would be regime consolidation which is very much linked to substantive democracy.

Another concept that is key to the analysis of regime change is *democratization*. Democratization is a complex process which begins with transition and matures into consolidation, in other words, the initial point where democratization starts is transition with the ultimate goal to reach a consolidated democracy. Huntington argues that "if popular election of the top decision makers is the essence of democracy, then the critical point in the process of democratization is the replacement of a government that was not chosen this way by one that is selected in a free, open and fair election."[11] He also points to the complex and prolonged nature of the overall process of democratization which involves bringing about the end of nondemocratic regime, the inauguration of the democratic regime, and finally the consolidation of the democratic system.[12] In that regard, democratization should be understood as a complex process which is far from having a clear route, means, and outcome.

Democratization can't be defined by some fixed and timeless objective criterion as democracy itself should be viewed as contextually variable and a deontological concept. It begins with the exit of an authoritarian regime and continues with competitive elections that lead to two successive peaceful transfers of government between contending parties.[13] Like democracy, democratization involves internal tensions as it incorporates facts and value. While democratization can be complex, protracted, or erratic, it could also result in a stable, predictable, or uniform outcome once democratization is over.[14]

Democratization is used to refer to the whole process of regime change from authoritarian or totalitarian rule to liberal democracy. Democratization is a multilevel and multidimensional process in which the dynamic of regime change can be analyzed by observing interactions between its different dimensions, and the nature and the intensity of these interactions may develop in a positive or negative way, thus determining the likely outcome of regime change.[15] Democratization is multilevel as it embraces liberalization and/ or authoritarian regime collapse through the transition phase and consolidation to the point where new democracies become established. Democratization is also multidimensional because the functioning of liberal democracies involves not only the creation of rules and procedures but also the societal level as well as intermediary linkages and interactions between different levels, especially elite-mass relations.[16]

Though democratization is about political regime change, often its prospects are influenced by economic developments as well as problems related to stateness, national identity, and international dimension. During postcommunist transition, for instance, economic and political transformation occurred simultaneously and in some post-Soviet states, it also included constructing national identity. In Eastern Europe, on the other hand, this process can't be analyzed without taking into account the role of European Union (EU) in transforming those states into liberal democracies. Thus, democratization should not be thought separate from multiple transformations occurring after regime change.

TRANSITION AND CONSOLIDATION

A major distinction in democratization literature exists between transition and consolidation. Transition is the interval between one political regime and another. Transitions are delimited, on the one side, by launching of the process of dissolution of an authoritarian regime and, on the other, by the installation of some form of democracy, the return to some form of authoritarian rule, or the emergence of revolutionary alternative.[17] Juan J. Linz and Alfred Stepan distinguish between transition and consolidation by pointing to the uncertain character of democratic transition, and they suggest that transition is the beginning phase of building democracy, in which politics is fluid, and democracy is not assured, whereas consolidation is a stage in which democracy becomes "the only game in town."[18]

Transition is a period marked by political struggles over defining rules and procedures which will eventually determine political advantages in the future. During transition, the rules of the political game are in constant flux, and they are usually contested; actors struggle to fulfil their immediate interests as well as interests of those whom they represent, they also try to define rules and procedures which at the end will determine prospective winners and losers.[19] Transition tasks include not only negotiating the constitutional settlement and settling the rules of procedure for political competition but also dismantling authoritarian agencies and abolishing laws unsuited for democratic life.[20]

To Guillermo O'Donnell, the overall change from an authoritarian to a democratic regime contains not one but two transitions: the first leads to the installation of a democratic government, and the second to the consolidation of democracy or to the effective functioning of a democratic regime. There is no specific formula or any event that distinguishes between the first and the second transition. Though these two transitions might overlap in certain areas, the authors argue that they differ in terms of the issues they deal with. Whereas the first transition focuses on the development of social and political oppositions to the authoritarian regime, the emergence of hard-liners and soft-liners within the circles of power, the formation of coalition demanding democratic change, the second transition deals with possible reverse of democratization and the makeup of democratic institutions that could cope with economic and social problems.[21]

On the other hand, the consolidation of democracy requires, first and foremost, the completion of democratic transition. Democratic transition is complete "when sufficient agreement has been reached about political procedures to produce an elected government, when a government comes to power that is the direct result of a free and popular vote, when this government de facto has to authority to generate new policies, and when the executive, legislative and judicial power generated by the new democracy does not have to share power with other bodies *de jure*."[22] Democratic consolidation is lengthier than democratic transition with possibly deeper effects involving mass attitudes and requiring legitimization of the new regime. To achieve democratic consolidation, it is essential that the uncertainties that surround transition are gradually removed, the new democracy is institutionalized, its rules are internalized, and democratic values are disseminated.

As democratization became widespread, it became evident that some countries successfully became democracies, while others failed or remained in the category of problematic democracies. This led to a renewed academic interest in identifying those factors that enables new democracies to endure or open the way for their weakness or volatility. As a result, the impact of political culture, political economy, and institutionalism on generating a democratic outcome became an integral part of democratization debate in addition to structure and agency, and their respective roles in causation.[23]

To O'Donnell, building a consolidated democracy involves in part an affirmation and strengthening of certain institutions, such as electoral system, revitalized or newly created parties, judicial independence, and respect for human rights, which have been created or recreated during the course of the first transition. However, there is no such linearity in many ways; building a consolidated democracy requires abandoning or changing certain arrangement, agreements, and institutions by providing guarantees to the authoritarian rulers and the forces backing them. Likewise, legislatures that include nondemocratically generated representation with military autonomy from control by the executive or with supreme councils empowered to review the actions of democratic governments are all set by the characteristics of the earlier transition phase whose effects are seen in later stage.[24]

If a democracy is consolidated, it is generally thought to be immune to disintegration and it is free from potentially destabilizing factors and regime reversals. However, the retention of democratic government doesn't necessarily indicate on its own that a democracy is consolidated. To illustrate, democratically elected governments may succeed one another for some time without any reversal simply because they don't challenge actors who don't show democratic accountability.[25] Guillermo O'Donnell refers to such situations as "slow death of democracy." Consolidated democracies are also exposed to destabilizing conditions such as racial and ethnic tensions, social unrest, urban riots, armed separatist movements, and terrorist attacks. They might face democratic breakdown as well. Therefore, the durability of a democratic regime is not sufficient to test whether it has achieved democratic consolidation.

Linz and Stepan suggest three minimal conditions that must be fulfilled in order to talk about democratic consolidation. First, in a modern polity, unless a state exists, free and authoritative elections can't be held, winners can't exercise the monopoly of a legitimate force, and citizens can't effectively have their rights protected by a rule of law. Second, democracy can't be thought of as consolidated until a democratic transition has been completed. A necessary condition, despite being insufficient for the completion of a democratic transition, is the holding of free and contested elections on the basis of broadly inclusive voter eligibility. Third, no regime can be regarded as a consolidated democracy unless its rulers govern democratically, that is, if elected executives infringe the constitution, violate the rights of individuals, interfere in the legitimate functions of the legislature, and they fail to rule within the boundaries of law, their regimes are not democracies.[26]

Linz and Stepan put emphasis on the three dimensions of democratic consolidation, namely, *behavioral, attitudinal,* and *constitutional*. Behaviorally, "democracy becomes the only game in town when no significant group seriously attempts to overthrow the democratic regime or to promote domestic or international violence in order to secede from the state."[27] In the absence of such attempts to topple democratically elected regimes, transition is free from the threat of democratic breakdown. Attitudinally, democracy becomes the only game in town when the majority of the people believe in the value of democratic procedures and that any political change must emerge from those procedures even in times of severe political and economic crises.[28] Constitutionally, democracy becomes the only game in town when all the actors in the polity are convinced that any political conflict within the state will be resolved according to the rules and norms established and violation of these norms will be costly.[29]

DEMOCRATIZATION AND LIBERALIZATION

The second important distinction related to transition concerns the difference between "liberalization" and "democratization." This conceptual differentiation is essential as it calls attention to the fundamental difference between democracy and changes within authoritarian regimes. Political liberalization and democratization are two concepts which are intertwined and have historical ties. If it weren't for the guarantees of individual and group freedoms inherent in the former, the latter risks converting into mere formalism, or so-called "popular democracy." On the other hand, if it weren't for the accountability to mass publics and constituent minorities institutionalized under the latter, liberalization could be easily manipulated and retracted by those in government arbitrarily. Nevertheless, liberalization considerably differs from democratization as the latter needs a certain level of institutionalization and legal framework that guarantee competition and separation among powers.

O'Donnell and Schmitter defines "liberalization" as the process of making effective certain rights that protect both individuals and social groups from arbitrary or illegal acts committed by the state or third parties. On the level of individuals, these guarantees include the classical elements of the liberal tradition: sanctity of private home and correspondence; the right to be defended in a fair trial according to preestablished laws; freedom of movement, speech, and petition; and so forth.[30] On the level of groups, these rights cover such things as freedom from punishment for expressions of collective dissent from government policy, freedom from censorship of the means of communication, and freedom to associate voluntarily with other citizens.[31] Political liberalization refers to a loosening of repression and extension of civil liberties in an authoritarian regime whereas a transition to democracy implies a change of regimes.

Liberalization can be observed in many authoritarian regimes. Authoritarian rulers may tolerate and even promote liberalization hoping that by opening up certain spaces for individual and group action, they can relieve internal and external pressures and gain support without altering the authoritarian structure of their rule. Liberalization is often used as a defensive strategy by authoritarian rulers. This form of rule has been given several labels such as "tutelary democracy" and "liberalized authoritarianism."[32] As will be discussed further in the upcoming chapters, Mubarak and Ben Ali regimes are striking examples of liberal autocracies where political liberalization is generated as a survival mechanism for the regime, rather than opening up reforms that would pave the way for democracy.

Liberalization can exist without democratization, that is, fundamental guarantees can be given to individuals and groups while obstructing them from participating in competitive elections, from access to policy deliberations and/or from exercising the rights that may make the rulers reasonably accountable to them. However, demands for democratization increases as liberalization advances though whether these demands will be strong enough to bring an authoritarian regression or a breakup is far from being certain. Based on the third-wave transition experiences examined, O'Donnell and

Schmitter argue that the attainment of political democracy was preceded by a significant, if unsteady, liberalization, thus, the overall transition can be conceptualized as a sort of "double stream" in which liberalization and democratization interact over time, each with its own hesitancies and reversions, and each with overlapping motives and constituencies.[33]

Linz and Stepan suggest that democratization entails liberalization, but it is a wider concept which requires "open contestation over the right to win the control of a government, and this, in turn, requires free competitive elections, the results of which determine who governs."[34] This suggests that there can be liberalization without democratization while there is likelihood that liberalization might facilitate the shift to democratization, however; liberalization is sometimes aborted and leads to a renewed repression. Transition process is often accompanied by constant flux in which the authoritarian elites are moving toward some liberalization to strengthen their own position or toward repression when they feel besieged by the threat of authoritarian crackdown.

DEMOCRACY AND POLITICAL LEGITIMACY

The explanatory value of the term "legitimacy" is quite significant in the context of regime change. Very often, breakdown in an authoritarian regime takes place as a consequence of declining political legitimacy. In brief, political legitimacy refers to broad acceptance of a political regime and providing regime legitimacy is key to the survival of any regime. In authoritarian regimes, legitimacy is more ideological, quasihistorical, charismatic, or functional, and the regime draws its identity and strength from the ruling ideology. In democracies, in contrast, legitimacy lies in formal mechanisms that determine the rules and procedures of transfer of power and the separation of powers.

Authoritarian regimes practice dictatorship and repression while promising democracy and freedom in the future, which allows them to justify themselves in political terms only as transitional powers, meanwhile, they attempt to shift attention to their immediate substantive accomplishments—typically, the achievement of "social peace" and economic development.[35] In that way, authoritarian regimes try to provide legitimacy for their prolonged authoritarian rule, yet this strategy might lead to the collapse of the authoritarian regime, given the easy access to the contemporary worldwide marketplace of ideas and communication technologies today. As Mainwaring argues, declining legitimacy[36]:

> Increases the costs of staying in power. In the post-World War era, Western authoritarian regimes have lacked a stable legitimizing formula. It is common

for authoritarian regimes to justify their actions in the name of furthering some democratic cause. This justification may be plausible to some sectors of the nation, and it may help legitimacy for a limited period of time. But appealing to safeguarding democracy is a two-edged sword for authoritarian governments, for their appeals, eventually calls attention to the hiatus between their discourse and their practice.

The notion of legitimacy and democracy are so closely related that the former is an essential prerequisite of the latter's stability. Democracy without legitimacy tends to be unstable. The institutions of government and the state can be said to be democratic only if there is popular consent, popular participation, accountability and a practice of rights, tolerance and pluralism, thus, citizens need to enjoy popular legitimacy and represent political community.[37] On the other hand, democratic legitimacy could be best understood as contextual as it is based on an understanding that at a particular historical juncture no other type of regime could provide a more successful pursuit of collective goals.[38] Political leaders in democratically elected governments need to be viewed as doing the best that can be done under the circumstances they face.

The notion of legitimacy is fundamental to understand why actors and citizens are less willing and less likely to undermine a democratic regime. Declining legitimacy can lead authoritarian governments to leave office, while in democracies rational actors would join a conspiracy against democracy to further their interests only if there is a reasonable likelihood of success. Otherwise, the costs of undermining democratic regime are so high in consolidated democracies that actors believe in the values of the system and they are likely to make compromise willfully to obey the rules of the game.[39] Likewise, if an authoritarian regime enjoys considerable support, it is less likely to face mass-mobilization from its people. That means if self-interest is the underlying cause of obedience, stability of the political system rests mostly on payoffs, particularly of a material nature.

DEMOCRACY AND UNCERTAINTY

One of the striking features of democratic transitions is its inevitable connection with uncertainty. Initially, outcomes of the democratic processes are uncertain because democracy depends not on a single force, but rather on interaction among a variety of competing forces which seem to maximize their own interests. Przeworski has highlighted the uncertainty of democracy as such[40]:

> The process of establishing a democracy is a process of institutionalizing uncertainty, of subjecting all interests to uncertainty. In an authoritarian regime, some

groups, typically the armed forces, have the capacity of intervening whenever the result of a conflict is contrary to their program or their interests In a democracy, no group is able to intervene when outcomes of conflicts violate their self-perceived interests. Democracy means that all groups must subject their interests to uncertainty.

The tendency to equate democracy with competitive multiparty elections is broadly criticized by scholars today. A transition to democracy can culminate in a liberal democracy, or it could terminate with a liberalized authoritarian regime (dictablanda), or a restrictive, illiberal democracy (democradura).[41] The inherent uncertainty and the variations in the outcomes of regime transitions have led many scholars in comparative democratization to investigate the regimes that fall into the gray zone and are referred broadly as "hybrid regimes." One of the most striking features of the third wave has been the rise of regimes that are neither clearly democratic nor totally authoritarian, but instead combine authoritarian governance with democratic rules in various regions of the world including Latin America, Eastern Europe, and the former Soviet Union. The boundaries between those regimes are so blurry that scholars are far from reaching a consensus on how to classify those ambiguous cases.

In the contemporary era, democracy is the only broadly legitimate regime form and thus, authoritarian regimes often feel pressure to adopt or pretend to adopt democratic form. To most scholars, it is inappropriate to label those regimes as "in transition to democracy," and we should begin thinking about those regimes as specific types. A variety of labels have been produced to define those ambiguous regimes such as semidemocracy, virtual democracy, electoral democracy, pseudodemocracy, illiberal democracy, competitive authoritarianism, electoral authoritarianism, and Freedom House's Partly Free.[42]

Not all hybrid regimes should be thought to be undergoing prolonged transitions, instead, they might move toward authoritarianism. For instance, some hybrid regimes (Mexico, Senegal, and Taiwan) underwent democratic transitions in the 1990s, whereas others (Azerbaijan and Belarus) moved in a distinctly authoritarian direction, and still others (Russia, Ukraine, Malaysia) either remained stable or moved in multiple directions.[43] Therefore, the term "transitional" doesn't imply unidirectional movement toward democracy.

For countries in transition, a great deal of caution is needed to avoid broad generalizations and conclusive presumptions. Even when transitions are complete, it takes decades for a democracy to consolidate. For consolidated democracies, the risk of democratic regression still lurks in the background. No matter whether democratization is in a transitional stage or a consolidation, any democracy is surrounded by a high level of uncertainty.

THEORETICAL FRAMEWORK

Theories of democratization are chiefly engaged with causation and identification of the main factors that set the stage for democratic transition. Particularly, the last quarter of the twentieth century witnessed significant democratic improvement globally. This led scholars to come up with theories accounting for factors that help to endure or hinder democratic transition. A basic distinction exists between structuralist theories and agency approaches because of their different approaches regarding structure and agency.[44] To this end, this section attempts to categorize theories in democratic transition into two distinct theories: the structural approach, and the strategic approach. These theories will be further discussed in chapter V.

Structuralist Approach (Modernization Theory)

Structuralist approach assumes that particular outcomes of the transition could be explained by economic development, political culture, class conflict, social structures, and other social conditions. These scholars are preoccupied with macrolevel analysis of social conditions as well as cultural and social prerequisites of democracy with their causal explanations based on quantitative analysis of a large number of countries. Under this approach, the most widely known and examined proposition is modernization theory which links the spread of democracy to economic development and capitalism.

Modernization theory was first proposed by Seymour Martin Lipset in his article on economic development and democracy in 1959. According to Lipset, countries that have undergone an extensive process of societal modernization such as industrialization, gross national product per capita, urbanization, increasing levels of education, and rising national income are more likely to be democratic. Lipset's work has inspired many scholars who have come up with a wide range of structural propositions to explain democratization. Some structural factors that are hypothesized to determine the democratic outcome are income inequality, economic crises, natural resources abundance, country size, religious composition, societal fractionalization, colonial heritage, social capital, mass political culture, democratic diffusion, and regional organizations.[45] Social and economic structure, according to the modernization theory, triggers democratic advancement. On this critical link between economic growth and democracy, Lipset noted, "perhaps the most widespread generalization linking political systems to other aspects of society has been that democracy is related to the state of economic development. Concretely, this means that the more well-to-do a nation, the greater the chances that it will sustain democracy."[46]

Economic growth in a country is correlated with a higher level of urbanization and education. With a stronger economy, the government is able to invest more money in education. which in turn prevents them from adopting monolithic and extremist doctrines and helps them to make rational choices. Likewise, with increasing wealth led by industrialization, the values of lower class shifted toward upper-class values. Economic growth generates an educated and entrepreneurial middle class that in time demands to have control over its own fate, which in turn forces repressive governments to give in to popular aspirations.[47]

Modernization theory has been criticized on various grounds. First, Lipset's claim that economic development eventually leads to a democratization of the country lacks empirical support today. Many developing economies in East Asia and the Middle East (e.g., China, Russia, and the Arab Gulf states) are far from being democratic. Indeed, authoritarian regimes use many tools and tactics to divert economic development to sustain their regime. O'Donnell's theory of "bureaucratic authoritarianism" links the deepening of capitalism with the emergence of dictatorships as these bureaucratic authoritarian regimes restructured political and economic institutions in an attempt to maximize their profits by using repressive means.[48] Based on the evidence of their research, Przeworksi and Limongi found that the chances for the survival of democracy are greater in wealthier nations, but the emergence of democracy is not a by-product of economic development and even the current wealth of a country is not decisive.[49]

Second, the distinguishing feature of this theory is that structural factors are attributed causal primacy and the causal process conveyed is rather mechanical, that is, change in the political regime is an outcome of a structural shift in the environment. However, these theories don't explain why different political actors make different political choices, why their preferences change over time and why one choice prevails over another in the same social and structural context. Therefore, the role of the human agency is missing in structural theories. In Huntington's words, the structural approach needs to move from causes to causers.

Third, another pitfall of the modernization theory is that it is ahistorical in that it presumes all societies can replicate a transition which occurred at a particular time and space.[50] On the contrary, trends to democratization are contradictory and partial across different countries and regions of the world. Given the same structural conditions, two countries might follow a different path toward or away from democratization. Finally, modernization theory has drawn a conclusion out of the experiences of the Western world and ignored the particularistic development patterns in the Third World.

The structural factors introduced by the modernization theory can have facilitating or constraining effects on the democratization process in a country, yet they can't generate a democratic outcome or democratic breakdown on their own. In a country, which is already democratic, structural factors help to prevent democratic regression or backsliding into authoritarianism. Modernization affects regime outcomes by hindering authoritarian reversals, rather than promoting transitions toward democracy.

Strategic Approach (Transition Theory)

Strategic approach, or transition theory, focuses on the interaction of elite strategic choices to explain the outcome of democratic transition.[51] Strategic approach takes an agent-centric view and focuses on the critical role of elites, their strategic choices, the splits within the authoritarian regime, and the compromise between the "hard-liners" and "soft-liners."[52] In contrast to the structural approach, it examines democratization in a micro level. The strategic approach sees democracy as a product of conscious and committed actors who convinced that democracy is the best possible regime, thus, economy, history, and development are not seen as determining political outcomes. The proponents of this approach emphasize the significance of political processes, elite calculations, and the interaction between their choices, although they do not deny the role of structural factors. The main hypothesis of the strategic approach or transition school is that successful outcomes for democracy could come true if elites learn the right way to proceed, independent of the structural context.[53]

Transition theory has brought a new perspective to comparative democratization as agency-centered approach situates the study of democracy within the mainstream political science methodologists and epistemologies rather than economic determinants. It prioritizes political choices over economic ones and restructuring political institutions over those aimed at reforming national systems of production and distribution.[54] By rejecting the deterministic view of the structuralists, they offer a process-oriented explanation of democratization, a process in which "choices are caught up in a continuous redefinition of actors' perceptions of preferences and constraints."[55] Thus, the task is to explain these processes.

Democratization could be depicted as a struggle between the authoritarian regime on the one side, and a unified society on the other, yet in reality divergent patterns of divisions exist among different groups with competing interests. A successful democratic transition is most likely to occur when competing forces in a society work together to bring down an authoritarian regime even while they are struggling with each other to have the best place in the new system. In this regard, Przeworski notes:

> The image for the campaign for democracy as a struggle of the society is a useful fiction dividing the first period of transition as a unifying slogan of the forces

opposed to the current authoritarian regime . . . . But societies are divided in many ways and the very essence of democracy is the competition among political forces within conflicting interests. This situation creates two dilemmas: to bring about democracy, anti-authoritarian forces must unite against authoritarianism but to be victorious under democracy they must compete one another. Hence the struggle for democracy always takes place on two fronts: against the authoritarian regime for democracy and against one's allies for the best place under democracy.[56]

The first phase of the transition in which opposition forces cooperate with one another is rather likely given the fact that they have a common goal to bring down the authoritarian regime. Yet, the second phase in which opposition forces need to negotiate in order to create a democratic order is rather challenging. The asymmetries and divisions among competing forces might prevent a democratic order from taking roots and bring about another authoritarian regime. This was the case in Iran where the Shah regime was toppled, but suppression took over negotiation leading to autocracy. Hence, the initial challenge for all parties in the opposition lies in making concessions to reach a compromise on the rules of the new system.

Given the presence of preferable alternatives, elites are likely to make calculations and adopt strategies based on cost–benefit calculations. Elites in the opposition will not be eager to take risks unless they are convinced that what they are likely to gain exceeds their potential risks. Elites in the regime, on the other hand, are likely to respond opposing elites either by suppression or regain legitimacy by using a strategy of liberalization.[57] Democratic transition is most likely to occur in cases where soft-liners in the ruling regime cooperate with the opposition in an attempt to regain legitimacy by opening space for liberalization. On the other hand, authoritarian breakdown is most likely case when hard-liners continuously attempt to suppress the opposition.[58] In a similar vein, O'Donnell and Schmitter found that all successful transition cases they examined depended upon agreements between elites and in none of their cases did democracy come out as a result of structural conditions or popular mobilization.[59] In the same manner, Przeworski drew our attention to the possible risks of popular mobilization and suggested that popular mobilization could be detrimental to democratization since it threatened the interests of powerful elites and then led them to close down tentative experiments in political liberalization.[60]

Democracy flourished in many parts of the world regardless of the structural factors indicating that the chances of spreading democracy in the contemporary world are rather good. It is clear that elite choices, compromise and their commitment to democracy could make it possible even in countries where structural factors are not favorable to democratic transition.

Nonetheless, the strategic approach is criticized on the ground that it focuses on the short terms calculations of actors during a short period of time and ignores the possibility of long-term forces, structural contexts, and constraints determining the outcome. Another shortcoming of the strategic approach is that it has never adequately addressed the conditions that determine actors' preferences, interests, and beliefs.[61] Understanding the underlying reasons or conditions that shape political elites' decisions, choices, and bargains is indeed as important as explaining the outcomes of the elite strategic interactions and negotiations in transition to democracy.

NOTES

1. John Keane, *The Life and Death of Democracy* (UK: Simon & Schuster, 2009), 865.
2. Giovanni Sartori, *The Theory of Democracy Revisited* (Chatnam, NJ: Chatham House Publishers, 1987), 206.
3. Samuel Huntington, *The Third Wave: Democratization in the Late Twentieth Century* (Norman: University of Oklahoma Press, 1991), 7.
4. Philippe C. Schmitter, and Guillermo O'Donnell, *Transitions from Authoritarian Rule: Tentative Conclusions About Uncertain Democracies* (Baltimore: John Hopkins University Press, 1996), 8.
5. Joseph Schumpeter, *Capitalism, Socialism and Democracy*, 2nd Ed. (New York: Harper & Brothers, 1947), 269.
6. Robert Dahl, *Polyarchy: Participation and Opposition* (New Haven: Yale University Press, 1971), 3.
7. Mary Kaldor, and Ivan Vejvoda, "Democratization in Eastern and Central European Countries," *International Affairs* 73, no. 1 (January 1997): 63.
8. Scott Mainwaring, "Transitions to Democracy and Democracy and Democratic Consolidation: Theoretical and Comparative Issues," *Kellogg Institute*, Working Paper 130 (November 1998).
9. Kaldor, and Vejvoda, "Democratization," 62.
10. Ibid.
11. Huntington, "The Third Wave," 9.
12. Ibid.
13. Laurence Whitehead, *Democratization: Theory and Experience* (Oxford: Oxford University Press, 2002), 26–28.
14. Ibid.
15. Geoffrey Pridham, *The Dynamics of Democratization. A Comparative Approach* (London and New York: Continuum, 2000), 4.
16. Ibid., 17.
17. Schmitter, and O'Donnell, "Transitions from Authoritarian Rule," 6.
18. Juan J. Linz, and Alfred Stepan, *Problems of Democratic Transition and Consolidation: Southern Europe, South America and Post-Communist Europe* (Baltimore: John Hopkins University Press, 1996), 5.

19. Ibid.
20. Pridham, *The Dynamics of Democratization*, 19.
21. Scott Mainwaring, Guillermo O.'Donnell, and J. Samuel Valenzuela, *Issues in Democratic Consolidation: The New South American Democracies in Comparative Perspective* (Notre Dame: University of Notre Dame Press, 1992), 4–5.
22. Linz, and Stepan, *Problems of Democratic Transition and Consolidation*, 3.
23. Jean Grugel, *Democratization: A Critical Introduction* (Houndmills, NY: Palgrave Macmillian, 2000), 3–4.
24. Guillermo O'Donnell, and Philippe Schmitter, "Tentative Conclusions about Uncertain Democracies," in *Transitions from Authoritarian Rule: Prospects for Democracy*, ed. Guillermo O'Donnell, Philippe Schmitter, and Laurence Whitehead (Baltimore: Johns Hopkins University Press, 1986), 8.
25. J. Samuel Valenzuela, "Democratic Consolidation in Post-Transitional Settings: Notion, Process and Facilitating Conditions," *Kellogg Institute*, Working Paper 150 (December 1990), 2–3.
26. In addition to a functioning state, Linz and Stepan state five mutually reinforcing conditions as prerequisites for consolidated democracy. These are civil society, political society, rule of law, state bureaucracy and institutionalized economic society. See Juan J. Linz, and Alfred Stepan, "Towards Consolidated Democracies," *Journal of Democracy* 7, no. 2 (April 1996): 1.
27. Ibid, 2.
28. Ibid.
29. Ibid.
30. Schmitter, and O'Donnell, *Transitions from Authoritarian Rule*, 7.
31. Ibid.
32. Schmitter, and O'Donnell, *Transitions from Authoritarian Rule*, 9.
33. Ibid., 10.
34. Linz, and Stepan, *Problems of Democratic Transition*, 3.
35. Schmitter, and O'Donnell, *Transitions from Authoritarian Rule*, 15.
36. Scott Mainwaring, "Transitions to Democracy and Democratic Consolidation: Theoretical and Comparative Issues," in *Issues in Democratic Consolidation: The New South American Democracies in Comparative Perspective*, ed. Scott Mainwaring, Guillermo O.'Donnell and J. Samuel Valenzuela (Notre Dame: University of Notre Dame Press, 1992), 324–325.
37. Grugel, *Democratization: A Critical Introduction*, 7.
38. Juan Linz, *The Breakdown of Democratic Regimes: Crisis, Breakdown and Reequilibration* (Baltimore: John Hopkins University Press, 1978), 18.
39. Mainwaring, "Transitions to Democracy and Democratic Consolidation," 306.
40. Adam Przeworski, "Some Problems in the Study of the Transition to Democracy," in *Transitions from Authoritarian Rule: Prospects for Democracy*, ed. Guillermo O'Donnell, Philippe C. Schmitter, and Laurence Whitehead (Baltimore: John Hopkins University Press, 1986), 58.
41. Schmitter, and O'Donnell, *Transitions from Authoritarian Rule*, 9.
42. Steven Levitsky, and Lucan Way, "The Rise of Competitive Authoritarianism," *Journal of Democracy* 13, no. 2 (April 2002): 51–2.

43. Ibid.
44. Grugel, *Democratization: A Critical Introduction*, 46.
45. Jan Teorell, *Determinants of Democratization: Explaining Regime Change in the World 1972–2006* (Cambridge: Cambridge University Press, 2010), 17–18.
46. Seymour M. Lipset, "Some Social Requisites of Democracy: Economic Development and Political Legitimacy," *American Political Science Review* 53, no. 1 (March 1959): 75.
47. George W. Downs, and Bruce Bueno de Mesquita, "Development and Democracy," *Foreign Affairs* 84, no. 5 (Sep.–Oct. 2005): 77.
48. Guillermo O'Donnell, *Modernization and Bureaucratic Authoritarianism: Studies in South American Politics* (Berkeley, CA: University of California Press, 1973), 1–39.
49. Adam Przeworski, and Fernando Limongi, "Modernization: Theories and Facts," *World Politics* 49, no. 2 (January 1997): 177.
50. Grugel, *Democratization: A Critical Introduction*, 49.
51. Both "strategic approach" and "transition theory" are used interchangably in literature on democratic transitions. Likewise, in this research they will be used interchangeably.
52. Sujian Guo, "Democratic Transition: A Critical Overview," *Issues & Studies* 35, no. 4 (July/August 1999): 136.
53. Grugel, *Democratization: A Critical Introduction*, 57.
54. Philippe Schmitter, "Transitology: The Science or the Art of Democratization," in *The Consolidation of Democracy in Latin America*, ed. Joseph S. Tulchin, Bernice Romero (Boulder, CO: Lynne Rienner Publishers, 1995), 33.
55. Herbert Kitschelt, "Political Regime Change: Structure and Process-Driven Explanations?" *American Political Science Review* 86, no. 4 (December 1992): 1028.
56. Przeworski, "Some Problems in the Study of Transition to Democracy," 66.
57. Hans Peter Schmitz, and Susan K. Sell, "International Factors in Processes of Political Democratization: Towards a Theoretical Integration," in *Democracy without Borders: Transnationalization and Conditionality in New Democracies*, ed. Jean Grugel (London: Routledge, 1999), 31–2.
58. Ibid.
59. Schmitter, and O'Donnell, *Transitions from Authoritarian Rule*.
60. Przeworski, *Some Problems in the Study of Transition to Democracy*.
61. Teorell, *Determinants of Democratization: Explaining Regime Change*, 21.

Chapter 2

Democratization in the Arab Middle East Context

For many decades until the outbreak of the Arab uprisings, the Middle East proved to be the only region where no democracy existed. According to the Freedom House, the Middle East and North Africa has historically been the least free region in the world.[1] What was surprising about the region was not the failure of democratic transition or consolidation, but the fact that no Middle Eastern and North African State had even initiated transition to democracy until the sudden outbreak of the popular protests in 2011. Until then, the MENA region proved to be an exceptionalism in terms of democratic change.

The democratic deficit in the region drew scholarly attention to the factors that hindered democratic outcome and political scientists came up with a wide range of variables to explain why democracy failed in the MENA region. The scholarly debates have ranged from low levels of economic growth to cultural and religious attributes of Islam and from political economy to the lack of regional and international organizations that would promote democracy in the region. The factors that could explain democratic deficit in one country failed to do so in another country with similar features, which indicated that there is no single direct answer to why democracy could flourish in one country but not in the other. Instead, the recent wave of uprisings and the political transitions indicated that democracy emerges and flourishes in any country randomly without any particular prerequisite being fulfilled.

While explaining the region's cultural exceptionalism in terms of democracy, some political scientists focused on the particular role of Islam to explain its authoritarian resilience. This group of political scientists associated the democratic deficit in the region with the values Islam promoted and came to the conclusion that an Islamic society would hardly accept democratic system and individual rights. They argued that Islam along with oriental despotism, patrimonialism, patriarchalism, and mass passivity were integral part of Arab political and social culture. In addition, participatory government and individual rights were seen as alien to the Muslim tradition because Islam is thought to vest authority in God, thus, society must be guided by divine law, or *Sharia* rather than popular will. According to this mainstream view, there is no legitimate base for liberal democracy which places sovereignty of man, and participatory government into the core of political life.

On the other hand, this argument over incompatibility between Islam and democracy is misleading in many ways. First, it would be anachronistic to question whether Islam endorses democracy and constitutionalism since the Holy Quran doesn't proscribe any particular system of government. In Islam, just like Christianity and Judaism, there are general ethical principles that have to be guaranteed under any system of government such as social justice, protection of life, property, honor of humanity, accountability of rulers to law, distribution of wealth, and protection of minorities. Besides, the Quran commands Muslims to decide on matters with *Shura*, consultative decision-making, and adopt *Ijma*, the principle of consensus. The early Muslim scholars referred to these ideas as governing with consent and creating a contract with the governed, which are key elements of a democratic system today. *Shura* in essence forbids one-man dictatorship, and the general principles of Islam which particularly emphasize the importance of equality and justice don't contradict with democracy.

Second, the autocrats that ruled the Middle Eastern states for several decades such as Ben Ali, Hosni Mubarak, Muammar Qaddafi, and Bashar Assad didn't place Islam in their political agenda. Instead, these rulers adopted secular ideology and attempted to design their societies with secular values. As political Islamist movements such as the Muslim Brotherhood and Ennahda gained widespread popular support in their societies, the autocrats viewed their growth as a threat to the survival of their own regime. They used various strategies to oppress and prosecute leading Islamic figures and contain the spread of such movements.

Third, various public opinion polls assessing support for democracy across the MENA region over the last decade have made it clear that Arab citizens want democracy and neither intellectuals nor ordinary citizens in the region believe that Islam and democracy are incompatible. In fact, a survey carried out by Jamal and Tessler in 2008 found out that more religious Muslims tend to believe that democracy is the best political system as much as less religious Muslims.[2] Another survey carried out by Afrobarometer teams in five countries—Tunisia, Morocco, Egypt, Sudan, and Algeria—in 2015 indicated that about two-thirds of respondents in four of the five countries see no contradiction between democracy and Islam: solid majorities in Tunisia (69 percent), Morocco (68 percent), Egypt (64 percent), and Sudan

(63 percent) disagree or strongly disagree with the idea that democracy contradicts the teachings of Islam.[3] According to the survey, the idea that non-Muslims should have fewer political rights than Muslims is rejected by majorities in Tunisia (73 percent), Morocco (72 percent), Egypt (58 percent), and Sudan (57 percent), and by a plurality (46 percent) in Algeria.[4] Similarly, a more recent survey conducted by the Arab Barometer that measured the level of democracy support in the MENA region from 2013 to 2016 found that regardless of regime type or experience with the Arab uprisings, across the region the vast majority of citizens ranging from 91 percent to 77 percent express that democracy is the best system despite its potential problems, and it is always preferable to any other kind of government.[5] The survey also found that in most countries surveyed citizens were more likely to say democracy is the best system compared to 2013.

Fourth, there are a number of countries with predominantly Muslim population which successfully transitioned to democracy such as Turkey, Malaysia, Albania, Bangladesh, Senegal, and more recently Tunisia. Political Islamic movements participated in legislative or regional elections in many countries, and they have contributed to the democratic processes in many cases.

Another argument concerning the democratic deficit in the MENA region has been the effect of political economy. Larry Diamond, a senior scholar in democratization studies, questions the cultural exceptionalism argument in an attempt to explain why there are no Arab democracies. He comes to the conclusion that the deficit of democracy lies neither in Islam nor in its cultural and religious aspects. To Diamond, it is political economy, particularly the so-called "oil curse" which accounts for the riddle of Arab democracy deficit.[6] He argues that the problem is not the economic level, but economic structure[7]:

> Of the sixteen Arab countries eleven are rentier states in the sense that they depend heavily on oil and gas rents to keep their states afloat. Most are so awash in cash that they don't need to tax their own citizens. And that is part of the problem—they fail to develop the organic expectations of accountability that emerge when states make citizens pay taxes.

Many political scientists increasingly believe that availability of natural resources, particularly oil revenues, prolongs or even promotes authoritarian forms of rule. Michael Ross has made a statistical research pooling cross-national data from 113 states between 1971 and 1997 to test whether oil impedes democracy. His key findings are that oil impedes democracy hypothesis is both valid and statistically robust and it does greater damage to democracy in poorer states than rich ones.[8] He also finds out causal mechanisms linking oil with authoritarianism; "a rentier effect," through which governments use low tax rates to dampen pressures for democracy; "a repression effect," by which governments build up their security forces to discard democracy; "modernization effect," in which populations become less eager to move into industrial and service sector jobs and this renders them less likely to push for democracy.[9] These states also don't create wealth through investment in other sectors. They are heavily centralized and oil and gas incomes accrue to the central state officers in the form of "rents."

Decline in competitiveness of nonoil sectors, volatility of revenues from oil and gas sector due to exposure to changes in the global market and governments' mismanagement of resources in a heavily centralized system are endemic in the region. Since the oil-rich Arab states don't depend on taxing their population, they have failed to develop a system which relies on accountability to the citizens and representation that emerges with taxation. Besides, resource curse hinders the development of other sectors through investment and risk taking, increases corruption, and enables Arab leaders to spend income extracted from natural resources on repressive security apparatus. From this point of view, Arab states which don't heavily export natural resources are more advantaged in terms of democratization. This also largely explains why the Arab uprisings bypassed the oil-rich Arab states in the Gulf region and in the short or long term, political change in oil-rich Arab states seems a long shot.

Just like oil rents, large revenue streams in the form of foreign aid have been regarded as key to the survival of those long-entrenched regimes. In the MENA region, foreign aid, both in the form of military aid and financial aid, helped autocrats to maintain their patronage systems and buy off protestors. The United States has provided large sums of aid to the military-backed regimes in the region as those autocrats were believed to ensure the Western interests in the region. Both the threat of radical Islamism and securing key Western energy interests in the area have made it tempting for Western actors to support authoritarian forces, and they will continue to give their support to the autocrats in the rest of the Arab world in some time to come.[10] The U.S. foreign aid has been particularly decisive in the case of Egypt, where the foreign aid to the military-backed regime strengthened its hand in confronting any possible opposition movement for decades, playing a very similar role to that of the oil rents in the Gulf region.

Viable regional and international organizations that implement the principle of conditionality and financial aid to promote democratization play a key role in facilitating democratic transitions. The Arab world lacks such a regional or international organization. In the region, there are some regional organizations such as the League of Arab States, the African Union, and the Gulf Cooperation Council, yet none of them managed to provide regional security, crisis management, or economic arrangements. These organizations have historically been more interested in the authoritarian regimes' survival and protecting the status quo. On the other hand, the authoritarian state systems in member states of the League don't make Arab League decisions toward supporting democracy credible. Hence, in the absence of Western support and a regional organization adherent to the democratic ideals, the Arab states have to depend almost entirely on their internal dynamics and domestic balance of power between democratic and anti-democratic forces.

Another major obstacle to the democratization in the Arab Middle East has been the mismatch between state and identity from the haphazard imposition of territorial boundaries under imperialism.[11] Artificial boundaries built during imperial period led to irredentism; in other words, dissatisfaction with the incompatibility between identity communities and a claimed territory. In the Middle East, this forced fragmentation within the Arab world into a number of small states resulted in the persistence of strong sub and supra-state identities that weakened identification with the state. Once the threat of exacerbating communal conflict and supra-state movements that could devastate the integrity of the state arise, elites are more likely to resort to authoritarian solutions.[12] Divided into many weak states, the Arab world sheltered popular movements, such as pan-Arabism and political Islam that were preoccupied with identity and unity problems. When the elite came into power, their priority was to create legitimacy through the triumph of Arab and Islamic identity over imperialism using authoritarian tools and tactics instead of democratization.

As Rustow stated, the consolidation of national identity is the only prerequisite of democratization; without national unity, electoral competition would only deteriorate the communal conflict. Thus, for decades, several Arab states gained little momentum for democratization as their political struggle had been diverted to building a nation-state. The imposition of artificial boundaries also created a security dilemma for the new states of the Middle East, where one state has perceived the other as a threat. This perception of threat has not only promoted ideological subversion such as Nasser's pan-Arabism which mobilized the populations of other states against their rulers but also it has been militarized on the Arab/non-Arab fault lines. In that regard, the Arab-Israeli conflict as well as the Iraq-Iran War were primarily over identity, territory, and security.[13] Security-oriented governments of the Middle East promoted the national-security states whose main concern revolves around security and stability rather than promoting individual freedoms and social injustice.

The prior settlement of nation question and managing social cohesion serve as prerequisites for democratic transition. Social cohesion refers to the glue that holds a society together with its multiple dimensions such as ethnicity, religion, sect, and shared history. The outbreak of uprisings brought an end to the forced stability provided by the authoritarian regimes and set the sources of old grievances and tension free. Polarization on various levels has emerged due to Islamists versus secular divide in Tunisia and Egypt, sectarian strife in Syria and Bahrain and clan divisions in Libya.[14] In Tunisia, cohesion problems are related mainly to the political sphere, in which moderate Islamist and secularist visions of governance are in conflict. A similar civic strife has existed between the liberal-secular forces and the Muslim Brotherhood members in Egypt. Besides, religious strife between Egyptian Muslims and Coptic Christians emerged as an important threat to stability in the period after the fall of the Mubarak regime.

The Middle East is usually considered fragmented, unstable, and war-prone region and as such, the region hasn't been hospitable to democratic change. The geopolitical contest between Saudi Arabia and Iran has shaped the politics of the region since the 2003 U.S. occupation of Iraq, each playing its hegemonic role out in the domestic politics of weak Arab states, such as Lebanon, Palestinian territories, Bahrain, and Yemen, and the contest has further intensified following the Arab uprisings. Both countries attempted to expand their sphere of influence in the construction of the New Middle East. The Iranian-Saudi confrontation, in the form of sectarianization of the geopolitical battle has manifested itself in Syria's case where the popular uprisings transformed from its democratic objective into a bloody civil war. As Salloukh points out sectarianization of the region's geopolitical battles and the instrumental use of some of the uprisings for geopolitical ends has hardened sectarian sentiments across the region and complicated post-authoritarian democratic transitions.[15] As a result, sectarianization of the geopolitical battle encouraged several regimes in the region to divert from democratization and move toward securitization.

In short, structural and historical conditions in the MENA region are not favorable to democratic transition while they have certainly affected some Arab states more than others. Tunisia and Egypt set an important example to other states in the region given that the uprisings started in Tunisia and spread over Egypt and transition to democracy was initiated in both countries unlike other Arab countries which went through authoritarian regime breakdown following the uprisings. The two countries' transitions will gain new insights to the study of comparative democratization and allow political scientists to reflect on the variables that enable or hinder a smooth transition to democracy. To this end, the next two chapters analyze the unfolding of the political transitions in Tunisia and Egypt, respectively.

NOTES

1. Freedom House, "Middle East and North Africa," https://freedomhouse.org/regions/middle-east-and-north-africa

2. In this Barometer, Jamal and Tessler identified the frequency of Koran reading as a valid and reliable measure of religiosity. Respondents were categorized according to whether they read the Koran every day, several times a week, sometimes, or rarely or never. Strikingly, at least 85 percent of the respondents in each category state that democracy is the best political system. Amaney Jamal, and Mark Tessler, "The Democracy Barometers: Attitudes in the Arab World," *Journal of Democracy* 19, no. 1 (January 2008): 101.

3. Thomas Isbell, "Separate or Compatible? Islam and Democracy in Five North African Countries," *Afrobarometer Dispatch* 188, February 14, 2018, https://afrobarometer.org/publications/ad188-separate-and-compatible-islam-and-democracy-five-north-african-countries

4. Ibid.

5. Natalya Rahman, "Democracy in the Middle East and North Africa: Five Years After the Arab Uprisings," Arab Barometer-Wave IV (October 2018).

6. Larry Diamond, "Why Are There No Arab Democracies?" *Journal of Democracy* 21, no. 1 (January 2010): 94.

7. Ibid., 98.

8. Michael L. Ross, "Does Oil Hinder Democracy?" *World Politics* 53, no. 3 (April 2001): 356.

9. Ibid., 340–356.

10. Lucan Way, "Comparing the Arab Revolts: The Lessons of 1989," *Journal of Democracy* 22, no. 4 (October 2011): 24.

11. Raymond Hinnebusch, "Authoritarian Persistence, democratization theory and the Middle East: An Overview and Critique," *Democratization* 13, no. 3 (June 2006): 378.

12. Ibid.

13. Ibid.

14. Anthony Shadid, and David D. Kırkpatrick, "Promise of Arab Uprisings is Threatened by Divisions," *The New York Times*, May 21, 2011, https://www.nytimes.com/2011/05/22/world/middleeast/22arab.html

15. Bassel F. Salloukh, "The Arab Uprisings and the Geopolitics of the Middle East," *The International Spectator: Italian Journal of International Affairs* 48, no. 2 (June 2013): 32.

Chapter 3

The Tunisian Revolution

January 14 revolution, or the Jasmine Revolution, was a remarkable turning point for not only the Tunisian history but also the wider Arab world. In the history of the modern Arab world, it was the first grassroots revolt that toppled an entrenched dictator and led the way to a democratic system. The Tunisian revolution was also a breakthrough for political scientists and analysts as it put an end to the obsolete orientalist approaches that viewed the Arab world as an exception to democratic change. Although analysts had long stressed on the stability and the robustness of Arab regimes with numerous strategies they used, the revolution was striking in terms of the pace of the events that unfolded leading to Ben Ali's ouster and the fact that Tunisia created a domino effect setting the stage for change in the wider Arab world. Moreover, Tunisia merits a particular attention as it is currently the only country with Muslim-majority population in the Middle East and North Africa (MENA) region that is democratic and has been rated as "Free" by the Freedom House from 2015 onwards.[1]

The Tunisian revolution was miraculous in several ways. First, it took Tunisian people less than a month of struggle to topple their dictator and patronage networks and to collapse democratic façade that Ben Ali spent twenty-three years to construct. Second, it was a peaceful revolution, and it didn't turn into a terror or civil war. The peaceful nature of the revolution convinced - Tunisians that they would achieve their goal of establishing democracy and restoring dignity and inspired other Arab publics to struggle against their authoritarian governments.[2] Third, the Tunisian revolution was not a classical one like that of French, which was a transition from feudal to bourgeois regime or a class-driven revolution like that of Bolsheviks in Russia. It was not a national liberation revolution like that of Algeria or the Kemalist revolution in Turkey. As Asaf Bayat described the popular demonstrations in the Arab world as collective actions of non-collective actors rarely guided by a clear ideology or recognizable leaderships and organizations, the Tunisian revolution lacked clear ideology, centralized leadership, and a pre-established political program.[3] With all these aspects, the diffusion effect of the Tunisian revolution over other Arab publics, Egypt, Syria, Yemen, and Libya made the Tunisian revolution merit world's attention and appreciation.

The self-immolation of Mohammed al-Bouazizi set off the wave of protests putting an end to the long uttered stability of the Arab regimes. The uprisings unveiled the deep-seated anger and resentment of the Arab publics. They were borne of the frustration and long-lasting dissatisfaction with the socioeconomic malaise and political repression. Upon a closer investigation, it is clear that the mass movements known as the Arab Spring are indeed the latest and most dramatic manifestation of a set of historical antecedents. As the Soviet leader Leon Trotsky once asserted "revolution is impossible until it is inevitable,"[4] the frustration over relentless oppression by Ben Ali regime and the long-lasting socioeconomic malaise in the country made it inevitable for Tunisians to rally around the public outcry against the ruling regime.

Since the January 14 revolution that ended up in the ouster of Ben Ali, Tunisia has embarked on a democratic transition process that is largely successful and promising. This chapter first explores the Tunisian transition with an extensive analysis of the historical developments that paved the way for the January 14 uprisings with an overview of the Tunisian economy and politics under Bourguiba and Ben Ali regimes. Second, the chapter explores the political transition in Tunisia since the outbreak of the uprisings referring the challenges and prospects for democratization in Tunisia.

HISTORICAL BACKGROUND

Any analysis of a revolution and its trajectory would be incomplete without an overview of the economic and political conditions that led the way to the popular uprisings. The Tunisian revolution isn't inseparable from its political and economic roots that led people to take to the streets in their struggle to end the long-entrenched dictatorship.

Tunisian Economy Prior to the Arab Uprisings

Under Bourguiba, Tunisian economy underwent four stages that shaped the country's postindependence economic life: an initial stage of economic decolonization, disastrous stage of socialist transformation, an attempt at state-managed and private-sector-funded industrialization, and finally the stabilization program of the mid-1980s.[5] After gaining independence, Bourguiba immediately moved to decolonize the economy which had been designed to benefit French rather than Tunisian interests. At the time, Tunisian agriculture and mining was heavily dominated and administered by French-owned firms. In the first few years after independence, thousands of French administrative staff with replaced with their Tunisian counterparts and those companies were brought under state control. The Tunisian government aimed to rebuild institutions and civil service that is Tunisian, rather than French.

In the 1960s, the country adopted a corporatist structure with a quasi-socialist (collectivist) economic orientation.[6] This economic orientation was in tune with the domestic demands for social justice and the wave of Nasserist Arab socialism of the era. Although main public utilities were nationalized and the public sector expanded. the spread of collectivist policies didn't attack on the private sector. Collectivization was primarily carried out in agriculture and mining sectors. However, at the end of the decade, quasi-socialist economic policies apparently failed due to gross inefficiency caused by top-down management and organization of the economy, little motivation for increased productivity, and increasing levels of corruption accompanied by growing unemployment.

In the 1970s, the failure of collectivism led to a new economic strategy, namely, protectionist market economy or a semi-liberal *infitah* policy under which a combination of import substitution and export promotion was fostered.[7] The *infitah* policy aimed at opening up foreign trade and promoting foreign investment and a more active role for the private sector. Nonetheless, the private sector consisted primarily of small businesses that were less capital-intensive such as textiles and tourism while public sector monopolized strategic sectors and controlled heavy industries and transport, water, and electricity.[8] Although the country experienced a period of economic growth during 1970s, an overreliance on oil export revenues and foreign borrowing as the engine for investment led to a sharp increase in external debt. By the end of the decade, growth and productivity had slowed down and Tunisia was unable to develop its domestic production or export competitive range of goods. However, the protectionist market economy largely resulted in failure as oil prices dramatically went down and severe droughts of 1982 and 1986 undermined tourism revenues, which in turn adversely affected annual growth rates.[9] As a result of this failure, unemployment increased at unprecedented rates, while austerity measures including reduction in government expenditure and restraining consumption brought about political problems accompanied with instability in the country. The UGTT (Tunisian General Trade Union) severely opposed to the continued wage freezes in the public sector and subsidy reductions. In 1984, Tunisia was swept by a series of violent demonstrations called as "Bread Riots" as a response to the government's ending long-standing price subsidies on grain products to reduce its heavy budget deficits.[10] Tunisia also faced growing social unrest and labor strikes during the last decade under Bourguiba.

In 1986, to stave off maladies caused by economic mismanagement, the Tunisian government introduced the Economic Recovery and Structural Adjustment Program (ERSAP) that brought numerous austerity measures including tariffs reduction, promoting restrictions on imports, and the reduction of personal income taxes and the devaluation of the Tunisian Dinar.[11] Under this program, privatization of state-owned companies was carried out on a vast scale. The Structural Adjustment program imposed by the IMF paid off restoring macroeconomic stability and reducing external debt and inflation. In addition, in 1987, Bourguiba was toppled in a peaceful and constitutional coup led by his prime minister, Zine el Abidine Ben Ali. Ben Ali was wholeheartedly committed to economic reform while promising a new era of political liberalization. He introduced a legislative framework that encouraged foreign investment and facilitated privatization measures while pursuing policies that targeted integration into European markets. Since 1996, the Tunisian government has gradually liberalized trade in manufacturing and played a significant role in making the private sector capable of competition in global markets. During the second half of 1990s, the labor and productivity gains contributed to economic growth and real GDP went up more rapidly than in the previous decade. In the course of two five-year development plans, his regime achieved macroeconomic stability, controlled inflation, and was able to diversify and reorient production from public to private sector and attain a GDP per capita equal to that of Europe's own poorer periphery and decrease country's debts.[12]

In the new millennium, various economic indicators including investments, GDP, and export volumes of goods and services indicated a steady growth in Tunisian economy. In addition, Tunisian political system under Ben Ali depended on the idea that political legitimacy could be based on economic growth. To this end, Tunisia underwent rapid modernization and economic growth as a result of market-oriented reform, private investment, and integration into regional economy. The country also adhered to the Washington consensus and Tunisian workers abroad also contributed to Tunisian economy by providing remittances.[13] The country was reputed as the Maghreb's healthiest economy as well as the MENA region's most successful economic liberalizer by the international creditors and investors.[14]

In the last decade under Ben Ali's rule, annual GDP growth in Tunisia averaged 5 percent and in terms of both GDP per capita and the annual rate of GDP growth, Tunisia performed far ahead of its neighbors. Besides, contrary to several other states in the region including Egypt, a large middle class that enjoys levels of material well-being (such as car and home ownership) existed in Tunisia. A number of reasons lie behind Tunisia's economic success in the region. Its growth under Ben Ali was driven by private sector development, rather than oil and gas exports as in the case of Algeria and Libya. The regime was capable of attracting direct foreign investment with its economic liberalization reforms. Above all, Tunisia closely adhered to the economic policies advocated by the West. It ranks second country with the smallest share in public sector employment in the MENA region after Morocco, which illustrates that the country embraced private enterprise.[15]

On the other hand, the growth of the Tunisian economy had masked several endemic problems engrained in the social unrests that emerged in numerous occasions. Despite the economic growth, the Tunisian government failed to address long-standing concerns about a more just distribution of growth across different socioeconomic groups as well as across different regions of the country. While privatization attempts benefited a small circle of business elite and Ben Ali family's known as Trabelsi clan, economic growth did little to address to the needs of the masses. The extent of Ben Ali family's share in the Tunisian economy was enormous with 220 companies owned by family members, and they controlled 21 percent of net private sector profits. His regulations for economic liberalization was structured to benefit a small circle of business elite linked to his family while he imposed restrictions to prevent other businesses from competing with his established firms.[16] Ben Ali and his family acquired fame for their mafia-style corruption that enriched the members of the president's family. The economic restructuring during his era was accompanied by a number of social costs such as endemic unemployment, intense pressure on public services due to austerity measures, and above all, the gap between rich and poor. These measures were articulated in public opposition to the government and its policies and they lied central to the growing social tensions reflected in the street protests during 2000s.

The major shortcomings that the Tunisian economic growth had masked such as the inability of the government to create jobs and the high unemployment rate among educated youth became more visible in the last decade in the lead up to the uprisings. The government's statistics illustrated a rise in employment among the university graduates from 8.6 percent in 1999 to 19 percent in 2007, yet unofficial data indicate figures twice as high as those derived from government statistics.[17] Unemployment was largely the consequence of the mismatch between the types of jobs available to the young people and their education level. Private sector investment which was tightly controlled by the government-generated jobs for low-skill employment, and most university graduates had to find jobs that they were overqualified for. Mohammed al-Bouazizi, the catalyst of the protest movements, was also part of unemployed educated youth, and he was forced to become a street vendor due to lack of employment opportunities for young people with a degree. Bouazizi's self-immolation might have not by itself triggered uprisings of this magnitude if it hadn't been for a number of suicide protests that preceded it. In March 2010, Abdesslem Trimech, a street vendor whose fruit cart was confiscated by the police and whose demand to meet the city major was rejected set himself on fire in the city hall in Monastır.[18] These suicide protests illustrate a chain of long-standing rebellious instincts of the Tunisian people, particularly the youth, which were repressed by the police.

Equally alarming to the political stability in Tunisia was the government's inability to generate enough jobs in the interior for a growing population. Since independence, economic development plans put into force by the government-fostered investments that would create jobs and increase living standards in the north and along the eastern coastline. This was because the development strategy adopted by the government since the early 1970s relied on private investment and export-oriented production. However, scarce natural resources, inconvenient climate conditions, and the need to reduce transportation costs made it challenging to attract investors to the interior regions.[19] As a consequence, a wide regional disparity emerged between the level of economic development and living standards in the rich coastal towns and the interior regions. A total of 80 percent of the national productions is concentrated in coastal areas from Bizerte to Sfax, while the interior regions host 40 percent of the population and can claim 20 percent of the GDP.[20]

In the years leading up to the 2011 revolution, there were a number of protests over deteriorating living conditions in the interior cities. To illustrate, Gafsa, a city located close to the Algerian border was shaken by an unprecedented social conflict in 2008. The revolt of Gafsa Mining Basin, the biggest protest movement since the Bread Riots of 1984, took place over a period of six months and attended by various categories of the population—the unemployed particularly the university graduates, high school students, families of the workers in the phosphate mines who had undergone a work accident.[21] The Gafsa riots indicated the first signs of a growing social unrest, and it was succeeded by a revolt in Ben Gardanne in southern Tunisia on the Libyan border, in August 2010. In addition to youth employment and regional disparities, the increasing living costs and food prices deteriorated the living conditions of the middle class. From 2003 to 2008, the number of Tunisians with credit card debts increased sixteen-fold, which clearly indicates the middle class increasing resorts to loans to make up for their shortfall in living expenses.[22]

The UGTT, Tunisia's sole trade union confederation, played a critical role in organizing prolonged protests in the Southern Gafsa Mining Basin in 2008 and early 2010. Though the government for long worked hard to bring the union under its control, union activists succeeded in remaining independent and taking a more confrontational stance. As was the case in the Bread Riots of 1984, the initial protests in late 2010 broke out in the interior cities starting from Sidi Bouzid and spread to the coastal areas. Education unions, some of the most independent and aggressive within the UGTT, took an active role in organizing unemployed workers against the government's inability to generate jobs, its corruption, and its rejection to engage in dialogue with civil society.[23] These protests were then joined by other unions, human rights organizations and opposition parties who connected economic grievances with mounting concerns over fundamental human rights and rule-of-law issues.

Tunisian Politics Prior to the Arab Uprisings

The political transition in Tunisia is closely related to historical legacies that have shaped Tunisian society for half a century. One of the most important legacies is that Tunisian society was depoliticized under a tight political control, which can be observed in weak party identification, low level of participation in democratic processes, and a lack of free press. Tunisia's political system was strongly authoritarian even when compared to other Arab states in the region.

Since Tunisia gained its independence from France in 1956 till the uprisings, Tunisia's political life was shaped by two authoritarian leaders: Habib Bourguiba and Zine el-Abidine Ben Ali. Under the guidance of Bourguiba, the Neo Destour movement was founded as a nationalist opposition movement to the French colonial rule in 1920. After Tunisia became a fully independent republic, Bourguiba became the first president in 1957, and his government implemented extensive reforms that would modernize and secularize the country, and develop its economy. Bourguiba holds a strong legacy and popular support among different fractions of the Tunisian society as he was the acknowledged leader of the nationalist movement, which confronted the colonial rulers and struggled for independence. He was strongly attached to French style *laicisme* and aimed to attach his young nation to the bandwagon of European modernity both socially and economically. From many respects, Bourguibaism has striking parallels with Kemalism though the former doesn't appear to be as well-developed ideologically as the latter and Bourguiba was a reformist rather than a revolutionist like Mustafa Kemal.

Under Bourguiba, Tunisia created an image of a modern and secular country, which adopted the values of the French colonial power. Bourguiba advocated a state-managed economy, provided strong social guarantees, and struggled hard to improve country's education and literacy levels. The school curriculums were modernized, designed on the principles of laicism while education was extended throughout the country.[24] Nationalism was at the heart of the government's policies and the administration at various sectors went through a process of "Tunisification" through which French workers were replaced by their Tunisian counterparts.

Bourguiba founded the Neo Destour (Constitution) Party which remained as the single political party that ruled the country till the constitutional coup in 1987.[25] Neo-Destour Party became an essential element of Tunisian government and as Kenneth Perkins noted, Tunisia under Neo-Destour was a "state in the service of the party, party in the service of the President."[26] Neo-Destour was a populist party that infiltrated deep into all levels of the society with the chief objective to rally public opinion in favor of government policies and to confine free political competition. Moreover, the Tunisian constitution introduced a highly centralized presidential system. According to the constitution of 1959, the president held extensive centralized powers including initiation and direction of state policies, appointment of judges, provincial governments, and other key bureaucratic positions. The presidential cabinet headed by the prime minister was also under the presidential control. In reality, all aspects of governance regarding the state and politics were dominated by the president and the Tunisian political institutions served to rubber-stamp the president's decisions.

Under Bourguiba, the constitution of 1959 was ahead of its Arab counterparts in many respects albeit authoritarian in terms of individual liberties. Although the constitution recognized Islam the religion of the state, the government introduced numerous restrictions on religious freedom such as banning women from wearing headscarves in public areas which is regarded as hostility to religion-by-religious factions.[27] Bourguiba emphasized Tunisian exceptionalism as the country differentiated itself from other Arab countries with the progressive personal status law that granted women with the right to vote and initiate divorce, banned polygamy, and introduced a legal minimum age for marriage, and several other reforms on education and gender equality.[28] His era was marked by developments in the era of healthcare, education, and women's rights at a level that could not be compared to any other Arab nation at the time. Bourguiba regime had a liberal image particularly due to the government's liberal policies on gender equality, emphasis on education, and its pro-Western foreign policy.

Tunisia under Bourguiba's presidency became increasingly authoritarian and repressive as opposition toward his efforts to reduce the role of religion in politics hardened. Bourguiba concentrated power in his own hands by co-opting and manipulating clientele networks. He intentionally appointed powerful individuals to important positions to serve their own clienteles while withdrawing others from those posts in a way that he became the "maker and breaker of political careers."[29] He struggled to support workers unrest among the unions and the Tunisian Human Rights League to undermine the union leadership and reunite those organizations under leaders who were loyal to Bourguiba. In 1975, to reassert his political power, Bourguiba declared himself president for life, a position he held until he was removed from power through a constitutional coup by his prime minister, Zine El Abidine Ben Ali in 1987. In his last decade of rule, the faltering economy and violation of political and basic individual rights created mounting dissatisfaction among the public.

By the mid-1980s, wage increases accompanied by the strong economic growth of the 1970s, extensive system of state subsidies, and the worker and students' reliance on public funds gave their way to economic deterioration and inability of the state to carry on providing subsidies and state funds. Bourguiba responded to the deepening political and social crisis by cracking down hard on the labor unions for their wage demands and students for demanding restoration of public funds. Meanwhile, the Islamic Tendency Movement, Nahda's precursor at the time, stepped in to fill the void created by repression of the unions and the movement soon became the regime's principal target for repression. Eventually, economic deterioration curtailed the government's ability to provide stability and buy social peace in return for economic growth. Besides, Bourguiba's refusal to initiate political and economic reforms, his efforts to destroy all sources of political opposition coupled with his health problems and advancing age cleared the way for the constitutional coup that brought Ben Ali to power with little public opposition.

With Ben Ali's accession to power, Tunisia stood at the forefront of democratic openings and political reforms in the late 1980s. Given that Tunisia had long-standing tradition of reform, Western-oriented elite and progressive social policies, in other words, several features that bode well for democratic transition, Tunisia was expected to embark on a trajectory of democratic change that would sooner or later bring multipartyism, competitive elections, and respect of human rights. Besides, Tunisia enjoyed a unique form of state-society relationship in that the state intervened to restore order and prosperity during times of economic and political crisis. The regime, at the same time, generated social forces such as the unions and civil society organizations that would counterbalance it when the state began to seize too much power.[30] Therefore, to many observers, Tunisia was regarded as one of the region's most promising countries in terms of democratic politics.

During his initial years in power, Ben Ali initiated several reforms that seemed to put Tunisia on the track of political liberalization. Ben Ali addressed long-standing aspirations for enhanced political pluralism by amending electoral and press laws. Several restrictions on the press were lifted and political parties were legalized while competition was introduced into the political system with the launch of the multiparty system. During this period, Ben Ali abolished presidency for life. Social and economic development and improving women's rights continued to be priority areas for policy-making. Furthermore, Ben Ali's government freed thousands of political prisoners with the 1989 Amnesty including Islamists, turned the death sentences of several opposition figures into life imprisonment, and encouraged political exiles that lived abroad to return Tunisia.[31] Ben Ali also enforced new legislation that made it easier to establish associations and parties, which enabled the emergence of a vibrant civil society in Tunisia. In line with these political openings, Bourguiba's Socialist Destourien Party (PSD) was renamed as the *Rassemblement Constitutionel Democratique* (Constitutional Democratic Rally) in 1988. Moreover, in 1988, the National Pact was signed with the country's sixteen political parties and interest groups and principal civil society organizations expressing collective commitment to the Code of Personal Status, freedom of expression and association and human rights.[32] Ben Ali's initial years in power seemed a promising trajectory toward democratic change in the country.

The National Pact seemingly aimed to overcome the shortcomings of the Bourguiba era by bringing oppositional forces to engage in dialogue on broad topics such as political system, economic development, and foreign policy. To this end, Islamists represented under the Islamic Tendency Movement (MTI) were invited to participate in the discussions, however, they were not one of the parties that signed the final document which ultimately aimed to pave the way for "a more elaborate corporatist formula with a growing pluralist potential."[33] On the other hand, the MTI conceded to fulfill the provisions in order to gradually integrate into the new political arena including the acceptance of *Shura* (consultation) and the renaming of the party to remove the religious connotation in its name at the regime's request. The movement changed its name from the Islamic Tendency Movement to *Hizb al-Nahda* or also known as "Ennahda" (Renaissance) anticipating that the regime would lay out competitive democracy that the Islamists would play a role.[34] However, Ben Ali refused to legalize Ennahda Party, although the party came to terms with the requirements of competitive democracy. Though opposition groups demanded proportional legislative elections, the old majority list system used under Bourguiba remained intact for the 1989 electoral code.[35]

Despite the illusory structural changes that Ben Ali's presidency came up with in response to calls for multiparty politics and genuine electoral competition, the National Pact was indeed an effort to create the appearance of political pluralism, yet it was in fact far from a compromise or bargain among equals.[36] By the 1990s, Tunisia's liberalization trend had begun to fade and this new decade marked the beginning of Tunisia's slide into deeply entrenched authoritarianism. In 1989, Islamists under the Tendency movement received up to 25 percent of the votes in the only elections they contested under Ben Ali, which made it clear that the real opposition to Ben Ali laid in the Islamist movement.[37] This electoral success of the Islamists culminated in Ben Ali's outlawing the Islamists in the political sphere.

Indeed, Ben Ali's electoral democracy was carefully and selectively designed to recognize his opponents that would make no real challenge to his regime and not allow any redistribution of power.

The exclusion of Ennahda from the parliament despite widespread grassroots support for their candidates running as independents led to intense protests by Ennahda activists. The government's ruthless campaign to crack down on Ennahda intensified in 1991 after the government accused Ennahda of a plot that intended to topple the regime. The government, thereafter, amplified the dose of its repression against Ennahda members. Torture under interrogation convictions carried out by military courts became common in this era. This led hundreds of leading Ennahda members to flee from the country to exile abroad. The government continually reminded the experiences of Algeria and Egypt arguing that political and economic stability would no longer proceed if any kind of Islamist party is tolerated within politics.[38] The government's repressive policies extended to other opposition groups including workers, students and activists. From 1990 onwards, Tunisia ever-increasingly witnessed arbitrary use of force to attack all opposition groups and widespread use of torture in prisons and countless political arrests and jailing.[39] Ben Ali's campaign to quash any form of opposition went parallel with the dramatic expansion of Tunisia's internal security forces.

Ben Ali's regime consolidated its power and provided legitimacy through economic performance rather than representative institutions and competitive elections. Early economic liberalization reforms have produced pressures on political liberalization which originate not only from the revival of competing social forces but also directly from the implications of economic liberalization itself. In many parts of the world, the process of liberalization occurred simultaneously with that of political liberalization and democratization. With a full-scale economic liberalization, new sociopolitical forces that challenge both state and party are expected to emerge and the mediatory role of the single party either becomes redundant or it ceases to function. Thus, regime is required to open space and new political opportunities for the upper classes initiating early political liberalization.

One consequence of this early liberalization is that the regime is forced to choose between its own survival and fulfillment of emerging popular demands in the route toward democratization which might challenge its survival. The Tunisian regime, like the other regimes in the MENA region, reacted by reinforcing authoritarianism as soon as tentative moves toward democracy had begun. Thus, the political liberalization was reversed, the media was heavily censored, the police and security services were given more freedom and political activities were limited or banned again. Therefore, Ben Ali's initial reforms, as Larbi Sadiki observes, represent another phase in the reproduction of hegemonic political practice which is about control rather than democratic power sharing.[40]

Ben Ali was, in fact, building a pseudo-democracy or a political order that allowed some freedom to express opinions and to organize within boundaries defined by the state while it changed very little of the authoritarian structures of the previous regime.[41] Though the new system enabled greater contestation and participation, the alternation of power was not possible. Ben Ali's political reforms were indeed manifestations of tightly controlled liberalization which was not accompanied by associational life, law-abiding government, free press, and freely organized opposition.[42] Over twenty-three years in rule, Ben Ali was never genuinely committed to fully opening the system to contestation; instead, he designed a tailored electoral system that would yield exceptionally high number of seats in the parliament in favor of the Constitutional Democratic Rally (RCD).

Under Ben Ali, Tunisian political system could better be described as "a hegemonic party system" where opposition parties could operate legally albeit with little or no chance to compete for power.[43] To create a democratic facade, Ben Ali wisely incorporated political opposition and potential challenges into a controlled and cooperative multiparty system by excluding the Islamist movement from the political arena on the one hand and promoting an essentially collaborative secular opposition to draw support away from the Islamists on the other. The Tunisian government carefully legalized only those parties which had little grassroots support from the masses and offered no real challenge to the regime such as the Communist and the leftist parties that had little ideological credibility after the collapse of the Soviet Union.

Under the veneer of a democratic language, Ben Ali took severe measures to curb any potential risks to his singular rule. To this end, charity activities were taken over by the state while the state struggled hard to bring the syndicates and civil society organizations under its control through several strategies including co-optation, intimidation, infiltration, and divide and rule. Moreover, in 1994, the regime decided to introduce a fixed quota of seats for opposition parties in parliamentary elections and municipal councils and gradually raised it till the quota reached 25 percent in the 2009 vote. RCD maintained a stranglehold in parliamentary elections and Ben Ali never polled below 90 percent of the vote. However, the fixed quota of seats for opposition parties not only created the pretense of competitive multiparty politics but also prevented any fractures within the ranks of the ruling RCD. There were also moments in Tunisian politics when this pretense of competitiveness was undermined by an explicit support to Ben Ali by an opposing candidate in a presidential debate.[44]

The electoral system was shaped in a way to serve as a mechanism to strengthen party unity and to buy off oppositionists through access to patronage. It also sowed disunity among the smaller parties which either chose to remain silent or mute their criticism in important political issues in return for access and patronage. The opposition parties had little chance and space to compete with RCD given that the party held sway over the legislature and municipal councils. Furthermore, electoral processes under Ben Ali were sham as ballot boxes were manipulated by the regime coercively and vote monitoring by independent parties was not allowed. From 1999 to 2010, Ben Ali and his party RCD won all the elections they contested—be they municipal, parliamentary and presidential—with landslide victory, over 90 percent of the votes in most elections.[45]

In the postdependence period, the Tunisian regime adopted a corporatist model in which the ruling party and the national labor union were channels that communicated people's demands. The ruling party RCD acted as an intermediary institution that reconciles different views reflected in its own texture rather than offering Tunisians a choice among political parties. The reasoning behind this is apparent in the party's name which describes it as a rally (*al-tajammu*), rather than a party (*al-hizb*) and in that regard, the party took on a broader role closing the political space for any potential competitor for power.[46] One consequence for this corporatist system is that the Tunisian society was highly depoliticized. In the first major poll after January 14, only half of the survey respondents could identify any political party including the ruling party by name, and in another poll conducted few months later, only a quarter of respondents said that they had sufficient knowledge about political parties or political situation in Tunisia.[47]

Tunisia was heavily policed during Ben Ali's rule. Based on the Amnesty International Reports, the country is almost akin to *un commissariat* (a police station) or a *mukhabarat* state and the exaggerated fear of "fundamentalist threat" have justified this commissariat.[48] The paranoia with the Islamist threat was frequently used as an excuse to justify excessive policing by the regime. Exclusion and harassment weren't confined to Islamists. Over the years, Muwaadah and Shammari, former MDS (Movement of Social Democrats) leaders, Marzouki, Mazali, and former Prime Minister Radiya Nasrawi all underwent regime harassment ranging from character assassination to police surveillance, passport confiscation, and interference with family members.[49] Violence was an integral part of the Tunisian political system since the country gained its independence. Amira Aleya-Sghaier, a professor at the University of Tunis, observed "Established in an atmosphere of fear, executions, trials and torture, the so-called 'modern' state created by Bourguiba and his successor Ben Ali was modern in nothing but its facade. All the government's ministries, meetings and legislation concealed a medieval despotism. The use of violence to counter popular demands was systemic."[50]

An additional factor regarding the democratic facade Ben Ali struggled to preserve since his early political liberalization efforts was to please his Western allies and potential foreign investors. Two cornerstones of the regime legitimacy were built on the creation of a secular state and improvement of women rights and gender equality. In the absence of a real participatory politics, the regime undertook policies such as quota for female parliamentarians and a ban on state wearing the headscarf for female state employees in an attempt to polish regime's credentials as modern, progressive, and secular state. Moreover, in the wake of 9/11, Tunisian police forces quadrupled since Bourguiba's presidency and Tunisia became a gigantic surveillance camp. The global war on terror and the so-called fundamentalist or Al-Qaeda threat were often articulated by Ben Ali though this threat was more of an exaggeration, rather than an actual reality. Ben Ali's vision of political Islam as a threat and his commitment to police Islamic currents and their mobilization in Tunisia served the Western, particularly the French and the U.S. security interests of curbing the influence of the Islamic movements in the name of preventing terrorism. In a recent cable in 2009, the U.S. Ambassador to Tunisia, Robert F. Godec, was reported to say, "we can't write off Tunisia. We have too much at stake. We have an interest in preventing al-Qaeda in the Islamic Maghreb and other extremist groups from establishing a foothold here."[51] Hence, the United States was complicit with Ben Ali's dictatorial rule and human rights violations in Tunisia, yet he would get away with the allegations of human rights violations in exchange for his commitment to fight against all Islamic currents in line with the American geostrategic priorities. By June 2008, the U.S. ambassador described Tunisia as a police state and gave signs of a potential explosion of public unrest in a top-secret report revealed by Wikileaks.[52]

> Tunisia has big problems. President Ben Ali is aging, his regime is sclerotic and there is no clear successor. Many Tunisians are frustrated by the lack of political freedom and angered by first Family corruption, high unemployment and regional inequities. Extremism poses a continuing threat . . . Despite Tunisia's economic and social progress, its record on political freedoms is poor. Tunisia is a police state, with little freedom of expression or association, and serious human rights problems. [. . .] But for every step forward there has been another back, for example the recent takeover of important private media outlets by individuals close to President Ben Ali.
>
> The problem is clear: Tunisia has been ruled by the same president for 22 years. He has no successor, and while President Ben Ali deserves credit for continuing many of the progressive policies of President Bourguiba, he and his regime have lost touch with the Tunisian people. They tolerate no advice or criticism, whether domestic or international. Increasingly, they rely on the police

for control and focus on preserving power, and corruption in the inner circle is growing. Even average Tunisians are now keenly aware of it, and the chorus of complaints is rising. Tunisians intensely dislike, even hate, First Lady Leila Trabelsi and her family. In private, regime opponents mock her; even those close to the government express dismay at her reported behavior. Meanwhile, anger is growing at Tunisia's high unemployment and regional inequities. As a consequence, the risks to the regime's long-term stability are increasing.

For decades, Ben Ali pursued a tacit social contract where the ruler emphasized stability and the ruled assented to it in return for the achievement of the second priority of economic well-being.[53] Most Tunisians reluctantly accepted Ben Ali's heavy-handedness through the 1990s as they bowed to authoritarian rule as a price for economic growth and political stability that could attract tourists and investors in the absence of a political unrest such as the one that plagued neighboring Algeria.[54] However, by 2000, this tacit social contract began to erode as Tunisians became more aware that Islamists no longer posed a serious threat and thus, less willing to accept Ben Ali's tyrannical authoritarianism. On the other hand, the government seemed to obstruct channels to engage in a dialogue with critics and opposition parties. While the social unrest was becoming more visible with labor strikes and street protests, the government amplified its brutal methods of repression including arbitrary arrests, passport confiscations, strict control of the print media and Internet access, and the imprisonment of journalists and human rights activists.

Among Tunisians, there was widespread discontent due to mounting social inequalities, wide-scale corruption, and particularly, the high rate of unemployment among the educated youth. Ben Ali's economic liberalization co-opted a small network of business elite instead of increasing benefits for the entire population. In the last decade of Ben Ali's rule, tensions rose, particularly among the youth as they perceived no possibility of upward economic and social mobility under the rule of Ben Ali.[55] Members of Ben Ali and Trabelsi family exercised extensive control over the private sector and many of the resources and jobs were distributed through clientalist networks. Nepotism and kleptocracy of the ruling elite became an important source of anger and frustration.

Ben Ali regime utilized its political mobility and coercive strategies to grab economic benefits through patronage and control at the expense of the entire nation. While privatization is expected to promote competitiveness and economic growth, in the Tunisian case, it generated the emergence of mafia-style clans close to Ben Ali who monopolized wealth. Since the private sector remained under state control and intervention, the line between the public and private was often blurry, which enabled various forms of corruption including the unregulated flows of assets accrued to the state traveling through the Tunisian Central Bank to the personal accounts of the ruling family.[56] Leila Trabelsi—Ben Ali's wife—was linked to a number of corruption scandals including stealing one and a half tons of gold from the country's central bank and "illegal appropriation of prime real estate, and acquisition of formally state-owned companies at substantially depreciated prices."[57] In addition, the embezzlement of funds normally allocated for public amenities and welfare services degraded the quality of public services such as education and health systems and the construction of roads and other infrastructure, which in turn led many Tunisians to refer to the ruling elite as thieves or mafia. Ben Ali's family and his close circles accumulation of enormous wealth through privatization of public assets accounts for the failure of egalitarian distribution of resources that was needed to alleviate economic grievances of the populations in the interior regions.

Although Tunisia under Ben Ali was among the economically better off than most countries in the MENA region in terms of GDP per capita, due to ever-widening gap between the rich elite and the poor, the coast and the interior, Tunisians were experiencing what James Davies called as "relative deprivation," a crucial prerequisite for a revolution.[58] Repression in the name of Ben Ali's often cited stability and one-sided social contract which benefits a small circle of elite was no longer tenable for Tunisian citizens who began to view the corrupt, unjust, and self-indulging behaviors of the ruling elite with abhorrence. Once Mohamed Bouazizi, a Tunisian street vendor set himself on fire, his self-immolation became a catalyst for the Tunisian revolution and the Arab Spring protests in the wider Arab world whose wick had long been waiting to be ignited. The insurrection began in Sidi Bouzid, a less-developed interior city of Tunisia, with demonstrations, strikes, and clashes with the police and it spread first to the west of the country, then to the south, and finally arrived the capital. The initial slogans made social demands for "work, freedom, and national dignity" (*shughl, hurriya, karama wataniyya*), and they called for Ben Ali regime and its entire apparatus to be ousted altogether with their famous slogan "We can live on bread and water, but no more Ben Ali" (*Khubz wa ma wa Ben Ali la*).[59]

The Tunisian Political Transition

Soon after Ben Ali was removed from power, the military withdrew to the barracks as soon as stability and security were restored. An interim government was founded to move the transition process toward elections and constitutional drafting. On the whole, the initial stage of the political transition was turbulent in Tunisia since it turned into a power play between the old regime forces and revolutionary factions. The transition process

Table 3.1 Timeline of the Key Events during the Tunisian Revolution

Date	Event
December 17, 2010	Mohammad al-Bou'azizi, a twenty-six-year-old supporting his family selling fruits and vegetables from a cart, sets himself on fire in protest over mistreatment from local authorities.
December 20, 2010	Protests break out over unemployment, political restrictions in Sidi Bouzid.
December 25, 2010	Demonstrations spread to other towns including Kairoun, Sfax, and Ben Guerdane.
December 27, 2010	The protests reach the capital city Tunis.
December 28, 2010	UGGT and Lawyers' Syndicate throw their weight behind protests. In a conciliatory measure, several governors and ministers are dismissed. Ben Ali promises a firm response to the protests in a televised address.
December 29 to January 3, 2011	The authorities' response to the protests turns increasingly violent and they attempt to shut down independent media.
January 6, 2011	Tunisian lawyers strike in protest over police brutality
January 13, 2011	Ben Ali promises not to seek reelection in 2014 and loosen restrictions on freedom.
January 14, 2011	After dissolving parliament and declaring a state of emergency, Ben Ali goes into exile to Saudi Arabia. Mohammed Ghannouchi, the prime minister, appears on state television to announce that he is assuming the role of interim president under chapter 56 of the Tunisian constitution.
January 15, 2011	The constitutional court rules that Fouad Mebazaa, the speaker of parliament, should be interim president, not Ghannouchi. Mebazaa tasks Ghannouchi with forming a new coalition government.
January 17, 2011	A new government is announced, but includes several Ben Ali loyalists in key posts—including the defense, interior, and foreign ministers—and few opposition members in lesser positions.
January 18, 2011	Unhappy with the lineup of the new government, Tunisians take to the streets in protest. Other opposition ministers threaten to quit, saying they do not want to be in a government with members of Ben Ali's former ruling party. Ghannouchi and Mebazaa resign from the RCD in a bid to placate protesters.
January 20, 2011	All ministers in the interim government quit Ben Ali's RCD Party but remain in their cabinet posts. The central committee of RCD is dissolved as many of the ministers were also committee members.
January 21, 2011	The protesters in Tunis demand the dissolution of the new government as they honor those who died in the unrest of previous weeks. In an effort to dampen the anger, Ghannouchi pledges to quit politics after legislative and presidential elections.
January 22, 2011	Thousands of protesters take to the streets yet again, continuing to ask for the removal of all RCD members from the interim government. Around 2000 police officers join the civilian protesters calling for better working conditions and a new union.

(Continued)

Table 3.1 (Continued)

January 26, 2011	The Tunisian General Labor Union holds a general strike in Sfax, Tunisia's second city and economic center, and thousands demand that the government resign
January 27, 2011	Tunisia's foreign minister, Kamel Morjane, announces his resignation. The prime minister later announces a reshuffle of the cabinet, dropping key ministers from the criticized government of ousted president Zine El Abidine Ben Ali.
February 20, 2011	Ghannouchi announced his resignation. Tunisians stage a demonstration on 20 February to demand the formation of a constituent assembly.
March 2011	The Higher Authority for the Realization of the Objectives of the Revolution, Political Reform, and Democratic Transition was created through the merger of various political factions. It was headed by Yadh Ben Achour.

Adapted from (Rifai 2011; The New Arab 2015)

was also characterized by deep polarization in the Tunisian society along religious-secular lines. Although the country has been deeply plagued by such divisions in several stages of the political transition, Tunisia was able to successfully move toward democracy as indicated in the electoral and constitutional processes that were fulfilled in a transparent, inclusive, and participatory manner. This section will investigate the political transition in Tunisia in the light of the key political developments that took place since the ouster of Ben Ali.

Tunisia under the Interim Government

Following the revolts that toppled Ben Ali's regime, RCD, the police, the Ministry of the Interior, and some elements of the army continued to operate. They held the belief that the popular uprisings was to oust the president, but it would not eventually displace the political system. Mohammed Ghannouchi, who served as Ben Ali's prime minister, declared that he would become the interim president in accordance with Article 56 of the Tunisian constitution. The Ghannouchi government and its RCD ministers announced they would elect a new president within sixty days. Upon this declaration, the popular uprisings became radicalized. Civil society organizations and lawyers expressed their deep concerns about a transition based on Article 56 as it could lead the way for Ben Ali's return. This second phase of the revolution was accompanied by the advent of young people from the interior of the country to Tunis in "caravans of freedom" in coordination with the revolutionary committees.[60] These young people occupied the prime minister's offices in a large sit-in that lasted from January 23 to January 28 which disrupted the operation of the government.

The second sit-in which was better organized and represented by various organizations including the UGTT and the Association of Lawyers managed to bring down the Ghannouichi government. They pressed for a transition based on Article 57 of the Tunisian constitution, which would close the door on Ben Ali forever but would call for the speaker of the parliament to become the interim president.[61] Thus, Ghannouichi stepped back into prime ministership, and Fouad Mbazaa became the interim president. The new government which included three ministers from the UGTT asked for cooperation of legal opposition parties and civil society activists. Ghannouichi announced the formation of three special commissions to meet people's aspirations and prevent further radicalization of the revolts: the Commission on Law Reform, the Commission of Inquiry on Corruption, and the Independent Commission of Inquiry (this last commission was later disbanded).

The new government took a number of initiatives aimed at addressing long-standing grievances of Tunisian people such as granting a general amnesty to political prisoners, welcoming home dissidents in exile, including Rachid al-Ghannouichi, the founder of Ennahda, freezing RCD activities and seizing its properties and legalizing new political parties.[62] However, these initiatives failed to gain the support of the organizations that acted as the protectors of the revolution. To many civil society organizations and the UGTT, Tunisian transition had the risk of diversion to authoritarianism as there were many holdovers from the old regime in Ghannouichi's government. Five ministers belonging to the opposition groups including two from the UGTT resigned from the interim government in an attempt to protest the inclusion of several holdovers from Ben Ali regime.

Protests shook the capital till Ghannouichi completely disbanded his government on January 27, 2011. The second government of Ghannouichi contained no officials from RCD Party and more representatives from civil society organizations. The prime minister announced his plans for moving forward with the UGTT. Despite these moves, Ghannouichi didn't prove to be a competent technocrat in the eyes of most Tunisians for two reasons: First, he failed to pursue the gangs of Ben Ali supporters who were involved in violent acts. Second, people were frustrated by the rather slow pace of change since the revolution.[63] In late February, Tunis was exposed to a new protest wave, the largest demonstration after Ben Ali's toppling. Amid unrest accompanied with outbreaks of violence and casualties, Mohammed Ghannouchi was forced to resign, and his resignation was followed by the appointment of a former Bourguiba minister, Beji Caid Essebsi as Prime Minister.[64] The interim government was responsible for managing the state's daily affairs and preparing for National Assembly elections.

A critical juncture emerged as concerns regarding the Article 57 were raised by the activists in civil society organizations and the UGTT. According to Article 57, a new president should be elected before a new legislature was set up and the constitution could only be amended after the elections, which left the commission in charge of political reform with very hard questions. The main controversy arose as regards to the sequence of the constitutional reform and elections. Many activists opposed holding presidential elections under an unreformed and undemocratic constitution that concentrated unchecked power in the executive's hands. Given Tunisia's long history of presidents who used constitutions as weapons to serve their interests, this concern was not without a reason. With the existing constitution, the remnants of the old regime could divert the transition to their own interests or the new elected regime could turn to authoritarianism by legitimizing its policies based on the constitution. Rachid Ghannouchi, the exiled leader of the Ennahda movement, maintained that a transition from an authoritarian system to a democracy would call for a democratic constitution in the first place given that the current constitution hands the executive, legislative, and judicial powers to the president. In one of his interviews in early 2011, Ghannouichi stated[65]:

> Basing the transition on the (current) constitution to build a democratic system is a futile attempt to build democracy from dictatorship because only God can bring out life from death. We cannot bring a democratic system out of this corrupt, dictatorial system. We have to put an end to the authoritarian system and start a new one. Basing this transition on Article 56 or 57 is a continuation of the old system. The constitution was a tyranny, the state was reduced to one man, who had in his hands the executive, judicial and legislative powers and was not accountable to anyone. How can such a constitution point towards building a democratic system, even as a starting point? The first step of building a democratic system is to build a democratic constitution. For this we need a constitutional council for rebuilding the state, one in which political parties, the trade unions and the civil society join. This council will rebuild the democratic constitution and will be the basis for building the democratic system.

On February 11, twenty-eight political parties and civil society organizations formed the Committee for the National Congress to Safeguard the Revolution and the committee agreed that saving the revolution is more important than obedience to an undemocratic constitution. The Tunisian solution to the gridlock was to dissolve the constitution and form a national constituent assembly to be elected on July 24, 2011, that would develop an entirely new constitution.[66] Civil society organizations and professional syndicates dissatisfied with the slow pace of reform used the Committee to consolidate protesters' demands and make pressure on the interim government to move forward with a national constituent assembly. Under Esssebsi, the Committee to Safeguard the Revolution and the High Commission for Political Reform was merged under Ben Achour's leadership, and it was renamed the High Commission for the Realization of the Objectives of the Revolution, of Political Reform and Democratic Transition, also known as the Ben Achour Commission.

The establishment of Ben Achour Commission and the decisions taken on the key issues regarding the transitional roadmap with the broad participation of civilian actors was an important step in moving the transition from an authoritarian rule toward democracy. The Commission was made up of 155 members including numerous (nonvoting) legal experts, representatives from political parties, civil society groups, prominent Tunisian intellectuals, and business leaders. The Ben Achour Commission first met on March 17 and with the involvement of members from a broad political spectrum drew a transitional roadmap for the country and the commission members took a "process-first" view privileging creating mechanisms for a democratic government that can carry out reforms legitimately based on public consent.[67] To this end, the commission members, first, decided the suspension of the 1959 constitution on the ground that it didn't ensure democratic, pluralistic, and impartial elections. Second, they came to an agreement on holding an election for a constituent assembly to draft a new constitution and writing a new electoral law based on an electoral system that would be antimajoritarian and coalition-encouraging. Third, the commission decided to create an independent electoral commission and invite many international electoral observers who would extensively monitor the elections. Finally, the commission decided on a gender-parity provision to ensure strong participation of women in the constitution-drafting process.

The 2011 Elections and Ennahda's Rise to Power

In April 2011, a new electoral law was drafted by the High Commission led by one of Tunisia's most-respected legal scholars, Yadh Ben Achour. The electoral law was based on a closed list Proportional Representation (PR) system with a zero-percent national threshold designed to promote plurality and inclusivity.[68] Three features of the electoral law were decisive on the outcome of the National Constituent Assembly (NCA) elections. First, the lustration[69] clause of the electoral law excluded officials who had been politically active in Ben Ali's RCD from the party lists. Second, there was no electoral threshold, which led to political fragmentation among left-leaning groups and the emergence of a vibrant multiparty politics.[70] Finally, the electoral formula used, that is, PR instead of Westminster style first past the post (FPTP) system had a significant impact on the seats allocated. The electoral system based on PR allows to include as many parties as possible and benefits smaller parties reducing the likelihood of a landslide victory by any one party.[71] The largest party was awarded less than a majority of seats and therefore had to negotiate with other groups while drafting the constitution.

In October 2011, Tunisians voted for representatives to the NCA, a transitional institution that is made up of 217 members and in charge of appointing a new transitional government, drafting a new constitution, and setting the stage for elections. In the elections for the NCA, eighty-one parties put forward candidate lists and twenty-seven parties won at least one seat. The voter turnout was about 51.9 percent of the registered voters. Over 80 percent of seats went to five parties; the Ennahda Party won the highest number of the seats (eighty-nine seats) in the assembly with 37 percent of the votes. The rest of the seats were shared among the four center left parties: Congress for the Republic (CPR), Popular Petition, Ettakatol, and the Progressive Democratic Party (PDP). After prolonged negotiations, Tunisia's new government was built on a coalition among three parties with the highest number of votes—Ennahda, Ettakatol, and the CPR, which came to be known as the "Troika" government.[72]

Through the elections, rhetoric of bipolarity, Islamists versus secularists held sway over Tunisian politics. In their first multiparty elections, Tunisians gave a majority to the Islamic political party Ennahda within the Constituent Assembly; however, they also voted for cooperation over polarization. For instance, the PDP, seen as Ennahda's chief competitor, pursued an anti-Islamist campaign aggressively and it rejected the idea of joining a coalition government with Ennahda. Contrary to the figures in the survey data carried out before the elections, the PDP's votes were far below the expectations indicating Tunisians' demand for moderate politics.[73] The holding of the elections for the NCA in 2011 was a breakthrough as it was not only the first free and fair election held in Tunisia since the country's independence, but also in the wider Arab world.

In the weeks following the elections, a deal was achieved among the three top parties in the election over sharing power and appointment of leading positions. Moncef Marzouki from Secular Congress for Republic (CPR) became the interim president of the republic, Mustafa Ben Jafar from Ettakatol was appointed as the president of the constituent assembly, and Hamadi Jamali from Ennahda was appointed as the prime minister.[74] The ease with which Islamists and the secular liberals reached a consensus and formed the troika government can be ascribed to their regular meetings that began eight years before Ben Ali's fall aiming to reduce mutual fears and agree-upon rules for democratic governance.[75] The heads of the Ennahda and the CPR, Rachid Ghannouichi and Moncef Marzouki had met about twenty times in London over eight years prior to Ben Ali's fall and their efforts bore fruitful outcomes in the post-Ben Ali period as the roughly 155 consensually selected members of the reform commission decided on six major rules and principles to govern the selection and proceedings of a constituent assembly.[76]

In January, the assembly began working on the new constitution by setting six commissions, each charged with a specific set of constitutional issues. In order for the draft to become Tunisia's new constitution, it needed to receive two-thirds of majority vote in the assembly. Once it failed to receive sufficient votes, the commission would revise it and the revised draft would be submitted to the assembly for a second vote. In the case of another failure to receive a two-thirds majority, the draft would go to the public for a national referendum and a simple majority vote in the referendum would allow the ratification of the new constitution. The Troika's division of power among Marzouki, Jebali, and Ben Jafaar obstructed the executive body of the country from taking a clear roadmap. The polarization between Ennahda and left-wing party representatives was also evident in the constitutional reform process. During the drafting process of the new Tunisian constitution, there was considerable debate between political Islamist groups, represented by Ennahda Party and secular and liberal groups, represented by Congress Party for the Republic (CPR) and Ettakatol on mainly four issues: (1) the role of religion in the constitution, (2) free speech, (3) the legal and constitutional rights of women, (4) the choice of a parliamentary or presidential system.

The Role of Religion in the Constitution

Shortly after NCA was set up, concerns arose as regards to the role of religion in the constitution among secular groups. Ennahda made mention of *Sharia* neither during its electoral campaign in 2011 nor prior to the elections. Rachid Ghannouichi, the leader of Ennahda, asserted that his party would not seek to insert religious law into the new constitution.[77] However, soon after the party's electoral victory in the NCA, a group of member of parliaments (MPs), belonging to a more conservative wing of Ennahda proposed adopting *Sharia* as a "source among sources" of legislation. At a protest in which thousands of Salafists rallied in support for adopting *Sharia* in the constitution, the president of the Ennahda parliamentary group, Sahbi Atig shouted that "*Sharia* would be the main source of legislation" and the crowd chanted "the only source!"[78] NCA speaker Ban Jaafar threatened that he would resign and withdraw Ettakatol from the ruling coalition should *Sharia* appear in the constitution in any form.[79] The risk of the Troika collapsing and growing pressure of the secular parties and nongovernmental organizations (NGOs) on Ennahda to clarify its position forced the party leadership to put an end to the debates announcing that it opposes adopting *Sharia* in the constitution but support retaining Article 1 of the 1959 constitution, which states that "Tunisia is a free, independent, sovereign state; Islam is its religion; Arabic is its language; and the Republic is its form of government."

Free Speech

The debates on blasphemy ban took place after the riots were triggered by an art exhibit considered as offensive to Islam by some conservatives. During these riots, one person died and hundreds injured while the government declared a three-day curfew. Following the riots, a bloc of Ennahda MPs announced the party's formal statement calling for criminalization of offenses against religion. The statement further demanded a judicial investigation into the acts of blasphemy against sacred values, and it urged the NCA to pass a law banning blasphemy in the new constitution.[80] The secular parties and civil society groups opposed to this proposal claiming that such an article would be constraint on free expression. Ennahda leadership later agreed with other parties in the coalition to drop this controversial blasphemy clause and following weeks of heated debates, the parties agreed on an article that criminalizes only speech causing harm to the public order and morals and prohibits charges of apostasy- or *takfir*- and incitement to violence and hatred.

The Legal and Constitutional Rights of Women

During the secular regimes of Bourguiba and Ben Ali, the status of women remained a domain that was unique in the Arab world.[81] Ennahda pledged to uphold the country's Personal Status Code, defining gender equality, outlawing polygamy, and granting equal rights to women in divorce, adoption, and other personal matters. However, Souad Abderrahim, a female Ennahda MP proposed that Tunisian laws shouldn't protect single mothers and 1998 law giving children out of wedlock equal rights should be eliminated arguing that the freedom granted to women should not be at the expense of Islamic principles.[82] Later, the constitutional subcommittee of the NCA on Rights and Liberties adopted its draft constitution thanks to the votes casted by Ennahda MPs stating "The State shall preserve women's rights and achievements under the principle of complementarity with men within the family and as partners of men in the development of the homeland."[83] Hence, the principle of equality in the 1956 constitution turned into the principle of complementarity in the draft constitution of 2012.

This draft constitution led to strong condemnations from NGOs including the Tunisian Association of Democratic Women, the Tunisian League of Human Rights, the Tunisian Branch of Amnesty International, and the UGTT as well as secular parties arguing that this equivocal draft defined women in relation to men rather than full citizens. The draft proposal also sparked a large-scale public protest on Tunisia's National Women's Day. After those protests, Ennahda MPs retreated from their initial position, and the draft was reformulated as "men and women are equal in rights and duties" and ratified in the assembly (Article 20 of the constitution).[84]

The Choice of a Parliamentary or Presidential System

A major point of contention emerged between Ennahda and secular parties as regards to the structure of power and adoption of parliamentary or presidential system. Ennahda MPs were in favor of a parliamentary power in the belief that they had a more unified voter base and a stronger national organization than the secular parties. They argued that a strong legislature with most executive power vested in cabinet of ministers would act as a shield against the concentration of power in a president who might have authoritarian tendency. On the other hand, the secular parties in the NCA advocated a presidential or semi-presidential system that would enable direct election of a president who has control over the legislature. They assumed that a presidential or semi-presidential system would serve their interests better given the strength of the Ennahda Party in the parliament and wanted to maintain a check on Ennahda's authority through a separation of powers. Ennahda's spokesman expressed that the party was open to reconsider its stance regarding the choice of political regime.[85] After negotiations among the secular parties and Ennahda, the constitution called for a semi-presidential system, which actually came closer to a power structure advocated by the Ennahda MPs. The directly elected president would exercise drastically reduced power only over areas of defense and foreign affairs but would share executive authorities with a prime minister from the party that has the largest number of seats in parliament.

During the drafting process of the new Tunisian constitution, political gridlock that originated from the ideological divisions between the secular and Islamist bloc of the Constituent Assembly and the politically fragmented nature of the coalition government, wide-scale protests, and violence dominated Tunisian politics through 2012 and the first half of 2013. The secularists accused the Ennahda MPs of being engaged in double-speak, making emphasis on tolerance, freedom of belief and expression, and respect for women's rights in their interviews to outside observers, while emphasizing commitment to Islamic values and rejecting Western values in their speech to their own base. Meanwhile, Ennahda blamed the opposition parties for reflecting ideological animosity, rather than principles of a democratic government.

As deputies in the NCA got stuck over language in the constitution dealing with civil liberties and rights, the status of women and the structure of power sharing, the Tunisian people continued to fight off the same social and economic challenges that catalyzed the revolution. Official unemployment rate rose from 14.9 percent to 18.9 percent and was more than 30 percent among the youth with higher education.[86] By January 2013, in a survey of public opinion 77 percent of Tunisians responded that the country was going in the wrong direction.[87] Tunisians were mainly concerned with high unemployment rate and financial stagnation and were annoyed at a government primarily engaged with cultural and ideological issues rather than coming up with policies to create jobs and managing prices. In addition to the worsening socioeconomic situation and a conflictual and increasingly polarized political scene, deterioration of public security decreased Tunisian public's trust in the Ennahda-led government. Amid the bipolarity in the political scene along the Islamists versus secularists line, the rise of Salafi violence, albeit a recent phenomenon, has brought a new security challenge in Tunisia.

Transitional Politics: The Peak of the Political Crisis (2012–2013)

Ennahda Party played a leading role in the drafting of the new constitution and had control over the executive from December 2011 to January 2014 under Hamadi Jebali and Ali Larayedh governments. Throughout this period, Ennahda was repeatedly charged with striving to "Islamize" society and monopolizing the key positions in state apparatus through the appointment of its members in the administration, the judiciary, and the media. Such endeavors were exposed to severe criticism from secular political opponents culminating in a deep societal split particularly with respect to the desirable separation between religious and political spheres by secularists. This split as well as a number of developments that took place over the course of 2012 and 2013 dragged the country into severe political turbulence.

Between 2012 and 2013, Tunisia witnessed various acts of intimidation and violence against artists, art galleries, theaters, embassies, journalists, and political opponents. To mention few, in September 2012, a crowd of almost 2,000 protesters attacked the U.S. Embassy in Tunis in their fury over a film denigrating Prophet Muhammad.[88] Five months later, in February 2013, Chokri Belaid, a poet, a lawyer, and the leader of the secular left Democratic Patriots Movement, was assassinated after months of harassment and surveillance by the militants.[89] Belaid's assassination led to the biggest political crisis in Tunisia since 2011 and his funeral was a manifestation of one of the largest outpourings of anger and grief in Tunisian history, with an estimated one million people taking to the street.[90] According to some critics, acts of violence were linked to the so-called "militias" in the Leagues for the Protection of the Revolution, which they described as Ennahda's military wing. The Ennahda-led government was accused of failing to investigate the attacks and assassination and imposing charges on their perpetrators.

The wave of protests after Belaid's assassination threatened Tunisia's stability and the opposition exercised pressure on the government to resign. Prime Minister Hamadi Jebali announced that his government would hand power over to a new government of technocrats; however, Ennahda leadership rejected this move on the grounds that the party enjoyed electoral legitimacy and it had not been consulted. Following several weeks of negotiation, Ennahda and the opposition agreed on a plan that would keep the government based on 2011 elections rather than appointing a team of unelected technocrats. Jebali resigned and Ali Laarayedh, who served as Jebali's interior minister and a member of the Ennahda Party, became the new prime minister. In turn, to end political crisis, Ennahda agreed to hand four key ministries—interior, foreign affairs, justice, and defense—to independent technocrats.

Amid the political and economic crisis, deep frustration and disappointment among the secular leaders with the government's failure to ensure security and transitional justice as well as increasing polarization in the country convinced them to develop a unified force to counter the electoral dominance of the Ennahda Party. In June 2012, former Prime Minister Beji Caid Essebsi announced the foundation of a new party, Nidaa Tounes (Call for Tunisia). Nidaa Tounes was an extremely heterodox party including secular leftists, progressive liberals, members of the UGTT and the Tunisian Union of Industry, Commerce and Handicrafts (UTICA) and Destourians (the supporters of old school Bourguibaism) and some former members of Ben Ali's RCD. Nidaa Tounes was formed, as the leaders described, as a response to postrevolutionary "instances of disturbing extremism and violence that threaten public and individual liberties as well as the security of the citizens."[91] The party has often been the target of accusations on the ground that its membership contains a large number of the old political elite that served during Ben Ali's ruling RCD Party.

The former regime officials in Nidaa Tounes excluded from running in the last elections distorted the criticisms on Ben Ali regime's rampant corruption and police state-attributes by pointing to the progress achieved in his era in areas like women's rights, education, and infrastructure development based on the statistical data on Tunisia's progress compared with other African states.[92] The liberal secularists, on the other hand, joined Nidaa Tounes as they viewed the party as the only possible way for non-Islamists to gain victory at the ballot box. In the 2011 elections, 60 percent of Tunisians voted for parties other than Ennahda, yet these votes were divided among a multitude of left-oriented parties. Hence, even the left-wing parties joined Nidaa Tounes despite their sharp opposition to the former officials from the RCD as they were convinced that they would not be able to challenge Ennahda otherwise.

In January 2013, Nidaa Tounes further engaged in talks to build an electoral alliance with four other leftist progressive parties to consolidate their position in the next election and they created the Union for Tunisia with a unified platform and candidate lists.[93] On the other hand, given that the Nidaa Tounes contained people from Ben Ali regime, activists on the far left did not join the party. Instead, in October 2012, they founded a coalition of far leftists and Arab Nationalists, the Popular Front, under Hamma Hammami.[94]

Five months after the assassination of Belaid, in July 2013, Tunisia was shaken by the assassination of another important opposition figure, Mohammed Brahmi who was the founder and the general secretary of the People's Movement and a member of the NCA. Brahmi was a vocal critic of Ennahda. His assassination enraged an immediate wave of massive protests and sit-ins in the capital and in front of the Constituent Assembly.[95] Protesters gathered in Tunis and other cities calling for the resignation of the government while the UGTT called for a general strike and Tunisair canceled all its flights to and from Tunisia for one day.[96]

In the same week, fourteen soldiers were killed in a terrorist attack near Mount Jebel Chaambi, on the Algerian border by a fundamentalist jihadist group. By the summer 2013, transition in Tunisia seemed to head toward a chaotic downfall. Increasing unemployment rate, rising labor unrest, deep ideological divisions, little progress on the constitution accompanied with escalating violence threatened the country to turn back into a form of new authoritarianism or a severe civil unrest.

A day after Brahmi's assassination, the Union for Tunisia and the Popular Front coalitions together announced the formation of a National Salvation Front (NSF), a coalition of parties and civil society organizations, to discuss the political situation in the country after the assassination of Brahmi. Opposition to Ennahda and dedication to a truly secular state provided the only glue that held all these leftist parties together. The NSF called the Ennahda-led troika government to step down and cede power to a technocratic government who would complete the work on the constitution, restore order, and lead the process up to the elections. Ennahda acknowledged that it could not manage the economy and security effectively; however, the party also claimed that those deficiencies did not justify disbanding the NCA and replacing the elected members of the assembly with unelected officials. The party initially refused calls for its resignation arguing that forcing an elected government to resign was against the basic principles of democracy and the will of Tunisian people.

Ennahda's resistance to calls for its resignation took thousands of Tunisians to the streets calling for the government to resign with the famous chant—that was often used during the Arab revolts in 2011—"the people want the fall of the regime."[97] The party offered to lead broadened National

Unity government and to leave more ministerial positions to the opposition, yet refused to step down, whereas the opposition parties refused to engage in a negotiation until the prime minister agreed to resign. In the midst of this political deadlock, polarization and instability reached its climax in Tunisia while the economy deteriorated drastically.

To break the deadlock, four civil society organizations—the Tunisian Union of Industry, Commerce and Handicrafts, also known as the Employers' Union (UTICA), the Tunisian Human Rights League (LTDH), the first independent human rights association in the Arab world, the Tunisian Bar Association (ONAT), and the UGTT formed an organization known as the Tunisian National Dialogue Quartet. The Quartet launched the "National Dialogue" to reach a compromise among political parties within the NCA. The political deadlock that swept the country over 2012 and 2013 came to an end only after the Quartet took over a mediating role and forced all the parties to negotiate under the national dialogue platform. In September 2013, the Quartet presented a "roadmap" which called for the government to hand power over to a caretaker government of independent technocrats. The roadmap included a timeline for completion of the new constitution within four weeks, selection of the members for an independent higher election commission within a week and the promulgation of an electoral law within two weeks starting from the opening session of the national dialogue. The roadmap also called for holding national elections two weeks after the establishment of the electoral commission.[98]

The Quartet announced that the roadmap required parties to accept all the conditions highlighted in the roadmap in order to participate in the national dialogue. Meanwhile, pressure over Ennahda to resign reached at a level that it could no longer resist since refusal to step down might be too costly for the party. The government could either be swept out by a similar wave of protest that toppled Ben Ali or the party's image would be so tarnished that it would face the risk of losing the next election. The moderates in Ennahda leadership decided that accepting the roadmap would serve the party's longer term interests. In January 2014, Prime Minister Laarayedh resigned, handing power over to an interim government of technocrats whose members weren't allowed to run for office in the next elections.

After weeks of negotiations, both ruling and opposition parties agreed to nominate Mehdi Jomaa, an independent member of the NCA as the prime minister of the caretaker government for a year until the next election. The national dialogue culminated in three outcomes: (1) an independent technocratic government, (2) an independent election commission, (3) a consensual constitution. The Quartet aimed to depoliticize the constitution-drafting process and protect the country against power vacuum by forming a nonpartisan technocratic government. The appointment of a technocratic government opened a dialogue that gave way to the competition of the final draft of the constitution and its adoption within a month. The Quartet's efforts were internationally recognized when the Tunisian National Dialogue Quartet, a key player in the attempts to build pluralist democracy, was awarded the Norwegian Nobel Peace Prize. The Nobel Committee declared:

> The quartet had secured the approval of the Tunisian population at large for the constitutional process that led to democratic elections. It paved the way for a peaceful dialogue between the citizens, the political parties and the authorities and helped to find consensus-based solutions to a wide range of challenges across political and religious divides.[99]

A MILESTONE IN TUNISIAN POLITICS: ADOPTION OF THE 2014 CONSTITUTION

One of the most important milestones of the Tunisian transition was the adoption of the new constitution in January 2014. The Tunisian constitution is an outcome of continuous struggle for negotiation and tradeoffs between the two main political poles. The Consensus Committee within the NCA was assigned with reviewing every article before presenting it to the general session of the NCA for debate and vote. If an agreement within the committee couldn't be reached, then the presidents of blocks within the assembly would meet the assembly president to hammer out a compromise. Unless an agreement was reached in this second phase, then party presidents and the Quartet would meet and come to a conclusion.[100] The final text of the constitution was adopted by the NCA in January 2014 with 200 votes for, twelve against and four abstentions, which was well over the two-thirds majority required and thus, it didn't need to be voted in a public referendum. The NCA agreed on the constitution after the Ennahda Party granted a number of concessions, the most critical of which was to drop references to Islamic law. In the new constitution, the contentious Article 1, 2 and 6 reads[101]:

> Tunisia is a free, independent, sovereign state; its religion is Islam, its language Arabic, and its system is republican. (Article 1)
> Tunisia is a civil state based on citizenship, the will of the people, and the supremacy of law. (Article 2)
> The state is the guardian of religion. It guarantees freedom of conscience and belief, the free exercise of religious practices and the neutrality of mosques and places of worship from all partisan instrumentalisation. The state undertakes to disseminate the values of moderation and tolerance and the protection of the sacred, and the prohibition of all violations thereof. It undertakes equally to

prohibit and fight against calls for Takfeer [calling someone an unbeliever] and the incitement to violence and hatred. (Article 6)

In the new constitution, Islam is not stated as a source of legislation since the Ennahda leadership gave up debates on integrating *Sharia* as a source legislation as early as 2012, yet Islam is recognized as the state religion. The constitution asserts Tunisia's Muslim identity and along with the Article 6, the state has the right to interfere in religious customs and traditions, which is against freedom of religious practice. Article 73 states that only Muslims may run for presidency recognizing no right for nomination of non-Muslim candidates.[102] Thus, the Tunisian constitution while not being truly secular, has become a sort of compromise between a secular state with a religious-oriented society model.

The constitution also recognizes gender equality in rights and responsibilities, which was achieved thanks to the women members of the NCA across different party lines. According to Article 45, the government not only protects women's rights, but also supports their achievements and ensures the equality of opportunities with greater engagement of women in politics, particularly in local politics. The article states: "The state works to realize parity between women and men in elected councils" which means every second candidate on the election lists has to be a woman, even in the regional elections.[103] Within the parliament, the new constitution imposed a quota of 30 percent representation for women.

Another contentious issue was over the independence of the judiciary. Ennahda advocated for some level of control by the executive over the judiciary, yet according to the Articles 102 and 124, the Supreme Judicial Council is in charge of the appointment of judges and it enjoys legal and financial independence. In the new political system, the role of the president of the republic is reduced owing to the negative experiences under the former presidents. The new constitution strengthens the role of the prime minister and of the parliament over the president and divides the executive power between the president and the prime minister in order to avoid any potential authoritarian backlash. The prime minister, according to the new constitution, will retain the dominant role and shares executive authority with the president while the president has important prerogatives in foreign affairs and defense.

New articles concerning freedom of association created novel provisions for civic engagement. Article 35 guarantees the freedom to establish political parties, unions, and associations while Article 36 ad 37 recognizes the right to join and form unions including the right to strike and peaceful demonstration.[104] The new constitution promotes further space for civil society organizations and unions. With the new constitution adopted, Tunisia became a decentralized and open government where separation of powers is guaranteed. The new constitution is viewed as the most democratic and progressive in the region both in terms of its content and the process by which it was drafted.[105]

ALTERNATION OF POWER: THE 2014 LEGISLATIVE AND PRESIDENTIAL ELECTIONS

Tunisian politics was dominated by two elections in 2014. The new parliament, called "the Assembly of the Representatives of the People" (ARP) was elected on October 26, 2004. The electoral turnout was 69 percent, higher than that of the 2011 election for the constituent assembly. The election was supervised by the Independent High Authority for Elections (ISIE), a neutral commission consisting of nine members. Tunisia's new electoral law, adopted in 2014 in advance of the election garnered praise from observers as a credible framework for reflecting the will of the voters.[106]

The clear winner of the election was Nidaa Tounes with 37.5 percent of the votes and the party won eighty-six seats in the 217 seat assembly. Ennahda won 27.8 percent of the votes and sixty-nine seats in the assembly (having lost twenty seats compared to previous election).[107] Building a government required an absolute majority of 109 seats. Nidaa Tounes built a coalition government with Ennahda, Afek Tounes, and Free Patriotic Union (UPL). Although the main objective of Nidaa Tounes was to hinder a second electoral victory of Ennahda, the party leadership decided that nonintegration of Ennahda into the coalition government might provoke anti-government protests and mobilization from religious voters.[108] The broad coalition including both small leftist parties and Ennahda served to hinder the exclusion of the Islamist political forces with strong electoral support from the new government and further polarization along the secular-Islamist divide. The new government included one minister (Minister of Employment) and three secretaries of state from Ennahda and some posts for Afek Tounes and the UPL.

There have been a number of factors determining the votes of citizens in the 2014 legislative election. First, the revolutionary forces that represent a complete break with the authoritarianism of the past were not able to form an alliance and the fragmentation in these political groups led to their decline. The CPR, for instance, split into three parties with some of its MPs who left the party to become independents or joined other parties because of the party's coalition and rapprochement with the Ennahda Party after 2011 elections. The Social Democratic Path and the Democratic Forum for Labor and Liberties were other leftist parties faced with internal fragmentation. Growing polarization between the secular and Islamist forces during the three years after the uprisings led many secular voters to cast their votes to Nidaa Tounes, which they think would win, in order not to waste their votes.

According to the 2014 Arab Opinion Index, over the three years Tunisian voters' priority has shifted from complete break with authoritarianism and nepotism of the former regime toward improving economy, ensuring law, order, and stability.[109] The political assassinations and various terrorist attacks in the previous years affected voter decisions-making the key criteria to restore security and stability and improve the economy regardless of the party members' relationship to the former regime. During the election campaigns, Nidaa Tounes portrayed terrorist attacks and assassinations as the failure of the troika government and its security apparatus. The party depicted itself as the most qualified party in restoring law and order given the members' political and security experience under Bourguiba and Ben Ali. On the other hand, the decline in Ennahda's votes could be explained by the rise of radical Islamist attacks and two political assassinations. The seculars often criticized the party for being too lax toward the ultra-conservative Salafists while the police repressed other demonstrations brutally. The Ennahda-led government was also accused of corruption, cronyism, and little progress in economic and financial reforms.

Two months after the legislative elections, presidential election was held in December 2014. According to the Article 75 in the new constitution, the president is elected for a five-year term by a simple majority of votes in a single nationwide district. In the event that an absolute majority is not achieved in the first round, the law provided a run-off election between the two leading candidates. Ennahda decided not to nominate a candidate for the presidential election in order to stay safe from the accusations of total power accumulation. In the first round of the presidential election, twenty-two candidates ran for the presidential election and no candidate could win an absolute majority of the votes. The two candidates with the majority of the votes were Beji Caid Essebsi and Moncef Marzouki. In the run-off election, Essebsi was elected as the first president of the second republic of Tunisia with 55.6 percent of the votes against Marzouki's 44.3 percent.[110] Essebsi's victory was regarded worrisome by many Tunisians as he served as a minister four times under Bourguiba. Likewise, for some analysts, the fact that many members of Nidaa Tounes served under Ben Ali might indicate a return to authoritarianism under the old regime while posing a threat to democracy and progressiveness in rights and liberties.[111] To many Tunisian and outside observers, the victory of Nidaa Tounes and Essebsi is seen a sort of soft restoration of the Ben Ali regime, as one Tunisian put it "old *boukha* [the traditional Tunisian homemade liquor] in new bottles."[112]

In late 2015, Nidaa Tounes party was riven by a deep split between the party's two wings: the party's formal general secretary Mohzen Marzouk who accused Hafedh Caid Essebsi —the president's son—of his attempt for a power grab and the supporters of the president's son who was appointed as the legal representative and the new general secretary of the party's central committee. The left-wing fraction of the party viewed his rise as an undemocratic attempt and nepotistic move by the president. They feared a hereditary transfer of power and a return to the days old politics under Ben Ali. Besides, the party was seen as gradually moving toward a business-oriented party, by which the elite from the former regime could use it as a vehicle for corruption.

Months of infighting culminated in the resignation of thirty-one members from the party, twenty-seven of those who withdrew from the party were deputies in the parliament. The resignations indicated deep divisions within the ruling party, bringing about the difficulty in addressing the country's key problems with a unified voice. The withdrawal of twenty-seven deputies from Nidaa Tounes led to a loss of parliamentary majority which the party gained following the 2014 elections, from eighty-five seats out of 217 to fifty-eight, falling behind Ennahda that retained sixty-nine seats. Eventually, Ennahda once again became the largest party in the Tunisian parliament.

TOWARD A CONSOLIDATED DEMOCRACY: PROSPECTS AND CHALLENGES

Since the Jasmine Revolution began in December 2010, Tunisia has accomplished major milestones on its way to become a democratic country. Those significant milestones include the end of the Ben Ali regime, free and fair elections that enabled peaceful transfer of power between divergent political forces, and the adoption of a democratic constitution. In 2015, upon a successful national dialogue that culminated in the passage of a progressive constitution in January 2014, the establishment of a new election commission, the formation of a politically neutral caretaker government under Prime Minister Mehdi Jomaa and the holding of free and fair elections, Tunisia's political rights rating improved from three to one and its status changed from Partly Free to Free according to Freedom House ratings.[113] With this significant improvement, as of 2015 Tunisia became the only free country in the Arab world and it has been the sole success story of the Arab Spring.

The consensual politics that broke the deadlock in late 2013 continued with the formation of a grand coalition government made up of the secular left and Islamist political parties following the 2014 elections. Over the years, Tunisia made substantial progress in consolidating its democracy by establishing democratic institutions and professionalizing the security forces. Civilian authorities effectively hold control over internal security forces and the military, a key challenge facing most Arab countries in the region. However, despite significant gains obtained in electoral politics and democratic institutions, endemic corruption, unjust distribution of wealth, high youth unemployment, security threats, and an inequitable regional development, in short, the factors that triggered the revolution in 2011 still remain as key challenges facing the post-revolution Tunisia. For democratic consolidation, Tunisia needs to fully achieve transitional justice and tackle with the unresolved issues.

In May 2018, Tunisia held its first free and fair local elections that had been delayed four times before due to logistic, administrative, and political obstacles since the revolution. Tunisian politics before the revolution had been characterized by a rigid centrist structure that took over issues of local governance while local authorities had little control over regional development.[114] With the new constitution, Tunisia took tangible steps toward decentralization and sought to bring decentralization into state governance as a pivotal instrument for change. Decentralization is expected to remedy the ills of the long-standing regional disparities in resource allocation and governance. Yet, the municipal elections saw a low turnout with 35.6 of the registered voters in stark contrast to the previous elections in 2014. This low turnout resulted from national dissatisfaction with the government's austerity policies, stalled anti-corruption and decentralization efforts due to controversial draft laws and partisan struggle.[115]

Fighting corruption has become one of the priority areas of the current National Unity government. In Article 14 of the Tunisian Constitution of 2014, the fight against corruption is defined as a national objective and policy-makers agreed to establish National Anti-Corruption Authority to come up with effective policies to fight against corruption. Over the last two years, Tunisia passed significant laws including the Law on Access to Information and the Law on Reporting Corruption cases and Protecting Whistleblowers.[116]. While the former aimed to provide free access to information, the latter was an attempt to develop a strategy to fight corruption and promote good governance. Following the passage of these laws, a wide-scale anti-corruption campaign led by the prime minister was initiated and a series of arrests and investigations targeted numerous public officials, politicians, police officers, customs, and prominent businessmen with corruption charges. The authorities took measures including freezing their bank accounts and seizing their property assets.[117] More recently, the Tunisian parliament passed a law against illegal enrichment that requires high government officials and institutions to declare income and assets and criminalizes illicit gains and conflicts of interest. By enacting such progressive legislation, the government apparently aims to promote transparency and good governance and to deter individuals from engaging in corrupt practices. However, the current government restrained from holding the Ben Ali era officials engaged in corruption accountable for their acts.

In September 2017, the parliament passed a controversial "Reconciliation Law" proposed by Essebsi that would grant amnesty to business people and Ben Ali era officials accused of corruption in exchange for returning ill-gotten money and paying a fine.[118] Due to growing public anger, the text was revised to cover only former civil servants implicated in economic crimes under Ben Ali. Though the law was depicted as an attempt for national reconciliation by the government, it was met with strong opposition from the civil society groups who claimed that there would be no reconciliation without accountability and the law would undermine transitional justice.[119] The law's passage signals an impunity for officials who served under Ben Ali and precludes a complete rupture from the corrupt practices of the old regime. On the other hand, a poll conducted in September 2017 by the International Republican Institute indicated that 89 percent of Tunisians maintained that corruption is higher today than it was before the revolution.[120] The survey research revealed that poor economic conditions coupled with corruption drove intense public dissatisfaction and led to a declining interest in participating in the electoral process.

Tunisia is plagued by unfair distribution of wealth, economic inequality, inflation, public indebtedness, high unemployment, and economic and social marginalization of the interior and the southern regions of the country remain endemic. The National Unity government has repeatedly failed to meaningfully address socioeconomic grievances and the living standards have deteriorated since the revolution. In January 2018, Tunisia was swept by a new wave of protests that began in the two months leading up to the anniversary of the Jasmine Revolution. In a subsequent stage, protests turned into violent confrontation between young demonstrators and police force. The protests came as a reaction to the 2018 Finance Act, a package of austerity measures adopted by the government to solve the rising inflation issue and to minimize the country's public deficit and the Act was approved by the legislature on December 9, 2017. The measures included an increase in consumer prices, especially for fuel and value-added tax on various goods and services including cars, phone calls, the Internet, hotel accommodation, and other items. While protesters demanded the unjust financial law be dropped, the government is in a tight squeeze as the Tunisian economy is in constant decline with its public debt that has risen sharply and purchasing power that has dropped by 25 percent.[121] Tunisia is in a dire need of structural economic reforms to generate more jobs, to tackle the power of smuggling and other black market lobbies, and to attract foreign investors to the country.

A survey carried out by the International Republican Institute between November and December 2017 revealed that 83 percent of Tunisian respondents stated the country was going in the wrong direction and the main reason for this response was identified as economic problems, whereas only to 13 percent of respondents, the country was going in the right direction.[122] According to the survey, over the three years, from November 2015 to November 2017, Tunisians increasingly view economic prosperity as more important than democratic system of government. In other words, Tunisians began to view economic growth under an authoritarian rule superior to democracy without economic growth, which might tempt Tunisians to aspire for a new strongman rule unless the government succeeds in addressing the country's long-standing economic problems.

In addition to the decline in economy, Tunisia is facing security destabilization which might have severe consequences for Tunisian democracy. Radicalism and extremist violence is rising among Tunisian youth which is strongly correlated with unsustainably high youth employment. An estimated 6,000 Tunisians have departed their country to join the ranks of the Islamic State of Iraq and the Levant (ISIS) in Syria, Iraq, and Libya, which is the highest per capita rate of foreign ISIS recruits in the world.[123] The collapse of the central state in Libya made Tunisia vulnerable in the face of constant terrorist attacks. Ansar Al-Sharia Tunisia (AST) and Okba Ibn Nafaa are the two main terrorist groups that are associated with the terrorist incidents in Tunisia. Both extremist groups aligned themselves with Al-Qaeda previously and as of 2014 with ISIS and targeted foreign tourists, secular political officials, and Tunisian security forces. AST and Okba Ibn Nafaa carried out numerous attacks against military mainly in the Kasserine region, mountainous border area with Algeria where most jihadist groups are based.

In 2015, Tunisian security and political stability was shattered by three major terrorist attacks associated with the Islamic State in touristic areas including the Bardo National Museum attack, the gunman killing of dozens of tourists in Sousse and an explosion that targeted a bus carrying members of president's security guard in Tunis. These successive terrorist attacks deeply hurt tourism sector, a backbone of the Tunisian economy and prompted Essebsi to declare a state of emergency and suspend several of citizens' rights.[124] Meanwhile, since the ISIS was defeated on the battlefields of Syria and Iraq, thousands of ISIS fighters of Tunisian origin are struggling to return home, which is another destabilizing factor for the country's fragile security. Tunisian politicians are at odds over the kind of policy they should adopt in the face of a returning wave from the ISIS and Essebsi's proposal of amnesty for those returners was vigorously opposed. Since the government has no program to reintegrate returning fighters into society and suspects of terrorism and their families are faced with the threat of imprisonment and torture, the cycle of radicalization and extremist violence might continue and even escalate.[125]

In July 2015, the government passed a new counterterrorism law that opened the way for the use of repressive tactics against suspects in terrorism-related cases, reminding of the robust police state under Ben Ali. The counterterrorism law increases surveillance powers of security forces, stipulates prolonged period of detention without access to legal counsel, restricts freedom of movement, imposes house arrest without proper judicial review, and includes a vague and broad definition of terrorism open to abuse.[126] In the name of security and stability, emergency laws and counterterrorism measures brought back the brutal tactics of the past including arbitrary arrests and detentions, harassment of suspects and their families, ill-treatment, and torture under detention. The state of emergency based on 1978 decree allows authorities to ban strikes or demonstrations endangering public order and prohibits gatherings that are likely to provoke or sustain order while it grants the government extensive powers to restrict freedom of expression and media.[127] The counterterrorism law and other legislative acts are used to undermine press freedom. Journalists and activists at times practice self-censorship to avoid violence mainly from security forces for the fear of being charged with supporting terrorism.

Though the 2011 revolution was a manifestation of Tunisians' rejection of Ben Ali's police state which had legitimized repression by claiming to provide security and stability, Tunisia is gradually moving toward the old regime politics in which the language of counterterrorism was widely used to force the public with a stark choice between accepting the heavy tactics of the government or facing the violence of extremist Islamists. The political discourse on terrorism was also channeled into Essebsi's presidential election campaign in which he called Marzouki's supporters as "Salafist Jihadists."[128] In addition, the association of opposition politicians, particularly Ennahda and journalists and activists raising criticism against the government's heavy-handed practices with terrorism inflicted by jihadist groups jeopardizes Tunisia's consensus-oriented politics and the democratic gains of the revolution.

Violations of basic individual rights as well as freedom of media takes place on the plea of fight against terrorism. More alarming is the Essebsi's struggle to grab an overreaching executive power and play an outsized role in governance, which contradicts with the semi-presidential system outlined in the constitution. According to the constitution, the president is responsible for setting state policy on defense, foreign relations, and national security, while the prime minister is the head of the government who governs the administration, concludes international agreements (Article 77). When controversy emerges as to the division of power between two executive leaders, it's within the responsibility of the constitutional court to settle the issue (Article 101). However, as constitutional court has not been created, President Essebsi has sought to centralize power around the presidency and his cult making use of Nidaa Tounes as a vehicle, which reminds the strong presidential system under Ben Ali and Bourguiba regimes.[129]

President Essebsi appointed numerous political figures from Ben Ali's governing party, the Constitutional Democratic Rally (RCD) as presidential advisors. Moreover, the cabinet reshuffle in September 2017 under the Prime Minister Youssef Chahed enabled the replacement of thirteen of twenty-eight cabinet ministers. In the new cabinet, Nidaa Tounes allies were appointed to six of the thirteen cabinet changes, while three ministers in the new cabinet served in the same posts under Ben Ali.[130] Essebsi was believed to be the real architect of this change and struggled to bring back many ministers from the old regime and officials from the RCD inside the government. By this move, he planned to consolidate Nidaa Tounes' position and enhance the power of his own circle. It was seen as an alarming move, by many observers and civil society groups, since the return of old business tycoons and political elite into the new system might usher a new era of authoritarianism. In addition, the failure of Tunisians to break with the past has precluded achieving the goals of the revolution including fighting against corruption, prosecuting the crimes of the Ben Ali regime, and providing transitional justice.

In short, with a democratic constitution and free elections Tunisia has made remarkable progress since ousting its dictatorship in 2011 and became a model of democracy in the entire region. Following the ouster of Ben Ali, thousands of political prisoners were granted amnesty and Ennahda movement was granted party status and integrated into Tunisian political life. Besides, the post-uprising government decided not to exclude members of Ben Ali's ruling party from the newly emerging system, which saved the country from a potential wave of violence witnessed in other countries in the region. In post-revolution Tunisia, freedom of religion and religious practice was guaranteed with the new constitution and Tunisians were able to wear expressions of religious identity in public for the first time after several decades. During the most precarious moments of the transition, when political groups within the troika government clashed over ideological issues in constitutional drafting and designing of the transition, key civil society groups launched a national dialogue to mediate between divergent political forces which successfully culminated in a peaceful political settlement. This indicated that Tunisia has a political culture characterized by pluralism, compromise, and a vibrant civil society, thus, the country is well-positioned to maintain its democratic credentials.

Despite those important milestones in transition to democracy, economic conditions are worsening and socioeconomic justice is still beyond the reach while transitional justice has not been fully achieved since human rights violations and the corruption crimes under the old regime have not been prosecuted. In other words, the problems that led to the fall of Ben Ali regime largely remain intact. Therefore, popular discontent with economic conditions and lack of notable progress in fighting corruption prevail in Tunisia as was apparent in the nationwide protests in January 2018 and the significant decline in the voter turnout in the local elections in the same year.

The arbitrary arrests of protesters calling for economic and social justice and police abuse under detention were alarming. They indicated a return to the repressive practices of the old regime and the incapability of the new political elite in solving the country's economic woes.

The popular discontent that is so strong among Tunisians has the risk of alienating citizens from the political system and the democratic process since the fate of democratic transition largely hinges on tangible economic outcomes in the first place.[131] Without economic growth and employment prospects, people could easily lose faith in democracy and look for a new strongman who could provide economic prosperity and political stability. Indeed, the rise of Nidaa Tounes in the second legislative elections in 2014 was an indicator of an old regime nostalgia in the search of security, economic growth, and political stability. In addition, Tunisia has to deal with ISIS or Al-Qaeda linked terror attacks targeting its military installations along the Algerian border and tourist resorts, which requires the government to find the right balance between its responsibility to restore security and its commitment to ensure religious freedom.[132]

Last but not the least, Tunisian democracy depends on how far politics is institutionalized through parliament. An empowered and transparent parliament that reflects the popular will and has popular legitimacy will make it less likely to concentrate power in the presidency. If parliament's power is wiped out and most of the power is concentrated in presidency and his inner circles including business elite and media barons, Tunisia might once again fall into the trap of an authoritarian regime with a democracy facade. In this regard, a lot depends on how far political dissent and civil society could protect their democratic gains and push for institutional reforms to consolidate the country's young democracy.

It is certain that democracy needs time to be consolidated and the future path of democratic transitions is far from being certain, and Tunisia is no exception. On the other hand, as a role model for democratic transition for the region, Tunisia's consolidation of democracy does not only have national importance. Tunisia could be an inspiring success story indicating how democratic change is possible in the Middle East. In a similar vein, its potential democratic backsliding toward authoritarianism might strengthen the old orientalist views that democracy is not compatible with the underlying cultural, social, and political influences in the region.

NOTES

1. Freedom House, "Freedom in the World 2018-Country Reports: Tunisia," https://freedomhouse.org/report/freedom-world/2018/tunisia

2. Amira Aleya-Sghaier, "The Tunisian Revolution: The Revolution of Dignity," *The Journal of the Middle East and Africa* 3, no. 1 (2012): 19.

3. Asaf Bayat, *Life as Politics: How Ordinary People Change the Middle East* (Stanford: Stanford University Press, 2009), 14.

4. Bruce Crumley, "Tunisia Pushes Out Its Strongman: Could Other Arab Countries Follow?" *Time Online*, January 14, 2011, http://content.time.com/time/world/article/0,8599,2042541,00.html

5. Emma C. Murphy, *Economic and Political Change in Tunisia: From Bourguiba to Ben Ali* (New York: St. Martin's Press, 1999), 30.

6. Mohamed Ayadi, and Wided Mattoussi, "Scoping of the Tunisian Economy," *WIDER Working Paper* 074 (2014): 1.

7. Ibid., 1–3.

8. Eva Bellin, "Tunisian Industrialists and the State," *World Development* 22, no. 3 (1994): 427–436.

9. Murphy, *Economic and Political Change in Tunisia*, 85–92.

10. James Rupert, "Tunisians Riot Over Bread Price Rise," *Washington Post*, January 4, 1984, https://www.washingtonpost.com/archive/politics/1984/01/04/tunisians-riot-over-bread-price-rise/a5aa4a75-9651-4a30-919e-9c297b3fdb38/?utm_term=.8923cf5026cc

11. Ayadi, and Mattoussi, "Scoping of the Tunisian Economy," 1.

12. Murphy, *Economic and Political Change in Tunisia*, 5.

13. The Washington consensus is a set of economic policy prescriptions that promote economic reform for crisis torn developing countries. The program was set by Washington, D.C. based institutions such as the International Monetary Fund and World Bank.

14. The International Bank for Reconstruction and Development/World Bank, *Unlocking the Employment Potential in the Middle East and North Africa: Toward a New Social Contract* (Washington, DC, 2004), 5–9. ; Christopher Alexander, "Tunisia's Protest Wave: Where it Comes from and What it Means," *Foreign Policy*, January 3, 2011, https://foreignpolicy.com/2011/01/03/tunisias-protest-wave-where-it-comes-from-and-what-it-means/

15. The International Bank for Reconstruction and Development/World Bank, *Unlocking the Employment Potential in the Middle East*, 5–9.

16. Tristan Dreisbach, and Robert Joyce, "Revealing Tunisia's Corruption under Ben Ali," *Aljaazera*, March 27, 2014, https://www.aljazeera.com/indepth/features/2014/03/revealing-tunisia-corruption-under-ben-ali-201432785825560542.html

17. Maria Cristina Paciello, "Tunisia: Changes and Challenges of Political Transition," *MEDPRO Technical Report* 3 (May 2011): 5.

18. Nouri Gana, *The Making of the Tunisian Revolution: Contexts, Architects, Prospects* (Edinburgh: Edinburgh University Press, 2013), 12.

19. Alexander, "Tunisia's Protest Wave: Where it Comes from and What it Means,"

20. Julia Clancy-Smith, "From Sidi Bou Zid to Sidi Bou Said: A Longue Duree Approach to the Tunisian Revolutions," in *The Arab Spring: Change and Resistance in the Middle East*, ed. Mark L. Haas, and David W. Lesch (Boulder, CO: Westview Press, 2013), 22.

21. Eric Gobe, "The Gafsa Mining Basin between Riots and a Social Movement: Meaning and Significance of a Protest Movement in Ben Ali's Tunisia," *HAL Working Paper* (2010): 1–3, https://halshs.archives-ouvertes.fr/halshs-00557826

22. Miller, Laurel E., Jeffrey Martini, F. Stephen Larrabee, Angel Rabasa, Stephanie Pezard, Julie E. Taylor, and Tewodaj Mengistu, *Democratization in the Arab World: Prospects and Lessons from Around the Globe* (Santa Monica, CA: RAND Corporation, 2012).

23. Alexander, "Tunisia's Protest Wave: Where it Comes from and What it Means".

24. Steven A. Cook, "Tunisia: First Impression," *Council on Foreign Relations*, November 12, 2014, https://www.cfr.org/blog/tunisia-first-impressions

25. Later the Neo Destour Party was renamed as the "Socialist Destourian Party" (PSD in its French acronym) in 1964 to signal the government's commitment to a socialist phase of political and economic development. In 1988, the party was again renamed under President Ben Ali as "Constitutional Democratic Rally" or "Reassemblement Constitutionel Démocratique" (RCD).

26. Kennett Perkins, *A History of Modern Tunisia* (Cambridge: Cambridge University Press, 2004), 130.

27. The Constitution of Tunisia, 1959, http://www.wipo.int/edocs/lexdocs/laws/en/tn/tn028en.pdf

28. Ibid.

29. Christopher Alexander, "Authoritarianism and Civil Society in Tunisia," *Middle East Report* 205, Vol. 27 (Winter 1997).

30. Alexander, "Authoritarianism and Civil Society in Tunisia."

31. Christopher Alexander, *Tunisia: Stability and Reform in the Modern Maghreb* (New York: Routledge, 2010), 53.

32. Ibid.

33. Nicola Pratt, *Democracy & Authoritarianism in the Arab World* (Boulder, CO: Lynne Reinner Publishers, 2007), 94.

34. Alaya Allani, "The Islamists in Tunisia Between Confrontation and Participation 1980–2008," *The Journal of North African Studies* 14, no. 2 (June 2009): 263.

35. Alexander, "Authoritarianism and Civil Society in Tunisia."

36. Lisa Anderson, "Politics in the Middle East: Opportunities and Limits in the Quest for Theory," in *Area Studies and Social Science: Strategies for Understanding Middle East Politics*, ed. Mark Tessler, Jodi Nachtwey, and Anna Banda (Bloomington, IN: Indiana University Press, 1999), 4.

37. Larbi Sadiki, "Political Liberalization in Bin Ali's Tunisia: Façade Democracy," *Democratization* 9, no. 4 (Winter 2002): 125.

38. Alexander, "Authoritarianism and Civil Society in Tunisia."

39. Murphy, *Economic and Political Change in Tunisia*, 5–9.

40. Larbi Sadiki, "Bin Ali's Tunisia: Democracy by Non-democratic Means," *British Journal of Middle Eastern Studies* 29, no. 1 (2002): 57–78.

41. Alexander, *Tunisia: Stability and Reform in the Modern Maghreb*, 54.

42. Sadiki, "Bin Ali's Tunisia: Democracy," 58–59.

43. Abdelbaki Hermassi, "Socio-economic Change and Political Implications," in *Democracy Without Democrats? The Renewal of Politics in the Muslim World*, ed. Ghassan Salame (London, New York: I.B. Tauris, 1994), 238.

44. Michael Willis, "Political Parties in the Maghrib: The Illusion of Significance?" *The Journal of North African Studies* 7, no. 2 (2002): 1–22.

45. Miller et. al., *Democratization in the Arab World: Prospects and Lessons*, 67.

46. Ibid., 59.

47. Ibid.

48. Sadiki, "Bin Ali's Tunisia: Democracy," 68.

49. Ibid., 72.

50. Aleya-Sghaier, "The Tunisian Revolution: The Revolution of Dignity," 28.

51. "U.S. Embassy Cables: Finding a Successor to Ben Ali in Tunisia," *The Guardian*, January 17, 2011, https://www.theguardian.com/world/us-embassy-cables-documents/49401

52. "U.S. Embassy Cables: Tunisia- a U.S. Foreign Policy Conundrum," *The Guardian*, December 7, 2010, https://www.theguardian.com/world/us-embassy-cables-documents/217138

53. Sonia L. Alianak, *Transition Towards Revolution and Reform: The Arab Spring Realised?* (Edinburg Edinburg University Press, 2014), 24.

54. Alexander, "Tunisia's Protest Wave: Where it Comes from and What it Means,"

55. Alianak, *Transition Towards Revolution and Reform: The Arab Spring Realised?*, 28.

56. Béatrice Hibou, "Domination & Control in Tunisia: Economic Levers for the Exercise of Authoritarian Power," *Review of African Political Economy* 33, no. 108 (June 2006): 197.

57. Larbi Sadiki, "Engendering Citizenship in Tunisia: Prioritizing Unity over Democracy," in *North Africa: Politics, Region, and the Limits of Transformation*, ed. Yahia Zoubir and Haizam Amirah-Fernandez (London: Routledge, 2008), 123.

58. James Davies argues that "revolution is most likely to occur when a prolonged period of rising expectations and rising gratifications is followed by a short period of sharp reversal". This suddenness of the reversal in social conditions, according to Davies, triggers insecurity, discontent, and fear and the emerging relative deprivation creates revolutionary tendencies. See James C. Davies, "Toward a Theory of Revolution," *American Sociological Review* 27, no. 1 (February 1962): 5–19.

59. Vijay Prashad, *The Death of the Nation and the Future of the Arab Revolutions* (California: California University Press, 2016), 8.

60. Aleya-Sghaier, "The Tunisian Revolution: The Revolution of Dignity," 25.

61. Alexander, *Tunisia: From Stability to Revolution in the Maghreb*, 82.

62. Ibid., 83.

63. Ibid., 84.

64. Beji Caid Essebsi served as a Minister of Foreign Affairs from 1981 to 1986 during Bourguiba period. Essebsi was not a member of the Ben Ali's government since he took power in 1987 and his government didn't include any minister affiliated with the RCD Party. "Tunisian Prime Minister, Mohammed Ghannouichi Resigns

Amid Unrest," *The Guardian*, February 27, 2011, https://www.theguardian.com/world/2011/feb/27/tunisian-prime-minister-ghannouchi-resigns

65. "Tunisia in Turmoil, Interview Transcript: Rachid Ghannouchi," *Financial Times*, January 18, 2011, https://www.ft.com/content/24d710a6-22ee-11e0-ad0b-00144feab49a

66. Jason Gluck, "Constitutional Reform in Transitional States: Challenges and Opportunities Facing Egypt and Tunisia," April 29, 2011, United States Institute of Peace, *Peacebrief 92*, https://www.usip.org/sites/default/files/PB92.pdf

67. Alfred Stepan, "Tunisia's Transition and the Twin Tolerations," *Journal of Democracy* 23, no. 2 (April 2012): 92.

68. "Final Report on the Tunisian National Constituent Assembly Elections," *National Democratic Institute*, October 23, 2011, https://www.ndi.org/files/tunisia-final-election-report-021712_v2.pdf

69. Lustration is a policy imposed by the law and court judgment that seeks to cleanse the new regime from the remnants of the past and thus, it bans officials from taking certain positions in central or local government authorities since they abused their official positions under the former regime.

70. Daniel Tavana, and Alex Russell, "Tunisia's Parliamentary and Presidential Elections," *Project on Middle East Democracy* (October 2014), http://pomed.org/wp-content/uploads/2014/10/Tunisia-Election-Guide-2014 .pdf

71. "The Islamist Conundrum," *The Economist*, October 22, 2011, http://www.economist.com/node/21533411

72. National Democratic Institute, "Final Report on the Tunisian National Constituent Assembly Elections."

73. Alexander, *Tunisia: From Stability to Revolution in the Maghreb*, 90.

74. Hamadi Jabali, the Secretary-General of Ennahda party before his position as a prime minister, had been the editor of *Al-Fajr*, the banned Ennahda newspaper. In 1992, Jabali was charged with being member of an unauthorized organization and having the intention to change the regime, thus, he was sentenced to sixteen years' imprisonment.

75. Alfred Stepan, and Juan J. Linz, "Democratization Theory and the Arab Spring," *Journal of Democracy* 24, no. 2 (April 2003): 23–24.

76. Ibid.

77. "Tunisian Constitution Will Make No Place for Faith," *Reuters*, November 4, 2011, https://af.reuters.com/article/commoditiesNews/idAFL6E7M42ND20111104

78. Duncan Pickard, "The Current Status of Constitution Making in Tunisia," *Carnegie Endowment for International Peace*, April 19, 2012.

79. Ibid.

80. Sarah J. Feuer, "Islam and Democracy in Practice: Tunisia's Ennahda Nine Months In," *Middle East Brief* 66 (September 2012): 3.

81. Tunisia adopted the most protective women's rights legislation in 1956, and it was seen as the Arab world's most liberal country as regards to the status of women. The pioneering personal status code in the 1956 constitution abolished polygamy, instituted judicial divorce, granted women the right to choose a marriage including

non-Muslim free from coercion and equal rights not only to dissolve marriage but also to become the principal guardian of their children, regardless of gender. It also granted Tunisian women the right to vote. Later in 1973, abortion was legalized within the first three months of pregnancy. During Ben Ali period, children born out of wedlock were protected by law and granted equal rights with other children. Today, 99 percent of Tunisian women are literate, mostly educated, participating actively in various sectors such as politics, law, medicine, academia, business, and media. Women organizations actively took part in the uprisings ousting Ben-Ali. See Samar El- Masri, "Tunisian Women at a Crossroads: Co-optation or Autonomy?" *Middle East Policy Council* 22, no. 2 (Summer 2015), https://www.mepc.org/tunisian-women-crossroads-co-optation-or-autonomy

82. Kouichi Shirayanagi, "Ennahda Spokeswoman Souad Abderrahim: Single Mothers are a Disgrace to Tunisia," *Tunisia Live*, November 9, 2011, http://allafrica.com/stories/201111281676.html; Amal al- Hilali, "Ennahda Members Make Conflicting Statements about Women's Rights in Tunisia," *Al- Arabiya News*, November 13, 2011, https://www.alarabiya.net/articles/2011/11/13/176916.html

83. Synda Tajine, "Will Tunisian Women Become 'Complimentary' to Men by Law?" *Al-Monitor*, August 14, 2012, http://www.al-monitor.com/pulse/politics/2012/08/tunisia-are-womens-rights-fading.html

84. Duncan Pickard, "Identity, Islam and Women in the Tunisian Consitution," *Atlantic Council*, January 24, 2014, http://www.atlanticcouncil.org/blogs/menasource/identity-islam-and-women-in-the-tunisian-constitution

85. Samia Fitouri, "Tunisia Still Undecided Over Form of Government for New Democracy," *Tunisia Live*, February 10, 2012, http://www.tunisia-live.net/2012/02/10/tunisia-still-undecided-over-form-of-government-for-new-democracy/

86. Laura Guazzone, "Ennahda Islamists and the Test of Government in Tunisia," *The International Spectator* 48, no. 4 (December 2013): 33.

87. "Survey of Tunisian Public Opinion," *International Republican Institute* (February 2014) http://www.iri.org/sites/default/files/2014%20April%2023%20Survey%20of%20Tunisian%20Public%20Opinion,%20February%2012-22,%202014.pdf

88. At least two people were killed and twety-nine were wounded in the attack to the U.S. Embassy. Tarek Amara, "Two dead as protestors attack U.S. Embassy in Tunisia," *Reuters*, September 14, 2012. http://www.reuters.com/article/us-protests-tunisia-school-idUSBRE88D18020120914

89. Belaid's two e-mail accounts and his Facebook account were hacked. Militants tracked his phone with GPS. The sophistication of his murder raised suspects among many people that the killers received assistance from the state apparatus, particularly from individuals in the Interior Ministry.

90. Yasmine Ryan, "Who Killed Tunisia's Chokri Belaid?" *Aljazeera*, September 12, 2013, http://www.aljazeera.com/indepth/%20features/2013/09/201394183325728267.html

91. Daniel Tavana, and Alex Russell, "Previewing Tunisia's Parliamentary& Presidential Elections," *Project on Middle East Democracy* (October 2014): 9, https://pomed.org/wp-content/uploads/2014/10/Tunisia-Election-Guide-2014.pdf

92. Erik Churchill, "The Call for Tunisia," *Foreign Policy*, June 27, 2012, http://foreignpolicy.com/2012/06/27 /the-call-for-tunisia/

93. The Union for Tunisia originally included Nidaa Tounes, Al- Massar (Social Democratic Path), the Socialist Party, the Patriotic and Democratic Labor Party and the Republican Party (Joumhouri).

94. The Popular Front, in its full name the Popular Front for the Realization of the Objectives of the Revolution, is a leftist political and electoral alliance in Tunisia, made up of nine political parties and numerous independents. The Founding parties of the Popular Front included the Worker's Party, the Democratic Socialist Movement, the Baathist Movement, the Vanguard Party, the Tunisian Green Party, as well as others.

95. According to the ballistic tests, both politicians, Brahmi and Belaid, were killed by the same gun and the perpetrator was linked to a Salafi-Jihadist organization.

96. "Tunisian Politician Mohammed Brahmi Assassinated," *BBC News*, July 25, 2013, http://www.bbc.com/news /world-africa-23452979

97. "Tunisia Protestors Urge Government to Resign," *Aljazeera*, October 24, 2013, http://www.aljazeera.com/news/africa/2013/10/tunisia-protests-urge-government-resignation-2013 10237 2524 126573.html

98. "Dialogue Dashed," *Al-Ahram* 117, November 7, 2013, http://weekly.ahram.org.eg/News/4574/-/-.aspx

99. Julia Borger, Angelique Chrisafis, and Chris Stephen, "Tunisian National Dialogue Quartet Wins 2015 Nobel Peace Prize," *The Guardian*, October 9, 2015, https://www.theguardian.com/world/2015/oct/09/tunisian-national-dialogue-quartet-wins-2015-nobel-peace-prize

100. Mohamed Salah Omri, "Tunisian Constitution: The Process and the Outcome," *Jadaliyya*, February 12, 2014, http://www.jadaliyya.com/Details/30221/The-Tunisian-Constitution-The-Process-and-the-Outcome

101. "The Constitution of the Tunisian Republic," trans. UNDP and International IDEA, January 26, 2014, http://www.constitutionnet.org/files/2014.01.26_-_final_constitution_english_idea_final.pdf

102. Ibid.

103. Sarah Mersch, "Tunisia's Compromise Constitution," *Carnegie Endowment for International Peace*, January 21, 2014, http://carnegieendowment.org/sada/?fa=54260

104. "The Constitution of the Tunisian Republic," Article 35–37.

105. "Tunisia Signs New Constitution İnto Law," *Aljazeera*, January 27, 2014, https://www.aljazeera.com/news/%20africa/2014/01/tunisia-assembly-approves-new-constitution-201412622480531861.html

106. "Freedom in the World 2016-Tunisia," *Freedom House*, https://freedomhouse.org/sites/default/files/FH_FITW_Report_2016.pdf

107. "Final Report on the 2014 Legislative and Presidential Elections in Tunisia," *National Democratic Institute* 53, https://www.ndi.org/sites/default/files/Tunisia%20Election%20Report%202014_EN_SOFT%20(1).pdf

108. Isabel Schafer, "The Tunisian Tradition: Torn Between Democratic Consolidation and Neo-Conservatism in an Insecure Regional Context," *European Institute of the Mediterranean*, no. 25 (August 2015): 27.

109. Ibid., 7.

110. Voter turnout in the presidential election was around 63.2 per cent and 60.9 in the run-off election.

111. "Essebsi Wins Tunisia Presidential Vote," *Aljazeera*, December 23, 2014, https://www.aljazeera.com/news /middleeast/ 2014/12/essebsi-declared-tunisia-presidential-winner-2014122212464610522.html

112. Monica Marks, "Tunisia Opts for an Inclusive New Government," *The Washington Post*, February 3, 2015, https://www.washingtonpost.com/news/monkey-cage/wp/2015/02/03/tunisia-opts-for-an-inclusive-new-government/?utm_term=.307df1b7184e

113. "Freedom in the World 2015: Tunisia," *Freedom House*, https://www.refworld.org/publisher,FREEHOU,,TUN,5502f33b9,0.html

114. Ramy Allahoum, "Will Tunisia's Municipal Elections Change Anything?" *Aljaazera*, April 16, 2018, https://www.aljazeera.com/indepth/features/tunisia-municipal-elections-change-180416155940797.html

115. "Tunisia's Municipal Elections," *Carniege Endowment for International Peace-SADA Debate*, May 10, 2018, http://carnegieendowment.org/sada/76299

116. In 2017, the parliament passed a comprehensive Whistleblower Protection Law that clearly defines a whistleblower and outlines procedures for reporting corruption and protection those who report corruption cases.

117. Tarek Amara, "Tunisia Approves Illegal Enrichment Law to Strengthen Anti-Corruption Fight," *Reuters*, July 18, 2018, https://www.reuters.com/article/us-tunisia-corruption-law/tunisia-approves-illegal-enrichment-law-to-strengthen-anti-corruption-fight-idUSKBN1K72QJ

118. "Anger as Tunisia Grants Amnesty to Officials accused of Corruption,' *The Guardian*, September 15, 2017, https://www.theguardian.com/world/2017/sep/15/anger-as-tunisia-grants-amnesty-to-officials-accused-of-corruption

119. Simon Speakman Cordall, "Amnesty of the Corrupt: Tunisia's Move to Heal Old Wounds Branded A Sham," *The Guardian*, October 27, 2017, https://www.theguardian.com/global-development/2017/oct/27/tunisia-reconciliation-act-dismissed-amnesty-of-the-corrupt

120. "Tunisia Poll: Underperforming Economy and Corruption Continue to Drive Intense Satisfaction," *International Republican Institute Center for Insights*, September 26, 2017, https://www.iri.org/resource/tunisia-poll-underperforming-economy-and-corruption-continue-drive-intense-dissatisfaction

121. "Tunisia Protests: Is there a Trade-off between a Strong Economy and Democracy?" *Deutsche Welle*, January 9, 2018, https://www.dw.com/en/tunisia-protests-is-there-a-trade-off-between-a-strong-economy-and-democracy/a-42087864

122. "Public Opinion Survey of Tunisians November 23 to December 2017," *International Republican Institute*, January 10, 2018, http://www.iri.org/sites/default/files/2018-01-10_tunisia_poll_presentation.pdf

123. Ian Bremmer, "The Top 5 Countries Where ISIS Gets Its Foreign Recruits," *TIME Magazine*, April 14, 2017, http://time.com/4739488/isis-iraq-syria-tunisia-saudi-arabia-russia/

124. Since 2015, despite severe measures taken to enhance security and decline in terrorist attacks targeting tourist areas, Tunisia has been exposed to deadly attacks on military and security posts staged by the ISIS in Ben Guardane near Libyan border in 2016 and in northwestern Jendouba province near Algerian border in 2018 leaving several soldiers and civilians dead.

125. Carlotta Gall, "The Return of Thousands of Young Jihadists," *The New York Times*, February 25, 2017, https://www.nytimes.com/2017/02/25/world/europe/isis-tunisia.html

126. "Tunisia: Abuses in the Name of Security Threatening Reforms," *Amnesty International*, February 10, 2017, https://www.amnesty.org/en/latest/news/2017/02/tunisia-abuses-in-the-name-of-security-threatening-reforms/

127. "World Report 2018: Tunisia," *Human Rights Watch*, https://www.hrw.org/world-report/2018/country-chapters/tunisia

128. Fadıl AliRiza, "Why Counterterrorism could be the Death of Tunisian Democracy," *Foreign Policy*, December 30, 2015, https://foreignpolicy.com/2015/12/30/why-counterterrorism-could-be-the-death-of-tunisian-democracy/

129. Fadıl AliRiza, "Old Political Habits in Tunisia," *Carnegie Endowment for International Peace*, June 16, 2015, http://carnegieendowment.org/sada/60406#comments

130. "Tunisia's Youssef Chahed Names New Cabinet," *Aljazeera*, September 6, 2017, https://www.aljazeera.com/news/2017/09/tunisia-youssef-chahed-names-cabinet-170906173802326.html

131. Abdullah Aydoğan, and Kadir Yildirim, "The Economic and Political Dissatisfaction behind Tunisia's Protests," *Carnegie Endowment for International Peace*, January 23, 2018, http://carnegieendowment.org/sada/75334

132. Sarah Feuer, "Tunisia, A Success Story? The Troubles Rattling Its Fragile Democracy," *Foreign Affairs*, July 6, 2017, https://www.foreignaffairs.com/articles/tunisia/2017-07-06/tunisia-success-story

Chapter 4

Egypt's Failed Revolution

Throughout much of its postcolonial history, Egypt has been regarded as a major power and leader in the Arab world in terms of political influence, military strength, education, culture, and religion. It has made up a significant portion of the Arab population and historically acted as an agent for mobilization of the Arab societies toward divergent ideological streams such as Arab nationalism, Arab socialism, Islamic modernism, Islamic Marxism, and the Muslim Brotherhood. From a religious perspective, Egypt exercised a leading role over the Islamic consciousness in the Arab world, owing to the presence of Al Azhar University in Egypt, the historical center of Muslim Sunni doctrine. Furthermore, Egypt's geopolitical importance is not comparable to any other country in the region. Its critical location for the Israeli security and the U.S. military aid for Egyptian cooperation in the region are indicative of this significance. Likewise, the social and political trends in Egypt were of utmost importance as they were often replicated in the rest of the Arab world such as the containment of Islam through repression and cooptation and upgrading authoritarianism to stave off prospects for democratic change. Therefore, political developments in post-revolution Egypt would inevitably impact the internal dynamics of the Arab world.

Egypt was a striking example for Arab autocracy and authoritarianism as it was governed by three successive regimes since the Free Officers coup in 1952 till the uprisings in 2011: Gamal Abdel Nasser (1956–1970), Anwar Sadat (1970–1981), and Hosni Mubarak (1981–2011).[1] Despite differences in their sources of legitimacy and legacies they depended on, all these regimes emphasized top-down rule and created a web of close relationships with the military, police, and other security apparatus. In particular, Mubarak regime has been a case study for many political scientists who explored dynamics of authoritarian stability. Most of the scholarly work reflected on how Mubarak, the ruling National Democratic Party (NDP), and the security apparatus of the state created an adaptive form of authoritarianism, and they used coercion and cooptation strategies to contain and manage emerging opposition forces.[2] The uprisings that ousted the Mubarak regime took many observers by surprise as their level of analysis was mostly based on the Arab state rather than society. However, the dynamics of state-society relationship in Egypt, including various actors such as the regime, civil society, military, security forces, have been particularly important to understand the process leading up to the revolution. Similarly, in the post-Arab Spring Egypt developments have been inseparable from the dichotomies of state-society, civil-military, and religion-state as well as their historical background.

The initial stage of the Egyptian transition appeared to be promising given the holding of the democratic elections, the establishment of a constitutional assembly, and approval of the constitution through a nationwide referendum. Nonetheless, this short-lived democratic experience was undermined by violent street clashes and eventually, brought to an end by the military coup only a year after the inauguration of the country's first democratically elected president. Various factors have contributed to Egypt's failed transition and the restoration of the *ancien* regime. This chapter first presents an overview of the Egyptian economy and politics prior to the January 25 uprisings. Second, it analyzes the political transition including the interim constitutional decrees by the Supreme Court of the Armed Forces (SCAF), parliamentary and presidential elections, constitutional drafting, and post-coup politics that marked an end to the rule of the first elected civilian government in Egypt's history.

HISTORICAL BACKGROUND

The January 25 uprisings has its roots in the gradual erosion of the Mubarak regime's political legitimacy and degradation of living standards for the middle and lower classes particularly in the last decade of Mubarak's rule. Upon a closer investigation, it becomes clear that there was a growing public discontent reflected in several opposition movements and demonstrations at a smaller scale prior to the January 25 uprisings. Hence, while January 25 marked the end of Mubarak's three decades long dictatorship by force, 2011 uprisings was indeed the last episode in the chain of grassroots opposition movements against the regime. An analysis of the political and economic situation prior to the uprisings will not only shed light on the causes of the 2011 upheaval and state-society relationship in a broader perspective but also help to analyze the developments during the transition and its aftermath.

Egypt's Economy Prior to the Uprisings

Economic grievances were evidently a driving factor of the discontent that led to the January 25 Revolution. Thousands of enraged Egyptians filled the Tahrir Square in Cairo and other cities with the public outcry of "Bread! Freedom! Social Justice!" Indeed, one of the protestors' initial demands was improvement in minimum wage. According to a poll conducted on the eve of the revolution in 2011 by the Pew Research Center, 82 percent of Egyptians considered improved economic conditions "very important" making it a top priority for Egypt's future. It was succeeded by fair judicial system, and law and order while freedom of speech was ranked as third priority in the same poll.[3] Hence, the public unrest started to become more visible owing to the mismatch between the ruled and the ruler on the perceived priorities. While Mubarak proceeded to emphasize stability with security as his top priority, inflation, rising economic inequality, and sharp increase in food prices were primary concerns of most Egyptians in the middle and lower classes.

By and large, all Egyptian rulers enjoyed a certain degree of political legitimacy which was closely linked to providing economic growth and security. However, by the early 1980s, the foundations of the regime's political legitimacy had been eroding for decades. Ironically, the origins of this erosion lied in the revolution begun by Abdel Nasser, in 1952. Nasser created a political order that was based on a tacit social contract: citizens would relinquish the political arena to Nasser and the ruling party and in exchange, the regime would provide material prosperity and security.[4] This informal social contract entailed the regime to build a massive public sector. By the early 1980s, the public sector had reached its peak and accounted for 50 percent of GDP and consumed three-quarters of gross domestic fixed investment. The Egyptian program of nationalization began with the nationalization of the Suez Canal and continued with all commercial banks, insurance companies, shipping companies, foreign trade agencies and later, with pharmaceutical companies, construction companies and public utilities.[5]

By massive nationalization program, Nasser attempted to put an end to the power of Egyptian and foreign oligarchs and instead, serve the interests of the middle and the lower classes. In an attempt to provide a more even income distribution, the state laid down high tax rates on higher incomes and salary limits on certain positions.[6] Meanwhile, to improve the living standards of the people in the lower ranks of the society, the state initiated a policy of consumption subsidies for basic commodities including food, gasoline, electricity, public transportation, education, medical care and other services either free or reduced prices. By the 1960s, the Egyptian state controlled all the primary sectors of the economy. The public sector served as the major employer of qualified technical personnel and the state guaranteed a job in the public sector for all the university graduates.

Within few years, the state-centered economic policies were faced with serious challenges. As medical care and nutrition improved owing to Nasser's economic policies, Egypt's population went up at unprecedented rates from 1970s onward. Consumption continued to rise due to material security and prosperity for the middle and lower classes while domestic savings and investment stagnated. Citizens expected the continuation of state subsidies promised by Nasser and a lifetime decent job, yet the state-centered economy failed to fulfill these demands. By 1965, it was clearly evident that this system based on subsidies and public sector expansion wasn't sustainable. Adding to the complexity of the economic downgrade, the fall of Khrushev in the Soviet Union in 1964 had severe consequences for the Nasser regime which, till then, relied on the Soviets both as financers of development projects and protectors of the regime.[7] Moreover, the Arab-Israeli War of 1967 had disastrous consequences for Egypt, leading to a more stagnant economy and political chaos.

Various groups were protesting on the streets to express their demands for better living conditions and the regime responded to these protests by repressive measures and mass arrests. As the regime was losing popular support, it became inevitable that the economy needed restructuring which emerged in the form of the March 30 Program. Measures were taken to shrink public sector and lift the restrictions on the private sector. Hence, the last few years of Nasser witnessed a shift from the state-centered to liberalized economy, however, the regime never attempted to eliminate the safety net from which it drove a certain degree of legitimacy. Instead, it attempted to overcome the economic challenges through borrowing from global financial institutions, which led Egypt to fall into a deep financial hole.

When Anwar Sadat came into power, he took the tentative steps of the late Nasser period further and adopted the open-door policy known as *Infitah* (opening) which required a dramatic economic change including decentralization and diversification of the economy as well as efforts to attract trade and foreign investment.[8] The idea was to open the country to foreign investment and technology transfer to bring about development and economic growth. In reality, economic performance under *Infitah* didn't fare well since most of the private investment went into tourism, finance, and luxury construction while the percentage of industrial activity was declining. This asymmetrical investment and growth led to a dramatic increase in consumption on the one side and stagnation in production, on the other. The government attempted to tackle with the domestic deficit by printing money, which resulted in a sharp rise in inflation roaring at double-digit levels. Under Sadat, Egypt heavily relied on foreign aid both from the global finance institutions and the oil-rich

Gulf states. While the Egyptian state economically fell into a state of emergency, income distribution and the class structure shifted to favor those who are in the upper ranks of the economic ladder because of the set of policy measures including tax reduction and in certain cases tax exemptions and various concessions.

In 1976, to overcome financial crisis, Egypt negotiated with the IMF for a credit, and in return, the IMF stipulated Egypt to comply with the Structural Adjustment Program (SAP) which required a set of measures including cutting subsidies and reducing government expenditures. In January 1977, the government raised the prices of subsidized basic commodities without parliamentary legislation culminating in 15 percent decrease in citizens' purchasing power. Consequently, growing discontent sparked food riots in 1977 leading to the death of nearly a hundred people and the injury and jailing of several thousands. The riots continued for two days until the government had to restore the subsidies and suspend the IMF plan. Under Sadat, the living standards of the middle class were deteriorating day by day, and the lower class was faced with poverty. His initiatives to liberalize economy led to growing inequality and uneven distribution of wealth.

Once Mubarak came into power, he carried on the open-door policy and implemented a set of policies to encourage industrial growth including lower interest rates on industrial loans and reduced tax rates on industrial projects. Despite the First Five Year Plan encouraging production, Egypt was on the verge of an economic crisis. While public sector and food subsidy spending kept growing, oil prices collapsed in the 1980s leading to a sharp drop in the revenues from oil exports as well as Suez Canal fees with lesser traffic and foreign aid considerably reduced due to recession in the donor countries. Thus, Mubarak was faced with the same dilemma as Sadat and Nasser: On the one hand, to weather the storm, Egypt had no choice but comply with the SAP to get credit from the IMF. On the other hand, any cut on the expenditures and subsidies could bring about a massive revolt.

By the late 1980s, Egypt was one of the countries that had the largest debt burdens which accounted for 184 percent of GDP.[9] In the early 1990s, Mubarak had no choice but receive bilateral or multilateral assistance from Europe and the United States, which required the regime to create a market-driven and export-oriented economy integrated to global economy.[10] Hence, in consultation with the IMF, Egypt embarked on a neoliberal reform plan. This neoliberal reform plan entailed the privatization of public sector, ending of subsidies, and reduced role of the state in economy, which in turn meant the dismantling of the tacit social contract that formed the basis of regime's legitimacy. For some time after the negotiations, Egypt failed to fulfil its pledges and tried to meet the deficit by printing money instead cutting down on public spending.

International finance institutions such as the IMF and World Bank made enormous pressure on Egypt, and at times withheld the loans until the government cut price subsidies. By 1990, Egypt had almost gone bankrupt. By exploiting its strategic importance during the Gulf War, Egypt managed to cancel half of its external debt and began to implement the structural reform agreement demanded by the IMF.[11] Eventually, in the 1990s Egypt's economic stabilization program was hailed by many observers including the IMF as a remarkable success story[12]:

> By the standards of recent experience with economic stabilization Egypt in the 1990s is a remarkable success story. Determined macroeconomic policy, together with some favorable external developments, has brought much reduced inflation, led to improved public finances, a stable currency, and a strengthened banking system, together with a sound balance of payment positions.

Egypt was praised as the economic 'Tiger of the Nile' and named by the IMF as a top economic performer.[13] The IMF economist Arvind Subramanian remarked: "Egypt's economy has come a long way since the 1980s. Growth is recovering and confidence is rising. Tough macroeconomic policies and deep structural reforms are doing the trick."[14] Egypt during Mubarak era saw a general improvement in economic conditions. The country progressed well and kept up with the pace of economic growth among the developing countries in the MENA region.

Despite the much-touted GDP growth, in hindsight, it became evident that the neoliberal program neither boosted productivity nor produced long-term economic growth and prosperity. There was no dramatic reduction in public spending. In the short term, the devaluation in the Egyptian pound increased the value of exports carried out in Egyptian pounds. Egypt's growth performance as noted by the global finance institutions was mostly due to domestic demand growth particularly in the construction sector and the financial assistance for siding with the coalition forces during the Gulf War. In addition to the lop-sided growth, the neoliberal program carried out in the 1990s had adverse effects on employment through the privatization program and sharp rise in food prices, leading to a dramatic increase in the levels of poverty.

Mubarak regime took a number of precautions to minimize the social and political repercussions of dismantling the state-centered economic structure. Public sector firms would be sold only to buyers who agreed not to fire workers for several years and if they were made redundant, they would receive training that would allow them to find new jobs. Meanwhile, they would benefit from subsidized housing.[15] However, in reality, public sector firms were sold to businessman with close connections to Mubarak, and they ignored promises dismissing thousands of workers. The Egyptian state, on the other hand, cut its subsidies and sharply reduced its investment in the public sector.

The by-product of the privatization program was the rise of a new class of oligarchs and business elite that have close connections to Mubarak and his family. Neoliberal reforms combined with corruption placed resources into a small circle of business elite instead of privatizing state-led companies in a competitive manner as required by free market regulations. Many businessmen with close connections to the regime were able to reap the benefits of the privatization program. They were enriched through using cheap credits and land and transportation infrastructure provided by the state. While the government was giving a boost to the rich and politically connected, the middle class was excluded from government support, and the poor were neglected and antagonized.

Timothy Mitchell observed[16]:

> The neoliberal program has not removed the state from the market or eliminated "profligate" public subsidies. These achievements belong to the imagination. Its major impact has been to concentrate public funds into different, but fewer hands. The state has turned resources away from agriculture, industry and the underlying problems of training and employment. It now subsidizes financiers instead of factories, speculators instead of schools.

Despite the fact that anti-corruption laws existed in Egypt, there were structural limitations due to the fact that Mubarak exercised his executive power to intervene and prevent the investigation of offenders.[17] The case of Ahmad Ezz is a typical example for the Mubarak's cooptation of some of the businessmen that were supporters of the regime. Ezz was able to purchase a stake in Alexandria Iron and Steel Company (AISCD) which previously belonged to state-affiliated petroleum companies and banks. He gradually consolidated his ownership of the company by using cheap state credits until he eventually owned the company himself and controlled two-thirds of Egypt's steel industry. Being a close friend of Gamal Mubarak, the son of Hosni Mubarak, he entered politics and became a leading figure in NDP, where he later served as the chairman of the party.

The level of corruption rose to new heights within the inner circles of Mubarak. Both Alaa and Gamal Mubarak were rumored to have amassed fortune using their father's connections.[18] Mubarak family and the leading businessmen of the country took advantage of the open-door policy through their partnerships with foreign companies. Under Egyptian law, foreign businesses have to give local partners a 51 percent stake in their investments, which led the members of Mubarak family and powerful people in the ruling party to enrich themselves through securing stakes in foreign investments. In addition, they amassed money through taking commission from every foreign company that invests in Egypt. Businesses that wanted to operate in Egypt needed to pay commission to a company formed by Gamal Mubarak who was an investment banker. Through his connections, he purchased a portion of Egypt's international debt and sold it back to the government receiving massive commission for himself and the bank.[19]

Corruption charges against Mubarak and his family also include creating a company in Cyprus named Bullion with a murky ownership structure, exporting Egyptian gas to Israel below market prices, insider trading in the European stock markets, misusing public funds, securing illicit gains, and receiving bribe while in office.[20] Following the uprisings, Ahmad Shafiq, the former Interior Minister, was accused of using his position to sell the land owned by an association of air force officers to Gamal and Alaa Mubarak at below-market prices.[21] The magnitude of corruption within Mubarak's family was manifested in the family's enormous wealth estimated to reach 70 billion dollars, according to experts, with much of their wealth in British and Swiss Banks or tied up in real estate in the West.[22]

The neoliberal economic policies encouraged by the IMF in the name of macroeconomic growth and stability resulted in a huge gap and apartheid between the super-rich elite and the rest of the Egyptians whose salaries remained largely stagnant while inflation proceeded at double-digit rates for much of the 2000s. The rising national wealth and GDP growth didn't correlate positively with the well-being of an average Egyptian citizen. Most Egyptians felt that they weren't benefiting from this economic progress, having little or no opportunity for upward mobility. On the eve of the uprisings, more than 40 percent of Egyptians were categorized as "extremely poor" (unable to meet minimum food needs), "poor" (unable to meet basic food needs), and "near-poor" (able to meet basic food needs, but not much more), according to the World Bank data.[23] In particular, the rate of absolute poverty increased from 16.7 percent in 2000–2001 to 23.4 percent in 2008-2009.[24] Unemployment reached 25 percent among the university graduates in 2009.[25] As Abu Dhabi Gallup Center Poll findings indicated, it was the perceived difference between what was in reality and what should be that created a driving force for the country's historic uprisings.[26] Moral anger and sense of social injustice, the prerequisites of a mass movement as Barrington Moore puts it, eventually took Egyptians to the streets with the calls "Bread, freedom, social justice."[27]

Egyptian Politics Prior to the Uprisings

Egypt prior to the uprisings didn't fall into the classical archetypes of the Arab state. Despite the significant rents it has derived via controlling the

Suez Canal and large revenue streams in the form of foreign aid particularly from the United States, Egypt was not a classical rentier state. It doesn't possess natural resources that would enable the regime to make an implicit bargain with its citizens to cede their right for political representation in exchange for the distribution of rents as in the case of Persian Gulf states. On the other hand, Egypt cannot be easily classified as a "*mukhabarat state*" or "*fierce state.*"[28] The Egyptian state resorted to coercion and repression in an attempt to confront opposition groups, particularly the Islamist groups such as the Muslim Brotherhood in the 1960s and 1970s. The broad powers granted under the emergency law imposed by President Anwar Sadat were used by Mubarak with an attempt to crush Islamists in the political arena.

Though Mubarak resorted to coercion to fend off pressures for democratic change at times, he also initiated economic and political liberalization to respond to the threat of global democratization trend and market economy. By the early twentieth century, Mubarak expanded space for multiparty politics, electoral arenas in which controlled forms of political contestation could occur. The regime softened its opposition to Islamist groups and Muslim Brotherhood gained historic success with 20 percent of the total number of parliamentary seats in 2005 elections. Mubarak regime selectively implemented reforms for economic liberalization and expanded opportunities for business and social elite. The regime also improved public access to the new communication technologies which had been until then seen as a threat. The era that witnessed several political openings continued till the 2005 elections which were followed by a new phase of autocracy.

In 2006, the Egyptian authorities renewed the state of emergency endowing extraordinary power to the security apparatus and repressed civil society actors brutally. Hundreds of members of the Muslim Brotherhood were arrested, and Muslim Brotherhood candidates were prevented from running as a candidate in local elections including student and labor union elections.[29] These policies produced repression and practice of illegal measures under the veneer of democratic institutions and multiparty politics. Mubarak regime, thus, could be best classified as an example of a hybrid form of authoritarianism where features of authoritarianism—coercion, surveillance, patronage, and corruption—coexisted with those of democracy—legitimacy, multiparty politics, elections and contestation. What enabled Mubarak regime to survive for three decades was his ability to adapt his authoritarian governance to accommodate and manage changing political, economic, and social conditions, a process called as "authoritarian upgrading" by Steven Heydemann.[30] This process emerged in several Arab states including Tunisia, Egypt, Jordan, and Morocco as a response to challenges originating mainly from the demands to democratize prior to the Arab uprisings. Ironically this adaptability and flexibility were meant to bring about a robust authoritarianism instead of producing a democratic change.

One of the fundamental aspects of the hybrid form of authoritarianism in Egypt was that since the Free Officers Coup, Egyptian political leaders, despite their authoritarian nature, derived certain degree of legitimacy and popular support albeit on different grounds. The toppling of the monarch by a group of junior military officers led by Gamal Abdel Nasser began a new era in Egypt. The Revolutionary Command Council (RCC) led by Nasser didn't have any preestablished policies or programs, nor did they have a political agenda. They had to create a set of policies as they took charge of governing the country. The RCC made a number of pledges among which giving an end to imperialism and its agents, feudalism, capitalistic control, and monopoly came to the fore. The Council also pledged to establish a powerful army, social justice, and sound democracy.[31]

In the postcolonial period, ideologies such as nationalism, anti-imperialism, and massive industrialization through public sector expansion were common among many newly independent states. It was also an era in which the Soviet Union proved to be the sole legitimate ally for these states. Hence, the RCC embarked on a major political and structural transformation of its institutions in order to fulfill its goals and built closer ties with the Soviet Union. While maintaining the private sector, Nasser initiated a program of mass nationalization and the state took control over the major means of production.

Nasser gained popular support by promoting ideologies such as Pan-Arabism, anti-imperialism, and Arab socialism. In this era, suspicions toward the West due to colonial past and struggle against Zionism formed the basis for Arab nationalism which would be meaningless without a political and military victory against Israel. Nasser challenged the Western dominance by bringing Egypt closer to the Soviet Union, nationalizing the Suez Canal, adopting Arab socialism and centrally planned economy, and struggling for the Palestinian cause. He was regarded as the leader of the Arab world as he fulfilled Pan-Arabist sentiments by taking the first step, which was to found the United Arab Republic with Syria. However, the defeat in 1967 Arab-Israeli War, which most Egyptians referred as *Naksa* or setback, put an end to the glory of Arab nationalism in the region. From this episode onward, Arab states began to prioritize their individual security and national interests.[32]

With the advent of Anwar Sadat to power in 1970, a new era began in Egyptian history. Sadat's domestic and foreign policies targeted a shift from centrally planned economy to liberal economy and alignment with the West. Under Sadat, Egypt's foreign policy dramatically shifted from being a Soviet ally toward alignment with the West. Sadat firmly held the belief that making peace with Israel would serve Egypt's interests best. He revealed his willingness to reach a peace agreement with Israel if it returned the Sinai

Peninsula which was lost during the June 1967 war. As the peace initiative failed, Egypt launched a military attack in cooperation with Syria to retake Sinai Peninsula, leading to Yom Kippur War of 1973. A cease-fire was achieved under the guidance of the United States. Though Egypt didn't win Yom Kippur War in a military sense, the initial successes allowed it to engage in peace talks and regain the Sinai Peninsula and the Suez Canal after signing the Camp David Accords with Israel.

Most Egyptians view Yom Kippur War as a victory to regain both the land and the honor they lost in 1967 war. The treaty of peace allowed Sadat to restore national pride and develop closer ties with the West, particularly the United States. However, while Sadat's popularity rose in the West, the treaty of peace with Israel had negative consequences for Egypt within the Arab world. Egypt was expelled from the Arab League soon after signing the treaty and it lost the financial support of the oil-rich Gulf states. The political legitimacy under Nasser, which was based on a social contract requiring citizens to forgo their political freedoms in exchange for safety net including fuel, food subsidies, and employment started to erode during Sadat era. Meanwhile, the increase in the prices of basic commodities led to violent crashes.

To compensate economic challenges accompanied by liberalization policies, Sadat addressed people's aspirations for political liberalization to provide more space for political liberties. He dismantled the ruling party and created the NDP while allowing opposition parties to emerge around the fragments of the Arab Socialist Union (ASU).[32] Sadat's regime was faced with rising opposition forces despite his political and economic openings. Much of the internal opposition to Sadat was due to the peace treaty with Israel and deteriorating economic conditions in Egypt. In an attempt to suppress the public unrest, Sadat ordered a massive attack on his opponents arresting and jailing more than a thousand Egyptians. In 1981, Sadat was assassinated by a group of Islamist extremists who were fervently opposed to his peacemaking in Israel, in a military parade commemorating the Yom Kippur War.

A day after Sadat's assassination, his Vice President Hosni Mubarak assumed power. Mubarak openly supported limited presidential terms and pledged to open Egypt to democracy. The initial years of Mubarak as a president were promising as he took a more liberal turn than his predecessor. He released the political prisoners jailed during Sadat's presidency, loosened restrictions on freedom of expression and of the press, and even allowed critics to criticize his governance publicly. Mubarak also permitted opposition parties such as the liberal New Wafd Party and the Socialist Labor Party to participate in the elections. By allowing multiparty elections to take place, he managed both to create a democratic image and secure a second term as a president. The early years of Mubarak also opened some breathing room for Islamic movements and organizations to flourish, expand their institutions, and become a part of mainstream society. In this era, Muslim Brotherhood and other philanthropic Islamic organizations engaged in providing social service by operating schools, clinics, hospitals, day care, opening youth centers, and offering legal aid. They also participated in student bodies, professional associations, syndicates, and legislative elections despite not being allowed to establish a political party. Many of the Islamist political prisoners were released by 1984. Hence, the early years of Mubarak saw hardly any violence. An Islamist political prisoner, Montasir Al- Zayat noted[33]:

> Many of us who were arrested after Sadat's assassination were released by October 1984. Mubarak gave some political space so we were participating visibly and legitimately in professional associations, student bodies and legislative elections. Al-Islam Howa al-Hal (Islam is the solution) was a slogan used by all of us not just the Muslim Brotherhood. We were very popular with people because the state was tolerant, we didn't initiate any violence against the state between 1984–1987.

Meanwhile, the Mubarak regime confronted stiff opposition from the radical Islamist groups such as Gama'a Islamiyya and Islamic Jihad over its economic and foreign policies.[34] They were severely opposed to the IMF structural plan in 1992, Mubarak's liberal economic reforms, and his foreign policy agenda including maintaining peace with Israel and alignment with the USA. These radical groups were engaged in the assassination of high-profile political figures and garnering support from the impoverished masses in order to topple the regime. Mubarak regime's violent crackdown on Islamists including the moderate ones and closing all the channels for their self-expression and participation in politics played into the hands of radical groups to portray the regime as anti-Muslim and thus, needed to be overthrown. Radical Islamist groups led by some reputable Sheikhs marched against the regime through Cairo streets. These protests came as alarming to the government which had already prioritized fighting against Islamic militancy to ensure stability and security.

On the other hand, the parliamentary election in 1987 was a turning point for Mubarak's political reforms. According to the electoral law of 1984, the Islamist candidates were allowed to align themselves with other political parties despite not having the right to establish their own party. In accordance with the electoral law, the Muslim Brotherhood allied with the Socialist Labor Party and the Liberal Party leading to a large opposition bloc "the Islamic Alliance." In 1987 election, the Muslim Brotherhood won thirty-seven seats while 2000 members of the movement were arrested, a step taken by the government to undermine their political gains.[35] The regime found the electoral success of the Muslim Brotherhood threatening and decided to slow down the democratic reforms and reverted to authoritarian practices.

The Higher Constitutional Court announced that the electoral law which determined the procedure for the 1987 election was unconstitutional, upon which Mubarak dissolved the parliament two years before the expiration of its term and called for an early election.[36] In 1990, in the election run for the Shura Council (the upper house) the opposition parties didn't win any seat, hence, they blamed the government for wide-scale fraud and intimidation. The election results and the government's refusal to permit judicial monitoring of the election led the opposition parties to boycott the 1990 elections for the People's Assembly.[37] From the 1990 election onwards, Mubarak reacted firmly to the opposition forces that had the potential to challenge his authority. Among them, Islamists proved to be the main opposition force that could defy Mubarak and thus, political space for them was highly restricted.

While the rise of Muslim Brotherhood was witnessed in the political arena and civil society, from the mid-1990s onward, Egypt also saw signs of Islamist extremism. The June 1995 assassination attempt against Mubarak by the al-Gama'a al-Islamiyya during his visit to Addis Ababa enhanced Mubarak's efforts to ensure security by cracking down on Islamist extremists. Thereafter, Egypt faced a number of subsequent terrorist attacks by extremists Islamist groups. The attack in Luxor in 1997, in Taba in 2004, and in Sharm El-Sheikh in 2005 and Dahab in 2006 mostly targeted foreign tourists and heavily influenced the tourism sector, the backbone of the Egyptian economy. These attacks enraged the Egyptian public who believed Islamists extremists were threatening Egyptian economy, and most Egyptians supported Mubarak in his battle to fight against Islamist extremism. Mubarak's response was to suppress all Islamist groups including the Muslim Brotherhood and exclude them from political arena, rather than making a distinction between fundamental and moderate groups. Behind this move was the increasing gains of the Muslim Brotherhood in professional institutions and syndicates, influence in the media, and increasing leverage in civil society.

Toward the end of the 1990s, Mubarak resorted to authoritarian tactics and the use of coercive measures more frequently while introducing some superficial political openings at the same time. In 1994, he engaged in a political dialogue with the opposition groups except the Muslim Brotherhood and professional labor organizations which had remarkable grassroots support. In addition, in October 1995, Independent Commission for Election Review (ICER) was founded to monitor the whole electoral process. These political openings, despite being ineffective in substance, were significant to project a democratic image to domestic and international audiences. Mubarak reverted to politics of repression whenever he realized that his power would be challenged. The tools for politics of repression used by Mubarak regime were the repressive amendments to the penal code, the anti-terrorism law, continuous extension of the emergency law, interference of the government into the affairs of professional syndicates and trade unions, and electoral fraud.

The Emergency Law No.162 of 1958, amended in 1981, vested broad powers in the state to impose censorship and to order the closure and confiscation of newspapers on grounds of "public safety" and "national security" to try civilians in military courts, to prevent public gatherings and to monitor private communication.[38] According to this law, anyone regarded as a threat to public security and order could be detained without trial or charge for a lengthy period of time. The state of emergency was continuously renewed during Mubarak's presidency and indeed, in Egypt emergency legislation was in force from 1967 till 2011 except for the period from May 1980, following the Camp David Accords, to October 1981 when it was reimposed in the aftermath of Sadat's assassination.

In 1992, the penal code was amended and according to the new "anti-terrorist law," any kind of action that would disrupt public order, harm individuals, damage the environment, financial assets, transport or communications, or which involved the physical occupation of sites and places, or obstructed the application of the law, could be considered as a terrorist act.[39] Likewise, belonging to organizations considered to be undermining social peace, the rule of law or advocating the aims of these groups were considered a terrorist act and all crimes against the security of the state and public were to be tried in the Supreme State Security courts whose verdicts could not be appealed.[40] Thus, by using state of emergency and anti-terrorism law, the regime was able to refer an increasing numbers of political opponents to military courts and deprive them of the right to appeal. Increasing number of people were sentenced to death in these military courts while torture and ill-treatment of detainees became a systematic practice. The number of political detainees, among which members of the Muslim Brotherhood made up the majority, rose dramatically from 1993 onward. As of 2001, there were between 15,000 to 20,000 Islamist political prisoners in prison.[41]

In the 1990s, partly in an effort to keep Islamists under control, Mubarak made some constitutional changes that heavily limited Egyptians' ability to express themselves either through formal channels or informal venues. These included the 1993 Syndicates law and the 1999 Nongovernmental Associations Law which severely restricted the freedom of association and assembly by imposing new governmental regulations and harsh penalties for violations.[42] Mubarak regime also restricted freedom of expression and media by having the NDP-dominated parliament pass Press Law 93 of 1995 which imposed heavy fines and imprisonment for up to five years on journalists publishing false information with the aim of attacking the economy in order to accuse industrialists and politicians. A year later, another bill was passed, making it a crime for journalists to criticize Mubarak and his family. Under the new Press Law, arrest and detention of journalists, and police assaults and torture against media workers became common.

Electoral politics under Mubarak was another area where politics of repression had been systematically and rigorously practiced. Elections in Egypt till 2010, didn't have any potential to bring about a genuine multiparty system with alternation of power. In an interview in 1993, Mubarak declared that Egypt was very keen on democracy, but it would take generations.[43] Despite Mubarak's aspirations for democracy in his political rhetoric, Mubarak used elections only to project democratic image while ensuring an electoral victory for himself and his party. The NDP monopolized the political life in such a way that space allowed for opposition parties to campaign for elections and the way elections took place were no more than cosmetics. Opposition candidates faced several bureaucratic restrictions and harassment during campaigns while candidates belonging to the NDP could rely on public sector resources, launch advertisements before the official beginning of the election campaign, appear on state-controlled television. Moreover, the judges who would supervise elections were cautiously chosen by the minister of interior. Campaign workers and representatives of the opposition candidates entitled to observe voting in polling stations were either expelled or turned away from polling stations.[44] Finally, the government didn't declare the number or percentage of the votes obtained by candidates.

The elections were plagued by fraud and ballot box stuffing and paid thugs were placed in the polling stations by the NDP. For instance, in 1995 parliamentary election, thousands of nonexistent and nonresident names were found on voter's registers.[45] In this election, the NDP enjoyed a 95 percent majority victory. However, since fraud, intimidation, and ballot-stuffing were proven, the Egyptian court, for a second time, ruled that election procedures were unconstitutional and demanded the election of more than 200 deputies out of a total 444 be invalidated.[46] Yet, the new parliament refused to follow this recommendation arguing that parliamentary immunity was enjoyed by deputies. Moreover, the arrest of a considerable number of critics ranging from the Muslim Brotherhood to secular intellectuals on the eve of the elections, undermined the credibility of the elections in Egypt. In another shady election in 1999, Mubarak was reelected as president with 94 percent of the votes with an estimated 10 percent voter turnout. Hence, people constantly remarked that Mubarak was bound to win whether they voted for him or not. Due to this lack of transparency and fairness in elections, the voter turnout remained quite low and the electorate never exceeded 6 million, which is less than the 15 percent of the population.[47]

Mubarak regime fell into a popular fallacy widely accepted by the autocrats in the Middle East. His regime believed that Egyptians feared change as there was a potential threat of Islamic militancy, and they would renounce their freedoms in exchange for government's protection against radical Islamism.[48] Under this assumption, the regime continued to extend the state of emergency and exert coercion and repression in the name of providing security and stability. Mubarak gradually increased dose of repression and targeted not only the Islamist extremists, but all elements of population suspected to be against his policies. The appointment of Habib al-Adly as a minister of interior was a clear turning point in the emergence of Egypt as a police state. Adly's main priority was to strengthen the internal security apparatus while marginalizing the military establishment. During his office, the internal security forces grew in size considerably, from 250.000 in the early 1980s to 1.5 million in 2011.[49] On the other hand, President Mubarak disengaged from internal politics and his main focus was on foreign policy while he handed key issues regarding internal politics to Adly and Gamal Mubarak.

Beginning in 2002, President Mubarak gradually brought his plan to transfer power to his son into action. He first appointed his son to the position of General Secretary of the Policy Committee of the NDP which is the starting point for most key positions in the government. In 2004, following a cabinet shuffle, Ahmed Nazif was appointed as prime minister and the new cabinet was nicknamed "Gamal's cabinet" as most of the new ministers were chosen from the NDP's Policy Committee.[50] Besides, within the NDP circles, the political elite focused on positioning Gamal Mubarak as a future president since their self-interests were wedded to regime's preservation while a dramatic change could create a drift within the regime.[51] The president's steps toward a hereditary transfer of power like that of Syria exacerbated Egyptians' resentment toward Mubarak.

On the other hand, human rights violations and abuse of power by state officials were unfolded through modern communication media including independent satellite television channels such as Al Jazeera, mobile phones and social media in 2000s. In the last decade of Mubarak's rule, the dissatisfaction among the Egyptian public with the NDP-led governments rose to unprecedented level and domestic demands for political change started to gain more visibility with the emergence of *Kefaya* ("enough") movement. Kefaya was a grassroots movement for change drawing its support across a broad political spectrum ranging from Nasserists, Marxists to Islamists.[52]

In August 2004, a petition was circulated by prominent Egyptian activists and intellectuals demanding fundamental constitutional and economic reforms including the abrogation of the state of Emergency law and holding free and fair elections. A total of 300 signatories including Egypt's most respected judges signed Kefaya's founding declaration, "democracy and reform to take root in Egypt."[53] When the movement came into existence, it targeted mass civil disobedience which would eventually create a strong pressure on Mubarak regime to reform. In October 2004, a respected judge, Tariq-al-Bishri, presented the movement's first manifesto in which he called for Egyptians to withdraw their consent to be governed and engage in civil disobedience.[54] Kefaya's manifesto pushed for direct presidential elections with competing candidates as the presidential elections in Egypt were rather symbolic allowing no room for opposition candidates, instead the president was nominated and confirmed by the People's Assembly and reaffirmed via a public "yes-or-no" referendum at six years intervals. Mubarak had already completed his four terms as a president. The Kefaya movement emerged particularly as opposition to the status quo, the monopoly of the NDP over politics in Egypt and Mubarak's plans to transfer power to his son.

Meanwhile, the four principal opposition parties, the Wafd Party, the National Progressive Unionist Party (the Tagammu Party), the Arab Nasserist Party, and the Islamist Labor Party formed "Alliance of National Forces of Reform" calling for reforms in mainly six areas: an end to the state of emergency, a constitutional amendment to allow for a direct election of the president from among competing candidates and a limitation of any individual to two five-year presidential terms, free elections under judicial supervision, greater freedom to establish political parties, a loosening of the government's control over unions, syndicates and civil society groups, and an end to the ruling party's dominance of the state media.[55] Apart from domestic forces calling for change, Mubarak was faced with mounting criticism by the West and thus, he was forced to create a new, reformist image to calm down pressures coming from domestic and international forces.

In response to the mounting pressures, in his police day address in 2004 Mubarak stated that there was need to carry out reforms on human rights issues and the state security system would be put under review with the possibility of elimination.[56] He also proposed to amend Article 76 of the constitution to allow multiple candidates to run for presidential election. However, in spite of the direct popular election of the president, the constitutional amendment effectively enabled the NDP to decide who could run against the incumbent. According to the amendment, each candidate would be required to obtain the support of at least 250 elected officials from national and local institutions. In addition, political parties nominating candidates on the ballot would have to register for at least a minimum of five years and to hold at least 5 percent of the seats in the lower and upper houses of the parliament.[57] Since the ruling NDP enjoyed stranglehold on all national and local institutions, the constitutional amendment precluded any realistic possibility of an opposition candidate coming into power.[58] These restrictions were signals that the so-called "reforms" were made to project a reformist image while maintaining monopoly over political life.

Kefaya movement publicly condemned the amendment calling it theatrics and fake reform. Various demonstrations took place simultaneously across Egypt with the slogan "No constitution without freedom." The judiciary also endorsed Kefaya by making pressure on the government to carry out independent and transparent electoral monitoring and over a thousand judges threatened the government to withdraw their supervision of elections unless their demands were fulfilled. On the day of the referendum, Kefaya organized demonstrations at critical spots in Cairo and called for voters to boycott the referendum which would allow the ruling party to decide who could be a presidential candidate. The protestors were faced with police brutality while some female supporters of Kefaya were assaulted by thugs thought to have been hired by the NDP.[59]

The year 2005 was marked by two critical elections: the 2005 presidential election in which Mubarak gained an overwhelming victory with 88 percent of the votes and the parliamentary election in which the regime was rocked by the electoral success of the Muslim Brotherhood.[60] In the first of three rounds of parliamentary elections, independent candidates affiliated with the Brotherhood won thirty-four seats compared with sixty-eight won by the ruling NDP. This strong showing by the Brotherhood candidates had tremendous immediate effects on the second and third rounds. The state arrested almost 900 Brotherhood members before the second round took place and polling stations were closed in the next two rounds while some voters were prevented from entering polls by soldiers.[61] During the month of voting, polling stations in areas where Muslim Brotherhood had strong support were blocked by riot police.

Similar to the previous elections, 2005 parliamentary elections were characterized by electoral rigging and fraud, and plagued by violence which resulted in the death of twelve people. Muslim Brotherhood claimed that they would have been entitled more seats if it had not been for rigging and intimidation against their supporters during the elections. Eventually, the Muslim Brotherhood still won eighty-eight seats which made up 20 percent of the elected seats and the ruling NDP won 311 seats much less than 404 seats gained in 2000. Overall, the 2005 elections were regarded as largely sham by opposition groups and outside analysts.[62] The Kefaya movement and other opposition groups protested condemning both the forgery and the beating occurred during the elections. A spokesman for Kefaya stated that they returned to the street for the simple reason that the route of change through the election was blocked.[63]

Mubarak responded to the political crisis led by the anti-Mubarak demonstrations by initiating a new wave of repression. Mubarak proposed amendments to thirty-four articles of the constitution. The amendment of Article 179 would grant the president to interfere in the judiciary by bypassing ordinary courts, to refer suspected terrorism-related offenses to military and state security courts, to deprive terrorism suspects of the right to appeal while granting police powers of arrest, and the right to monitor private communications, correspondence, telephone calls, and other communications.[64] Furthermore, the amended Article 5 would preclude not only the establishment of political parties based on religion but also any political activity within any religious frame of reference.[65] This article aimed at closing off any space in political life for the Muslim Brotherhood and it was inserted as the regime's response to the group's showing in 2005 parliamentary elections.

The revised Article 88 would remove any provision for judicial supervision, instead, it would transfer the responsibility to an electoral commission. Given Egypt's past experience with an independent electoral commission, most regime critics argued that such a commission would not be a neutral body and this amendment would only reduce the role of judges in supervising elections and referendums.[66] With the amended article, the regime would easily evade accusations of electoral fraud which was at the heart of the debates in the previous year when two leading judges denounced the government's failure to respond to evidence of electoral fraud during the presidential and parliamentary elections. The amendments were carefully tailored by Mubarak regime to foil genuine competition. Amnesty International defined the proposed constitutional amendments "as the greatest erosion of human rights in 26 years."[67] Amendments were approved by People's Assembly and introduced to public referendum in 2007. Meanwhile, opposition deputies making up 20 percent of the parliament boycotted the vote. The amendments were ratified in a violence-ridden referendum in less than a week after they were passed in the People's Assembly raising questions as to its reliability.

State repression against opposition groups intensified following the elections. Contrary to the expectations for reforms, Mubarak took a harder line with his opponents. Ayman Nour, Al-Ghad (Tomorrow) party leader, a twice-elected member of the parliament and the first runner-up in the 2005 presidential election with 7.6 percent of the national vote, was imprisoned by a regime-friendly judge under allegations of forging signatures on the party's license application. The arrest of Nour, despite the parliamentary immunity enjoyed by members of the parliament, was believed to be politically motivated and based on corrupt charges. The act was widely criticized by the governments in the West and the United States. As a reaction, Condoleezza Rica postponed a visit to Egypt to protest Nour's arrest. In 2009, Nour was suddenly released from prison a year earlier than his imprisonment would expire. His release was interpreted as a political gesture to the United States.[68] This single case manifested the arbitrariness of law in Egypt where the president could directly interfere in judiciary outcomes in the direction of his political motives.

In April 2006, Mubarak extended the state of emergency for an additional two years.[69] The extension of state of emergency gained momentum to the state-sanctioned repression on the Muslim Brotherhood to neutralize their gain in the parliamentary election in 2005. The minister of interior began mass arrests of the Brotherhood members in 2006. The prominent members of the Brotherhood and two members of the People's Assembly, Rajab Abu Zeid and Sabri Amer, were arrested. Their parliamentary immunity had been lifted and despite being civilians, they were tried before the supreme military court on charges of terrorism and money laundering.[70] Human rights activists, journalists, and bloggers also fell victim to the authoritarian backlash of the Mubarak regime. In 2008, Amnesty International reported that there were at least 18,000 administrative detainees and some had been imprisoned for more than a decade despite repeated decisions in the civil courts that they should be released.[71] In 2009, Human Rights Watch reported that between 5,000 to 10,000 Egyptians were estimated to be held in prison without charge or trial, and use of torture and harassment against those suspects became systematic.[72]

In response to the escalating political repression and deteriorating economic conditions, Egyptian workers staged a general strike on April 6, 2008, in El-Mahalla El-Kubra, a large industrial town famous for its textile industry in Egypt. The workers were protesting rising prices, low wages, delays in payments, and privatization of public sector firms. The general strike was different from the previous one both in terms of its magnitude and sphere of influence. Few days before the strike, a group of activists spread the call for a general strike on social media and they reported on the strike, informed their networks of police activity and gained a nationwide attention, particularly among the youth. Between sixty to eighty thousand people took to the streets and rebelled against the government.[73] The strike lasted for three successive days until the representatives of the cabinet reached a consensus with strike leaders and promised to grant workers some of their demands. What makes this strike a turning point was the birth of the April 6 Youth Movement, which would play a decisive role in the January 25 Revolution. When strike ended in success, the activists decided to initiate April 6 movement as a political opposition.

While citizens were fervently urging for fundamental change, the regime kept being aloof and repressive. The renewal of state of emergency in 2008 for another two years gave security forces power to disperse election-related rallies, public gatherings, and demonstration, and arrest individuals without charge for exercising their rights to freedom of assembly and expression. The 2010 parliamentary elections took place in a very tense atmosphere, and the elections were marred by disruption of demonstrations, arrest of campaign activists, exclusion of opposition supporters, and allegations of fraud and state-sanctioned violence. The NDP won 96 percent of the seats, while only one independent candidate affiliated with the Muslim Brotherhood won a seat, eventually leading to a loss of eighty-seven seats by the Muslim Brotherhood candidates compared to the previous election. According to observers, this election was the most fraudulent in Egypt's history.[74]

With the constitutional amendment in 2007, the government drastically limited independent judicial supervision of polling and international monitors were prevented from overseeing the voting. Over a thousand people demanding to observe the vote-counting process in Mahalla were forcefully dispersed by the police.[75] Nine people were killed in the Election Day exacerbating tensions in the country. These developments renewed feelings of humiliation experienced by Egyptians and destroyed people's slightest hope in any change by peaceful means. The government deeply aware of Egyptians' restive mood invoked the Interior Minister to use security forces targeting any citizen opposing the regime.

In the chain of events leading up to the January 25 revolution, the most touching and pathetic one was the death of Khaled Said who used his phone to record police informers distributing drugs and talking about giving them to individuals and pushers so they could arrest them and get promotions while they would keep a portion of drugs for themselves to sell later.[76] Said was arrested before he could upload the video to the Internet, and he was tortured to death at a police station in 2010. After his death, his friends uploaded the footage recorded by Said so that people could see why he had been killed. In addition, a prominent Facebook group "We are all Khaled Said" brought together thousands of Egyptians and played a critical role during the uprisings. Coupled with the protests movements stemming from Bouazizi's death and ouster of the Ben Ali in Tunisia, the death of Khaled Said ignited the wick for the Egyptian revolution.

January 25 Revolution has deep roots in the erosion of the political legitimacy of Mubarak regime and its loss of touch with citizens. Mubarak failed to fulfill the legitimacy provided by some Arab autocrats who ensured rising prosperity and economic safety in return for lack of freedom. The regime also failed to initiate any tangible political reform and to expand space for individual freedoms. Mubarak assumed that Egyptians would forgo their freedoms in exchange for the stability and security provided by the government against Islamic extremism. However, in reality, the national security rhetoric employed by the political elite justified neither the continuous extension of state of emergency nor the draconian assaults on civilian activists in the eyes of most Egyptians. While promising reforms which would gradually move Egypt toward democracy, Mubarak only implemented superficial reforms accompanied by substantive restrictions and followed by a wave of repression. Eventually, an intolerable mismatch between the priorities of the regime and the values of citizens emerged leaving no hope for Egyptians except taking to the streets. Hence, the years leading to the revolution witnessed unprecedented wave of street protests and labor strikes reflecting the long-standing anguish experienced by the majority of Egyptians.

Tunisians' success in ousting their deeply entrenched dictator was a catalyst for Egyptians who witnessed that the authoritarian regime once believed to be robust and deeply entrenched was vulnerable in the face of people power. After the fall of the Tunisian dictator, a call was made by the cadre of young Egyptians involved in the April 6 movement, Kefaya and the National Association for Change (NAC) for a revolution on social media on 25 of January, a holiday honoring the police in Egypt. Around sixty thousand people gathered in Tahrir Square on the 25 January and the initial protests started with peaceful and minimalist slogans such as *eesh, hurriya, karamah* (live, freedom, dignity). The regime responded by resorting to wide-scale repression and initiated Internet blackout, which further inflamed the protestors' rage. The demonstrations had neither a clear ideology nor a leader, and they were made up of people from all political and socioeconomic backgrounds.

On February 1, 2011, Mubarak delivered a speech to the nation and declared that he would not seek reelection and he wanted to die in Egypt. He appointed Omar Suleiman, the director of military intelligence, as vice president and announced that he would charge him with the task of holding dialogue with all political forces and factions concerning political and democratic reforms and the constitutional amendments required to fulfill people's legitimate demands.[77] The military took an impartial stance during the protests and was deployed into the streets as a neutral party declaring that it would do nothing until Mubarak and demonstrators agreed on something. Mubarak's speech and the concessions he promised divided protestors as to whether they should give him a chance. On the next day, pro-Mubarak thugs riding camels and horses attacked protestors with sticks and knives, which turned the tide of the events irreversibly and contributed to the radicalization of protests.[78] The course of the popular uprisings which faced extortionate use of force by the security forces made it clear to Egyptians that Mubarak's promised reforms weren't a result of goodwill, but rather an interim remedy to survive the crisis. Protestors were convinced that very little would change unless Mubarak regime was overthrown.

Despite the largely peaceful nature of the protests, the security forces' response was brutal leading to the death of 840 people and over 6000 casualties during the eighteen days of the uprisings, according to a report by the Amnesty International.[79] The internal security forces failed to cope with the massive size of the demonstrations all across the country.

Table 4.1 Timeline of the Key Events during the Egyptian Revolution

January 25	Protests organized largely via social media and word of mouth were staged in Cairo and other major cities. Tens of thousands of Egyptians participated in unprecedented anti-government demonstrations urging for reforms on National Police Day. The event is termed *yawn al-ghadab,* or The Day of Rage. Police attempted to disperse demonstrations using batons, tear gas, and water cannons. Two protestors in Suez and a police officer in Cairo are killed.
January 27	Police clashes with protestors throughout Egypt and attempted to lock down Cairo's Tahrir Square in anticipation of another mass demonstration after Friday prayers on January 28. The government ordered Facebook and Twitter to be blocked.
January 28	Internet and mobile phone text message services were disrupted. The Muslim Brotherhood participated in demonstrations. Massive protests with hundreds of thousands of Egyptians spread throughout the country. Demonstrators won control of Tahrir Square. Clashes between the police and demonstrators turned deadly. Eleven civilians were killed and at least 1,030 people got injured countrywide. Mubarak deployed army troops and tanks into cities, but the army chose to remain neutral.
January 29	Mubarak addressed the nation and announced that he had fired Prime Minister Ahmed Nazif, replacing him with former Air Force Commander Ahmed Shafik tasked with forming a new cabinet. Mubarak also appointed intelligence chief Omar Suleiman as vice president in an apparent move to end speculation that the regime is grooming Gamal Mubarak to succeed his father. Meanwhile, Mubarak refused to step down.
January 30	Mubarak sacked the head of the ruling party and the minister of interior. Police forces were withdrawn from Tahrir Square. The army announced that it would not use force against demonstrators and that it recognized the legitimacy of their demands.
February 1	The turnout to the protests reached an estimated one million people from all walks of the Egyptian society. Mubarak addressed the nation again promising constitutional reforms and vowed that he would not seek reelection in September.
February 2	Hundreds of armed Mubarak supporters rode camels and horses into the Tahrir Square and attacked protestors in what came to be known as the "Battle of the Camel. The Muslim Brotherhood members were credited for their role in fighting against the attack and keeping the protestors organized.
February 5	Several NDP leaders including Gamal Mubarak resigned
February 6	Omer Suleiman met a variety of opposition groups including the Muslim Brotherhood to negotiate a way out of the crisis, but his reform proposals were rejected
February 7	Wael Ghoneim, a Google executive and the coordinator of the influential Facebook Page "All of Us are Khalid Said" was released from state custody. He gave a touching interviewing on live television adding momentum to the protest movement.

(Continued)

Table 4.1 (Continued)

February 9	Labor strikes throughout Egypt dragged the country into a deadlock.
February 10	The SCAF held a meeting without the participation of Mubarak and announced that it was monitoring the course of events in Egypt and would remain in continuous session. Mubarak gave his third speech to the nation which was widely expected to announce his resignation. Mubarak declared that he would remain in power until the expiration of his term. He also announced proposed constitutional reform including six articles that would be amended. Protestors got furious over Mubarak's speech.
February 11	Omer Suleiman addressed to the nation and announced that Mubarak had resigned and the SCAF would take over power led by Field Marshal Mohammed Hussein Tantawi.
February 13	The SCAF dissolved the parliament, suspended the constitution, and announced that it would rule for six months or until general elections were held, depending on whichever came first.

Adapted from (Irshad 2012; Aljazeera 2011)

Therefore, Mubarak had to turn to the military to intervene to put an end to the popular uprisings. In the course of events, the most critical to the overthrow of Mubarak regime was that the military didn't respond positively to Mubarak's demand and declared that the demands of the protestors were legitimate and the army would not use force against the Egyptian people.[80] On February 11, Mubarak was forced to resign opening a new chapter in Egypt's history.

EGYPT'S POLITICAL TRANSITION

The overthrow of Mubarak brought the military council as the main political actor in shaping Egypt's transition. The military's stance during the uprisings raised many hopes among Egyptians that Egypt would move forward in the direction of democracy under the auspices of the military. The initial roadmap of the military speculated that the elections would be held within six months following the fall of Mubarak. Nonetheless, the military leadership dragged their feet in the holding of elections and relinquishing power to a civilian government. The trajectory of the transition including the declaration of the interim constitution and other decisions by the military council clearly indicated that the military emerged as a playmaker setting the rules of the game, and it would in no way allow a genuine democratic transition. The following sections investigate the key political developments that shaped Egypt's political transition and hindered prospects for democratic outcome.

Egypt under the Rule of the SCAF

On the same day Mubarak resigned, the SCAF, led by Field Marshal Tantawi, Egypt's Defense Minister under Mubarak, took the reins of power declaring that it would rule the country until parliamentary elections were held and a new president was elected. Nonetheless, given that the interests of the SCAF and the former ruling regime were interwoven, the military preserved most of the old system of power and its institutions such as judiciary, media, local governorates, and some of the Mubarak loyalists.[81] The SCAF, which was composed of twenty senior generals, took over the legislative and executive powers, dissolved the parliament and suspended the constitution. The day after Mubarak fell, responding to the aspirations of the protestors, the SCAF vowed to ensure a peaceful transition of authority within a free and democratic system that allows for a civilian and elected government and the build of a democratic and free state.[82]

In the interim, a "Constitutional Declaration" which would function as a *de facto* constitution until the drafting of a new constitution, was delivered by a committee formed by the SCAF. The committee was headed by Tareq Al-Bishri, a former Judge and an Islamist intellectual. Subhi Saleh, a leading attorney affiliated with the Muslim Brotherhood was also a member of this committee. Other six members were professional jurists; however, the committee had no member from liberal or revolutionary forces. The *de facto* constitution was based on the 1971 constitution with amendments to eight articles which in general fulfilled the demands raised by opposition groups in the late Mubarak period.[83] The amendments enabled full judicial supervision of elections, imposed two consecutive four-year term limit on future president's incumbency, and limited the state of emergency to a maximum of six months depending on the approval of an elected parliament.[84]

The *de facto* constitution led to controversies between the two camps: Islamists including the Brotherhood and the remnants of the NDP in one camp and liberals and revolutionary forces in the other. The amendment mandating the elected parliament with drafting a constitution was opposed by liberal and revolutionary groups while it was supported by the Muslim Brotherhood and the veterans of the NDP. The debate over the sequencing of elections and the drafting of the new constitution was a critical issue determining the trajectory of the transition, as was the case in Tunisia. The Muslim Brotherhood, confident of its organization and wide-scale grassroots support, supported this amendment assuming that they would hold a majority in the parliament, which would ultimately enable them to draft the new constitution. Likewise, the NDP having ruled the country for many decades had the organizational and campaigning skills that would allow them to rival against the Brotherhood. On the other hand, the revolutionary and liberal forces maintained that the newly elected bodies could abuse their political powers unless a new constitution was drafted before elections. For the liberals who had little faith in people, a secular political order would bring out a democratic outcome and hence, they opted for the drafting of constitution by prominent judges in dialogue with politicians and civil society actors and prolongation of the interim period to win over Egyptian people as they were not as well organized as the Islamists.

The process of constitutional reform gave no chance for campaigning and national dialogue for the proposed amendments due to tight timeframe between the declaration of the amendments and the holding of the referendum. Therefore, the way constitutional amendments were made was harshly criticized by many experts, judges, and politicians who called for opening a broad national dialogue over the constitutional reform and giving the right of electing a constitutional commission to Egyptian people.[85] Despite proposed amendments, holding parliamentary and presidential elections under the 1971 constitution had the likelihood of leading to a system similar to the one under Mubarak. The 1971 constitution which gave too much power to the president and reduced the power of legislative and judicial branches was not suitable for managing a safe transition to democracy.[86]

Amid controversies, the referendum was held on March 19 and the amendments were approved by a 77 percent of the votes opening the way for the parliamentary and presidential elections. The turnout for the referendum was at 41 percent, the highest ever obtained in Egypt's history.[87] However, only eleven days after the referendum, on March 30, the SCAF unilaterally issued an Interim Constitutional Declaration (also known as the March 30 Constitutional Declaration) consisting of a slightly modified version of the eight amendments with 53 Articles from the 1971 Constitution to serve as a legal reference until a new constitution was drafted.[88] The declaration outlined a roadmap and timeline for the Egyptian transition phase and scheduled parliamentary elections before the writing of a new constitution. According to this roadmap, the elected members of the first People's Assembly and Shura Council would meet in a joint session within six months of their election to form a commission of one hundred members from both the Shura Council and the People's Assembly to draft a constitution within six months.[89] Besides, the Interim Constitutional Declaration allocated the executive and legislative power of the president and the parliament to the SCAF until these institutions were popularly elected. By this unilateral declaration of the interim constitution, the SCAF not only rendered the verdict of the referendum invalid, but it also decided to be the main actor determining the trajectory of the transition by entrenching its control over critical institutions of the state.

The interim constitution of March 30 eliminated previous legal restrictions on the establishment of parties. The declaration stated that it was not permitted to directly engage in a political activity of form political parties on the basis of religion, race, or origin, but it also omitted the clause on the prohibition of political parties based on religious background, which was inserted by Mubarak in the 2007 constitutional amendment.[90] Hence, the interim constitution cleared the way for the Brotherhood to establish a political party.[91] Besides, on March 28, the SCAF issued the New Political Parties Law, amending Law 40 of the 1977. Under the new law, political parties would be formed after notifying a seven-member judicial committee. Unless an objection was raised by the commission within thirty days, the party would be able to operate. The amended party legislation increased the founding members from 1,000 to 5,000 members from at least ten different governorates and required the witness of a notary of each member's signature. This legislation also required party founders to publish the names of 5,000 founding members in two widely circulated newspapers while the financial state subsidies provided for political parties were withdrawn.[92] In other words, it privileged the parties that already had financial resources and organizational structure while acting against the interests of youth movements and revolutionary groups.

The Muslim Brotherhood wanted the holding of parliamentary and presidential elections and the conclusion of a constitution with expedition fearing that the political turmoil and uncertainty could strengthen the military's hand and pave the way for a return to the former status quo. Particularly, constitutional drafting was a top priority for the Brotherhood members as it would be the only way to break from Egypt's long-standing autocracy. On the contrary, liberal groups and leftists parties didn't consider the extension of the transition period risky since their immediate concern was an Islamist takeover of the parliament following the elections which would bestow them with the power to shape the country's future constitution.

The SCAF's Constitutional Declaration of March 30 stipulated that only parties represented in parliament would nominate a presidential candidate. This clause came as a blow to newly established parties and revolutionary forces that were in the heart of the revolution. On September 25, the SCAF issued new amendments to the electoral law, introducing a mixed system of individual candidacy and closed party lists system for the upcoming parliamentary election. According to this new electoral system, one-third of the seats would be elected through individual candidacy as independents and two-thirds of the People's Assembly would be elected through closed party lists. This system allowed the party-affiliated candidates to compete in the one-third of the seats normally allocated for independents, which would ultimately lower the chances of the representatives of revolutionary groups and youth movements to win a seat in the parliament. Moreover, the individual candidacy was opposed by many political parties and youth movements on the ground that it allowed people from the old regime to get reelected through vote buying and propaganda and thus promoted the monopolization of a political body by the old guard.[93] They instead advocated for elections based on a party list system.

On November 1, the SCAF issued supra-constitutional principles intended to be binding on the constituent assembly under the "Declaration of the Fundamental Principles of the New Egyptian State." These principles, commonly known as Al-Selmi Communiqué gave the SCAF an increased role and political influence over the decision-making process in Egypt. According to the communiqué, the SCAF was the sole responsible for all matters concerning the armed forces for discussing its budget, which should appear as a single line in the annual state budget, hence, the defense budget and all military appointments would escape the oversight of the parliament.[94] The communiqué entrusted the military "to defend constitutional legitimacy," thus, bestowing the military with the constitutional right to overrule any clause that they regarded as contradictory to the basic tenets of the Egyptian state and the society. The communiqué further demanded the approval of the SCAF for the declaration of a war by the president, which strengthened SCAF's position with a veto power. It also stipulated that the constituent assembly that would draft the new Egyptian constitution would be composed of twenty members from the parliament and eighty members from other state institutions.[95]

Many political parties and civil society actors severely opposed to the Al-Selmi document which positioned the military as a state within the state. Islamists, liberals, leftists, and nationalists called for a march in Tahrir Square and the march was unmatched to any protest movement since the January 25 Revolution.[96] A weeklong clash between the protestors and security forces forced the SCAF to withdraw the document. Protestors' demands included the trial of Mubarak and all corrupt figures who served during his rule, dismantling the former ruling NDP, ending the state of emergency, immediate release of political prisoners, and replacing the incumbents in the local councils, governorates, and other state institutions appointed by the old regime.[97] In addition, they demanded the SCAF to impose penalty on those accountable for the killings and injuries during the upheaval. Despite having pledged to protect the revolution and realize its objectives when it took reins of power, the SCAF failed to properly investigate the perpetrators of the killings and injuries of thousands of protestors. As most cases were perpetrated by the old regime, the SCAF chose to turn a blind eye to the numerous incidents that needed investigation and trial. This, in turn, led thousands of protestors to retake Tahrir Square and organize protests, sit-ins, and march in an attempt to condemn the policies of the SCAF.

Throughout the transition, the SCAF failed to initiate any meaningful action in line with the objectives of the revolution. Military response to the public demands often arrived late and remained superficial in several cases. In fact, most of the meaningful steps were taken by the SCAF only under the mass pressure exerted by the revolutionary groups protesting at Tahrir Square or through court verdicts. For instance, Mubarak's trial was a key demand of protestors in the months following his ouster. In response to the military's reluctance to put Mubarak and other corrupt figures of the old regime on trial, on April 1 the "Save the Revolution" Day was launched by demonstrators who retook the Tahrir Square calling for the SCAF to respond to the objectives of the revolution. The protest was repeated on April 8 with the same calls, which eventually forced the SCAF to order Mubarak to stand trial on the charges of ordering the killings of protestors during the January uprisings.[98]

In a similar vein, the dissolution of the NDP and the NDP-dominated municipal councils materialized not by the SCAF but by the Supreme Administrative Court (SAC). On April 16, the SAC issued a ruling to dissolve the NDP and ordered its funds and properties to be handed over to the government.[99] On June 28, the court further issued another verdict to dissolve all municipal councils dominated by the NDP. Similarly, a series of court rulings barred former NDP officials from running in the post-revolution parliamentary elections. However, those decisions were overturned on appeal, and the SCAF refused to issue the decree blocking the old elite from public office.[100] Hence, despite siding with the protestors during the uprisings, the military kept aloof from realizing most of the critical objectives of the revolution. Members of the old regime were still remaining in their positions in several state institutions, companies and workers' unions.

Notwithstanding protestors' pleas for improvement in human rights, Egypt under the SCAF witnessed a serious derogation in human rights and individual freedoms. Mubarak's repressive policies were preserved and even strengthened in the disguise of security and stability.[101] The state of emergency was not lifted and the SCAF was blamed for many charges of abuse, torture, and misconduct. These included unfair military trials of thousands of civilians, the arbitrary arrest and conviction of peaceful protestors, torture and abuse of detainees. According to the Human Rights Watch, in 2011 more than 12,000 civilians faced unfair military trials which failed to provide the basic due process rights of civilian courts and the figure was more than the number of military trials of civilians during the thirty years of Mubarak's rule.[102]

Most cases involving violence and the killings of protestors remained uninvestigated even after they were submitted to the prosecutor general. In the year following the January 25 revolution, there were over fifteen major incidents in which hundreds of protestors were killed and injured and the military didn't conduct any investigation adequately.[103] More alarming was the escalating sectarian violence against Copts, often perpetrated by Salafists and numerous Coptic churches were subject to attacks by the extremist groups. On the other hand, demonstrations and sit-ins carried out by peaceful protestors were harshly suppressed by the military while the massacres perpetrated by the hard-line Islamist groups and the military didn't receive any response.

In line with its antirevolutionary stance, the SCAF issued Decree 34 of 2011 restricting freedom of speech and assembly by criminalizing strikes, sit-ins, and demonstrations that would impede public work. In the months following Mubarak's ouster, protests organized by civil society organizations escalated as the SCAF entirely ignored the demands and recommendations of civil society actors in its decision-making process. The SCAF sought to undermine the Egyptian NGOs by implicating that they were working on behalf of foreign agendas. Furthermore, the SCAF declared thirty-nine NGOs including many of Egypt's oldest and most respected human rights organizations "illegal" on the ground that they were not officially registered and received foreign funding.[104] Given that the declared illegal organizations' common denominator was their focus on democracy and human rights, the military's crackdown on these NGOs appeared to be rather politically motivated to silence and discredit its critics. It was also a tragic irony that the Egyptian military attacked human rights organizations for receiving foreign funding while by far the largest recipient of foreign funding in Egypt was the military itself.[105] Since it assumed power, the SCAF took most critical decisions and issued decrees and amendments unilaterally without consulting to the public. Having vested economic and political interests in determining the trajectory of the transition, the military kept its stranglehold over the three branches of the government; the executive, legislative, and judiciary while the interim government under Sharaf played almost no role in decision-making and acted as the secretariat of the SCAF.

Post-Mubarak Elections and the Rise of the Muslim Brotherhood

The first parliamentary elections in post-Mubarak Egypt were held in late 2011 and early 2012. Elections for the People's Assembly were carried out under judicial oversight and with the participation of international observers including the International Republican Institute, the US-based Carter Center, the National Democratic Institute, and a European observation mission. The elections were deemed as free and fair, and the voter turnout was the highest in Egypt's history with over 60 percent in all three rounds of the electoral process.

In compliance with the amendments to the electoral law by the SCAF, the election was carried out under a parallel voting system; two-thirds of seats were elected by party list proportional representation and the remaining one-third was elected by individual candidacy. Following a three rounds of electoral process, the parliamentary elections resulted in an overwhelming victory for Islamists. The Freedom and Justice Party (FJP), the Muslim Brotherhood's political arm, won 47 percent of the seats; 127 seats on party list and 108 seats on individual candidacy making up for 235 out of 498 seats in the People's Assembly.[106] The Salafist al-Nour Party won nearly 25 percent of the seats, which came as a surprise to many observers. Salafists weren't involved in Egyptian politics prior to the uprisings and their leaders opposed the uprisings holding the belief that accepting Mubarak's authority would be better than facing the risk of disorder and chaos that might result from a change of regime. The Wafd Party, the largest liberal party in Egypt, won 7.5 percent of the seats while the Egyptian Bloc, an alliance of other liberal parties secured 6.7 percent of the seats in People's Assembly. Ten seats were appointed by the SCAF including two women and five Copts.

Soon after the elections for the People's Assembly, the Shura Council elections were held in two rounds in January, 2012. Shura Council has 264 seats, two-thirds of which (176 seats) were elected in direct election, whereas the remaining one-third was appointed by the president after the presidential election was held. In Egypt, the Shura Council acted as a purely consultative and advisory body with very little influence on decision-making. Its role was further diminished by the SCAF's interim constitution. Similar to the People's Assembly elections, the Islamist parties gained a landslide victory in Shura Council elections. The FJP secured 58 percent of the elected seats, whereas the Salafi Al-Nour Party won 25 percent of the seats in the upper house of the parliament.[107]

The election results manifested the lengthy experience of the Brotherhood members who ran as independents under Mubarak and their superior organizational skills contrary to the fragmented liberal parties and youth movements. Beyond the ideological outreach, the Brotherhood's and Salafists' electoral success lied in their deep penetration into the Egyptian society through the charities they had run as social organizations for decades. In the absence of effective social services provided by the state, the strong grassroots networks built up through charity services appealed to the masses of lower-class voters. On the other hand, liberal parties and opposition groups were not unified and well organized. Failing to understand the priorities and values of the lower strata of the society, they took a more elitist stance and appealed only to the educated, secular, and upper-income voters. As one taxi driver in Aswan put righteously: "The Islamists cater for our needs and understand our traditions while the liberals and secularists are talking to each other on Facebook."[108]

The SCAF and the Brotherhood engaged in tacit alliance in the initial period of the transition. The Brotherhood members fervently campaigned for a yes vote in the referendum over the interim constitution and endorsed the military amendments in the March 30 Constitutional Declaration. The organization opposed to the demonstrations and sit-ins organized by the revolutionary forces reacting to the military's suppression of the protestors and unilateral decision-making process. This initial alliance came to a halt following the first parliamentary elections in post-Mubarak era. The first sign of this rift was seen when the FJP called for the dissolution of the incumbent government led by Kamal El-Ganzouri using harsh language for being incompetent and failing to fulfill its duties. The SCAF insisted on keeping the interim cabinet in place till the election of the president.

The legitimacy of this government was shady to most Egyptians supporting the revolution as it was composed of the politicians who served under Mubarak. The SCAF defended its impartiality and in a veiled threat, warned the Brotherhood to be aware of the lessons of history by implying the 1954 military crackdown on the movement.[109] Another setback to the Egypt's transition to a civilian government was the Supreme Constitutional Court (SCC)'s ruling which declared the parliamentary elections in late 2011 and early 2012 unconstitutional on the ground that one-third of the seats elected through individual candidacy were invalid[110]. Based on this ruling, the SCAF dissolved five-month-old parliament. The SCC's ruling and the SCAF's move to dissolve the parliament were regarded as politically motivated steps to deny the Brotherhood the political power it had earned in the election.

The first round of the presidential elections took place following the approval of the approvals of the thirteen candidates belonging to a wide spectrum of political ideologies by the Presidential Election Commission in May 2012. The results of the first round brought the two candidates forward: Mohammed Morsi, a senior Muslim Brotherhood member and the president of the FJP and Ahmed Shafiq, a former air force general who briefly served as a prime minister at the end of Mubarak's reign. Morsi obtained 24.8 percent of the votes, and he was followed by Shafiq with 23.7 percent. The run-off election was regarded as a contest between the remnants of the old regime emphasizing stability and Islamists who opposed to the three decades rule of Mubarak regime.

The campaigns for the presidential election was carried out in a political setting polarized between seculars fearing of religious radicalism and Islamists deeply worried about a return to the police state. The results were alarming to the youth movements and liberal groups as both candidates were seen far from achieving the goals of the revolution. While many secular and liberal groups were suspicious of the Brotherhood's intentions, Shafiq was the figure most associated with Mubarak-era politics and just like Mubarak, he campaigned with the rhetoric of providing stability. During the uprisings, Shafiq compared the protestors to a disrespectful child slapping his father.[111] Therefore, fearing of a possible return to Mubarak-era politics youth movements such as the April 6 movement urged its followers to vote for Morsi as the lesser of two evils.

On June 17, only a few hours before the closing of the polls, the SCAF issued a Supplementary Constitutional Declaration which included several amendments to the interim constitution limiting the coming president's powers while granting the SCAF with broad legislative powers previously held by the parliament and complete control over all military affairs including appointments and budget without any civilian oversight. More alarming was the amendment granting the SCAF the power to form a new constitution assembly if the existing assembly failed to complete its work on time. In another amendment, the SCAF granted itself and the Supreme Judicial Council veto power on any article should it be in conflict with "the goals and principles of the revolution" or "principles agreed on previous constitutions."[112] The declaration was an attempt by the military to get the upper hand in the drafting of the new constitution. The amendments meant that the SCAF could demand the Constituent Assembly revise any article and should the assembly refuse the article, the article would be referred to the SCC whose decision would be final one.[113] The declaration undermined the legislative power of the parliament and turned it into a consultative and advisory board. Hence, the tensions between the SCAF and the Muslim Brotherhood escalated as the Brotherhood officials called the constitutional declaration released by the SCAF null and unconstitutional. The military's power grab through a constitutional declaration indeed acted as a soft coup. Having casted itself the role of the guardian and the sole arbiter of the transition, the military set the stage for a future confrontation with the president.

In June, the second round of the presidential election resulted in a victory for the Muslim Brotherhood. Morsi was elected as the president with around 52 percent of the poll as against the 48 percent of the votes won by Shafiq. In his inaugural speech, Morsi promised to be a "president for all Egyptians" telling Egyptians that they were "the source of all authority" and declared that he would continue the revolution until all its objectives were met.[114] As Morsi took office, he progressed to form a new cabinet, which many Egyptians had hoped, would be a milestone in country's history. Contrary to the expectations, the makeup of the new cabinet included seven ministers that served in the outgoing cabinet and some under Mubarak and five ministers from the Muslim Brotherhood; namely, Information, Higher Education, Youth, Labor, and Housing. The cabinet was mostly made up of technocrat ministers indicating Morsi's effort to be conciliatory to the opposition. The new cabinet retained the Military Chief Field Marshal Hussein Tantawi, a key figure of the SCAF, as the defense minister while Hashem Qandil who served in the outgoing cabinet, was appointed as the prime minister by Morsi.

Morsi's cabinet was criticized for lacking diversity and failing to be inclusive as the cabinet included only two women, one of whom was also a Christian. Also, the cabinet didn't include any of the iconic figures of the youth movements. As for the liberal and leftist parties, they expressed their unwillingness to work with a government led by Morsi.[115] In the first cabinet formed following the election, key positions including finance and foreign affairs still remained in the hands of ministers who served in the interim government backed by the military. Evidently, the new cabinet seemed to be an outcome of compromise between the SCAF and Morsi. Faced with a series of mounting crises, Morsi made cautious moves to avoid antagonizing the military which still held most of the power following the elections.

Only a few days after Morsi assumed power, Egypt faced an attack in Sinai on the Israeli-Egyptian border by a Jihadist group leaving sixteen soldiers dead. In a highly unexpected move, following this attack, Morsi forced the retirement on several key SCAF members including the Minister of Defense Field Marshal Hussein Tantawi and the Army chief of staff, Sami Anan and the chiefs of the navy, the air force and the air defense branch of the armed forces, and he appointed a younger generation of officers in their place. As the forced retirements were associated with the failure in maintaining security on the Israeli border, they were deeply embarrassing to the generals and weakening them politically.[116] Morsi appointed Abdel Fattah Al-Sisi, the former chief of military intelligence, as the new defense minister of Egypt, who would later play a critical role in military's power grab.

At the outset of Morsi's presidency, several critical issues remained unresolved including the status of the dissolved parliament and the political power seized by the military. The administrative court, having ruled over the unconstitutionality of the newly elected parliament, also put the resolution of the Constituent Assembly into doubt as the assembly was chosen by the members of the parliament. As a response, the Brotherhood formulated its own strategy to protect its electoral gains and reclaim the political power allocated to the president previously. To this end, Morsi invalidated the June 17 Supplementary Constitutional Declaration by the SCAF and issued a new Constitutional Declaration consisting of four articles on August 12. The new constitutional declaration allocated full legislative and executive powers to the president and granted the president with the power to draw up a new assembly representing the full spectrum of Egyptian society who would draft a new constitution in case of the dissolution of the current one. The Muslim Brotherhood argued that this declaration would keep the constitutional drafting process on its track preventing any intervention from the SCAF and the SCC.

The alarming signs of Morsi's authoritarian imposition emerged on November 22 when he issued the constitutional decree that granted him broad powers and placed himself above law by making his decisions immune from judicial oversight until a new constitution was passed. The decree cleared the way for retrial of political and executive officials from the former regime including Hosni Mubarak for the killings of protestors and the use of violence. It also extended the Constituent Assembly's timeline for drafting the constitution by two months. However, the three articles in the decree raised doubts about Morsi's intentions. The Article 2, being the most controversial part in the decree, stipulated "All constitutional declarations, laws and decrees made since Morsi assumed power on 30 June 2012 cannot be appealed or canceled by any individual, or political or governmental body until a new constitution has been ratified and a new parliament has been elected. All pending lawsuits against them are void."[117] In a similar vein, according to Article 5, "No judicial authority can dissolve the Constituent Assembly or the Shura Council" and Article 6 asserted, "The president is authorized to take any measures he sees fit in order to preserve and safeguard the revolution, national unity or national security."[118]

Evidently, Morsi encountered numerous obstacles that had been thrown his way by the remnants of the former regime deeply engrained in the judiciary, military, and interest groups. This was reflected in their attempts to dismantle the first democratically elected parliament and block Morsi's appointments to significant positions. Morsi supporters defended the decree by arguing that it aimed to speed up a protracted democratic transition that had been hindered by legal obstacles and sweeping power grab by the president would be temporary until a new parliament was elected. Nonetheless, with this decree, Morsi concentrated too much power in his hands as the guardian of the revolution in a very fragile political setting plagued by polarization and mistrust between Islamists and all other groups. The liberal and secular opposition severely opposed the degree portraying it as imposition of new authoritarianism. The decree was reminiscent of some of the extra-constitutional practices that had characterized the former regime. Opposition groups in Egypt as well as outside observers portrayed the decree as a return to Mubarak style presidency under the Muslim Brotherhood.

In the days following Morsi's November Decree, a coalition of opposition parties and prominent political figures announced the establishment of the National Salvation Front (NSF) as an umbrella organization that united more than thirty-five political parties and social movements from a wide political spectrum in their rejection and resistance to power grab by Morsi. The Front demanded that the constitutional decree be rescinded, the referendum be postponed, and a new and more representative constituent assembly be formed. To these ends, the NSF instigated nationwide demonstrations and sit-ins that lasted for several days across Egypt. Moreover, the Egyptian Judges

Club severely condemned Morsi's constitutional declaration stating that it represented "an assault on the rule of law and judicial independence" and would push Egypt back to the "prehistoric era."[119] The Judges Club further threatened to close the courts across country in protest against Morsi's constitutional declaration and demanded the resignation of the Attorney General appointed by Morsi.

Amid protests and sit-ins, Egypt drifted into a state of chaos. The crisis escalated when hundreds of Morsi supporters besieged the SCC to prevent judges from convening to consider the constitutionality of the elections law. Egypt's political crisis was further deepened by a new wave of violence when thousands of Morsi supporters forcibly dispersed a sit-in around the presidential palace and tore down their tents resulting in death and injuries of several protestors.[120] The Brotherhood leaders failed to calm down rising tension in the country, instead, they exacerbated the ongoing crisis by denouncing protestors as thuggish minority striving for ousting of an elected president. Meanwhile, the military called for a national dialogue to resolve the constitutional crisis and annulment of the controversial decree by Morsi warning that failing to reach a consensus would drag the country into a dark tunnel, which the military would not allow.[121]

Under this intense pressure, Morsi rescinded the November Decree while keeping the referendum date unchanged. At this critical juncture, Morsi's decided to hold the referendum instead of postponing it as the opposition demanded. Since the first presidential and parliamentary elections, much of Egypt's political tensions revolved around the formation of the constituent assembly and the constitutional drafting process. The tensions that surrounded Egypt's constitutional crisis merit particular attention since it was the process of constitutional drafting in which most ideological clashes came to the fore and deeply politicized the transition.

The Constitutional Drafting under the Muslim Brotherhood

Following the elections, the most pressing issue was the formation of the Constituent Assembly. On March 25, 2012, the two houses of the parliament, the People's Assembly and the Shura Council met jointly to establish the Constituent Assembly, 100-member committee in charge of drafting Egypt's new constitution. In this process, the main issue revolved around the Article 60 of the March 30 Constitutional Declaration which remained unclear as to whether the members would be elected from the parliament and Shura council or from the electorate. While leftist and liberal groups argued that electing members from the parliament and the Shura council would promote favoritism and bring about a politicized organ, Islamists asserted that members of the parliament and the Shura council held the legitimacy in drafting the constitution as elected representatives of people. Eventually, both camps agreed on a formula that 50 percent of the assembly would be from within the parliament and Shura council and the rest would be from outside the parliament.[122] The makeup of the first constitutional assembly with around 70 percent of the members from the FJP and Al-Nour Party members was criticized by liberal and leftist members who resigned *en masse* to protests Islamists' dominance. This led to a vacancy in a third of the seats in the assembly. On April 10, the Constituent Assembly was dissolved by a court ruling on the ground that it was unrepresentative involving very few women and members from minority groups.

Once the first constituent assembly was dismantled, the SCAF and political parties embarked on negotiations on member selection process for the next constituent assembly. On April 28, the SCAF and political parties agreed on six criteria for forming the assembly. These included proportional representation for each societal group, the approval of each article by a two-thirds majority (if such a majority can't be reached then a 57 members out of 100 would be sufficient), the appointment of representatives by relevant parties, efforts to finish the drafting of the new constitution before presidential election was completed, a joint meeting to elect members of the constituent assembly and formation of a supervising committee to include representatives of each party.[123] Despite the agreement on the technical details, formation of the constituent assembly was at a stalemate. The political deadlock lied in the Constitutional Declaration of March 30 issued by the SCAF which left many critical issues regarding the composition of the constituent assembly unresolved. The declaration didn't specify whether the constituent assembly was meant to reflect the political composition of the parliament or the makeup of the Egyptian society and whether the members would be chosen from within the parliament or outside.

After months of gridlock, on June 5, the SCAF declared that it would take matters into its hands and amend Article 60 of the interim constitution and unilaterally intervene to form a new constitutional declaration of its own unless political parties came to an agreement in two days.[124] Despite the reluctance to obey the rules set by the SCAF in April, under this intense pressure, Islamists were forced to negotiate with other parties in a meeting on June 6 to determine the formulation of the new Constituent Assembly. Eventually, the FJP was forced to agree with liberal and leftist political parties on a 50–50 ratio dividing the seats equally between the two groups in the constituent assembly.

Based on the agreement, the number of assembly seats reserved for members of the parliament was reduced to thirty-nine from fifty, a concession made by the Muslim Brotherhood to those struggling to curb the influence of the Islamist-dominated parliament over the constituent assembly.

As for the remaining seats, the assembly would be composed of fifteen judges, five representatives from Al-Azhar, four from the Coptic Church, ten revolutionary youth representatives, seven members from workers and farmers unions, seven members from professional syndicates, fourteen representatives from the unions and syndicates, ten public figures, and one member from the military and the police and the Ministry of Justice each.[125] In the meeting, it was also agreed that any article drafted by the assembly would require the approval of the 67 percent majority and unless this majority was reached, a fifty-seven member approval would suffice.[126] While the compromise initially seemed satisfactory to all parties, controversy emerged over whether the 50–50 ratio would be applied to the seats allocated to the nonparty affiliated members. Both the interim constitution and the agreement among political forces remained vague over the composition of the members outside the parliament given that representatives of unions or public figures might also be Muslim Brotherhood or the Salafist party affiliated.

Amid the controversy, on June 12, a hundred members of the constituent assembly were elected in a joint meeting between the People's Assembly and the Shura Council. In the new constituent assembly, thirty-five elected MPs belonged to Muslim Brotherhood and Salafi Al-Nour Party while an additional twenty-five members identified as Islamists were elected within the other 50 percent of the seats allocated for independents.[127] Thus, around 60 percent of the constituent assembly was composed of Islamist members. Both the composition of the assembly and old ideological divisions and distrust between the two camps culminated in a highly polarized political atmosphere in the assembly. Of the 688 parliamentarians voting fifty-seven members of the parliament withdrew from the session including representatives of several leftist and liberal parties as well as independent candidates. Thereafter, the High Constitutional Court withdrew from the assembly arguing that there were many conflicts among political forces in the assembly and it didn't want to be forced to take sides.[128] The non-Islamist members of the assembly frequently asserted that the assembly was not representative of the Egyptian society in its entirety and accused Islamists of their efforts to monopolize the constitution drafting process.

Eventually, the constituent assembly gathered the sufficient members and on June 18 held its first session. The constitutional drafting process took place in five different committees; state and society, rights and freedoms, public authorities, independent authorities, and a fifth one consisting of legal experts in charge of editing draft articles. All drafts were to be discussed within the committees first, submitted to the fifth committee later for editing, and finally put together to be presented to all members in the assembly for preliminary discussion within the plenary session.[129] After the articles were discussed and amendments were made, a final draft was brought to final voting in a long plenary session of the assembly.

Throughout the constitution writing process, non-Islamist members criticized the assembly's Islamist majority on the grounds that there was lack of transparency in the process of constitutional drafting, and the process was rushed up. It was the manner in which constitution was adopted rather than its content that became the focal point of protests within the assembly and on the streets. Islamist members were accused of showing no real willingness to reach a consensus on major disagreements and of placing specific emphasis on religion in state affairs. According to leftists and liberal members, the initial draft didn't fulfill the demands for social justice and the goals of the revolution. For instance, labor rights were not included in the draft while the draft allowed legislators to shut down newspapers with administrative decrees.[130] The draft also failed to end military trials of civilians, which was a key issue following the wide-scale detentions and arrests both under Mubarak and the SCAF's rule. They demanded an extension of another three months for the drafting to engage in more discussion and debate.

At the time, the SCC announced that it would rule on the lawsuits regarding the constitutionality of the constituent assembly. Although November 22 Decree extended the timeline of constitutional drafting another two months, the FJP and other Islamist members decided to rush the final draft through voting. In response, seventeen members of the assembly including the representatives of the Coptic Church and liberal and secular parties, withdrew from the assembly to protest over Islamist members' avoiding to engage in serious debates, ignoring their suggestions and hastening the process.[131] This wave of withdrawals was followed by another wave when Morsi issued November 22 Decree stating that his decisions were to be final and unchallengeable until a new constitution was ratified. The decree led to the withdrawal of Wafd Party leaders and Ghad Al-Thawra representatives, leaving four parties represented in the assembly; the Freedom and Justice Party, the Nour Party, the Al-Wasat Party, and the Civilization Party, the only secular party.

The rushed nature of the writing of the constitution hardly left any time for a nationwide debate and discussion among legal experts. Despite the boycott of the leftist and liberal members of the assembly, voting took place without a total of a hundred members in the final session. The ratio of the voting needed for the approval of the draft constitution also played a role in Islamists' ignorance of the boycotts. Given that 57 percent of the votes would be sufficient in the second round to approve the draft constitution in the assembly, Islamist groups ensured the approval of the draft at any case with their 60 percent majority. The constitution was approved in the assembly on November 29, in less than two months after the first draft had been submitted. Then, it was quickly approved by the Shura Council and ratified by the president announcing that the referendum would take place in two rounds. Despite the approval of the constitution with 63.8 percent of the votes, the turnout was only 32.9 percent of total electorate which means that the constitution was approved by a mere 21 percent eligible voters.[132]

The 2012 constitution brought a number of improvements in the system of government and protection of certain rights, yet it also failed to fulfill much of the revolution's demands. The Constituent Assembly opted to use the 1971 constitution as the basis for the new constitution, thus, the new constitution failed to mark a clear departure from the autocratic past. An important factor in using the former constitution as a starting point, rather than starting from scratch was the challenge faced by the assembly in meeting the timeframe imposed by the SCAF. The six-month timeframe was not sufficient in the Egyptian context to draft a modern constitution that would be both conciliatory and responsive to the past's failures. In the end, the constituent assembly made more effort to meet the deadline than struggling for solutions to Egypt's chronic problems.

In terms of the system of government, the 2012 constitution put an end to all-powerful presidency by limiting presidential terms and granted the parliament with a significant authority in the formation and dismissal of government. The parliament was also protected from arbitrary dissolution and the president's authority to declare state of emergency was restricted, which was one of the much-touted objectives of the constituent assembly from its inception. The new constitution also imposed restriction on the presidential power that could be exercised during state of emergency. On the other hand, the president still had more power and was above checks and balances in many respects. The new constitution authorized the president to appoint 10 percent of the upper chamber of parliament giving the president much leverage over legislative process.

Another unjust distribution of power was the president's responsibility for appointing the heads of every independent agency in the country including those charged with supervising the president (Article 202), which would inevitably limit independence of these institutions while creating challenges for transparency resulting from increased nepotism. The president was also granted with the power to appoint and dismiss civil and military personnel (Article 147), appoint the judges of the SCC including its Chief Justice (Article 176) and veto laws legislated by the parliament (Article 104). Hence, the president would emerge as a dominant political power and some observers pointed to the risk of perpetuated authoritarianism under a new form.

Like Tunisia, one of the most controversial issues over the new Egyptian constitution was the role of religion in state affairs. During the constitutional drafting process, the opposition camp frequently accused the Islamist majority of their intention to create a religious state instead of a civil one. However, a close reading of the constitution gives the notion that while putting more emphasis on religion than former constitutions, it could not establish an Islamic state per se. Out of 236 articles, only seven contain an explicit reference to religion and a mere three refer to Islam.[133] According to the Article 2, which remained the same as in the 1971 constitution, Islam is the religion of the state and "the principles of Islamic *Sharia* are the principal source of legislation."[134] The article was not changed by the Islamist members of the assembly to assure that Egypt was not headed toward becoming an Islamic state. However, this clause remained vague as to the meaning of the term "principles of Islamic *Sharia*," and the authority which would interpret those principles.

According to Article 219, the principles of Islamic *Sharia* included "general evidence, foundational rules, rules of jurisprudence, and credible sources accepted in Sunni doctrines."[135] In addition, Article 4 stated that Al Azhar, Egypt's oldest university and the most prominent institution in Sunni Islam, "is to be consulted in matters relating to Islamic *Sharia*."[136] While the new constitution manifested that the new Egyptian legislation would be heavily inspired by Islamic *Sharia*, it became clear that Al-Azhar would assume a critical role in observing the application of law. Article 4 didn't specify the weight that would be attributed to court's consultation to Al-Azhar while stating that the opinions of Al-Azhar would not be legally binding. Contrary to the allegations of the opposition camp, Egypt wasn't directed toward becoming an Islamic state. The new constitution made limited reference to religion notwithstanding the dominance of Islamist members in the constituent assembly. Clerics were bestowed with counseling role rather than any hard political power and sovereignty was granted to citizens rather than God. Therefore, the constitution could not be said to lead to theocratic state, yet evidently religion would play a significant role in inspiring legislation and many state affairs.

In the 2012 Egyptian constitution, dozens of articles appealed to individual rights and liberties while individuals were portrayed as the objects of the state that needed to be cared and protected. The conservative, patriarchal, and statist worldview of the assembly was reflected in several articles. For instance, according to Article 10, the state and society shall commit to the genuine character of the Egyptian family, its cohesion, stability, and the consolidation and protection of its moral values. Similarly, Article 11 stated that the state would safeguard ethics, public morality and public order. The constitutional draft promised to reinforce a social contract, reminiscent of the Nasserist period and subsequent governments.[137]

Much of the controversy on individual rights focused mainly on freedom of expression and the status of women. Despite the objections of the liberal members of the constituent assembly, a provision that pointed to women's obligations toward family appeared in Article 10 while attributing no such role on men. In addition, the constitution's conservative and patriarchal worldview was openly reflected in its introduction part where women were depicted as "sisters of men."[138] The 2012 constitution didn't introduce any specific provision to forbid discrimination on the basis of gender and provide safeguards for gender equality, which disappointed civil society organizations. The constitution calling for freedom from discrimination in general terms also didn't specify any measure for the protection of religious minorities.

In a similar vein, freedom of expression under the new constitution was another point of contention among Islamist and non-Islamist members of the assembly. Article 45 guaranteed freedom of thought, opinion, and expression; however, blasphemy was forbidden by Article 44 which stated, "defaming all religious messenger and prophets is prohibited."[139] This article could lead to several restrictions on speech such as preventing theological debates between religious denominations.[140] Finally, freedom of religion was guaranteed by the state according to Article 43, yet the article limited the right to practice religion and establish places of worship for heavenly religions; namely, Islam, Christianity, and Judaism while excluding non-Abrahamic religions such as Egyptian Bahais, Ahmadis, and Shia. Hence, freedom of religion was biased in favor of the three religions resulting in discrimination toward some of Egypt's religious minorities.

The darkest side of the constitution lied in the provisions on civil–military relations. The articles regarding military and defense remained largely unchanged including the stipulation that the military's budget would be free from parliamentary oversight and it would be entered as a single line in the national budget. Likewise, the establishment of a national defense council consisting of eight military members and seven civilians, and the powers granted to the council aimed at maintaining military's autonomy. The national defense council would be responsible for discussing the armed forces budget and the council must be consulted in relation to draft laws on the armed forces (Article 197). In addition, the defense minister, according to the new constitution, must be a military officer who would be approved by the SCAF (Article 170). Another pitfall regarding the 2012 constitution was that it didn't end military trial of civilians. In the previous drafts, the relevant article stated "no civilian shall be tried before the military justice system," yet the provision was deleted when military justice officials formally objected.[141] The new constitution stated "civilians can't stand trial before military courts except for crimes that harm the armed forces" and the article went on to state "members of the military judiciary are autonomous and cannot be dismissed" (Article 198).[142] The article was open to manipulation as the broad statement "crimes that harm the armed forces" might be interpreted in different ways.

Hence, 2012 constitution didn't lay the groundwork for bringing military under civilian oversight, instead, its powers and immunity were preserved.

Overall, the 2012 constitution had several shortcomings. The language used in drafting was mostly vague and open to interpretation. The text left much of the revolution's goals unfulfilled and didn't point to a complete rupture from the autocratic past as the president was still granted with a great authority and the new constitution created imbalanced civil–military relations favoring the latter. Above all, the drafting process of the constitution was tainted from its inception given the withdrawals of most of the liberal and leftist members and the time limitation. In that regard, Egypt's new constitution didn't bring about a social contract based on a broad consensus.

The June 30 Uprisings and the Military Coup

Throughout constitutional drafting and its aftermath, Morsi emphasized stability which he thought, would be achieved through the ratification of Egypt's constitution. The biggest threat in the way of the new constitution, according to Morsi, was the judiciary made up of Mubarak-era appointees who would dissolve the constituent assembly tasked with the drafting of the constitution. It was under this assumption that Morsi, as the Muslim Brotherhood put it, passed the November Decree and took much of the political power into his hands temporarily to hasten the constitutional drafting and its ratification. Egypt's hastily drafted and approved constitution further exacerbated tensions that had already plunged the country into a political chaos. Egypt following the constitutional referendum was marked by political uncertainty, mounting ideological polarization, a weak economy and violent street protests. The majority of Egyptians were not satisfied with the trajectory of the transition in their country and the public opinion was turning increasingly negative.

Various public opinion polls manifested Egyptians' dissatisfaction with the ongoing political and economic situation in their country. The approval rating of presidential performance after his one year in office sharply declined according to opinion polls. The results of a poll conducted by the Egyptian Center for Public Opinion (Baseera) indicated that the percentage of respondents who approved the president's performance declined from 78 percent at the end of his 100 days in power to 42 percent after eleven months in office and further to 32 percent at the end of one year.[143] The poll also displayed that if elections were to be held the next day, only 25 percent intended to reelect him while 62 percent didn't intend to reelect him and the remaining 13 percent stated that reelecting Morsi depended on the other candidates.[144] In a similar vein, a poll conducted by the Pew Research Center evinced only 30 percent of Egyptians thought the country was headed in the right direction in May 2013, a figure down from 53 percent in 2012, and 65 percent in 2011 following the uprisings.[145] Roughly three-quarters of Egyptians stated that the economy was in decline and optimism about the country's economic situation went down significantly. In addition, 49 percent of the respondents viewed the nation's new constitution as a source of division for Egyptians.[146]

Similarly, the findings of the Zogby Research Services based on a poll conducted between April 4 and May 12 revealed that the two main Islamic parties—the FJP and the Nour Party—had the confidence of just under 30 percent of Egyptian adults and the major opposition groups had a support base of almost 35 percent of the adult population while the remaining 40 percent had no confidence in either the government or any of the political parties.[147] The research further indicated overall only about one-quarter of Egyptian respondents were satisfied with the performance of the Morsi government with respect to guaranteeing rights and freedoms, creating economic opportunity, maintaining safety and order and providing social services.[148]

There were a series of political mistakes by Morsi that led to a fall in his approval ratings in the polls. Indeed, the January 25 uprisings were rallied against torture, human rights violations, lack of freedom, corruption, poverty, and unemployment. Nonetheless, each of these political deficiencies maintained and even intensified since the accession of Morsi to power. For instance, one of the most important slogans of the January 25 uprisings was *hurriya* (freedom), and the protests were declared against Mubarak's mounting authoritarianism. The November Decree which led him to assume sweeping powers was regarded as regeneration of a new form of authoritarianism by the opposition parties In addition, individual freedoms including freedom of expression, media, and assembly were restricted through legal arrangements by the Brotherhood. The constitution recognized military trials of civilians while it was not openly recognized even in 1971 constitution despite its application in various cases.

In May 2013, the FJP proposed a bill on civil society organizations that would impose harsh restrictions on them and subject civic entities to executive oversight through a coordinating committee including representatives from the security apparatus and endowed with powers to interfere in all matters related to foreign funding of local civil society groups and the licensing and operations of foreign NGOs working in Egypt.[149] Thereafter, forty Egyptian NGOs, severely criticizing the draft law, issued a joint statement entitled "The Muslim Brotherhood lays the foundations for a new police state by exceeding Mubarak-era mechanisms to suppress civil society."[150] In the same vein, press freedom faced a serious crackdown under Morsi. Nearly, seventy articles in eight different laws that restricted freedom of press and expression in the former constitution were left intact by the Morsi government. Various aspects of public discourse were limited under a legal framework including prohibitions against blasphemy, anti-state propaganda, insults to public officials, and the state, incitement to disobedience in the army and disruption of national peace. The number of journalists arrested went up dramatically and a great many of journalists were wounded while reporting on the street protests. An analysis by the Committee to Protect Journalists found that Brotherhood supporters unleashed a wave of criminal complaints against media critics on vague allegations of "spreading wrong information," "disrupting peace," insulting the president," and "insulting religion," and six hundred criminal defamation cases were reported in the first nine months of Morsi's presidency, a figure that far outpaced the rate of such cases during Mubarak's rule.[151]

Torture and abuses of individual rights were at the core of the political grievances that poured people to the streets during January 25 uprisings. Thus, one of the goals of the revolution was to put an end to torture and ensure fair trial of individuals under detention. Despite the concrete proposals made by Egyptian lawyers and human rights activists on how to reform security establishment including new laws that delineated role for the police force, shifting hierarchies at security bureaus and the appointing of civilian regulators and lawyers at police stations, Morsi lacked political will to implement such reforms in the security apparatus. Instead, the Ministry of Interior pursued the same policies toward protests and extorted disproportionate use of force under Morsi as it did under Mubarak. A report by El Nadeem Center for Rehabilitation of Victims of Violence documented 359 cases of torture and 217 cases of torture-related deaths during the eleven months of Morsi's tenure while the report didn't include those victims who didn't report or weren't identified because of threat or fear.[152] Likewise, a joint press release by twenty rights organizations in Egypt harshly accused Morsi regime of mounting authoritarianism and of brutal suppression of social and political protest movements. The release stated[153]:

> One year after Morsi became president, it is now clear that the priority of the presidency—and, of course, the Muslim Brotherhood—was to firmly establish the underpinnings for a new authoritarian regime in place of the Mubarak regime. It is no surprise, therefore, that the past year witnessed widespread human rights crimes, on a scale that rivaled than under the Mubarak regime. The brutal suppression of political and social protest movements did not cease; indeed, the security forces are no longer the only party to use of excessive force against demonstrators, as MB supporters have also been given free rein to use violence to punish and intimidate their opponents, including through torture and even killings, whether at the gates of the presidential palace, in front of the main MB headquarters in Muqattam, or in squares in other governorates.

Another source of public discontent was economic stagnation that didn't indicate any sign of progress. On the eve of the uprisings, economy was the top priority for Egyptians with 82 percent emphasizing improved economic conditions as their most-immediate concern for Egypt's future. A poll conducted by the Pew Research Center in March 2013 illustrated that 56 percent of respondents believed their standard of living was deteriorating in contrast to 12 percent of respondents who reported improvement while 30 percent reported that there was no change in their standard of living.[154] Indeed, immediately after coming into power, Morsi issued a 15 percent raise to all public sector employees and increased the minimum social security pension by 50 percent to the benefit of more than a million and a half citizens. On the other hand, Egyptian annual GDP growth was only 2.2 percent in the first quarter of 2013, which was far below 7 percent for several years before the uprisings. The fall in the tourism revenues and foreign investment caused by protests and political instability accounted for much of the GDP fall, hence, the government projected a deficit of 135 billion pounds for the year under Morsi's tenure and by the end of May 2013, the total deficit had already reached 202.9 billion pounds.[155] The deficit was exacerbated by the rise in civil servant labor costs and the system of food and fuel subsidies, by which Morsi aimed to minimize public discontent and appease the street. Structural reforms including cutting off the subsidies and reducing public spending were needed to tackle with the budget deficit, yet Morsi avoided to implement such reforms as it would prove politically risky.

While it could not be denied that the Brotherhood made a series of tactical mistakes in the transition, it was often overlooked that Morsi faced a formidable opposition from the "deep state" engrained in the bureaucracy, military, judiciary and the security services. The Muslim Brotherhood held *fulool*, the remnants of the Mubarak regime, responsible for the street protests and undermining government's effort to implement reforms. To the Brotherhood, it was the fervent resistance from the judiciary, bureaucracy, and media that obstructed Morsi from changing the country in the targeted direction. From the onset of the political transition, the SCC was used by the SCAF to restrict and control Morsi's efforts to restructure the state or expand his power. The SCC acted in a politicized and obstructionist manner in various junctures as it was the case with its controversial decision to dissolve the country's democratically elected parliament. Brotherhood members argued that it was the "deep state" that allowed law and order to lapse, religious violence against Coptic Christians to go uninvestigated and notorious thugs called *beltagaya* to be sent out to cause chaos on the streets.[156]

Evidently, Morsi government didn't have full control over the intelligence services, the military, police, judiciary, banking institutions, the diplomatic corps which were staffed under Mubarak. As David Kirkpatrick noted,

"Morsi was sort of perched on top of the machinery, of the old regime, the bureaucracies of the old regime and security forces of the old regime- and he was gradually trying to change that . . . But there was always an element of at least foot dragging in every part of bureaucracy and open revolt among the security forces."[157] For instance, during the last few weeks of Morsi's tenure, public discontent was aggravated with the shortages in fuel resulting in long queues in petrol stations and daily electricity cuts. The sudden end to the crippling energy shortages immediately after Morsi's downfall seemed to support the conspiracy that the artificial interruption of energy sources was intended to undermine overall quality of life by the bureaucracies of the old regime.[158] The real powerbrokers were the elements of the old state looking forward to a set of conditions and popular support for a counterrevolution and the Brotherhood's critical decisions at various junctures and failure to address to revolutionary demands played into their hands for such a move. In the end, the public discontent and widespread opposition was used by the military to stage a coup and legitimize its actions. Ashraf El-Sherif noted[159]:

> With the military, police and judiciary on its side, the old state could knock the Brothers out. However, such a step needed popular support and backing from key non-state actors, such as the business class, private media, political elites, prestigious national religious institutions (al-Azhar and the Coptic Church) and revolutionary movements. Ultimately, the old state was able to secure this support thanks to the Brother's policy of alienating all other actors.

In response to Morsi government's failure to fulfill revolution's goals, declining living standards and deteriorating public quality services, in May 2013 a grassroots opposition movement in the name of "Tamarod" (rebellion) was founded by a number of youth activists calling for early presidential elections. The movement quickly garnered support from the elements of the deep state -judiciary, military, police, and bureaucracy—along with the mainstream opposition groups such as the NSF, the April 6 movement, and the Kefaya movement, much of the Mubarak-era public media and some Muslim and Coptic religious leaders. By the end of June 2013, Tamarod movement announced that they had collected over 22 million signatures in their petition to withdraw confidence from President Morsi and hold early presidential elections.[160] The movement accused Morsi and the FJP of their attempt to "Brotherhoodize" the state institutions, appointing seven governors from the Brotherhood and one from the Gamaa Islamiyya, the extremist group known for a notorious massacre at Luxor in 1997. Their accusations also included the issuing of a constitutional decree that sacked the prosecutor general and immunized presidential decisions from judicial review, failing to fulfill election pledges to reform the security sector, and failing to build consensus.[161]

The campaign further blamed Morsi for the sale of Suez Canal to Qatar, deterioration of economic conditions, and lack of security. In hindsight, it became clear that the movement was heavily financed by the business elite who prospered under Mubarak, the United Arab Emirates (UAE), and Saudi Arabia.[162]

Tamarod movement proposed a six-month transitional roadmap calling for transfer of power to an independent prime minister to head a technocratic government and assigning the duties of the president to the head of the constitutional court until the holding of presidential elections. On June 30, the first anniversary of Morsi's election, wide-scale uprisings took place in many cities across Egypt demanding the ouster of their first democratically elected president. On July 1, violent clashes broke out in several cities around the country leaving at least eight people dead and injuring hundreds. Protestors ransacked Brotherhood offices around the country and set the empty Brotherhood headquarters on fire, yet the police and security forces did nothing to counter the assault and the arson.[163] Tamarod called Morsi to resign by 17:00 on the next day or face a civil disobedience campaign and it also rejected the president's offer of national dialogue.[164] Thereafter, the Egyptian Armed Forces issued an ultimatum that gave forty-eight hours to all political parties to meet the demands of Egyptian people, or else the military would intervene and impose a roadmap.[165] On the following day, Morsi addressed Egyptians announcing his rejection of the ultimatum and called on people to guard democracy and the legitimate government that came to power through democratic elections. The Muslim Brotherhood and some of its allies established the National Coalition for Supporting Legitimacy, an umbrella group of forty Islamist parties and groups to call on opposition leaders to condemn the ongoing political violence and break ties with corrupt figures of the Mubarak regime.[166] The coalition released a statement asserting that Egyptian people wouldn't accept anything less than democratic legitimacy nor the reproduction of the corrupt Mubarak regime.

On July 3, military officers ousted the country's first democratically elected president. The defense minister and military chief Abdel-Fattah Al-Sisi unveiled Egypt's political roadmap which included the suspension of the constitution, the formation of a new technocratic government, and the appointment of Adly Mansour, the Chief Justice of the SCC as the interim president.[167] The proposed roadmap was advocated by the old state, the NSF, April 6 Youth Movement, Al-Azhar, the Coptic Church, and the Salafi Nour Party. On the other hand, the generals surrounding themselves with religious leaders and the spokesman of opposition movements on the media gave the image that the overthrow of Morsi had a broad consensus by civilian and religious leaders.[168] In a similar vein, protests were depicted as an analog to the uprisings that ousted Mubarak in 2011 on the media, thereby pointing to a second revolution by the Egyptian people. In hindsight, it became clear that the military coup marked the launch of a "counterrevolution" by the military junta, the elements of the deep state in security apparatus, judiciary and the bureaucracy who made use of Egyptians' dissatisfaction with Morsi regime on several grounds. In July 2013, the Egyptian military ensured that no civilian government would rule Egypt in the near future and dimmed prospects for democratization in Egypt over the long haul.

EGYPT UNDER SISI: REASSERTION OF AUTHORITARIANISM

Egypt under Sisi is a continuation of electoral authoritarianism that was an important tool for regime survival for many decades under Sadat and Mubarak who manipulated multiparty elections to maintain status quo. Electoral authoritarianism served the interests of the military junta aiming to depict Egypt as *en route* to democracy. Having seized power on July 3, Sisi portrayed himself as "the savior of democracy." In a similar vein, the political roadmap declared by Sisi aimed to create a democratic facade that was reminiscent of the liberal autocracy under Mubarak. Therefore, the holding of the elections and the drafting of a new constitution were high on Sisi's agenda. Creating a democratic facade was apparently important for the military junta to maintain military's legitimacy as "the defender of the nation" for another generation. Furthermore, the military junta had to satisfy the youth groups and revolutionary movements who were at the forefront of the June 30 uprisings and gave a green light to the military to intervene. The proposed roadmap also enabled Sisi to consolidate his "democracy rhetoric" and appease Egypt's Western allies.

The political roadmap issued after Morsi's ouster required the drafting of a new constitution and the holding of a referendum in the first place.[169] The constitution drafted in 2013 and adopted by popular referendum in early 2014 was based on the Egyptian constitution of 1971. The manner in which the new constitution was drafted could in no way be defined as consensual or inclusive. Contrary to the original promise, only parts of the political spectrum were involved in the amendment process, whereas Salafists only received one seat in the fifty-member committee despite having a broad public base. The committee was composed of the representatives of state institutions and youth movements, while liberal groups didn't have representation.[170] Egypt's 2013 constitution expanded the powers of the country's three key institutions—the military, the judiciary, and the police—which had served as the cornerstones of the deep state for several decades.

The core of the constitution ensured a strong president and a powerful army with an economic and political role. The new constitution consolidated the presidential system to the extent that the president would have the right to appoint 5 percent of the members of the legislative body and the key posts of ministries of interior, defense, foreign affairs, and justice. The president was also granted with the right to call for a referendum to dissolve the parliament. Some articles calling for checks on the presidential powers were inserted in the new constitution, to a great extent, due to the youth activists' advocacy. Article 159, for instance, opens the way to impeachment of the president on the charges of violating the provisions of the constitution, treason and any other felony which must be based on a motion signed by at least the two-thirds majority of the parliament and an investigation carried out by the prosecutor general.[171] Likewise, Article 161 enables the parliament to withdraw confidence from the president and holding of early presidential elections based on reasoned motion to be signed and approved by the two-thirds majority of the members of parliament.[172]

The 2013 constitution obliged all decrees issued by the president to be approved by the parliament within fifteen days of their first session. Ostensibly, the articles seemed to give greater role to the parliament, yet in hindsight, it became clear that the fragmented and weak parliament served only to legitimize the policies of the military-backed government. Given that the parliament approved almost all of the 342 presidential decree laws issued by then Interim President Mansour and the President Al-Sisi without revision manifested how submissive the legislative branch is to the executive power.[173] Similar to the 2012 constitution, the military retained its political power and its economic privileges and guaranteed its right to try civilians in military courts for the undefined concept of "national security."[174] Moreover, with the new constitution, the military retains more decisive power over the issues of national security, military budget, and military justice. Particularly, Article 234 which stipulates that the minister of defense should be appointed with the SCAF's approval is an indicator of the military's efforts to ensure its institutional autonomy within the emerging political order.[175] In 2013 constitution, the responsibility to appoint the prosecutor general shifted to the Supreme Judicial Council instead of the president.

The 2013 constitution differs from the former constitution mainly in its removal of the Islamist-leaning provisions inserted under Morsi and its expansion of rights and freedoms to women and religious minorities. Both 2012 and 2013 constitutions stated, "the principles of *sharia* are the principal source of legislation"; however, the 2013 version eliminated an article that sought to define the "principles of *sharia*" which the secularists severely objected fearing that it could be used to impose a specific understanding of Islam. In addition, the 2013 constitution removed the provision which granted Al-Azhar a legislative role requiring lawmakers to consult in matters pertaining to the Islamic law. Similarly, the controversial provision on blasphemy which criminalized insulting any prophet was eliminated in the 2013 constitution. Indeed, the provision was indeed severely criticized for being contradictory to the freedom of speech by liberals in 2012. The new constitution also explicitly forbids the foundation of political parties on the basis of religion. The 2013 charter explicitly states that women are equal to men and "the state is committed to the protection of women against all forms of violence and to empower women to balance their family and work duties."[176] As to religious minorities, the new constitution paves the way for building and renovating churches and guarantees Copts the freedom to practice their religion. Overall, despite some improvements in individual freedoms, the new constitution didn't indicate a fundamental change compared to the previous constitutions.

Almost a year after Morsi was ousted, presidential elections were held on May 26, 2014. The new constitution made it more difficult to run for presidential election for potential candidates. It mandated the support from at least twenty-five thousand voters instead of twenty thousand and in at least fifteen governorates instead of ten to be accepted as a candidate for presidency.[177] These tough requirements combined with shrinking space for political dissent left only one opposition candidate, Hamdeen Sabahi who ran against Sisi in the presidential election in stark contrast to the 2012 elections for which nine candidates vigorously competed. Just like under Mubarak, the emergence of Sabahi created a democratic facade while for many Egyptians Sabahi was destined to lose.

Sisi won the presidential election with 96 percent of the votes. The voter turnout was reported to be around 47. 5 percent by the electoral commission while the figure's accuracy was a matter of debate according to some outside observers.[178] Despite the military coup and violent crackdown on political dissent and the member of the Brotherhood, President Sisi remained popular among millions of Egyptians. The most likely reason for Sisi's popularity was that Egyptians were in need of an individual leader who would manage to control all state agencies and bring much-needed stability to the country. Given the political turmoil and state of chaos since the fall of Mubarak, the initial euphoria surrounding thousands of Egyptians in the hope of freedom, justice, and economic welfare had vanished, and it gave way to expectations for stability and social order, which to millions of Egyptians, could be restored by a powerful man from the military.

Parliamentary elections marked the end of Egypt's transition roadmap adopted by the interim government following the coup. Adly Mansour, before handing authority over to Sisi, issued a new parliamentary election law for the upcoming parliamentary elections. The new electoral law tilted the balance toward the president and undermined prospects for a strong parliament while abolishing the upper house of the parliament (Shura Council) and expanding the number of seats in the People's Assembly.[179] The most controversial provision was the imbalance in the distribution of seats for individual candidates and party representation. Under the new legislation, out of 567 seats, a significant majority—420 of them—would be elected by an individual candidate system while 120 would be elected via a party list system and the remaining twenty-seven would be appointed by the president.[180] The new law discarded the proportional representation which was also used in 2012 elections and it stipulated that only the list that won an absolute majority in each district would receive seats in the parliament. Independent candidates were allowed to form their own lists and compete within the quota allocated for party list system.

Candidates elected to independent lists would enable cooptation by the regime and facilitate the return of the rent-seeking old elite and the powerful figures who served under Mubarak while undermining party politics. Political parties were further weakened by diversity quotas imposed exclusively on the party lists; out of 120 seats, 56 were women, 24 Copts and 16 workers and farmers, 16 youth, 8 Egyptians abroad, and 8 Egyptians with disabilities.[181] Smaller political parties that could not fulfill the diversity quota requirement due to having insufficient numbers of members in all categories weren't able to run for parliamentary elections. Hence, most of Egypt's political parties opposed the electoral law campaigning for greater weight to be attributed to party representation. Opposition movements and leftist parties called for boycotting the election.

The new election system had been designed in such a restrictive way for party representation that it virtually eliminated ideological competition and policy debate. It only facilitated a throwback to Mubarak-era politics bringing Sisi loyalists to a legislative body to rubber-stamp the president's decisions. Many candidates were the former members of the ruling party under Mubarak, the military officers who served under Sisi and powerful local figures without known ideologies or platform. An alliance of socialist parties and some liberal parties representing the main opposition choice withdrew from the parliamentary elections in an attempt to boycott the new election system.[182] Thus, the election results came as no surprise and served the ultimate goal of Sisi's government to reinforce authoritarianism while creating a democratic facade. No political party was able to guarantee enough seats to create a majority in the 2015 elections. The Free Egyptians obtained sixty-five seats, the Nation's Future Party won fifty-three seats, and the New Wafd Party secured thirty-six seats in the new parliament. All political parties when combined obtained around 40 percent of the total seats. Besides, former army and police officers gained an unprecedented ground in the parliament with seventy-five seats.

The 2015 elections recalled the parliamentary elections under Mubarak in many ways. In the elections under Mubarak, the dominance of individual candidacy resulted in the weakening and marginalization of political parties and money, family, and tribal loyalties were key elements of a successful candidacy. Likewise, the parliamentary elections under Sisi led to a weak party politics and prioritized wealthy, powerful elite over party competition with a political agenda. As was the case with the elections held under Mubarak, the voter turnout was low with 28.3 percent of the voting population according to the High Election Committee, and it was speculated to be around 10 percent by some outside observers.[183] This low voter turnout came out despite the fact that the government encouraged voter participation by declaring half day holiday for state workers on the Election Day and threatening a fine for not voting. In addition, the 2015 elections were marked by vote buying as notified by local and international election monitors.[184]

EGYPT'S FAILED REVOLUTION: REVERSION TO THE ANCIEN REGIME

What has been taking place in Egypt from July 2013 onward signified the restoration of the *ancien regime,* or *counterrevolution*. In Egypt, for many decades, the military was a political and economic force that had effectively steered the country's politics behind the curtains; however, following the coup, the generals are now at the helm. The widespread public discontent due to political instability and economic stagnation under Morsi government played into the hands of the military. Many politicians in the opposition naively held the belief that the military would turn to the barracks, set the stage for a civilian rule and Egypt's failed democratic transition would be back to track. As events unfolded, it became clear that the military had no intention of leaving the political stage to civilians; instead, generals replaced Mubarak's crony business elite with a crony military elite. Thus, as Sahar Aziz aptly put it, Egypt shifted from a civilian electoral authoritarian system to a military electoral authoritarian system.[185]

Two key differences distinguish Sisi's reign from his predecessors: First, civilians under Sisi have much less control over governance and the national economy than Mubarak. Second, the parliament is controlled by the military elite composed primarily of individual rent-seeking individuals and weak small parties having little potential to mobilize the citizenry against the regime.[186] The Egyptian state imposed control over all state and non-state institutions including the parliament, judiciary, party politics, civil society, and the media. In many respects, restrictive policies and decree laws that were frequently resorted during Mubarak's rule reemerged under the military-backed government. However, in stark contrast to the relatively liberalized authoritarianism of the Mubarak era in which there was limited space for political opposition, civil society, and media, under Sisi regime, public space has shrunk dramatically, and the state has attempted to monopolize all aspects of politics and economy.

The military takeover on the first anniversary of Morsi's election marked not only a fatal blow to Egypt's short-lived democratic experience but also an end to the moderate political Islam within Egypt's electoral arena. Immediately after the military takeover, the regime launched a violent crackdown on the Muslim Brotherhood, prosecuted the FJP, suppressed anti-coup protests, and issued presidential decrees to gain legal image to their regime. The Muslim Brotherhood was outlawed upon being declared a "terrorist" organization, its assets were frozen by a court order, and its activities were criminalized. Programs and channels belonging to the Brotherhood and other Islamist groups as well as the two channels of Al Jazeera were suspended. The wide-scale arrests and death sentence of its members once again forced the Brotherhood underground. By closing down all the channels for the Brotherhood to express itself, the military regime incited the movement to marginalize and to develop its own strategies to counter the state-sanctioned crackdown.

The military regime perpetrated several mass killings of the protestors denouncing Morsi's ouster. One of the first signs of the bloody face of the military regime was witnessed on July 8 when the army massacred fifty-one Muslim Brotherhood supporters protesting at the Republican Guard, where they believed Morsi was in detention. Upon this incident, the Brotherhood took an unyielding stance in its defiance to the military-backed government and declined any potential offer to join the interim government.[187] The security forces routinely opened fire with live ammunition on crowds of protestors opposing the military coup. Meanwhile, thousands of Morsi supporters called for counter-protests and established sit-in protest camps in two districts of Cairo, at al-Nahda and near Raba'a Al-Adawiya Square.[188] The protestors assumed that the sit-in would succeed pressuring the military to reinstate Morsi as president. On August 14, 2013, the military-backed government ordered the dispersal of the protest camps in Raba'a Al-Adawiya and Al-Nahda which envisioned opening fire and large-scale and disproportionate use of force on largely peaceful protestors. Human Rights Watch documented 817 people killed in the August 14 dispersal of the Raba'a Al-Adawiya sit-in camp alone, and given the strong evidence of additional deaths without accurate record or known identity as well as individuals still missing, it is very likely that more than a thousand civilians were killed in a single day.[189] Security forces detained more than 800 protestors from the sit-in, some of whom were beaten, tortured, or executed. Kenneth Roth, the executive director of Human Rights Watch, pointed to the scale of ferocity of the incident with these words[190]:

In Raba'a Square, Egyptian security forces carried out one of the world's largest killings of demonstrators in a single day in recent history. This wasn't merely a case of excessive force or poor training. It was a violent crackdown planned at the highest levels of the Egyptian government. Many of the same officials are still in power in Egypt and have a lot to answer for.

The Egyptian authorities failed to hold even a single officer from the army or the police accountable for the killings and the security forces continued to brutally suppress dissent while enjoying complete impunity for their actions. The secular elite and leftist groups which had a sort of hysteria toward the Brotherhood tried to excuse the military attack by depicting the Brotherhood supporters as armed criminals. On the side of the Brotherhood, the dark legacy of the Raba'a massacre developed a powerful narrative of martyrdom and established a ground for the young Brotherhood members to vow for revenge against the regime and its people. As Ashraf El- Sherif stated Raba'a massacre "closed of the possibility of reconciliation between Islamists and the state and of national cohesion and stability."[191] Though violent suppression and mass killings of the Brotherhood members has been prevalent under the military rule in Egypt, the Raba'a massacre, given the extent of mass killings, is probably the most iconic and will continue to be a tragedy whose legacy would not erase over decades.

With the military-backed government in power, there is a revival of Mubarak-era policies which relied on the political rhetoric of emphasizing stability. The elements of the deep state made use of the stability rhetoric to shield the status quo from the potential gains of the revolutionary unrest. Egyptian authorities engaged in unprecedented repression including imposing legal restrictions on freedom of association, expression, and assembly, carrying out mass arbitrary arrests, torture, and sentencing political opponents to long-term jail or death. Egyptians' strong support for the military in their urge for stability and economic growth and the absence of a parliament during the three years after the coup allowed the interim president Mansour and President Sisi to issue hundreds of presidential decrees unilaterally.

In line with the security and stability rhetoric, the interim government adopted a number of legislative and legal measures to effectively isolate voices of dissent and fend off citizens from the public space. First, the new protest law issued on November 24, 2013, also known as "anti-protest law," required Egyptians to seek approval days in advance before organizing a demonstration. While in theory, the law didn't outlaw demonstrations and protests, it gave the Ministry of Interior discretion to prohibit any protest on vague grounds such as violations of public order and disrupting public interests, even any action that could impact the flow of traffic.[192] The protest law failed to adequately define what would constitute an act of violence in demonstrations or what would lead to the violation of public order specifically, hence, the vague provisions enabled the authorities to arbitrarily use the law to close channels for peaceful opposition. Besides, the new protest law allowed the police forcibly disperse the protests at the slightest indication of disorder giving the government much-needed pretext for widespread crackdown on dissent.

Second, on October 27, 2014, following a deadly attack on North Sinai, Sisi issued a military jurisdiction law that placed all public and state facilities under military court jurisdiction and directed prosecutors to refer any alleged crimes occurring on public land to their military counterparts. In June 2016, a presidential decree was passed to expand the military jurisdiction to include public lands up to 2 kilometers from the nation's public roads. Human Right Watch reported that since Sisi issued the decree, nearly 4,000 civilians have been charged or sentenced in military courts that deprived civilians of basic due rights including the right to be informed of the charges against them, the right to access a lawyer and to be brought promptly before a judge following arrest.[193]

Another law that paved the way for rights abuse is counterterrorism law enacted on August 15, 2015. The major pitfall with the law is that it defined a terrorist act so broadly as to encompass acts of civil disobedience and enhanced authorities' power to impose heavy sentences including death penalty for crimes under the definition of terrorism. Under the new law, incitement to terrorism and propagating ideas that advocate terrorism were treated just like perpetrating terrorist acts. However, linking incitement to the vague and broad definition of terrorism would inevitably have the risk of extending to civil disobedience or peaceful opposition to the regime under the same category. Egyptian authorities have prosecuted and arrested thousands of Brotherhood members as well as human rights activists on terrorism charges for engaging in sit-ins or blocking roads during protests.

The new terrorism law heavily restricted freedom of expression and media through Article 35 which criminalized publishing or promoting news about acts of terrorism that contradict the Defense Ministry's official statement and authorized the courts to temporarily ban journalists from practicing their profession for having violated the law. Press freedom was further undermined by another law ratified by Sisi which ordered the creation of a Supreme Council for Administration of the Media, a state institution authorized to revoke media licenses and fine or suspend publications and broadcasters. These laws made it almost impossible for news agencies and channels critical of Sisi's government to operate.

In a similar vein, the freedom of association was heavily restricted with a draconian NGO law ratified by Sisi in May, 2017. The new law prohibits NGOs from conducting opinion polls, publishing the results of a survey or study and cooperating with an international organization without obtaining permission from the authorities.[194] Under the new law, NGOs are only allowed to engage in activities in line with national development plans while engagement in human rights work is banned under the veil of national security, law and order, and public morals. Besides, NGOs are required to register and operate under the National Authority for the Regulation of Non-Governmental Foreign Organizations, a body composed of representatives from several state institutions including army and intelligence representatives who would monitor the foreign funding received by Egyptian NGOs and the activities of foreign NGOs. The state authorities were granted with broad powers to control NGO activities and budget and to impose harsh punishment and fine in case of violation of the NGO law. Under the disguise of national security, the new legislation has attempted to bring civil society under state control and silence all independent voices.

Egypt's counterrevolution has been highlighted by deterioration in human rights conditions, mass arrests, and trials civilians in military courts, death sentences, and closure of the space for all democratic forces. Under Sisi, Egypt has been gradually turning into a police state. The lengthy periods of pretrial detention for the accused Brotherhood members and the dramatic increase in the number of people imprisoned or sentenced to death were some indicators of the severity of human rights abuses in Egypt. According to various human rights organizations, from 2013 to 2017, the number of those imprisoned has reached approximately 60,000, a figure far above the capacity of Egypt's prisons.[195] Local and international human rights organizations documented reports of forced disappearances at an average of three to four cases a day.[196] Incidents of torture and ill-treatment in police stations and prisons became systematic and routine. Numerous secular activists also fell victim to the crackdown and arrest campaign that began after the coup. In February 2015, a judge sentenced 230 activists to life in prison for participating in December 2011 protests.[197] The April 6 youth movement was banned while Ahmed Maher and Mohamed Adel, two of the movement's leaders, were jailed. More alarming was a pair of court rulings issued by a judge in March and April 2014 sentencing 720 Muslim Brotherhood members to death and the remaining 429 to 25-year jail terms.[198] The mass trials were carried out upon rushed proceedings without basic guarantees of a fair trial.

The counterrevolution in Egypt seems to be at its height when Mubarak, his sons, and political and business elite under his rule were acquitted of charges including murder, embezzlement, and corruption by the court. The prominent figures of the old regime are holding on to key positions under Sisi who surrounded himself with former Mubarak advisors and officials. While some of the most prominent activists, who were the backbone of the revolution in 2011, are in prison and the thousands of Brotherhood members and supporters, who won the first free democratic elections, are jailed, the release of Mubarak and several corrupt figures of his era and the return of many Mubarak-era figures back to their positions dashed Egyptians' dimmest hopes of a democratic change and justice in their country.

On the other hand, the economic situation has deteriorated dramatically under the governance of Sisi. Sharp decline in tourism revenues, lack of economic growth and foreign investment due to the political instability resulted in economic stagnation and huge budget deficit which the government has tried to overcome by receiving IMF loan. The government embarked on an economic program designed to address structural issues as a prerequisite for the loan. However, despite the IMF program which targets attracting foreign investment and increasing employment through enlargement of private sector, the military regime is consolidating its monopoly over many parts of the economy and adopting policies that run counter to opening the market to competition and investment. Egypt's external debt has been on the rise and the poor segments of the population are suffering from high inflation rates and sharp price rises as a consequence of the IMF program.

Many of the government's economic and development policies failed to produce a favorable outcome to reduce poverty. The government invested massive public resources in funding mega building projects such as the Second Suez Channel and the New Administrative Capital managed directly by the military. These projects haven't generated expected economic returns despite having cost massive amount of money for the state. The economic malaise has further been exacerbated by the decline in the financial support which Saudi Arabia, the UAE, and Kuwait have provided to the Egyptian government since the 2013 coup.

As time progressed, it became clear that the priorities of the ruling junta have never matched to the expectations of the revolutionary forces. Sisi's governance failed to bring prosperity while closing all the channels for democratic participation. Thus, the legitimacy of the ruling junta has relied on inducing fear among citizens particularly as to the so-called "Islamist threat." Furthermore, the political instability surrounding the Middle East, rising terrorist attacks in the region, and the ongoing civil wars in countries swept by the Arab Spring such as Syria, Yemen, and Libya also inflicted heavy blows to Egyptians' democratic aspirations. The long-lasting instability and chaos in the countries following the authoritarian breakdown reinforced Egyptians' demands for stability and security in the first place.

NOTES

1. The Egyptian Revolution of 1952 was initiated by the Free Officers Movement, a group of army officers led by Muhammed Naguib and Gamal Abdel

Nasser. The revolution initially aimed at overthrowing King Faruq, however, later the movement adopted more political ambitions and soon moved to abolish the constitutional monarchy of Egypt. The revolutionary movement pursued a nationalist, anti-imperialist agenda expressed through Arab nationalism during Nasser era and international nonalignment.

2. Bruce K. Rutherford, "Egypt: The Origins and Consequences of the January 25 Uprisings," in *The Arab Spring: Change and Resistance in the Middle East*, ed. Mark L. Haas, and David W. Lesch (Boulder, CO: Westview Press, 2013), 35.

3. In the same poll, 79 percent considered fair judicial system "very important," whereas 63 percent considered freedom of speech and law and order as a priority. "US Wins No Friends, End of Treaty with Israel Sought; Egyptians Embrace Revolt Leaders, Religious Parties and Military, As Well," *Pew Research Center*, April 25, 2011, http://www.pewglobal.org/files/2011/04/Pew-Global-Attitudes-Egypt-Report-FINAL-April-25-2011.pdf

4. Rutherford, "Egypt: The Origins and Consequences of the January 25 Uprisings," 35.

5. John Waterbury, *The Egypt of Nasser and Sadat: The Political Economy of Two Regimes* (Princeton, NJ: Princeton University Press, 1983), 74.

6. Ibid., 75.

7. Karatholuvu Viswanatha Nagarajan, "Egypt's Political Economy and the Downfall of the Mubarak Regime," *International Journal of Humanities and Social Science* 3, no. 10 (May 2013): 25.

8. Amy Mckenna, *The History of Northern Africa* (New York: Britannica Educational Publishing, 2010), 96–97.

9. Khalid Ikram, *The Egyptian Economy, 1952–2000: Performance, Policies and Issues* (New York: Routledge, 2006), 56.

10. Rutherford, "Egypt: The Origins and Consequences of the January 25 Uprisings," 35.

11. Nagarajan, "Egypt's Political Economy and the Downfall of the Mubarak Regime," 30.

12. Howard Handy et al., *Egypt: Beyond Stabilization, Toward a Dynamic Market Economy* (Washington, DC: International Monetary Fund, 1998), 1.

13. Adel Abdel Ghafar, *Egyptians in Revolt: The Political Economy of Labor and Student Mobilizations 1919–2011* (New York: Routledge, 2017), 120.

14. Arvind Subramanian, "Egypt: Poised for Sustained Growth?" *Finance and Development* 34, no. 4 (December 1997): 44.

15. Rutherford, "Egypt: The Origins and Consequences of the January 25 Uprisings," 35.

16. Timothy Mitchell, "Dreamland: The Neoliberalism of Your Desires," *Middle East Research 210*, no. 29 (Spring 1999), https://www.merip.org/mer/mer210/dreamland-neoliberalism-your-desires?em_x=22

17. Alianak, *The Transition Towards Revolution and Reform*, 57.

18. "Mubarak Sons Stand Trial For Corruption," *Al Akhbar*, July 9, 2012, http://english.alakhbar.com/content/mubarak-sons-stand-trial-corruption

19. Marcus Baram, "How the Mubarak Family Made Its Billion," *Huffington Post*, November 2, 2011, http://www.huffingtonpost.com/2011/02/11/how-the-mubarak-family-made-its-billions_n_821757.html

20. Gamal Essam El-Din, "Tightening the Grip," *Al-Ahram Weekly*, no. 1053, June 23–29, 2011, http://weekly.ahram.org.eg/Archive/2011/1053/eg5.htm

21. "Judge Orders Mubarak Sons Detained in New Case," *Hurriyet Daily News*, August 2, 2012, http://www.hurriyetdailynews.com/judge-orders-mubarak-sons-detained-in-new-case--26930

22. Philip Inman, "Mubarak Family Fortune Could Reach 70 Billion Dollars," *The Guardian*, February 4, 2011, https://www.theguardian.com/world/2011/feb/04/hosni-mubarak-family-fortune

23. Joel Beinin, "The Working Class and the Popular Movement," in *The Journey to Tahrir*, ed. Jeannie Sowers, and Chris Toensing (New York: Verso, 2012), 105.

24. Absolute poverty is calculated according to expenses less than needed to cover absolutely minimal food and non-food needs. Maria Cristina Paciello, "Egypt: Changes and Challenges of Political Transition," *Mediterranean Prospects Technical Report*, no. 4 (May 2011): 7.

25. "Egypt Human Development Report," United Nations Development Program, 2008, 296.

26. "Egypt: The Arithmetic of the Revolution: An Empirical Analysis of Social and Economic Conditions in the Months before the January 25 Uprising," *Abu Dhabi Gallup Center* (March 2011), http://www.gallup.com/poll/157043/egypt-arithmetic-revolution.aspx

27. According to Barrington Moore, people don't revolt for poverty or unemployment; rather, mass movements emerge when people feel that the distribution of pain in their society is unfair and suffering is not inevitable. Hence, revolutions come out when there is a huge socioeconomic gap between the super-rich elite and the rest of the society and as a result, people start to feel relative deprivation. See Barrington Moore, *Injustice: The social Bases of Obedience and Revolt* (New York: White Plains, 1967).

28. A *fierce* state (or *mukhabarat* state) doesn't enjoy any popular legitimacy through political participation, political representation, development of institutions, and growth of economy, patrimonialism or kinship. Rather the state uses surveillance and repression as a strategy for survival. A fierce state is so opposed to society that it can only deal with it via coercion and raw force. See. Nazih N. Ayubi, *Overstating the Arab State: Politics and Society in the Middle East* (London: I. B. Tauris, 2009).

29. Joshua Stacher, "Egypt: The Anatomy of Succession," *Review of African Political Economy* 35, no. 116 (June 2008): 301–314.

30. Steve Heydemann, "Upgrading Authoritarianism in the Arab World," *Saban Centre for Middle East Policy Analysis Paper*, no. 13 (October 2007): 1–38.

31. Waterbury, *The Egypt of Nasser and Sadat*, 48.

32. Muge Aknur, and Irem Askar Karakır, "The Reversal of Political Liberalization in Egypt," *Ege Academic Review* 7, no. 1 (2001): 313.

33. Maye Kassem, *Egyptian Politics: The Dynamics of Authoritarian Rule* (Boulder, CO and London: Lynne Rienner Publishers, 2004), 148.

34. Yakub Halabi, *US Foreign Policy in the Middle East: From Crises to Change* (New York: Routledge, 2016), 94.

35. Kassem, *Egyptian Politics: The Dynamics of Authoritarian Rule*, 148–150.

36. Eberhard Kienle, "More Than a Response to Islamism: The Political Deliberalization of Egypt in the 1990s," *Middle East Journal* 52, no. 2 (Spring 1998): 223.

37. Najib Ghabian, *Democratization and Islamist Challenge* (Boulder, CO: Westview Press, 1997), 90.

38. "Egypt: Continuing Arrests of Critics and Opponents "Chill" Prospects for Reform," *Amnesty International*, May 27, 2005.

39. Kienle, "More Than a Response to Islamism: The Political Deliberalization of Egypt in the 1990s," 221–222.

40. Ibid.

41. Kassem, *Egyptian Politics. The Dynamics of Authoritarian Rule*, 156.

42. Marina Ottoway, and Julia Choucair-Vizoso, *Beyond Façade: Political Reform in the Arab World* (Washington: Carnegie Endowment, 2008), 19.

43. Larisa Epatko, "Mubarak in 1993: Egypt Keen on Democracy, But It Will Take Time," *PBS Newshour*, February 4, 2011, http://www.pbs.org/newshour/rundown/mubarak-on-democracy

44. Kienle, "More Than a Response to Islamism: The Political Deliberalization of Egypt in the 1990s," 226.

45. Ibid.

46. John L. Esposito, Tamara Sonn, and John Obert Voll, *Islam and Democracy after the Arab Spring* (Oxford: Oxford University Press, 2016), 206.

47. Ibid., 202.

48. Shafeeq Ghabra, "The Egyptian Revolution: Causes and Dynamics," in *Routledge Handbook of the Arab Spring: Rethinking Democratization*, ed. Larbi Sadiki (London and New York: Routledge), 199.

49. Ibid., 200.

50. Sherif Mansour, "Enough is Not Enough: Achievements and Shortcomings of Kefaya, the Egyptian Movement for Change," in *Civilian Jihad: Nonviolent Struggle, Democratization and Governance in the Middle East*, ed. Maria J. Stephan (New York: Palgrave Macmillan, 2009), 206.

51. Jason Brownlee, "A New Generation of Autocracy in Egypt," *The Brown Journal of World Affairs* 14, no. 1 (Fall/Winter 2007): 78.

52. A series of opposition groups such as Journalists for Change, Doctors for Change, Workers for Change, and Youth for Change, merged under the umbrella of Kefaya movement. Kefaya, mainly composed of middle-class constituents, was involved in 3,000 strikes and sit-ins between 2004 and 2010.

53. Mansour, "Enough is Not Enough: Achievements and Shortcomings of Kefaya," 207.

54. Mona El-Ghobashy, "Egypt Looks Ahead to Portentous Year," *Middle East Research*, February 2, 2005, http://www.merip.org/mero/mero020205

55. Tareq Y. Ismael, Jacqueline S. Ismael, and Glenn E. Perry, *Government and Politics of the Contemporary Middle East: Continuity and Change* (New York: Routledge, 2016), 466.

56. Sonia L. Alianak, *Middle Eastern Leaders and Islam: A Precarious Equilibrium* (New York: Peter Lang, 2007), 192–193.

57. Mansour, "Enough is Not Enough: Achievements and Shortcomings of Kefaya," 209.

58. The amendment requiring the nomination of party for candidates, some prominent figures not affiliated with a political party but drawing support from across the political spectrum such as Mohamed El Baradei, the former International Atomic Energy Agency Chief, and Nobel peace prize winner in 2005, would be precluded from making candidacy.

59. "Downtown Showdown," *Al Ahram*, no. 154, August 4–10, 2005, http://weekly.ahram.org.eg/Archive/2005/754/eg7.htm

60. In its initial phase, the 2005 elections marked an advance compared to previous elections as political criticism, and protests were allowed albeit in a limited manner. Muslim Brotherhood candidates were allowed to campaign far more openly, and elections were monitored by NGOs.

61. Denis Sullivan, "Will Egypt's Muslim Brotherhood Run in 2010," *Carnegie Middle East Center*, May 5, 2009, http://carnegie-mec.org/sada/23057

62. "Egypt's Imitation Election," *New York Times*, September 11, 2005, http://query.nytimes.com/gst/fullpage.html?res=9E07E5D61331F932A2575AC0A9639C8B63

63. "Protestors Say Egypt Elections Rigged," *CNN*, December 12, 2005, http://edition.cnn.com/2005/WORLD/africa/12/12/egypt.election.protest/index.html?iref=allsearch

64. "Egypt: Proposed Constitutional Amendments greatest erosion of human rights in 26 years," Amnesty International Press Release, March 18, 2007, https://www.amnesty.org/en/documents/mde12/008/2007/en/

65. Nathan J. Brown, Michele Dunne, and Amr Hamzawy, "Egypt's Controversial Constitutional Amendments," *Carnegie Endowment for International Peace*, March 23, 2007, https://carnegieendowment.org/files/egypt_ constitution_webcommentary01.pdf

66. Ibid.

67. "Egypt: Proposed Constitutional Amendments greatest erosion," Amnesty International Press Release.

68. Michael Slachman, "Egyptian Political Dissident, Imprisoned for Years, is Suddenly Released," *The New York Times*, February 18, 2009, http://www.nytimes.com/2009/02/19/world/middleeast/19egypt.html

69. Daniel Williams, "Egypt Extends 25-Year-Old Emergency Law," *Washington Post*, May 1, 2006, http://www.washingtonpost.com/wp-dyn/content/article/2006/04/30/AR2006043001039.html

70. More than 500 members of the Muslim Brotherhood were detained, many of them without charge or trial. "Egypt: Continuing Crackdown on Muslim Brotherhood," *Amnesty International Public Statement*, August 30, 2007. https://www.amnesty.org/download/Documents/64000/mde120282007en.pdf

71. "Egypt: Amnesty International Report 2008. Human Rights in the Arab Republic of Egypt," *Amnesty International*, May 28, 2008, http://www.refworld.org/docid/483e2788c.html

72. "World Report 2010: Egypt," *Human Rights Watch*, https://www.hrw.org/world-report/2010/countrychapters/egypt

73. Ekram Ibrahim, "6th of April 2008: A Workers' Strike Which Fired the Egyptian Revolution," *Ahram Online*, April 6, 2012, http://english.ahram.org.eg/NewsContent/1/64/38580/Egypt/Politics/-/th-of-April--A-workers-strike-which-fired-the-Egyp.aspx

74. Gregg Carlstrom, "Explainer: Inside Egypt's Recent Elections," *Aljazeera*, November 15, 2011, http://www.aljazeera.com/indepth/spotlight/egypt/2011/11/201111138837156949.html

75. Evan Hill, "Election Day in Mansoura," *Aljazeera*, November 29, 2010, http://archive.is/20120708001856/blogs.aljazeera.com/blog/middle-east/election-day-mansoura

76. Ghabra, The Egyptian Revolution: Causes and Dynamics," 204.

77. "Hosni Mubarak's Speech," *The Guardian*, February 2, 2011, https://www.theguardian.com/world/2011/feb/02/president-hosni-mubarak-egypt-speech

78. The camel raid lasted for two days and left 11 people killed and over 600 injured. "Battle of the Camel," *The Tahrir Institute for Middle East Policy*, February 2, 2011, https://timep.org/timeline/feb2-11

79. "Egypt Rises: Killings, Detentions and Torture in the 25 January Revolution," *Amnesty International*, May 19, 2011, https://www.amnesty.org/en/documents/mde12/027/2011/en/

80. "Egypt Set for Mass Protest as Army Rules out Force," *The Guardian*, January 31, 2011, https://www.theguardian.com/world/2011/jan/31/egyptian-army-pledges-no-force

81. Ahmed Shafiq who served as the prime minister for a brief period during late Mubarak's era, remained in office until he was forced to resign following a wave of protests. The new cabinet headed by Essam Sharaf gained public acceptance and approval of the opposition. However, the interim government still included some ministers who served under Mubarak or had strong ties to him.

82. "Egypt Supreme Council of the Armed Forces: Statements and Key Leaders," *New York Times*, February 14, 2011, http://www.nytimes.com/interactive/2011/02/10/world/middleeast/20110210-egypt-supreme-council.html?mcubz=0

83. The concerned amendments were made to the most controversial articles during Mubarak's rule; namely, Article 75, 76, 77, and 139 on the conditions for presidential nominations and limitation of the president's terms; Article 88 on the judicial oversight over elections during the entire electoral process; and Article 93 was amended to ensure that the Court of Cassation becomes the sole arbitrator of contested parliamentary memberships. M. Cherif Bassiouni, *Chronicles of the Egyptian Revolution and Its Aftermath: 2011–2015* (Cambridge: Cambridge University Press, 2016), 82–83.

84. Extending the state of emergency would require a public referendum according to the de facto constitution. "Brotherhood Leader: Proposed Constitutional

Amendments Mostly Reasonable," *Egypt Independent*, February 27, 2011, http://www.egyptindependent.com/brotherhood-leader-proposed-constitutional-amendments-mostly-reasonable/

85. According to Tahani Gebali, Vice-President of Egypt's Supreme Constitutional Court, Article 189 requiring the elected parliament to choose a constitutional assembly took away the right of people to elect the commission and gave it to the parliament. Noha El-Hennawy, "Controversy Heightens over Proposed Constitutional Amendments," *Egypt Independent*, March 3, 2011, http://www.egyptindependent.com/controversy-heightens-over-proposed-constitutional-amendments/

86. Amr Hamzawy, "Egypt: Evaluating Proposed Constitutional Amendments," *Los Angeles Times*, March 7, 2011, http://carnegieendowment.org/2011/03/07/egypt-evaluating-proposed-constitutional-amendments-pub-42923

87. "Egyptian Voters Approve Constitutional Changes," *The New York Times*, March 20, 2011, http://www.nytimes.com/2011/03/21/world/middleeast/21egypt.html?mcubz=0

88. Mara Revkin, and Yussef Auf, "Beyond the Ballot Box: Egypt's Constitutional Challenge," *Atlantic Council Issue Brief* (June 2012): 4. https://www.files.ethz.ch/isn/145484/94969_ACUS_Egypt_Challenge_final-rev.pdf

89. Citizens would vote on the draft constitution in a referendum and power would be transferred to an elected president by June 30 as popular demands indicated.

90. "Constitutional Declaration of Egypt," March 30, 2011, http://www.wipo.int/edocs/lexdocs/laws/en/eg/eg04 6en.pdf

91. With this amendment, after decades of repression, the Muslim Brotherhood was able to establish the Freedom and Justice Party (FJP) and the party headed by Mohammed Morsi achieved legal status on June 6, 2011.

92. Gamal M. Selim, "Egypt under SCAF and the Muslim Brotherhood: The Triangle of Counter Revolution," *Arab Studies Quarterly* 37, no. 2 (Spring 2015): 181.

93. Ibid., 86.

94. Mahmoud Hamad, "The Constitutional Challenges in Post-Mubarak Egypt," *Insight Turkey* 14, no. 1 (2012): 54–55.

95. Ibid.

96. The protestors decided to stage a sit-in in Tahrir to grab attention to their suffering under military rule. The sit-in was dispersed by the security forces and the army. The clash between the protestors and the security forces lasted for a week and tens of protestors were killed and hundreds got injured.

97. "Tens of Thousands Attend 'Save the Revolution' Day," *Ahram Online*, April 1, 2011, http://english.ahram.org.eg/NewsContent/1/64/9055/Egypt/Politics-/Tens-of-Thousands-attend-Save-the-Revolution-day.aspx

98. Mubarak, his two sons, and several prominent figures in his inner circles during his rule such as the former ministers together with well-connected businessman were placed on trial yet the process dragged on for years due to lengthy adjournments. Mubarak was sentenced to life in prison in 2012, while in 2015 in a separate case over corruption, he was sentenced to three years and his sons, Gamal and Alaa Mubarak, to four years in prison.

99. "Egypt Dissolves the Former Ruling Party," *Aljazeera*, April 16, 2011, http://www.aljazeera.com/news/middleeast/2011/04/2011416125051389315.html

100. Gregg Carlstrom, and Evan Hill, "Scorecard: Egypt since the Revolution," *Aljazeera*, January 24, 2012, http://www.aljazeera.com/indepth/interactive/2012/01/20121227117613598.html?xif=;Protests

101. "No Joy in Egypt," *Human Rights Watch*, January 25, 2012, https://www.hrw.org/news/2012/01/25/no-joy-egypt

102. "Egypt: New Law Keeps Military Trials of Civilians," *Human Rights Watch*, May 7, 2012, https://www.hrw.org/news/2012/05/07/egypt-new-law-keeps-military-trials-civilians

103. Some of the major incidents in 2011 were Port-Said Football massacre on February 2; the cabinet attacks that lasted for four days in December, 2011; the Battle of Mohamed Mahmoud which took place from 19 to 25 November and left forty-one dead and over one thousand injured; the case of Essam Atta (a twenty-four–year old boy tortured to death by prison guards and died on October 27); the Maspero Massacre that took place on October 9 when Coptic Christians poured into the streets to protest the destruction of church in Aswan; the Battle of Abbasiya on 23 July (attack on the thousands of protestors marching from Tahrir to the Ministry of Defense to decry the SCAF for the unmet demands of the revolution); Nakba Day Protests on 15 May (the attack on the protests outside the Israeli Embassy in Cairo in solidarity with Palestinians left 350 people injured and 150 arrested); the clashes over the Imbaba church attack on May 7 which left 186 people injured; mass arrests and torture over a sit-in at Tahrir Square on March 9 (the military attack on the sit-in drew widespread attention as virginity tests were carried out on female detainees as reported by several organizations including the Amnesty International). Wael Eskandar, "Year of the SCAF: A Time-line of Mounting Repression," *Ahram Online*, February 11, 2012, http://english.ahram.org.eg/NewsContent/1/64/34046/Egypt/Politics-/Year-of-the-SCAF-a-timeline-of-mounting-repression.aspx

104. These NGOs included Egypt's most prominent organizations such as the Cairo Institute of Human Rights Studies, the El-Nadeem Center for Rehabilitation of Victims of Torture, the Egyptian Initiative for Personal Rights, the Hisham Mubarak Law Center, and the Washington-based organizations working to support democracy such as the National Democratic Institute (NDI), The International Republican Institute (IRI), and Freedom House.

105. Stephen Mcinerney, "SCAF's Assault on Egypt's Civil Society," *Foreign Policy*, September 28, 2011.

106. "Egypt's Brotherhood Wins 47% of Parliament Seats," *Egypt Independent*, January 21, 2012, http://www.egyptindependent.com/egypts-brotherhood-wins-47-parliament-seats/

107. "Results of Shura Council elections," *Carnegie Endowment for International Peace*, February 29, 2012, http://egyptelections.carnegieendowment.org/2012/02/29/results-of-shura-council-elections

108. Angy Ghannam, "Islamists in Egypt's Tourist Spots Win Surprise Support," *BBC News*, December 28, 2011, http://www.bbc.com/news/world-middle-east-16348229

109. "In Sunday Statement SCAF Hits Back at Brotherhood Criticisms," *Ahram Online*, March 25, 2012, http://english.ahram.org.eg/NewsContent/1/0/37691/Egypt/0/In-Sunday-statement,-SCAF-hits-back-at-Brotherhood.aspx

110. "Egypt Court Orders Dissolving of Parliament," *Aljazeera*, June 14, 2012, http://www.aljazeera.com/news/middleeast/2012/06/2012614124538532758.html

111. David D. Kirkpatrick, and Karem Fahim, "Egypt Race Pits Aide to Mubarak against Islamist," *New York Times*, May 25, 2012, http://www.nytimes.com/2012/05/26/world/middleeast/egypt-presidential-election-runoff.html?mcubz=0

112. "SCAF Expands Its Power with Constitutional Amendments," *Egypt Independent*, June 17, 2012, http://www.egyptindependent.com/scaf-expands-its-power-constitutional-amendments/

113. Gamal M. Selim, *The International Dimensions of Democratization in Egypt: The Limits of Externally-Induced Change* (Switzerland: Springer International Publishing, 2015), 45.

114. "Egypt President-Elect Mohammed Morsi Hails Tahrir Crowds," *BBC*, June 29, 2012, http://www.bbc.com/news/world-middle-east-18648399

115. Kareem Fahim, and Mayy El Sheikh, "New Egyptian Cabinet Includes Many Holdovers," *New York Times*, August 2, 2012, http://www.nytimes.com/2012/08/03/world/middleeast/new-egyptian-cabinet.html?mcubz=0

116. Kareem Fahim, "In Upheaval for Egypt, Morsi Forces out Military Chiefs," *New York Times*, August 12, 2012, https://www.nytimes.com/2012/08/13/world/middleeast/egyptian-leader-ousts-military-chiefs

117. "Morsi Issues New Constitutional Declaration," *Egypt Independent*, November 22, 2012, http://www.egyptindependent.com/morsy-issues-new-constitutional-declaration/

118. Ibid.

119. "Judges Club Lashes Out at Morsy's Decisions," *Egypt Independent*, November 22, 2012, http://www.egyptindependent.com/judges-club-lashes-out-morsy-s-decisions/

120. "Morsi's Supporters Clash with Protestors outside Presidential Palace in Cairo," *The Guardian*, December 5, 2012, https://www.theguardian.com/world/2012/dec/05/morsi-supporters-protest-presidential-palace-cairo

121. Abdel-Rahman Hussein, "Egypt: Mohamed Morsi Cancels Decree that Gave Him Sweeping Powers," *The Guardian*, December 9, 2012, https://www.theguardian.com/world/2012/dec/09/egypt-mohamed-morsi-cancels-decree

122. Gamal Essam El-Din, "Islamists Dominate Egypt's Constituent Assembly," *Ahram Online*, March 25, 2012, http://english.ahram.org.eg/NewsContent/1/0/37606/Egypt/0/Islamists-dominate-Egypts-constituent-assembly.aspx

123. "SCAF, Political Parties Agree to 6 Criteria for Forming Constituent Assembly," *Ahram Online*, April 28, 2012, http://english.ahram.org.eg/News/40374.aspx

124. Mara Revkin, and Yusuf Auf, "Egypt's Constitutional Chaos," *Foreign Policy*, June 14, 2012.

125. "Political Forces Reach Uneasy Agreement on Egypt's Constituent Assembly," *Ahram Online*, June 7, 2012, http://english.ahram.org.eg/NewsCon

tent/1/64/44134/Egypt/Politics-/Political-forces-reach-uneasy-agreement-on-Egypt
s-.aspx

126. "Egypt's Army Ends Deadlock on Constituent Assembly," *Ahram Online*, June 8, 2012, http://english.ahram.org.eg/NewsContentP/1/44212/Egypt/Egypts-army-endsdeadlock-on-constituent-assembly.aspx

127. Cornelis Hulsman, Diana Serodio, and Jayson Casper, "The Development of Egypt's Constitution: Analysis, Assessment and Sorting through the Rhetoric," *Arab-West Report* (May 2013): 43.

128. "High Constitutional Court Withdraws from Constituent Assembly," *Ahram Online*, June 12, 2012, http://english.ahram.org.eg/NewsContent/1/64/44669/Egypt/Politics/High-Constitutional-Court-withdraws-from-constitue.aspx

129. Diana Serodio, "Internal Dynamics of the Second Constituent Assembly," in *Development of Egypt's Constitution: Analysis, Assessment and Sorting through the Rhetoric*, Cairo: Arab-West Report (May 2013), 45–46.

130. "Secular Figures Withdraw from Constituent Assembly, Call Draft Egypt's Downfall," *Egypt Independent*, November 18, 2012, http://www.egyptindependent.com/secular-figures-withdraw-constituent-assembly-call-draft-egypt-s-downfall/

131. Ibid.

132. Zaid Al-Ali, "The New Egyptian Constitution: An Initial Assessment of Its Merits and Flaws," *OpenDemocracy*, December 26, 2012, https://www.opendemocracy.net/zaid-al-ali/new-egyptian-constitution-initial-assessment-of-its-merits-and-flaws

133. Holger Albrecht, "Egypt's 2012 Constitution: Devil in the Details, Not in Religion," *PeaceBrief* 139, United States Institute of Peace, January 25, 2013, https://www.usip.org/sites/default/files/PB139-Egypt%E2%80%99s%202012%20Constitution.pdf

134. The New Constitution of the Arab Republic of Egypt, 2012. Art. 2. trans. International IDEA. http://www.constitutionnet.org/sites/default/files/final_constitution_30_nov_2012_-english-_-idea.pdf

135. The New Constitution of the Arab Republic of Egypt, 2012. Art. 219.

136. Ibid., Art. 4.

137. Albrecht, "Egypt's 2012 Constitution: Devil in the Details, Not in Religion."

138. The New Constitution of the Arab Republic of Egypt, 2012. Preamble, Principle 3.

139. Ibid., Art. 44.

140. Al-Ali, "The New Egyptian Constitution: An Initial Assessment of Its Merits and Flaws."

141. "New Constitution Mixed on Support of Rights," *Human Rights Watch*, November 30, 2012, https://www.hrw.org/news/2012/11/30/egypt-new-constitution-mixed-support-rights

142. The New Constitution of the Arab Republic of Egypt, 2012, Art. 198.

143. Magued Osman, "The President's Approval Rating after 11 Months in Office," *Egyptian Center for Public Opinion Research* (Baseera), May 29–30, 2013, http://baseera.com.eg/EN/PressPoll-Ar/24_En.pdf

144. Ibid.

145. "Egyptians Increasingly Glum," *Pew Research Center*, Global Attitudes Project, May 16, 2013, http://www.pewglobal.org/2013/05/16/egyptians-increasingly-glum/

146. Ibid.

147. "After Tahrir: Egyptians Assess Their Government, Their Institutions and Their Future," *Zogby Research* Services (June 2013), https://static1.squarespace.com/static/52750dd3e4b08c252c723404/t/52928b8de4b070ad8eec181e/1385335693242/Egypt+June+2013+FINAL.pdf

148. Ibid.

149. "Egypt's Presidency's Civil Society Bill 'Hostile to Freedom': NGOs," *Ahram Online*, May 31, 2013, http://english.ahram.org.eg/NewsContent/1/64/72807/Egypt/Politics-/Egypt-presidencys-civil-society-bill-hostile-to-fr.aspx

150. Ibid.

151. Sherif Mansour, "On the Divide: Press Freedom at Risk in Egypt," *A Report by the Committee to Protect* Journalists (CPJ), August 14, 2013, https://cpj.org/reports/2013/08/on-divide-egypt-press-freedom-morsi.php

152. "Torture in Egypt during a Year of Muslim Brotherhood Rule," *El Nadeem Center for Rehabilitation of Victims of Violence*, June 26, 2013, https://alnadeem.org/en/content/torture-egypt-during-year-muslim-brotherhood-rule

153. "One Year into Mohammed Morsi's Term Manifold Abuses and the Systematic Undermining of the Rule of Law," *Cairo Institute for Human Rights Studies*, June 26, 2013, http://www.cihrs.org/?p=6849&lang=en

154. "Egyptians Increasingly Glum," Pew Research Center.

155. Patrick Werr, and Andrew Torchia, "Analysis: New Egypt Government May Promote Welfare, Not Economic Reform," *Reuters*, July 17, 2013, https://www.reuters.com/article/us-egypt-economy-policy-analysis /analysis-new-egypt-government-may-promote-welfare-not-economic-reform-idUSBRE96G0IP20130717

156. Bessma Momani, "In Egypt, 'Deep State' vs. 'Brotherhoodization'," *The Brookings Institution*, August 21, 2013. https://www.brookings.edu/opinions/in-egypt-deep-state-vs-brotherhoodization/

157. Interview with David Kirkpatrick "Morsi's Ouster in Egypt: A "Bookend" for the Arab Spring," *NPR*, July 22, 2013, http://www.npr.org/2013/07/22/203616418/morsis-ouster-in-egypt-a-bookend-for-the-arab-spring

158. Ben Hubbard, and David Kirkpatrick, "Sudden Improvements in Egypt Suggest a Campaign to Undermine Morsi," *New York Times*, July 10, 2013, http://www.nytimes.com/2013/07/11/world/middleeast/improvements-in-egypt-suggest-a-campaign-that-undermined-morsi.html

159. Ashraf El-Sherif, "Egypt's Post-Mubarak Predicament," *Carnegie Endowment for International Peace*, January 29, 2014, https://carnegieendowment.org/2014/01/29/egypt-s-post-mubarak-predicament-pub-54328

160. Salma Abdullah, "Tamarod Surpasses 22 Million Signatures," *Daily News Egypt*, June 29, 2013, https://dailynewsegypt.com/2013/06/29/tamarod-surpasses-22-million-signatures/

161. Ian Black, "Mohammed Morsi: The Egyptian Opposition Charge Sheet," *The Guardian*, July 3, 2013, https://www.theguardian.com/world/2013/jul/03/mohamed-morsi-egypt-president-opposition

162. Walaa Hussein, "Egypt's Tamarod Outlives Its Purpose," *Al-Monitor*, May 8, 2015, http://www.al-monitor.com/pulse/originals/2015/05/egypt-tamarod-movement-political-campaign-mubarak-sisi.html

163. David D. Kirkpatrick, Kareem Fahim, and Ben Hubbard, "By the Millions, Egyptians Seek Morsi's Ouster," *New York Times*, June 30, 2013, http://www.nytimes.com/2013/07/01/world/middleeast/egypt.html

164. "Profile: Egypt's Tamarod Protest Movement," *BBC News*, July 1, 2013, http://www.bbc.com/news/world-middle-east-23131953

165. Matthew Weaver, Paul Owen, and Tom McCarthy, "Egypt Protests: Army Issues 48-Hour Ultimatum-As it Happened," *The Guardian*, July 1, 2013, https://www.theguardian.com/world/middle-east-live/2013/jul/01/egypt-stanoff-millions-protest

166. "Egypt Islamist Coalition Urges Opposition to Break from Mubarak Regime Figures," *Ahram Online*, June 29, 2013, http://english.ahram.org.eg/NewsContent/1/64/75211/Egypt/Politics-/Egypt-Islamist-coalition-urges-opposition-to-break.aspx

167. "Egypt Military Unveils Transitional Roadmap," *Ahram Online*, July 3, 2013, http://english.ahram.org.eg/News/75631.aspx

168. "Egypt Army Topples Morsy," *Egypt Independent*, July 3, 2012, http://www.egyptindependent.com/egypt-army-topples-morsy/

169. In January 2014, the constitution was approved in a popular referendum with 98 percent of the voters. Voter turnout was low at 38.6 percent of registered voters, less than the 50 percent predicted by officials. "Egypt Constitution Approved by 98.1 percent," *Aljazeera*, January 24, 2014, http://www.aljazeera.com/news/middleeast/2014/01/egypt-constitution-approved-981-percent-2014118163264 70532.html

170. Samer Atallah, "Egypt's New Constitution: Repeating Mistakes," *Aljazeera*, January 14, 2014, http://www.aljazeera.com/indepth/opinion/2014/01/egypt-new-constitution-repeating-mistakes-201411255328300488.html

171. Constitution of the Arab Republic of Egypt, 2014, Unofficial Translation, Art. 159. http://www.sis.gov.eg/Newvr/Dustor-en001.pdf

172. Ibid., Art. 161.

173. Amr Hamzawy, "Egypt's Parliament Opens Doors for More Repression," *Washington Post*, September 22, 2016, https://www.washingtonpost.com/news/global-opinions/wp/2016/09/22/egypts-parliament-opens-the-door-for-more-repression/?utm_term=.4694e755e641

174. Atallah, "Egypt's New Constitution: Repeating Mistakes."

175. Constitution of the Arab Republic of Egypt, 2014, Art. 234.

176. Ibid., Art. 11.

177. Another alternative was to obtain the recommendations of at least twenty elected members of the parliament. Constitution of the Arab Republic of Egypt, 2014, Art. 142.

178. It is not plausible to figure out the exact voter turnout and the election results as the administration of the electoral process was carried out by the Presidential Elections Committee composed of Mubarak-era presidents and senior members of the judiciary. Patrick Kingsley, "Abdal Fatah Al-Sisi Won 96.1% of Vote in Egypt Presidential Election, Say Officials," *The Guardian*, June 3, 2014, https://www

.theguardian.com/world/2014/jun/03/abdel-fatah-al-sisi-presidential-election-vote-egypt

179. Egypt's former parliamentary election law dates back to 2011, but it was overturned by the Supreme Constitutional Court's ruling in June 2012, leading to the dissolution of the People's Assembly. From June 2012 to October 2015, Egypt was governed without a parliament.

180. Scott Williamson, Nathan J. Brown, "Egypt's New Law for Parliamentary Elections Sets up a Weak Legislature," *Atlantic Council*, June 24, 2014, http://www.atlanticcouncil.org/blogs/menasource/egypt-s-new-law-for-parliamentary-elections-sets-up-a-weak-legislature

181. Sahar F. Aziz, "Military Electoral Authoritarianism in Egypt," *Election Law Journal* 16, no. 2 (2017): 294.

182. Over ten political parties announced that they would not participate in the election and these included Al-Dostour (Constitution) Party, Popular Socialist Alliance Party, Popular Current Party, Al-Wasat Party, Reawakening of Egypt Party, Revolutionary Socialist Party, Bread and Freedom Party, Building and Development Party, Social Justice Coalition, Freedom Egypt, and Strong Egypt Party. All these parties opposed to the electoral law on the ground that it would not lead to a just representation in the parliament and would provide opportunity for the wealthy and powerful member of the elite to use their resources to manipulate election results.

183. Ahmed Aboulenein, and Eric Knecht, "Turnout Low in Egypt's Long-Awaited Parliamentary Election," *Reuters*, October 18, 2015, http://www.reuters.com/article/us-egypt-election-idUSKCN0SC07420151018

184. Yussef Auf, "Egypt's New Parliament: What Do the Results Mean?" *Atlantic Council*, January 7, 2016, http://www.atlanticcouncil.org/blogs/menasource/egypt-s-new-parliament-what-do-the-results-mean

185. Aziz, "Military Electoral Authoritarianism in Egypt," 290.

186. Ibid.

187. Sherif Khalifa, *Egypt's Lost Spring: Causes and Consequences* (Santa Barbara, CA: Praeger Publishers, 2015), 189.

188. Sit-in protests soon developed into a sprawling tent city that where protestors slept, ate, prayed, and even received medical care. The protest camp near Rabaa Al-Adawiya Mosque had barricades, its own volunteer security guards, field hospital, media center, and some parts of the camp were allocated for street art and street vendors. According to the Human Rights Watch (HRW), approximately 85.000 protestors joined the sit-in which lasted for over forty-five days. "Protest Camp: Raba'a Al-Adawiya," *BBC News*, July 18, 2013, http://www.bbc.com/news/world-middle-east-23356389

189. "Egypt: Rab'a Killings Likely Crimes against Humanity," *Human Rights Watch*, August 12, 2014, https://www.hrw.org/news/2014/08/12/egypt-raba-killings-likely-crimes-against-humanity

190. Ibid.

191. A Conversation with Dr. Ashraf El Sherif "A Dangerous Deterioration: Egypt under Al-Sisi," *Project on Middle East Democracy* (June 2017). http://pomed.or

g/pomed-publications/a-dangerous-deterioration-egypt-under-al-sisi-a-conversation-with-dr-ashraf-el-sherif/

192. "Full Translation of Egypt's New-Protest Law," *Ahram Online*, November 25, 2013, http://english.ahram.org.eg/News/87375.aspx

193. "Egypt: New Parliament Should Fix Abusive Laws," *Human Rights Watch*, January 12, 2016, https://www.hrw.org/news/2016/01/12/egypt-new-parliament-should-fix-abusive-laws

194. "Egypt's Sisi Approves Controversial NGO Law," *Aljazeera*, May 29, 2017, http://www.aljazeera.com/news/2017/05/egypt-sisi-approves-controversial-ngo-law-170529182720099.html

195. Amr Hamzawy, "The Tragedy of Egypt's Stolen Revolution," *Aljazeera*, January 25, 2017, http://www.aljazeera.com/indepth/features/2017/01/tragedy-egypt-stolen-revolution-170125062306232.html

196. Ibid.

197. "Egypt: Year of Abuses under Al-Sisi," *Human Rights Watch*, June 8, 2015, https://www.hrw.org/news/2015/06/08/egypt-year-abuses-under-al-sisi

198. Patrick Kingsley, "Egyptian Judge Sentences 720 Men to Death," *The Guardian*, April 28, 2014, https://www.theguardian.com/world/2014/apr/28/egyptian-judge-sentences-720-men-death

Chapter 5

Democratic Divergence between Egypt and Tunisia in the Post-Arab Spring Context

Arab Spring initially instilled hope as to the fundamental change of political systems from authoritarianism toward democracy and freedom. These hopes were dashed only a few years after the outbreak of the Arab uprisings in all the countries where giant masses of people revolted against their rulers. With the exception of Tunisia, in each of those countries, the Arab Spring was brought to a halt with the engagement of the counterrevolutionary forces designed and financed by local, regional, and international actors. Democratic transition prospects were overthrown by a military coup in Egypt in 2013; the uprisings in Libya, Syria, and Yemen were succeeded by protracted civil wars among rival factions seeking control over territory; the protest movements were suppressed to consolidate a minority-led regime in Bahrain. In the Arab states affected by revolutionary protests, political and economic instability has taken root and violence has become normalized, and no progress has been witnessed as to democratic reforms and freedoms. In other words, the Arab Spring gave way to the long-standing Arab winter.

In the initial period after the revolution, both Tunisia and Egypt raised optimism, given their success in toppling their former regimes in rather a short time, and relatively peacefully. Their transition from authoritarianism hosted a number of referendums and elections with participation of various political forces. Both countries followed transitologists' classical pattern for democratization. The authoritarian breakdown gave way to increased pluralism, the enacting of a new constitution, and the holding of competitive elections in both countries. Yet, almost a decade in retrospect, transitions in Tunisia and Egypt present divergent outcomes in terms of democratization. While democracy began to take root in Tunisia, the model of democratic transition carried out in Egypt hasn't really allowed a regime change, and eventually generated a hegemonic military authoritarianism. According to the Freedom

House ratings in 2020, Tunisia is rated as "Free" with overall freedom rating of seventy out of hundred (political rights are rated as thirty-two out of forty and civil liberties are rated as thirty-eight out of sixty), while Egypt is rated as "Not Free" with overall freedom rating of twenty-one out of hundred (political rights are rated seven out of forty and civil liberties are rated fourteen out of sixty).[1]

Given that the uprisings' starting point and the initial transition bear striking similarities in Tunisia and Egypt, why democratic outcome has diverged substantially between the two countries is an important question for transition studies and comparative democratization. Before moving to a comparison between the two countries, the chapter follows with an overview of the similarities between Tunisia and Egypt in terms of their historical, political, social, and economic aspects. The following section continues with an analysis of the divergence in democratic outcome between the two countries in the post-Arab Spring context. In the next section, democratic divergence between Tunisia and Egypt is investigated in relation to the structural approach concluding that structures alone don't suffice to account for the complex character of a transition process. Finally, an extensive analysis is carried out as to the divergence in the democratic outcome between Tunisia and Egypt based on the assumptions of the transition theory (or agent-centered approach).

The analysis comes to the conclusion that it is the agents and the nature of interactions and compromises among them that make democracy come out, yet those agents, to some extent, can be encouraged or constrained by a set of structural conditions while designing the transition process. While agent lies central to success or failure of democratization in a transition, structures are vital in determining the choices, interactions, and consensus-making tendency of those agents. In other words, the structural context in which the transition takes place, such as the power equilibrium among political forces, institutional setting, civil society mobilization, and external factors, influences attitudes and decision-making process of the political elite.

WHAT DO TUNISIA AND EGYPT HAVE IN COMMON?

Of all the states swept by the popular protests and faced regime change in 2011, Tunisia and Egypt share many features in common, and they witnessed similar trajectories in the initial phase of their transition. To begin with, mass street protests toppled the long-entrenched autocrats in a rather short period of time without significant violence involved in street protests. Compared to other Arab countries which underwent regime change, uprisings in both countries were largely peaceful.[2] Not surprisingly, the peaceful nature of both revolutions and the short time span in which the authoritarian regimes were ousted in Tunisia and Egypt were largely due to the role played by the armed forces in two countries. In both Tunisia and Egypt, the generals decided to side with people in the face of growing public anger and gave a very clear message to the rulers that the armed forces were no longer a guarantee for their protection.

In both countries, youth took the lead in the uprisings, and they shaped the trajectory of the protest movements. Besides, the use of social media was an important feature of the Arab Spring movements, and those revolutions were portrayed as "Twitter revolutions" by many observers. Efforts by the Tunisian and Egyptian governments to suspend the Internet and preclude people from communicating through social media failed and activists found different ways to communicate and mobilize people. The widespread use of social media during the uprisings gained new momentum to the revolutionary change, and for the first time in history, social media was regarded as an important aspect of a revolution.

Unlike other Arab states shaken by popular protests in 2011, Tunisia and Egypt didn't face direct external intervention and threat of civil war for some reasons. First, the two countries, unlike Syria and Libya, enjoyed a coherent and unified national identities and strong statehood which relied on the historical legacy of state building from the Ottoman Empire to the postcolonial period.[3] Second, in both countries, the ethnic makeup of population seems to be homogenous. Approximately 98 percent of Tunisian population are Sunni Arabs. Likewise, about 90 percent of the population of Egypt are Sunni Arabs. However, though Tunisia and Egypt appear to enjoy homogeneity in their societal composition, they remain largely stratified along tribal, regional, sectarian constituencies. A number of different religious, tribal, and sectarian groups exist in Tunisia and Egypt including Amazigh, Copts, Nubians, Bedouins, Salafis, Sufis, Bahais, Ahmadis, and Egyptian Shia, coastal and rural. Despite the stratification along tribal and sectarian lines, the protest movements in 2011 neither diverted from aspirations for democracy and freedom to ethnic and sectarian issues nor played into the hands of the former autocrats to garner support from a portion of population by appealing to their sectarian or tribal affiliations as happened in Syria, Libya, and Yemen. On the other hand, Egypt faces the divide between Salafis and other Sunni groups as well as between seculars and Islamists which is just as visible. Secular tendencies are even far stronger in Tunisia along with an established leftist political tradition including labor unions and leftist political groups.

In terms of their political systems and economy policies prior to the Arab uprisings, Tunisia and Egypt had several distinctive features in common. The two countries were governed by republican systems, and the former regimes in both countries were portrayed as "liberal autocracies" in which civil liberties were granted by facially liberal constitutions, multiparty elections were held, and a certain degree of freedom was allowed for civil society and the media. An important feature of these liberal autocracies is to allow a set of liberties that wouldn't affect the survival of the regime and in no way bring about any radical change in the political system. In that regard, controlled elections, selective repression, and partial inclusion of Islamists (in Egypt), guided pluralism were used both as a survival strategy by the former regimes and a type of political system that would defy any linear model of democratization.[4] Civil society and opposition political parties were persistently manipulated by the state, and they remained inherently weak. Most nongovernmental organizations were co-opted by the government and determined their policies in line with the government's agenda while opposition nongovernmental organizations and unions were either delegitimized by state corporatist practices or precluded from operation.[5]

Both Ben Ali and Mubarak regimes took refuge behind political openings initiated during periods of political liberalization while ensuring their ruling party's dominance over political life without any real rotation of power. Besides, they both engaged in a protracted cycle of liberalization and deliberalization in which rulers widened or narrowed the boundaries of participation and expression in response to changing social, political, economic, and geostrategic challenges facing their regimes.[6] Political reforms were often carried out in order to stave off crises of legitimacy, challenges to the rulers' hold on to power or under serious pressure from Western allies to stick to their democracy promotion programs. These reforms aimed to manipulate the public by introducing some superficial and cosmetic changes. To illustrate, Mubarak regime had to introduce some political reforms in the face of growing Western pressure in 2005. The ruling party amended the constitution to allow for multicandidate presidential elections for the first time in Egypt's history. Nonetheless, it also imposed certain restrictions in a way that controlled liberalization would not risk its dominance over politics. It was clear to all parties from the outset that the NDP would not allow free and fair elections where all candidates had equal opportunities.[7] In a similar vein, with Ben Ali's accession to power in 1989, a form of electoral democracy took root in Tunisia, but it was through a carefully tailored and constitutionally mandated opposition integrated into parliament since 1994 elections.[8]

In the absence of associational life, free press, and freely organized opposition, electoral democracy only served the ruling parties to maintain power without altering their authoritarian structures while giving a facade of democracy to its Western allies. Behind the veneer of democracy, the autocrats in both countries sought to control civil society, thriving patronage networks, economy, and media ,while judiciary and government agencies were highly influenced to serve the ruling elite's interests and help to ensure monopoly of power. The outcome of political liberalization were routinely held elections without any chances for alternation of power, effective political parties, independent judiciaries, and freedom of press and organization. The two countries were examples of a facade democracy where the ruling regimes prevented emergence of democracy with genuine deepening (contestation) and widening (participation), the two dimensions of Dahl's polyarchy by manipulating the trappings of democracy.[9]

In addition, Tunisia and Egypt were remarkable examples of economic liberalization over the last three decades till the outbreak of the uprisings. Egypt under Anwar Sadat initiated the trend for open-door policy in the early 1970s which marked the beginning of a new wave of economic liberalization followed by Morocco, Jordan, and Tunisia. Both Ben Ali and Mubarak regimes adopted neoliberal economic policies as a response to the economic crisis of the early 1970s and 1980s, the failure of the state-planned economies and reliance on the public sector. The two countries were continuously hailed as success stories by the IMF in terms of economic reforms and economic growth. The IMF praised the Mubarak regime for implementing successful neoliberal policies prior to the global financial crisis, remaining committed to resuming financial consolidation broadly and its adjustment to preserve macroeconomic stability.[10] Similarly, in 2007, the IMF endorsed Ben Ali regime's economy policies proclaiming "efficient economic management has helped achieve relatively strong growth while preserving macroeconomic stability, thereby positioning Tunisia among the leading economic performers in the region."[11] Ironically, only few months before the uprisings, both countries were praised by the IMF for having sound economy policies and market reforms.[12]

There are a number of similarities with regard to effects of neoliberal programs in Egypt and Tunisia. First, neoliberal economic reforms aimed to shrink government and encourage competitive market and private enterprise to pave the way economic growth and create more jobs. While markets became more capitalist and freer since the 1990s, they were not competitive. Neoliberal policies were manipulated to serve the interests of a small circle of political and economic elite. In both Tunisia and Egypt, privatization concentrated in the hands of a class of crony capitalists with close connection to the regime. Thus, neoliberalism and privatization in particular bred a new class of business elite whose interests became increasingly interwoven with the ruling elite.[13] The business tycoons surrounding Gamal Mubarak in Egypt and the Trabelsi clan in Tunisia made use of their political power to acquire wealth. Second, an important consequence of the neoliberal reforms over the three decades in the lead up to the uprisings was the material decline of the middle and working classes accompanied by decline in real purchasing power, uneven wealth distribution, growing regional disparities, and rising poverty.[14] The neoliberal program in Tunisia and Egypt eliminated the state subsidies for basic provisions and job security especially for the educated young people. Meanwhile, neoliberal policies exacerbated the gap between the rich and the poor, creating tensions that manifested itself in the years leading to the uprisings. For instance, Egypt was cited as one of the top ten reformers in the world based on its economic growth by the World Bank from 2006 to 2008, while over 40 percent of its population was noted as extremely poor in the given period.[15]

Neoliberal policies led to the erosion of political legitimacy of the regime as the social contract which relied on state developmentalism and co-optation of the working and middle classes by provision of material wealth and job security in return for their allegiance to the regime was no longer valid. As a consequence, urban mass protests called "Bread Riots" broke out in Egypt (in 1977) and Tunisia (1984) as an expression of growing discontent with neoliberal policies and austerity measures including government cuts to bread subsidies. In addition, since the late 1990s, Egypt and Tunisia experienced numerous labor strikes in response to growing inequality caused by widening gap between the classes and uneven regional development in the case of Tunisia.

Tunisia and Egypt shares common features with respect to the composition of political parties and ideological division between secular and Islamist factions in the society. In both countries, the two major Islamist movements, namely Ennahda in Tunisia and the Muslim Brotherhood in Egypt constituted the main opposition groups for several decades. Both movements were subject to repressive measures by their respective governments. Since independence, Habib Bourguiba was deeply attached to the vision of Tunisian state strictly secular and nationalist in nature and he viewed Islamists as an existential threat to the very nature of the Tunisian state. Ben Ali took a similar path and both leaders never attempted to co-opt Islamists by allowing their participation into the political system, instead, they entirely excluded them from politics.[16] Unlike their counterparts in Tunisia, Anwar Sadat and Hosni Mubarak were willing both to utilize Islamic imagery to gain legitimacy to their rule and to accommodate Islamists in the political system, albeit in a limited scale, and keep them under control. In Egypt, Mubarak initiated periods of political liberalization in which Islamists were relieved from harsh repression yet these periods were succeeded by harsh crackdowns on the Islamist movements.

In the first free and fair elections, the two major Islamist parties, the FJP and Ennahda won an electoral victory and morphed from an opposition group which mainly engaged with resistance and survival into ruling parties in charge of shaping their countries' political transition. In both Tunisia and Egypt, in a short while after the revolution, the political debates surrounding constitution drafting revolved around the question of adopting *Sharia* as a basic source of legislation. The political tensions that arose during constitutional and electoral processes unveiled the long-standing ideological divide between seculars and Islamists and turned out to be an important challenge to national unity in the two countries.

The origins of the uprisings have also much in common in Tunisia and Egypt. The former authoritarian regimes ran short on political legitimacy. Rampant corruption, repressive policies, lack of equal economic opportunities, political freedoms, and independent judiciaries were pervasive. In both countries, long-entrenched autocrats were viewed as inept and corrupt with no ability to provide progress in social and economic welfare. A broad coalition of opposition groups from all segments of society, rural and urban, Islamists and seculars, lower and upper classes unified to mobilize against the regime demanding its ouster. In both countries, the success of revolutions lied to a large extent in the military elite's support for peaceful protestors.

HOW HAVE TUNISIA AND EGYPT DIVERGED POST-ARAB SPRING?

Tunisia has emerged as the only country where Arab uprisings ended up in transition to democracy and the political goals of the revolution were largely attained. It has successfully evolved from an authoritarian state to an electoral democracy whose political actors are committed to moderation, civil liberties, and the rule of law. In Tunisia, since the fall of the Ben Ali regime, power changed hands through free and fair elections and the elected government runs the country free from any tutelage. Civil society has blossomed and important steps have been taken to tackle corruption and ensure press freedom. From the point of democratization, there are a few prerequisites of democratic transition to be regarded as complete, and Tunisia seems to have fulfilled each of these criteria. First, a sufficient agreement has to be reached about political procedures to produce an elected government.[17] The Tunisian interim government established Ben Achour commission that provided a significant platform for political parties and civil society actors to negotiate about the sequencing and timing of the elections and constitution drafting as well as the procedures governing the elections for the NCA. Second, democratic transition is complete when a government comes to power as the direct result of a free and popular vote.[18] In Tunisia, in 2011, a constituent assembly was elected to be in charge of the writing of the new constitution. In 2014, Tunisia elected a pluralist and inclusive parliament and a president through free and fair elections. The 2014 elections was an indicator that Tunisia passed the "Huntington two-turnover" test; that is, the party that dominated the government after the ouster of Ben Ali peacefully handed power over to the opposition and all political actors accepted the results of the ballot box.[19] Third, transition to democracy is achieved "when the government *de facto* has the authority to generate new policies, and when the executive, legislative and judicial power generated by the new democracy doesn't have to share power with other bodies *de jure*."[20] The new Tunisian government has generated policies since the elections and it doesn't share power implicitly or explicitly with any authority such as a religious leader or military. In 2014, despite difficulties, Tunisian political parties and civil society managed to draft a constitution that provides civil and political rights unambiguously.

Tunisia can be said to have successfully completed its transition to democracy and now faces a more protracted challenge which is democratic consolidation. Nonetheless, it still remains premature to come to a conclusion that Tunisia will consolidate its democracy. Given the turmoil and the strong, if not the dominant, participation of the old guards in the new parliament and government, the political situation remains volatile in Tunisia where structural reforms face stiff resistance from the old guards. In addition, economic problems and security challenges could lead the society to prioritize stability over democratization, requiring additional precautions in attributing final success to democratic consolidation in Tunisia.

Egypt provides a stark contrast to the case of Tunisia in all several respects surrounding the transition. Soon after Mubarak was ousted, the country found itself engulfed in a protracted conflict between the military tutelage that has ruled the country behind the curtain for decades and the Brotherhood supporters who have the deepest bonds with the society but were isolated from the political sphere under Mubarak. Egypt failed in every single step regarded as condition for a democratic transition. Political parties and civil society actors didn't reach a consensus about the rules and procedures that would govern the transition. The country moved into electoral politics immediately after the fall of the regime with little attention paid to the electoral law and constitutional drafting process. Egyptians were called to the polls for a total of five national elections or referenda, some of which had multiple rounds between 2011 and 2013. None of the elections or referendums paved the way for designing the country's political transition along the popular will. Each election and referendum only helped to magnify the polarization between the two opposing camps. Since the fall of Mubarak, the country drafted and ratified two constitutions neither of them was an outcome of a broad national dialogue and truly reflected popular will. The result was the country's reversion to a fully fledged military authoritarianism.

Despite various similarities between the two countries, the divergence between Egypt and Tunisia in their post-revolution period has stimulated a wide-ranging debate among political scientists and observers. Some political scientists have found the explanation in structural factors such as a relatively well-educated population, a large middle class, and higher industrialization levels in Tunisia. Others have pointed to a fundamental difference between the leading Islamist movement in the two countries; Ennahda party in Tunisia and the Muslim Brotherhood in Egypt. Still others have tried to explain this divergence by looking at the institutions of those countries, such as military and judiciary and concluded that Tunisia accommodates institutions that are more hospitable to democratic transition.

In the light of those arguments, the next section offers an analysis into the inadequacy of structural factors in accounting for the democratic divergence between Tunisia and Egypt. In the upcoming section, agency is brought to the core of the research and the democratic divergence between the two countries is investigated through the agents' role in designing the transition as well as their identity, historical evolution, interests, and restraints. It is also important to note that during the initial phase, while agents are central to the success or failure of the transition as their decisions, interactions, beliefs, and commitment to democracy enable the unfolding of the democratic processes, structures could create a political environment more conducive to democratization in the long run.

THE INADEQUACY OF THE STRUCTURAL APPROACH

While trying to account for the divergent trajectories of Tunisia and Egypt in the post-Arab Spring context, Tunisia's greater success in democratic transition could seem to originate from the country's superior structural factors and better socioeconomic standing. It is assumed that democratization would follow from socioeconomic development. Lipset's theory correlates democratic progress with higher economic development. To his theory, economic development goes hand in hand with societal modernization, urbanization, industrialization, rising levels of literacy and education, and rising national income, which make up an environment conducive to democracy.[21] More recently, Huntington indicated a different correlation between democracy and development suggesting that regimes gain legitimacy by prospering economically.[22]

As indicated in figure 5.1, modernization theory is concerned with structural and societal conditions especially in the socioeconomic domain that would pave the way for democratic governance. Lipset's modernization theory broadly argues that various aspects of economic development such as industrialization, urbanization, wealth, and education are "so closely interrelated as to form one major factor which has the political correlate of democracy."[23] The underlying logic behind the correlation between economic development and democratization is that higher per-capita income and GDP

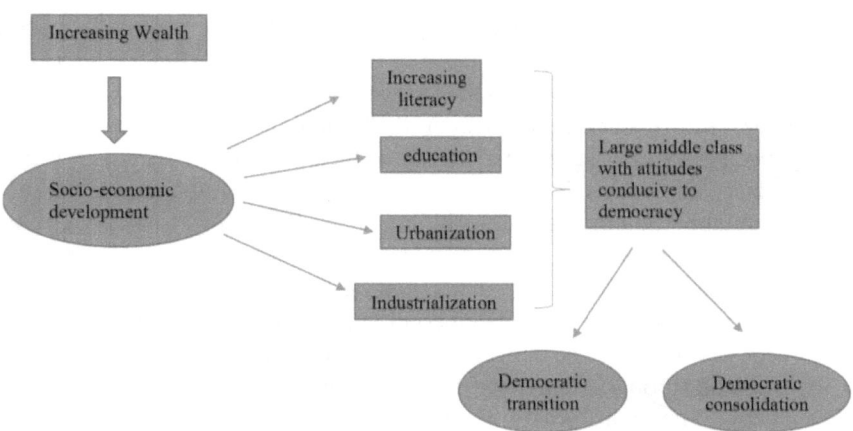

Figure 5.1 Lipset's Modernization Theory. *Source:* Author

growth would create structural and societal conditions conducive to democracy, though these conditions are not necessarily causes for democracy. In other words, modernization is assumed to bring the ideal conditions that would result in mass political participation. First, economic development goes hand in hand with industrialization and urbanization which lead to physical mobility of citizens. According to Lerner, industrialization leading to urbanization and physical mobility of citizens (migration) eventually generates social mobility. Social mobility, in turn, breeds high levels of empathy, a crucial skill for moving out of tradition.[24] Second, industrialized societies inevitably needs more investment in human capital through education and upgrading workforce to produce high-tech goods, which results in the enlargement of educated middle class.[25] Modern societies are also assumed to shift from traditional to secular-rational values. Third, a viable middle class acts as a catalyst to democracy. Being stronger in human capital and especially education and exposed to wider and diverse audiences (e.g., voluntary organizations and trade unions), workers in developed countries, are more receptive toward democratic values.[26] The increased levels of literacy and education are prerequisites of democracy as educated people are more likely to take part in the rational compromises that democracy requires. It is the middle class that internalized norms and values such as tolerance, empathy, secularism, openness to new ideas that allow democratic culture to materialize. Thus, once the middle class becomes large and empowered, it is assumed to push for liberal democracy.

Looking through the prism of modernization theory, by some analysts Tunisia's successful transition to democracy was attributed to factors such as wealth, urbanization, education, population, and the dominance of the middle class. Tunisia is a small country with a population of about 11.6 million, while Egypt is the Arab world's most populous country with a population of over 98 million. In addition, Tunisians are on average wealthier than Egyptians, and in 2010, their GDP per capita was almost twice as high as that of Egyptians.[27] At the time of the uprisings, the Tunisian middle class amounted to nearly 81 percent of the population, while in Egypt, the size of the middle class declined substantially to just under 10 percent by the end of 2010.[28] Besides, Tunisia is more urbanized than Egypt, given that 66.5 percent of the Tunisian population was urbanized (as of 2012) as opposed to Egypt's 43.6 percent.[29] Tunisian population also seems to be more educated than that of Egypt based on adult literacy rate and attendance in secondary education though the difference in figures has been slight.[30] Eventually, statistics illustrate that Tunisia is wealthier, more urbanized, more developed, and more educated than Egypt, and many political scientists have put emphasis on these structural factors that are assumed to make Tunisia more conducive for democracy to take root.

The assumptions of the modernization theory, on the other hand, don't apply to the Arab world when looked into the region from a socioeconomic perspective. The countries with highest per-capita income in the region are the Arab Gulf states, where social mobilization for democratic aspirations were nonexistent or not of any particular significance, if any. In addition, when we look at Egypt and Tunisia, both countries fall into the category of lower-middle-income developing countries—a category that many analysts consider an "indeterminate zone" for political transition and the political trajectory of the countries in this zone could go either way, as Eva Bellin noted.[31] In 2010, Egypt maintained an average 5 percent annual GDP growth rate and in Tunisia, the average GDP growth rate was slightly lower at 3.5 percent.[32] The similarity in the growth rates eliminates the alternative explanation that economic well-being fostered democratic transition in Tunisia. Third, modernization theory assumes that the high level of urbanization would be accompanied by rising levels of literacy and education, which would inevitably make people receptive to common correlates of democratic attitudes and demand democracy over other systems of governance. However, the data obtained from the Pew Research Center, indicated that support for democracy was high in both countries with little difference in the support ratings for democratic governance between two countries. In 2012, 67 percent of Egyptians supported democracy over other kinds of government and the support for democracy in Tunisia was rated as 63 percent in the same year.[33]

From 2012 to 2014, support for democracy declined in both countries: in Egypt, from 71 to 59 percent between 2011 and 2014, and in Tunisia, from 63 to 48 percent between 2012 and 2014. As of 2014, a quarter of interviewees contended that a nondemocratic government could be preferable in both countries. In addition, people's preference shifted from democracy toward stability over the three years succeeding the uprisings. Economic stagnation, political and economic instability accompanied by rising unemployment and inflation were the roots of citizens' grievances and, to a large extent, determined people's priorities favoring economic and political stability over democracy in the post-Arab Spring Tunisia and Egypt. The findings of the Pew Research Center indicate that support for stability over democracy rose in both countries. In Tunisia, 62 percent of respondents preferred stable government even without democracy in 2014, while the figure was only 38 percent in 2012.[34] Likewise, in Egypt, the supporters of a stable government rose from 32 percent in 2011 to 54 percent in 2014.[35] Consequently, we see similar rates and patterns in people's support toward democracy in both countries though the middle class is substantially larger and more empowered in Tunisia, and the country is more urbanized than Egypt. According to the modernization theory, Tunisians are assumed to be more inclined to support democracy at all costs. The similar ratings in both countries in 2014 indeed illustrate that the assumption that urbanization and high education rates which accompany modernization would lead to attitude change in people doesn't account for the democratic divergence between Tunisia and Egypt.

While it could be acknowledged that higher economic development, industrialization, urbanization, and education could create a political and social environment that is more conducive to democratic transition and consolidation, socioeconomic factors alone don't determine the fate of democratic or authoritarian regimes. Based on their extensive study on the experiences of 135 countries between 1950 and 1990, Przeworkski *et al.* came to the conclusion that democracies come into being with similar chances at all levels of development and economic development doesn't generate democratic transition, however, they also found that democracies are more likely to survive in wealthy societies.[36] In a similar vein, the third wave of democratization experiences have indicated that the fall of authoritarian regimes led countries with low socioeconomic development to transition to democracy and consolidate their democratic system while some countries with much higher socioeconomic development reverted to authoritarianism or became hybrid regimes.

TRANSITION THEORY AND THE CENTRALITY OF "AGENT"

In 1970, Dankwart Rustow criticized modernization theory on the ground that it mistakes the functional feature of mature democracies—what make them flourish—for genetic causes of new democracies— brings them into being.[37] In contrast, he argues that the only prerequisite for democracy is a unified national state: "the vast majority of citizens in a democracy-to-be must have no doubt or mental reservations as to which community they belong to."[38] In his seminal work *Democracy's Third Wave*, Huntington also noted that economic development is a driver for democratization, but it is the political leadership that is a must to make it real.[39] For democracies to come into being, future political elites must at least be convinced that democracy is the least bad form of government for their societies and for themselves. In addition, those elites also need the skills to bring about transition to democracy, while radical oppositionists and authoritarian hard-liners would possibly seek to undermine their efforts.[40]

In examining transitions to democracy or reversion to authoritarianism, the determinant of political change first and foremost lies in choices, behaviors, and strategies of principal political agents. Transition theorists appreciate the complex interaction of elites and institutions in the process of democratization. To understand what leads to democratic transition or authoritarian revival, it is essential to investigate the way how regime change takes place, negotiation or clash among the political elite, and the way new system, institutions, and political norms are settled. Giuseppe di Palma explored the conciliatory political undertakings, termed as "democratic crafting," a process that involves negotiated agreements between ruling and opposition elites. For democratic crafting, there are various reasons such as stalemate, the high costs of repression, a loss of goals, international constraints that may encourage all parties to accept democracy as the best possible regime form under given conditions.[41] The Third Wave of Democracy illustrates that successful democratic transitions took part in countries which accommodated negotiations and pacts among the political elite. These former transition experiences also proved that elite commitment to democracy is the key to a smooth and successful transition, while their resistance to change would lead to falling back to an authoritarian regime or a failed state.

In the same vein, the different paths taken by Egypt and Tunisia could be best analyzed by looking at the agency-based factors such as important decisions taken at strategic points of transition, political actors' commitment to democracy, and their compromises at the critical junctures. Besides, interactions between the hard-liners-old regime forces—revolutionary factions and whether they opted to accommodate or exclude each other in designing transitional phase have been an important aspect of democratic outcomes. However, while elite commitment and support to democratic transition is key to a successful transition, the roles played by political actors during the transition are not isolated from structural factors. Political actors often make calculations and take their decisions considering structural contexts and constraints. For instance, civil society is not thought to be an agent in the construction of democracy, yet associational life and a vibrant civil society have the potential to make pressure on political actors to fulfill essential reforms on the way to democratization. Likewise, external influence is not regarded as an agent; however, political actors' behaviors are greatly influenced by external political or financial support for democratic transition or reversion to the old regime. Similarly, balance of power among political forces significantly impacts the willingness of political actors to negotiate with their opponents. Those structural factors indeed help us to understand the underlying reasons why actors make certain choices but not others and conditions under which they make those choices. Hence, political and historical structures lie central to agents' decision-making processes as they allow agents to become more compromising or remain firm in their political decisions. Against this backdrop, analyzing structural factors interwoven with calculations of political actors helps us to bridge the gap left by the transition theory.

EXPLAINING DEMOCRATIC DIVERGENCE BETWEEN TUNISIA AND EGYPT

This section investigates the drivers or factors that eroded Egypt's path to democratic transition in contrast to a negotiated and consensual model of democratic transition in Tunisia. To this end, there are mainly six factors that account for the democratic divergence between the two countries in the post-Arab Spring context: (1) elite consensus, (2) leadership styles of the transitional actors, (3) civil society, (4) institutional endowment, (5) power equilibrium among the political forces, and (6) external influence. The former two variables directly indicate the significance of choices, decisions, and compromises among political actors, while the latter four variables manifest the structural constraints or strengths that drastically alter interactions among them and thus, significantly influence their strategic decisions. The two models of transition with their key variables are examined in figure 5.2.

ELITE CONSENSUS

Democratic transition in any country is successful to the extent that political elites reach a consensus on the ultimate objectives of the transition and choose to collaborate and compromise to accomplish those objectives. Transition from an authoritarian regime takes place through two phases: extrication from the authoritarian regime and crafting a democratic constitution.[42] In this initial phase, extrication could be achieved when political actors in the transition support democracy and hold the view that democracy is the system that would benefit them most. Another precondition of extrication would be

Variables	Tunisia	Egypt
Elite consensus	Consensual	Non-Consensual
Political Interaction and Bargaining Between opposing political forces	Strong	Weak
a. Pluralism and competitiveness	High	Low
b. Polarization	High	High
c. Interaction among political parties	High	Low
Leadership of the Transition	Inclusive Compromising	Exclusionary Uncompromising
Distribution of power among political Forces	Even	Uneven
Civil society participation/ popular Mobilization for democratic transition	High	High
Contribution of civil society and labor to democratic processes	Decisive	Non-decisive
Role of military during the transition	Neutral & Non-decisive	Politically Motivated & Highly Decisive
Role of the Old Regime	Non-decisive	Decisive
Role of External Actors	Non-decisive	Decisive

Figure 5.2 Models of Transitions in Tunisia and Egypt. *Source:* Author

building trust and carrying out negotiation among elites, particularly, moderates and reformers (soft liners). On the other hand, hard-liners are likely to resist to transition and hold on to the status quo which they believe would serve their interests best.[43] A successful extrication from the old regime is feasible when political actors build a political pact, reach a consensus on sharing power and office, and on a roadmap that would move the country toward democracy. A crucial factor determining the success of transition is whether prodemocracy forces remain united against the old regime. Especially if they divide at an early stage, democratic transition would be jeopardized as it would play into the hands of the incumbents of the old regime who would take advantage of this division and play one actor against the other.[44]

The consolidation of democratic transition entails more than removing the authoritarian ruler; it necessitates a conciliatory stance by the respective political elite to build accountable institutions and determine post-authoritarian transitional policies. When an authoritarian regime breaks down, the challenge lies in paving the way for more permanent arrangements for the resolution of potential conflicts. O'Donnell and Schmitter regards initial elite pacts as central to democratic transition. They define a pact as "an explicit, but not always explicated of justified agreement among a set of actors which seek to define or redefine rules governing the exercise of power on the basis of mutual guarantees for the vital interests of those entering into it."[45] A pact is built on negotiated compromise through which actors eliminate violent confrontation as an alternative to handle disagreements. At the core of a pact lies a situation that no social or political group is dominant enough to impose its ideal project, yet competing groups are interdependent, and they can't unilaterally determine the rules of the game following the regime breakdown. Therefore, they have to address each other's divergent interests and the outcome is often the "second-best solution" that doesn't completely satisfy one particular actor while offering something which all of them can agree.[46] Pacts foster abstention from violence and commitment to resolving future disputes by dialogue thereby closing the space to nonpolitical elite. Pact-making is a substantial sign of political will among the elite to create mechanisms for democratic governance and to build effective and accountable political institutions.

On the other hand, pact-making essentially requires a political culture that involves political maturity among the political elite to make compromise to come to terms with one another. While it is of great significance to maintain dialogue and take a conciliatory stance in the post-authoritarian setting, the political culture of the MENA region has rarely witnessed such cooperation and consensus building. Instead, the region accommodates winner-takes-all political mentality which eliminates chances for creating a platform to reconcile divergent ideologies. In the region, power parties that promise to remove illiberal regimes viewed losers in the electoral game "not as minorities to be protected but as enemies to be silenced."[47] This political mentality limits democracy only to the realization of electoral politics which is only democratic in the strictest procedural sense. In Egypt, for instance, the Brotherhood and the military viewed electoral politics as a zero-sum game where the winner is entitled to take all and the loser is destined to acquiesce to the ruling faction. The absence of toleration and compromising is what accounts for the inability to generate and maintain a democratic government in Egypt.

Ideological moderation is vital for religious parties to engage in talks and negotiations with their ideological opponents, which allows them to embrace the norms and values essential for emergence of pluralist democratic culture. Schwedler defines moderation as "movement from a relatively closed and rigid worldview to one more open and tolerant of alternative perspectives."[48] In this context, moderates can be defined as those political actors who aspire for gradual change by working within the existing political system contrary to radicals who seek to overthrow the entire system. Ideological moderation, in this light, can be viewed as a gradual change from radical to a moderate standpoint on which religious parties respect and adopt liberal notions of individual rights and democratic notions of tolerance, pluralism, and cooperation.[49] As Schwedler notes, mere participation in elections and democratic processes is not sufficient as an indicator of moderation since political actors might adopt this behavior for purely strategic purposes while pursuing a more radical political agenda.[50] Ideological moderation requires substantive commitment to democratic principles, including peaceful alternation of power, ideological and political pluralism, and citizenship rights.[51] In other words, the prospect of democratization is in line with the capability of religious parties to moderate their political discourse and behaviors so as to enable coexistence with ideological opponents in political setting peacefully.

In Tunisia and Egypt, in the post-authoritarian setting, party systems were characterized by cleavages along religious lines—secular versus Islamist forces—ideological lines—mainly, liberal, leftist, and conservative. The societies in both countries were also highly polarized and fragmented. However, despite this fragmentation, Tunisia had a higher level of elite consensus; political elite were able to form alliances not only along their ideological affinity but also with political forces that were on the other end of the political spectrum. Transition in Tunisia was built on consensual politics and bargaining among the elite, particularly between seculars and Islamists on the basic rules of the transition. In Egypt, on the contrary, transition started in a partisan manner and focused on electoral politics rather than taking a process-first view approach and unifying political actors from political spectrum to decide on the key issues regarding the future of the new Egyptian state. Hence, political actors made use of their bargaining skills to reach a consensus in Tunisia whereas in Egypt they opted to use their institutional weight to force a transition in line with ideological and political interests.

The first requirement of democratic transition, according to Linz and Stepan, is "sufficient agreement on procedures to produce an elected government."[52] Tunisia has accomplished transition to democracy since political actors reached consensus on the procedures on how to design the transitional phase to produce a representative, inclusive and accountable government that came to power through free and fair elections. In addition, political elite in Tunisia, both Islamists and seculars, had a shared desire to break with the authoritarian past and its remnants, and to embrace free and fair elections which was evident both in their declarations and political choices. To illustrate, soon after the ouster of Ben Ali, the Higher Authority for the Realization of the Objectives of the Revolution, Political

Reform, and the democratic transition was established. This commission involved members from all political factions in addition to legal experts, civil society groups, intellectuals, and business elite who agreed on a transitional roadmap identifying the key decisions over the timing, sequencing and the model of the transition. The commission decided to suspend the 1959 constitution, to hold elections for a constituent assembly to draft a new constitution and to create the ISIE, an independent electoral commission. In addition, commission members privileged decisions that concerned electoral system, voting rules, and guarantees of electoral freedom and fairness. The creation of the High Commission enabled critical decisions to be taken based on consensus among divergent political forces and the institutionalization of the transition. As Alfred Stepan aptly put it, the Higher Authority for the Realization of the Objectives of the Revolution, Political Reform, and the democratic transition turned out to be "one of the most effective consensus-building bodies in the history of crafted democratic transitions."[53]

In the same vein, following the first elections for the Constituent Assembly, Ennahda party which gained plurality of the votes but fell short of a majority, formed a coalition government with two secular parties, the Congress for the Republic (CPR), and Ettakatol. The three parties also reached a deal on sharing power and the appointment of leading positions. Moncef Marzouki from the CPR was appointed as the interim president of Tunisia, Mustafa Ben Jafar from Ettakatol became the president of the Constituent Assembly, and Hamadi Jamali from Ennahda was appointed as the interim prime minister. On the other hand, the ease with which divergent political parties were able to establish the troika government resulted from the gradual construction of a dialogue that began in 2003 when representatives from Tunisia's four opposition groups met in France to negotiate on the two fundamental principles of a future government: sovereignty of people as the source of legitimacy and ensuring liberty of beliefs to all while respecting people's Arab-Muslim values.[54]

An important aspect of the dialogue between seculars and Islamists in Tunisia is that both camps came to an agreement on the shared values and principles regarding the state-religion-society; that is, the seculars agreed the Islamists would be part of democratic politics and the new government would be free from any form of tutelage, whereas the Islamists agreed that the new Tunisian state would be a civic and democratic state whose legitimacy would be popular sovereignty. In the words of Stepan, in Tunisia political elite, whether seculars or Islamists embraced "twin tolerations," that is, an agreement that ensures religious authorities won't intervene in the political sphere as longs as democratic officials act constitutionally while democratic officials won't interfere in the religious sphere so long as religious actors respect other citizens' rights.⁵⁵

Another characteristic of the Tunisian transition was that opposition forces whether Islamists or seculars, managed to remain united in the face of the efforts by the old regime's vestiges to seize the revolution and restore their privileges. The secularist and the Islamist camps participated jointly in demonstrations at the Casbah plaza to demand the resignation of the interim prime minister Mohamed Ghannouchi, a veteran of the old regime and a holdover from Ben Ali's party— RCD.⁵⁶ The Casbah protests opened the way for the dissolution of Ben Ali's party, the legalization of Ennahda, and holding of the election for a constituent assembly. These protests illustrated how Tunisian demonstrators managed to turn street activism into concrete political objectives by remaining united and saved the revolution from falling into the hands of the old regime.

In July 2013, the Tunisian transition reached a complete impasse given the political deadlock surrounding the drafting of the new constitution, the assassination of the political opponent Mohamed Brahimi and continual street protests demanding the resignation of the troika government. At this critical turn, it was the Tunisian National Dialogue Initiative launched by the four main trade unions of the country that saved the revolution. The Tunisian National Dialogue Initiative serves as a successful example of pact-making and offers an important lesson on how the elite bargaining and pact-making advanced democratic transition. The national dialogue served as a vital platform for elite talks allowing Islamists and secular forces to overcome the political stalemate and mounting street protests.

During the summer 2013, the bloody coup that overturned the revolution in Egypt enabled the Tunisian political elite to learn from the Egyptian experience and come to the conclusion that parties can't win by confrontation and violent conflict, and thus, must choose dialogue and compromise instead.⁵⁷ The Tunisian national dialogue drew a "Road Map" for the country and managed to convince political parties to accept it in order to take part in the national dialogue. The deal paved the way for the resignation of the Islamist-led troika government, the creation of new interim government of technocrats and a calendar for the completion of the new constitution and the upcoming parliamentary and presidential election. The initiative succeeded to bring the political deadlock to an end by finding a middle ground between the Islamist-led government and the left-wing and secular opposition.

The success of the national dialogue in relieving Tunisia from the deadlock has greatly altered the two leading opposing parties' policy priorities. While soon after the revolution Islamists have chosen to use ideological polarization to their advantage, they realized that they would lose the thread and might face the risk of exclusion from the political arena. Therefore, through the national dialogue, they came to the conclusion that a negotiated approach undermining ideological issues enabled them to stay in the game.[58] Likewise, during his party campaign, Essebsi stated that Nidaa Tounes would not govern alone even in the case that the party received an absolute majority.[59] Following the 2014 parliamentary elections in which Nidaa Tounes won eighty-six seats and Ennahda sixty-nine seats in the 217 seat legislature, both parties chose to cooperate and came to a power-sharing agreement in which Nidaa Tounes assumed the presidency of the parliament and one of the vice presidential post was allocated to Ennahda while the other one went to the UPL. This reconciliatory attitude between parties became an important trait of the Tunisian political culture.

On the other hand, the case of Egypt following the uprisings stands in stark contrast to that of Tunisia in terms of elite bargaining and compromise. What the Egyptian transition has taught us has been the simple fact that elections alone don't guarantee a democratic transition.

The Egyptian case illustrated how limited agreement and compromise between the opposition groups thwarted prospects for a successful democratic transition. This was partly because Egypt didn't experience a political platform in which opposition political forces came to a common understanding on the principles of a new state, similar to the October 18 Coalition in Tunisia. The lack of consensus and negotiation among the political elite, first and foremost, resulted from the lack of a common understanding as to the meaning of democracy and the form of state they aspired to build. The Brotherhood, unlike Ennahda, was not eager to compromise on the character of the state, and when they talked about democracy, they referred to Islamic democracy which draws its legitimacy from *Sharia* and the sovereignty of God rather than sovereignty of people. In contrast, Ennahda leadership asserted that *Sharia* would not be the source of legislation and embraced a civic democratic state that guarantees freedom of religious practice.

In this regard, the form of Islamic constitutionalism that appeared in 2007 draft party platform of the Muslim Brotherhood was a clear indication of the restrictive and exclusive approach adopted by organization's hard-liners.[60] The draft party platform raised three controversial positions: First, the draft proposed a body of religious scholars to review draft legislation to determine its compliance to *Sharia*. Second, the draft opposed a female candidate for the office of presidency. Third, it opposed allowing a Copt to hold the office of presidency or prime ministry on the ground that the state plays a fundamental role in implementing *Sharia* and building the Islamic character of individuals and society.[61] Despite the calls from the reformist wing of the organization, the Brotherhood's senior leaders were not eager to align themselves with a political platform that would drastically differ from their agenda. Without a common understanding on the type of state to be established and the root of legitimacy it would derive from, Egypt's transition strayed from its intended path and faced precarious setbacks.

From its outset, post-Mubarak Egyptian politics focused exclusively on electoral politics instead of creating a platform for political elite to decide on the principles of the Egyptian state and its institutions. The deep problems embedded in the long-authoritarian system and the institutional endowment in Egypt were not to be overcome by elections, but by building a broad agreement among the political elite on the rules of the transition. From the ouster of Mubarak to the military coup, a total of five national elections or referenda were held. Indeed, after the authoritarian breakdown, frequent elections with short intervals aggravated the country's political woes by deepening the existing polarization and undermining prospects for dialogue among political actors to reconcile their differences. Exclusive focus on elections also deepened divisions rather than resolving them. While in Tunisia, political elite and civil society groups merged to establish institutions to talk about how to achieve a democratic system and a constitution, Egyptians were left with successive elections and referenda.

Elections by their nature mean parties' interests in maximizing their electoral gains. They also meant the exclusion of nonpolitical elite, youth movements, and labor unions from the political process in the Egyptian context. The outcome was a great imbalance between the Brotherhood and other political forces in terms of social base, organizational capacity and the lack of a political force that would counterbalance them, which facilitated the run-alone attitude of the Brotherhood, on the one hand, and exacerbated suspicion and fear on the part of secular circles, on the other.[62] In the end, a vicious circle arose in Egyptian politics in which Islamists blamed non-Islamists for refusing to accept election results while non-Islamists charged Islamists with using those elections to impose their political agenda unilaterally and undermine the development of democratic processes.[63]

In Egypt, the chances for elite consensus and compromise were undermined in the initial stage of the transition when the MB engaged in a tacit alliance with the military considering that Brotherhood's political interests would be ensured by a tacit alliance the military. To the Brotherhood's mindset, the military served as the sole political force that could challenge the organization and thus, a power-sharing agreement with the military would secure its interests in the long run. To this end, the Brotherhood carried out a campaign in favor of the interim constitution issued by the SCAF.[64] Once revolutionary groups took to the streets demanding investigation and fair trials of individuals killed by security forces during the uprisings and an end to trials of civilians in military courts, the Brotherhood organized pro-SCAF demonstrations and portrayed protestors as foreign agents aspiring to divide the country. Yet, the honeymoon between the SCAF and the MB came to an end shortly after the SCAF issued Al-Selmi document which granted the SCAF with broad powers while weakening the powers of the future president.

The initial alliance between the military and the Brotherhood divided the prorevolutionary forces, Islamists, and secularists who stood against the old regime together during the uprisings. It also allowed the military to take an advantage of this division and eliminate any prospect of a strong and united revolutionary force as it happened during the 2011 protests. To put it another way, if Muslim Brotherhood chose to reach a compromise with the revolutionary groups and other political parties and make concessions at critical points of the transition, the military would have harder time mobilizing the street against the Brotherhood and staging a coup would have been too costly for generals.

On the other hand, opposition parties and revolutionary groups failed to come up with a common strategy to stand against Morsi while protecting the revolution from the military tutelage. For instance, in Tunisia, under the 18 October Coalition, secular parties and opposition groups as well as Islamists came to an agreement that the new state would be free from any tutelage. Besides, secular parties united under an umbrella party Nidaa Tounes to counterbalance Ennahda in the elections. In Tunisia, the political elite were committed to stay within the realm of democratic processes. On the contrary, in Egypt secular political parties and revolutionary movements were too fragmented to unite against the Muslim Brotherhood while the umbrella organization *the National Salvation Front* made up of a number of opposition groups only operated as an agent for street protests and mobilizing people against Morsi and the Brotherhood. Just like in 2011 when the political stage was left to the military council after Mubarak was ousted, revolutionary groups and secular parties reprised the same mistake in 2013 by handing the revolution over to the military. Hence, Egypt suffered not only from the lack of consensus between Islamist and secular political elite against the old regime but also from the lack of a united opposition against the military.

LEADERSHIP STYLES OF THE TRANSITIONAL ACTORS

One of the underlying factors that determined the course of transition in Tunisia and Egypt has been Islamist parties' sudden and unexpected move from being political outsiders under the former authoritarian regimes to the political center in the new political system. Both the Brotherhood and

Ennahda emerged as underground movements to resist the authoritarian injustice with a religious agenda to establish Islamic society through grassroots activism. Unlike traditional political parties, these movements were not designed for open participation in a pluralist political landscape and democratic competition in their origin. When they moved to the political center, it was essential for their leaders to transform their movements from being an Islamic organization that aims at proselytism to a political party that both embraces democratic norms and conservative sensibilities of their base. Without such transformation, it would be very unlikely for Islamist parties to find a common ground with their ideological rivals and to engage in dialogue to establish democratic institutions.

Despite the fact that Ennahda and the Brotherhood share many common features and Ennahda is thought to be an offshoot of the Brotherhood, over decades the two movements have evolved in different directions and with different understandings of Islam and its relations to state and society. The crackdown on Islamists in Tunisia in 1989 forced Rachid Ghannouichi, the founder of Ennahda together with several leading figures of the movement to leave Tunisia for exile for two decades till the uprisings. Under Ben Ali regime, Islamists were banned from founding a party and taking part in politics, thus, the political space for Islamists was totally closed. In Egypt, on the contrary, despite brutal crackdowns on the Brotherhood, Mubarak regime granted the movement a limited space for political participation. Though the Brotherhood members were not allowed to found a political party, they managed to run as independent candidates in the legislative elections. Through their electoral success, Brotherhood members were able to obtain a certain degree of political clout in the Egyptian parliament. Nonetheless, the internal governance of the organization was tight-knit, inward-looking, and full of suspicion regarding the outside world.[65] In the years leading up to the uprisings, the Brotherhood's reformist wing aspiring for the evolution of the movement toward a more open, democratic, and pluralist movement was either repressed or excluded from the organization.

The Brotherhood's senior leaders were too concerned with ideology. In line with the movement's slogan "Islam is the solution," they maintained an Islamist ideology of state and society. Under the Guidance Bureau dominated by the Supreme Guide and the old guard, the Brotherhood held a strict and narrow minded worldview particularly on issues regarding the rights of women and non-Muslim minority groups. Morsi was a reflection of this current and in his speech, he continually stated his personal opposition to a women or Copt candidate for the presidency. Morsi also advocated for a constitution in which the role of Islam is dominant and *Sharia* is the source of legislation. On the contrary, despite the emergence of different factions within the Ennahda movement, Rachid Ghannouichi managed to reconcile different currents within the party and adopted a more consensual and pragmatic vision in his party's relation to the secular opposition. Under Ghannouichi, the movement portrayed itself a civic organization.

The Islamist discourse and practice witnessed in Tunisia and Egypt indicated considerable divergence. In Tunisia, Ennahda went through substantial moderation in the decade leading up to the uprising and the movement aspired for the establishment of a new system which reconciled Islam and democracy while ensuring the rights of women and religious minorities. Ghannouichi and other senior leaders reached out to the wider Tunisian public to ensure that if elected, they would not alter the civil character of the state into a religious state. Besides, Ennahda's discourse was in compliance with the political culture of the Tunisian society at large and the party laid the groundwork for pragmatic alliances with liberal and leftist parties. According to an analysis by the Arab Center for Research and Policy Studies (ACRPS)[66]:

> Renaissance (Ennahda) presented a clear-cut political platform that defined its preferred form and principles of government, and adopted a general approach despite the intellectual variations within its vast political spectrum. It also generated a political discourse that is open to secular parties and seeks to preserve the real national gains of both Tunisian society and the Tunisian state, including the establishment of institutions during the country's modern history. The party also addressed the Code of Personal Status and the rights of Tunisian women.

Ghannouchi is a farsighted leader who has internalized both the teachings of Islam and the principles of democracy. His life in exile in Europe for two decades might have also contributed to his broad vision of Islam and democracy. Under his leadership, Ennahda movement transformed itself from an underground resilience movement to a political Islamist party. With the ratification of the constitution in 2014, Ghannouichi announced that the new constitution ruled out the need for political Islam and the party was rebranded as a party of Muslim democrats.[67] The evolution of the movement's identity ensured Islamists would embrace the principles of democracy and democratic culture. Ghannouchi was aware that after Ben Ali's fall, one of the biggest challenges facing Tunisia's democratic transition was the polarization between Islamist and secular forces. To fend off secular circles' fears regarding Ennahda, he continually stated that the new Tunisian state would be a civil one and include all citizens.[68] Ghannouichi gave precedence to the build-up of a pluralist democratic system and vibrant multiparty politics in which Ennahda would be one of the political players within the system. Ennahda's discourse reflected their desire for a democratic state that could coexist with Islam. To this end, Ghannouichi advocated for an electoral formula (PR with Hare Quota-Largest Remainders

Formula) which substantially reduced the number of seats won by Ennahda in the Constituent Assembly. Ghannouichi convinced the party base that during the transition Ennahda wasn't ready to govern alone expressing that Tunisia should not be ruled by one dominant party and even an absolute majority was not enough in the times of transition.[69] Ghannouichi's support for coalition government after the first parliamentary elections saved Ennahda from being the scapegoat for the ills of the country during the transitional period.

On the other hand, Morsi's discourse was ideological and his leadership was shortsighted. While the Ennahda party approached politics in a consultative manner and didn't allow divisive ideological issues to jeopardize the continuation of dialogue, the Brotherhood brought ideology to the core of political agenda and focused more on consolidating power. Besides, the Brotherhood's political discourse was alarming to a great many seculars. The Brotherhood together with other Islamist parties issued a statement in 2011 in which it threatened opposition groups for calling for the introduction of supra-constitutional principles to govern the drafting of the future constitution with "unbearable consequences if they persisted in articulating these demands."[70] Sobhi Saleh, one of the senior leaders of the Brotherhood, threatened Al-Selmi, the deputy minister in the first interim government who drafted Al-Selmi document, that he should resign or else he "would bear the consequences of his nonresignation."[71] Al-Selmi had to resign after this explicit threat. Likewise, Azab Mustafa, a member in the Political Bureau of Ikhwan, also threatened that if any Brotherhood member were excluded, the Brotherhood would sabotage elections.[72]

The Brotherhood leaders at times labeled secular forces as anti-Islamic (*kafir*). The divisive and threatening political discourse used by the Brotherhood leaders closed the doors for dialogue with secular forces. One of the biggest mistakes of the organization was to underestimate the opposition groups' resistance to its policies and to ignore the demands of the revolution. Instead, the Brotherhood wrongly assumed that a power-sharing agreement with the military would ensure their governance based on election results. This was simply a wrong assumption. Though Mubarak was removed from power, the legacy and the holdovers of the old regime were still powerful. Behind their power lied the fact that the deep state (military, the security forces, and the judiciary) had much stake at a regime change while preserving the status quo served their political, economic, and ideological interests. Morsi undermined any type of policy disagreement with the political opposition as violation of the will of the Egyptian people or an attempt by the old regime supporters to overthrow the revolution.[73] By doing so, he detached the Brotherhood from any potential coalition against the old regime and found themselves in complete isolation when the transition reached an impasse.

Morsi didn't try to reach out to opposition groups and broader Egyptian civil society to find a common ground on the constitution drafting, the single most important document which would act as the basis of the future Egyptian state. Instead, confident of their social base and electoral success, the Brotherhood chose to dominate the Constituent Assembly with Salafists and struggled to finalize the constitutional process to meet the deadline despite the unrest and dissatisfaction continually expressed by opposition groups. The attempts to form a constituent assembly created several frictions as it was heavily dominated by Islamists. While the first assembly was dissolved by a court order for not being truly representative, the second assembly ended up with a similar outcome as most of the nonpartisan drafters who were supposed to be representatives of various institutions were chosen from people with Islamist inclinations. This nonconciliatory attitude of the Brotherhood aggravated the already existing gap between the two camps.

A further polarizing move was the November Decree issued by which Morsi granted himself broad powers and declared himself above any court in Egypt as the guardian of Egypt's revolution. The Brotherhood members tried to legitimize this decree by expressing the need for protecting the Constituent Assembly from a forced dissolution by the Supreme Constitutional Court. The effect was to ignite a new wave of protests, this time not against the military and the old regime but against the Brotherhood and the president. The decree also opened the way for mobilization of the street demanding the resignation of Morsi by opposition groups united under an umbrella organization, National Salvation Front (NSF) and those street protests set off the process which would culminate in military coup.

Islamists in both Egypt and Tunisia were confronted with similar set of problems, yet the way how the leadership of the power parties, Ennahda and the FJP, approached these problems made difference in the course of the transition. To begin with, in order to assure secular groups of their not having the intention to monopolize power, during their electoral campaign both Ennahda and the FJP announced that they would not run for presidency. Ennahda abided by its pledge and looked more credible and consistent in the eyes of opposition groups. On the other hand, the Brotherhood nominated Morsi for presidency. Furthermore, prior to the elections, the Brotherhood announced that they would compete for only half of the seats in the parliament and aimed to win roughly one-third of the seats.[74] The Brotherhood failed to keep this promise as well and raised suspicions as to the sincerity of the organization in the eyes of secular circles.

In addition, two parties took divergent paths during the political impasse in the constitution drafting process. Once the secular opposition threatened Ennahda to withdraw from the Constituent Assembly, Ennahda made a compromise and gave up any reference to *Sharia* in the constitution. In contrast, the Brotherhood simply turned a blind eye to all objections of the opposition and inserted *Sharia* to the constitution. When the opposition walked out of the Egyptian Constituent Assembly *en masse*, the Brotherhood went on to work alone and hastened the process to have a constitution written and ratified. In Tunisia, each time the opposition objected to certain articles, the work of the assembly slowed down and Ghannouichi and other senior figures engaged in dialogue with the opposition parties' leaders.

The most critical turning point emerged in both Tunisia and Egypt when the political impasse reached its climax in 2013. In Egypt, the opposition insisted on a governmental reshuffle, yet Morsi refused to compromise and he added more Brotherhood affiliates when a new ministerial reshuffle took place.[75] A political deadlock emerged and continuous street protests challenged the legitimacy of the president. Despite massive street protests, Morsi neither attempted to call for a broad national dialogue nor was willing to make concession to soothe the opposition. When the conflict reached to a point of no return with several violent clashes across the country and the military issued an ultimatum announcing that all political parties should meet the demands of the people or the military would intervene, Morsi rejected the ultimatum and responded by calling the Brotherhood members to the streets to guard democracy and confront the old regime forces. Increasing violence, in turn, handed the military the golden opportunity to take the matters into its own hands on a silver platter.

On the contrary, during the climax of the political crisis in Tunisia, Ennahda took part in the national dialogue initiated by the UGTT and three other unions. The national dialogue was not a linear path, and it was full of ups and downs. Even though the party base and several party members initially opposed the roadmap drawn by the Quartet, following the anti-Ennahda demonstrations and the second political crisis that erupted after the assassination of secular opposition leader Chokri Belaid, the party leadership agreed to step down and leave power to a technocratic interim government. Ghannouichi had an important role in convincing his party base that it was necessary for Ennahda to make compromise and to lose in the short term in order to win in the long one. By leaving the stage to the technocratic government till the next election, Ghannouchi assured that Ennahda would maintain its presence in the electoral game while at the same time he prevented his party from losing vote in the ballots when the country was facing a real political and economic instability.

The Egyptian transition indicated that a majoritarian democracy through which a political party governs based on the "will of the majority" argument at the expense of the sensitivities and demands of a sizeable minority doesn't allow for a smooth democratic transition. One important miscalculation of the Brotherhood leadership was perhaps their assumption that they would be allowed to govern based on their electoral success in the ballot box as long as they didn't confront the military. To this end, the Brotherhood legitimated and even mobilized public support for the military's interference in constitution writing when prodemocracy groups took to the streets protesting against the SCAF's constitutional declaration in March 2011.[76] Likewise, when military suppressed civilian protestors violently and tried around ten thousand civilians in military courts, or when virginity tests were conducted on female protestors detained, the Brotherhood didn't break their silence.[77] Morsi failed to challenge the status of the military elite and hold them accountable for the attacks on peaceful protestors, which were among the central goals of the revolution. The effect was that the public opinion sharply turned against the Brotherhood, and many liberals and non-Islamists who voted for Morsi in the second round of the presidential elections turned to the military for intervention.[78]

POWER EQUILIBRIUM AMONG POLITICAL FORCES

An important factor in transition from authoritarianism to democracy is equilibrium among existing power structures; in other words, democracy flourishes best in a country where power is evenly distributed among political forces. As early as 1939, Walter Lippmann noted that the survival of the national unity of a free system depends upon "a sufficiently even balance of political power to make it impracticable for the administration to be arbitrary and for the opposition to be revolutionary and irreconcilable; where that balance no longer exists, democracy perishes."[79] This kind of power equilibrium which offered competing political forces the opportunity to come to power didn't exist in Egypt. Instead of a vibrant political arena where divergent political parties and interest groups operated, in the aftermath of the uprisings Egyptians were faced with well-organized Islamists, on the one hand, and old regime forces, on the other. Non-Islamist and liberal parties had just begun organizing their networks and had a long way to reach out to Egyptians and gain their confidence. This was the very reason for the secular and leftists parties' constitution-first approach in contrast to Islamists' elections-first campaign.

The Egyptian social fabric is mostly composed of poor, conservative, and rural population whose traditional values go hand in hand with the Islamist institutions based on faith and family. In addition, Islamists enjoyed much better organizational skills and resource advantage given the long history of the Brotherhood. The political forces that could serve as a counterweight to Islamists were the secular left and labor unions as their backbone. Yet, the secular left was far from building ties among the political groups belonging to the same ideology and labor unions were weakened by the former authoritarian structure to be made to serve as a tool for surveillance. Thus, both groups were weak and fragmented, and they had little chance to counter the Brotherhood in the ballot box. The only force that could provide counterweight in this power equilibrium was the former ruling NDP with its well-organized political networks and business elite who could reach out to the party base. Nonetheless, the NDP was dissolved by a court order after the fall of Mubarak and the incumbents of the former regime were scattered along other political parties and didn't have the capacity to coordinate a unified electoral campaign that would challenge Islamists.

Eventually, the ouster of Mubarak created a political landscape where Islamists would dominate with Egyptian politics under a democratic system and their opponents would continually seek military intervention.[80] From the outset of the transition, the uneven balance of power favoring Islamists discouraged the secular leftist parties from confining their political aspirations to democratic means. Having realized that their parties had very little chance, if any, to grab power under democracy, those parties aligned themselves with the deep state and sought to overturn the democratic gains of the Brotherhood by undemocratic means. This uneven distribution of power explains why the courts intervened in political processes to impose some horizontal accountability on Islamists and opposition parties resisted Islamists' calls for parliamentary elections. In other words, Islamists' possible domination of Egyptian politics seemingly for a long time to come led the secular opposition to become revolutionary and irreconcilable as observed in the Tamarod movement's campaign and the military coup on July 3, 2013.[81]

The electoral outcome and power distribution among political forces in Tunisia created a context which gave incentives to divergent political groups to negotiate very early in the transition process. Ennahda won a plurality rather than a majority of the votes with 37 percent while 60 percent of Tunisian voters chose to support secular parties. Ennahda had to seek allies with secular parties and could only play a role in governance and the drafting of the constitution. Ghannouchi convinced his party members and the party base to seek reconciliation with secular parties, initially by referring to the fate of the political Islamists in Algeria in the 1990s and later to the Egyptian experience after the 2013 coup. Therefore, the distribution of power encouraged both seculars and Islamists to negotiate and come to a compromise on the key political issues surrounding the new constitution.

In the Egyptian case, uneven power distribution among political forces precluded all parties to play a role within the rules of the democratic game. FJP won an overwhelming victory in every electoral constituency they contested since March 2011. While it is true that they didn't get a massive majority, the electoral results clearly indicated that they could count on the support of their ideological fellows, Salafists.[82] The FJP and the Al-Nour Party together won 78 percent of the vote on the constitutional referendum in March 2011; 73 percent of the vote in the first parliamentary election in late 2011 and early 2012; 51.7 percent of the vote in the second round of the presidential elections in June 2012 and 64 percent of the vote in the constitutional referendum in November 2012.[83] These electoral outcomes convinced the Brotherhood leaders that they could easily win an absolute majority with the support of Salafists and thus, they didn't really manifest political commitment to negotiate with secular parties. They believed that their electoral gains gave them the legitimate authority to come to terms with the military on the direction of Egypt's transition.[84] Seeing the military as an opposition to their rule, they substantially ignored the secular and Coptic Christian communities' concerns while setting their political program.

The divergence in the democratic outcome between the two countries could also be attributed to the emergence of a breakdown in the mechanisms that generated and maintained the old distribution of power. Marina Ottaway notes a transition from an authoritarian regime to a democratic regime requires a redistribution of power, thus, a break in the status quo.[85] The removal of the president itself doesn't constitute a break in the status quo. In Tunisia, the ouster of Ben Ali created a power vacuum that no single actor could fill on its own, whereas the deposition of Mubarak didn't. In Tunisia, three competing social forces intervened in the transition process after the outbreak of the uprisings and the departure of the president: the UGTT, Ennahda, and a small group of veterans of the Bourguiba period.[86] Since Tunisia has a small and nonpoliticized army both unable and reluctant to have control over politics on the one hand, and divergent political forces and a robust civil society, on the other, a political context in which no single group could eliminate the others came out. This, in turn, facilitated the emergence of a pluralist society and political culture of negotiation and consensus making.

Contrary to Tunisia, Egypt had a giant military which was both able and willing to intervene in politics. Immediately after the departure of Mubarak, the SCAF assumed executive and legislative powers for the interim period until the election of a president. With the election of Morsi as the president, those powers were transferred to the president in theory. However, in reality, the military together with the elements of the deep state, the intelligence, the police, the judiciary, and the bureaucracy, had the upper hand in controlling politics and daily governance of the country. While the military allowed Morsi to govern for some time, the deep state was working behind the scene to turn public opinion against Morsi.

In Egypt, there existed a well-embedded state with a powerful and politically engaged military and the judiciary and unlike Tunisia, there was one socially embedded political force outside the state. Secular parties didn't have much popular support and mostly addressed to a small circle of elite. No political context came out like that of Tunisia where no actor was able to dominate and set rules on its own and thus, divergent political forces with similar chances had to compete for power. Hence, the Egyptian transition turned into a zero-sum game between the Muslim Brotherhood and the military and the other elements of the deep state.

INSTITUTIONAL ENDOWMENT

Institutional endowment, or state structure and character of the state institutions, is central to account for the different trajectories of transitions in Tunisia and Egypt. In terms of institutional design of the state bureaucracy, military stands as the most pivotal institution that matters to state survival and no revolution can succeed without the backing of the military. Theda Skocpol once argued that the success of a revolution lies in the state's capacity to maintain monopoly on the means of coercion.[87] In other words, if a state's coercive apparatus remains coherent and it has the capacity and the will to crush popular protests, a revolution has no chance to occur. Similarly, Eva Bellin argues that democratic transition can take place successfully only when the state's coercive apparatus lacks either the will or the capacity to suppress any sort of protestation from the public.[88] Accordingly, the very reason why the MENA region had been an exception in terms of democratic transition for decades lies in the robust coercive apparatus in these states. Bellin explains the variations in the outcomes of the Arab uprisings by the divergence in these states' coercive apparatus' will to repress the popular movements.[89]

In the context of the Arab Spring, the role of military has been a determining factor to the success or failure of revolutions. In each country, the ruler ordered the military to suppress protests by using force, however, the Arab militaries didn't respond uniformly. The uprisings only culminated in the demise of the authoritarian regime in relatively short time and peacefully in Tunisia and Egypt, where the armies sided with the protestors or at least didn't intervene in favor of the regime's survival. Tunisian and Egyptian militaries acted as rational actors based on cost-benefit calculations and sided with people calculating that it would be more costly to fire against their people in terms of legitimacy in the eyes of people since the size of popular protests had reached an unprecedented level.

Transition from an authoritarian rule to a democratic system can be carried out by the establishment of democratic civil-military relations. Even if democratic transition takes place and free and fair elections are held, a full-fledged civilian authority will not emerge and democracy will hardly consolidate unless democratic civil-military relations are established and the military steps down entirely out of the political sphere. Nonetheless, military's return to barracks doesn't ensure establishing democratic civil-military relations per se particularly if the military establishment tends to retain a measure of autonomy. The case of Egypt has manifested how officers in the Middle East can rule but not govern without ever having to step beyond the boundaries of their barrack.[90]

There seems to be a correlation between the military's departure from governance and politics and the process of liberalization and democratization.[91] The third wave of democratization indicated that those countries that have established a balanced and democratic civil-military relations and where the military establishment has focused primarily on external threats and national territorial integrity (e.g., former Communist States of Eastern and Central Europe) managed to undergo swift and successful democratic transitions. On the other hand, strong military forces and robust security apparatus have been generally regarded as a main obstacle to political reform and democratic transition. The previous transition experiences in the globe also indicate that militaries have often proved to be the last institution willing to allow for democratization.

Military establishment in much of the Middle East has acted as the guardian of authoritarian regimes and shared vested interests interwoven with those of the regime. Besides, in the Middle Eastern societies the image of the military as the guardian or the defender of the fatherland played into hands of military officers who have aspired to position themselves within the realm of politics. Military institutions often acted above politics and beyond civilian control fulfilling many functions which go beyond their standard mandate of defending the country. Military has often acted as the most resistant institution toward democratic change as such a change indeed involves potential dangers to the military's institutional interests. Thus, society-led revolutions are likely to culminate in a caretaker military junta which pledges to organize elections while not being interested in extricating themselves from power.[92]

Establishing civilian control over military has been the most arduous task of democratic transitions. Military officers attempt to retain as much control as they could at the expense of civilian authorities who struggle to design a new political system and determine military policies in the aftermath of a regime breakdown. In addition, a fully fledged democratic regime should outline military's role and its subordination to elected government officials in the constitution, leaving no space for provisions suggesting military tutelage. The central challenge for democratic consolidation lies in whether the transition succeeds in ruling out or preventing the emergence of a military coup. Nikolay Marinov and Hein Goemans have found that "three out of every four failures of democracy are the result of a successful coup d'état" posing the biggest threat to the success of democratic transitions following a regime breakdown.[93]

The resistance of militaries toward democratic change depends on the degree to which they are professional, institutionalized into authoritarian regime, and they are directly involved in policy-making and repression; in other words, the degree to which they are politicized. Institutionalized military has a corporate identity distinct from the state and the regime, and it is rule-governed, predictable, and meritocratic. In such military establishments, career advancement and promotion is based on performance, discipline is maintained through enforcement of merit-based hierarchy.[94] Military professionalism, on the other hand, requires a military establishment to be politically neutral and controlled by civilian authorities. According to Huntington, military professionalism involves three attributes such as expertise referring to education of military personnel, responsibility referring to the role of military as the defender of state, and corporatism which indicates the existence of a shared sense of unity among military personnel.[95]

Military institutionalism and professionalism often go hand in hand, that is, institutionalized militaries are the ones that are professional. The level of military institutionalism and professionalism determines the will of military establishment to disengage from power and allow political reform to proceed. Institutionalized military establishments assume that their power would not be ruined by political reform and are more likely to transfer power to a civilian authority to save the institutional integrity of military.

Politicization of a military also determines the extent to which civilian control over the military establishment could be achieved. Politicized militaries are characterized by the fact that the military elite exercise effective control over governance and play a role within extra-military areas within the state apparatus.[96] As it was the case in Egypt where the military is professional and institutionalized, if the military has historical legacy by successfully delivering on public goals like national defense and economic development, it is also likely to hold on to power by popular election. In general, politicized militaries have often played an important role in a country's independence struggle and have held the executive power through a military coup. The politicization of military poses a major threat to the consolidation of democratic processes and institutions as they are more likely to stage a coup when a civilian political party in power runs counter to the military elite in terms of ideological and political interests.

There are some more variables that enable necessary or sufficient conditions for the retreat of military from political power such as fiscal health, international support, popular mobilization, and the existence of a credible threat.[97] First, military establishment would be forced to open up the political space for democratic change when it can no longer maintain fiscal health.

Second, international support is also an important indicator of the robustness of security apparatus. High level of international support in the form of military aid by the Western countries to assure oil and gas supply security and to contain the Islamist threat has played into the hands of the military elite who aspire to position the military within politics and make them more unlikely to compromise for reform. Third, high level of popular mobilization for reform enable the military elite to give way to gradual implementation of demanded reforms as repressing thousands of people violently is costly for military risking its institutional integrity, international support, and domestic legitimacy. Fourth, the existence of a credible threat posed by a neighbor, such as the threat posed by Israel to its Arab neighbors, makes it more likely for the military to grow in size and enjoy broad popular support while reinforcing its robustness in the face of reform demands.

The high level of institutionalization and professionalism of the Tunisian and Egyptian militaries played a critical role in the removal of the autocrats. Generals in the army supported mass protests not because of their commitment to democratic norms and values but because they calculated that their interests would be served better in the case of a regime breakdown while siding with the regime in the face of massive popular mobilization might cost their legitimacy and popular support. Yet, once the authoritarian leader was deposed, Tunisian military elite announced that they would leave the political scene to civilian control, whereas the SCAF in Egypt was determined to take the matters into its own hands and run the country alone. While the Tunisian transition is characterized by civilian-led transitional mechanisms, the SCAF shaped the course of the transition by considerably liming the space left to civilian mechanisms. Even when space for civic interaction among political forces was created, the SCAF continually stepped in the transition as an arbitrator. The different roles played by the two armies have remarkably changed the destination of the two countries' political transition.

The military establishments in Tunisia and Egypt have different characteristics in terms of their size, historical legacy, political engagement, and institutional capability. Tunisia has a small, professional, and depoliticized army with little experience in political engagement and over time it has acquired an institutional culture that accepts civilian supremacy.[98] Tunisian independence didn't take place through a military coup and military officers played a negligible role during the independence and instead, it was driven by civilian resistance fighters led by Habib Bourguiba who was a lawyer. To fend off the threat of a military coup, Bourguiba intentionally kept the military small and granted it a minimal role, if any, in the political affairs of the country. Once in power, Ben Ali also maintained this strategy and kept the military on the periphery while relying on internal security forces which were more generously funded and bigger in size. On the other hand, the Tunisian military is poorly equipped and funded and Tunisia has the least defense spending in North Africa.[99]

The military in Tunisia acted on the sole mandate of border defense and aid supply to civilians in need. Since independence, Tunisian Armed Forces didn't engage in a major war and ward off a security threat that could gain the army prestige and popular support. Therefore, historically the Tunisian military hasn't stood as an institution that is of great significance and weight. Besides, the army enjoyed weak relationship with the presidential family, which paved the way for the army's increased institutionalization and professionalism and little incentive on the generals' side to protect the president and his family on the eve of the uprisings. Decades of deliberate policy to starve the military of resources and to limit its operations by Bourguiba and Ben Ali paid off following the regime breakdown. Once Ben Ali was removed from power, the Tunisian military had neither the political will nor the capacity to impose itself as the sole authority and to reap the benefits of the revolution. Instead, early in the transition, the Tunisian military withdrew to its barracks and left the political scene to the interim government made up of civilian political elite.

By contrast, Egypt possesses a very large military that is highly institutionalized and professional with a long history of political engagement and an institutional culture that doesn't accommodate the notion of civilian supremacy. To begin with, the politicization of the military in Egypt is closely linked to the leading role played by the military officers during the independence struggle of the country. British colonizers were dismissed from the country after the Free Officers Coup in 1952. Since then, the military's strongmen took control of the country's political life. Second, under Nasser the Egyptian military nationalized economic enterprises of the country and carried out massive infrastructure and development projects, thus, the military acted as the vanguard of economic modernization and progress. The military also developed vested economic interests by building economic enterprises and having them managed by its own cadres. The Egyptian military is predicted to control around one-fifth of the economy.[100] Third, thanks to Egypt's strategic position in the Middle East and the security threat posed by the Israeli-Palestinian conflict, the Egyptian military enjoyed a long-standing political support and financial aid by the United States, which strengthened the army's role in political affairs. Therefore, Egyptian military had various economic and political interests at stake on the eve of the uprisings.

Bringing the SCAF as the main powerbroker, the military-led transition in Egypt was tainted from the outset. At this point, Atef Said pointed to two paradoxes: First, the army leaders could be seen as part of the regime that the revolution was aimed at replacing. Second, it was the military which is an institution based on hierarchy, strict regulation, and obedience, leading the transition to democracy.[101] The military's institutional interests were embedded in preserving the status quo. It was the massive size of the popular mobilization against Mubarak that left little choice to generals but reluctantly bow to people's will. To protect and further its privileged position and institutional interests, it took the reins of power once Mubarak was toppled.

During the transition, the SCAF has taken significant steps to ensure that ultimate power, be it political or economic, lies in the hands of the military. First, it refused any call to share power with civilian representatives of political forces in a presidential council.[102] Instead, the SCAF assumed executive and legislative powers until the presidential elections of June 2012. Ahead of the elections, the SCAF issued Al-Selmi document which outlined supraconstitutional principles that gave the military immunity from civilian oversight and enabled it to dominate the constitutional process even after election of a new parliament. In addition, the SCAF shaped the transitional period by appointing successive technocratic governments composed of SCAF loyalists and Mubarak-era incumbents so that the power structures of the Mubarak era could remain largely intact. It also acted as a veto player through its cooperation with the judiciary. The Supreme Constitutional Court passed a controversial verdict by announcing the dissolution of the elected parliament on the ground that part of the electoral law was unconstitutional granting the SCAF full legislative powers until the election of a new parliament. The attempt by the judiciary to disqualify the Brotherhood dominated parliament from operating was indeed a judicial coup and it was an outcome of the long-standing engagement of the judiciary in politics with its politically motivated and ideologically driven court rulings. The judiciary acted in line with the military given that the institution was dominated by Mubarak-era holdovers with its political and ideological interests embedded in preserving the status quo.

From the standpoint of democratization, what matters to democratic transition is not the military itself, but the nature of civil-military relations. Stepan noted, "the less inclined civilians are to abdicate their right to rule to soldiers in exchange for military protection against the perceived threats from class or sectarian rivals newly empowered by democracy, the better the chances for a successful democratic transition not constrained by excessive influence or privileges in the hands of the military."[103] As indicated in various opinion polls, average Egyptians viewed the military as a symbol of unified national power, determination, and a remedy to the problems of civilian disunity, partisanship, and uncertainty. A closer look into the larger political scene reveals a problem that is deeply engrained in the Egyptian politics: a widely shared belief that the arbitration role of the military as a strongman is essential to have things on track. Almost all political parties and groups not only acquiesced but also embraced the SCAF as the leader of the transition process. The Brotherhood's attempts to ally itself with the SCAF in 2011, the opposition political forces' turning to the military for a takeover in 2013 and the rise of Al-Sisi to presidency as a national hero all reveal the problematic nature of civil-military relations in Egypt. In addition, pro-democracy groups and political forces refused to meet the President Morsi during the political crisis of 2012, instead asked to meet with the defense minister who is chosen from among the top generals in the military.[104] The fact that SCAF emerged as an arbiter between increasingly polarized political factions stamped out the potential emergence of civilian-led mechanisms and coalitions like the Ben Achour Commission in Tunisia.

The contrasting cases of Egypt and Tunisia served as striking examples for potential constraints and opportunities posed by the strong legacy of military during transitions. A well-institutionalized military and security apparatus in Egypt encouraged political actors with divergent ideologies to separately negotiate with the military rather than with themselves in an attempt to maximize their political gains while alienating other political actors from the negotiation process.[105] The political crisis at the end of 2012 and early 2013 allowed the military to easily manipulate the democratic processes by positioning itself as the guardian of the revolution as each opposition party turned to the military for intervention. In Tunisia, on the other hand, a full autocracy that lacked the legacy of a similar arbiter before the uprisings created a context in which opposing political forces had to either fight or negotiate, thus, increasing their incentives for pact-making process.[106]

Under the patronage of the military, the transition implemented in Egypt has not allowed a real regime change, instead, it brought a structural change to the regime replacing the political and business elite associated with Mubarak with those of the military in the post-revolution. The authoritarian institutions and the way how they operated were kept intact. Political actors solely focused on power grab rather than creating democratic mechanisms and essential checks and balances over legislative, executive, and judiciary branches of the government. Without these checks and balances, elections alone didn't bring a genuine power transfer to a civilian authority. On the other hand, the long-standing legacy and political engagement of the military makes it extremely costly for political actors to struggle to bring the military under civilian control. The strong and politicized military establishment easily stepped in to overturn the democratic transition for the fear that the new president would strip them of their powers. As Stepan and Linz aptly noted, should the coercive apparatus find it difficult or unpleasant to coexist with democratic elements, a transition toward fully fledged authoritarianism via military coup is the most likely scenario.[107] The result was reversion to *ancien* regime in Egypt where the emergency law is reinstated, military trials of civilians were expanded, civil society and opposition forces are repressed, and human rights violations become more of a norm rather than the exception.

CIVIL SOCIETY

Since the end of the Cold War, Western scholars have embraced the concept of civil society as a precondition for democratic transition. The successful transition experiences of Latin American and Eastern European countries in the 1980s and 1990s, respectively, demonstrated that civil society is an important agent of democratization. Later, from 2000 onwards, popular upheavals in Georgia, Ukraine, and Kyrgyzstan, and more recently in the Arab world have once again manifested people power versus the power of authoritarian rulers. Both democratic transition and consolidation entails a vibrant civil society through which political participation is promoted, space for public engagement is opened, the power of government is controlled and in certain ways limited and above all, a sense of democratic values is developed.

In broader terms, civil society can be defined as an open public sphere, where individuals discuss and coordinate their interests, identify with the common good and reconcile their conflicting interests by making use of voluntary associations. Hence, three elements are vital to the concept of civil society: being independent from the state and the market, unrestrained space, and a set of shared values and interests. Nonprofit organizations, religious organizations, labor unions, business associations, interest, and advocacy groups as well as more informal political, social, and religious movements fall into the sphere of civil society.

Civil society offers various social and cultural underpinnings that set the stage for democratic governance. Through involvement in civil society, citizens acquire and disseminate certain values fundamental to democratic participation and collective action. Larry Diamond points to the two generic ways civil society advances democracy: First, it helps to generate a transition from authoritarian rule to at least electoral democracy. Second, it helps to deepen and consolidate democracy once it is established.[108] Various types of civic organizations play a key role in how transition occurs, violently or peacefully, gradually or abruptly and whether it results in democracy or to some new form of authoritarian or hybrid regime.

Gabriel Almond and Sidney Verba stressed the connection between democracy and civil society in that democratic order requires civil culture which develops through civic engagement. They argued that civil society organizations can be considered as micro-constitutions as citizens get accustomed to the formalities of democratic decision-making through them.[109] Besides, civil society allows individuals the opportunity to express, institutionalize, and mediate their divergent interests by means of voluntary associations, hence, it enables peaceful settlement of conflicts by reconciling conflicting interests.[110]

Civil society and democratization thesis assumes that an energetic associational life composed of voluntary organizations distinct from the state, economy, and family can trigger democratic transitions by challenging autocratic leaders and forcing the state to accept liberal reforms. This thesis has been challenged by various tactics of the entrenched autocrats in the MENA region. Civil society has witnessed a renaissance by the late 1980s in much of the Arab world when economic regression, rising youth population, and increasing level of education combined to bring about widespread frustration with the state. However, the increase in civil society activism in the region could rather be seen as state-led processes of controlled liberalization instead of autonomous associational activity. This was more a function of authoritarian rulers' strategy of "authoritarian upgrading" through which they responded to social, economic, and international changes by modifying their modalities of rule as a substitute for, rather than a step forward full democratization.

Despite the fact that civil society was seen to boom in numbers, its effectiveness was undermined by a number of factors. First, there was a restrictive legal framework under which civil society organizations (CSOs) were heavily regulated, restricted, and banned. Regimes often allowed the remaining CSOs to create a democratic facade and as a party of wider strategy of survival while using various strategies such as containment, control and cooptation to undermine the effectiveness of those organizations. In several states in the region including Tunisia and Egypt, CSOs must register with the Ministry of Interior or Social Affairs which make use of complicated "Associations Laws" to bring those organizations under tight state control.[111] Besides, provisions related to maintenance of public order and national security granted authorities the right to dissolve CSOs and harass activists. Authoritarian regimes also undermined the effectiveness of CSOs by creating a state-monopolized civil society framework in which civil society organizations were run by civil servants and relied on government funding, thus, their agenda were largely determined by the government. Finally, civil society in the MENA region is characterized by the secular-Islamist divide due to conflicting visions of both parties over various issues including liberal democratic norms and values, the role of Islam in state and society relations, and the role of women. The secular-religious divide in civil society has been exploited by the authoritarian rulers to eliminate threats to the status quo.

In a similar vein, in the context of the Arab transitions, the existence of civil society both prior to and during the transition phase looms large. Indeed, a very powerful explanation for the divergent outcomes of the post-Arab Spring MENA countries lies in the existence and engagement of civil society actors in the transition. In the Arab countries, where the authoritarian regimes maintained the tightest control over the society and used the harshest methods to suppress the opposition, such as Syria and Libya, the regime change was the most chaotic with high level of violence involved or the country turned into civil war. In contrast, in the countries which enjoyed a vibrant civil society and trade unions prior to the uprisings despite the restrictions they faced, the transition phase was much smoother and promising. In that regard, both Mubarak and Ben Ali regimes pursued more liberal politics than their predecessors. In turn, in both Tunisia and Egypt, civil society had tremendous role during the transition though there has been significant differences between the two countries, particularly in terms of the evolution of trade unionism and their impact on the transition process.

By the turn of the new century, controlled liberalizing reforms initiated in most countries stalled while in several countries like Egypt and Tunisia, they gave their way to tighter restrictions on civil liberties and political pluralism. Hence, neither the surge in civil society nor enhanced support from external actors culminated in any tangible outcome toward substantial democratic reform in the years leading up to the uprisings. The outbreak of the Arab uprisings were characterized by the emergence of new social movements that were leaderless, nonideological, and free from organizational structures.[112] In both Tunisia and Egypt, popular participation in the protests was very heterogeneous including ordinary citizens without political affiliation, political parties, trade and labor unions, women's associations, Islamic organizations, human rights movements, and other opposition movements. Once mass protests broke out, CSOs were mobilized against the regime, yet no group emerged as overwhelming or was in a position to set forth an alternative political project to the former regime.[113]

In Tunisia and Egypt, popular mobilization continued after the ouster of autocrats because of the deep divide between revolutionary factions and the transitional rulers, substantial deterioration in the economies, disruption of essential public services, as well as security challenges. In Egypt, in addition to these reasons, there were other factors lying behind demonstrations: violent sectarian attacks, the SCAF's monopoly over the transition, disagreement, and ideological clashes over the constitution. In Tunisia, there was a widespread civil political unrest due to dissatisfaction with the interim government' little progress in line with the goals of the revolution, yet compared to Egypt, demonstrations remained more peaceful in nature and response from security forces didn't involve much violence. Similar to Egypt, NSF, an umbrella of opposition parties and Tunisian Tamarod movement, albeit much smaller in size and weaker in effect, called for the resignation of the government and the dissolution of the parliament. Unlike Egypt, in Tunisia civil society groups, particularly labor unions, took a leading role in conciliating social unrest through bringing political actors to the table for negotiation.

Compared to Egypt, the civil society framework in Tunisia was better situated to contribute to its democratic transition. Tunisian civil society is heterogeneous in that it is composed of religious groups, nonreligious organizations, and labor unions. This heterogeneity enabled mobilization of voters into the first democratic elections through civil society networks of political contestants from across the political spectrum. Besides, Tunisia's vibrant civil society in which labor unions and non-Islamist civil society groups posed counterbalance to Islamist groups was well-grounded to ensure political pluralism and create a setting in which no single group could dominate the political and constitutional processes. By contrast, Egypt's civil society was largely constructed around religious ideals and it predominantly relied on the Islamist communal activism and charities through mosques or Islamist NGOs. Islamist organizations had much stronger efficiency and social base compared to their secular counterparts. Yet, these organizations are guided by Islamist ideology, the belief that Islam should dominate social and political as well as personal life, and they have sought stricter religious observance and a revolutionary transformation of their societies in the light of Islam. The challenge in the Egyptian transition lay in the fact that a significant portion of Islamist organizations, majority of which belonged to the Brotherhood, embraced democracy as far as it would bring them political power, hence, as a tool rather than an end. On the other hand, secular NGOs and human rights organizations were co-opted by the Mubarak regime and relied on either government funding or external aid. Most of those organizations are elitist in structure with weak ties with the society to coordinate with and they failed to channel the demands of the society, which was evident in their trivial role during the uprisings and its aftermath.

Alfred Stefan aptly points to the distinction between the tasks of resistance movements within the civil society that help to deconstruct authoritarianism and the tasks of political society that help to construct democracy. In Stepan's terminology, a political society refers to organized groups of political activists who not only rally resistance to dictatorship but also negotiates among themselves on how to overcome mutual fear and agree upon the rules for a democratic outcome.[114] A political society also helps to construct democracy by bringing opposition leaders into agreement on plans for interim government and elections that would generate constitution-drafting bodies.[115] Tunisia had a political society that developed in parallel to civil society whereas in Egypt political society was nonexistent.

In Tunisia, a political society flourished far before the authoritarian regime's crackdown. The consensus-oriented tradition in Tunisia results from the gradual construction of a dialogue between the secular groups and Ennahda, a political rapprochement which began eight years before the fall of Ben Ali. In June 2003, representatives from four of Tunisia's major non-regime parties—Ennahda, the CPR, Ettakatol, and the PDP—met in France and signed "A Call from Tunis" (*Appel de Tunis*) in which they negotiated on fundamental principles of the future Tunisian state: any future government would draw its sole source of legitimacy from the sovereignty of the people and the state while showing respect for the people's identity and its Arab-Muslim values would provide the guarantee of liberty of beliefs to all and the political neutralization of places of worship.[116] This dialogue among leftist, liberal democrats, and Islamists enhanced and in 2005, "The 18 October Coalition for Rights and Freedoms" was formally established among political parties and CSOs of diverse, and even contradictory ideological orientations on the basis of a common goal: achieving the rule of law and basic rights and liberties. In its manifesto, the October 18 coalition stated that it struggled to "lay the foundations for a democratic transition aimed at ending dictatorship and building the institutions of the state on the basis of democratic legitimacy rooted in respect for the sovereignty of the people, free from any form of tutelage, the practice of democratic succession of leaders, intellectual and political pluralism, and the safeguarding of human rights" and the manifesto touched upon liberal family code and building a strong civil society.[117]

The manifesto illustrates that a dialogue among disparate political forces began far before Ben Ali's fall and it enabled those actors to decide on the key issues surrounding the transition such as forming an interim government and holding elections with much ease. This political society extended to the formation of the Ben Achour Commission soon after the authoritarian breakdown and the commission acted as a platform where representatives of civil society groups as well as political parties discussed critical issues on the electoral and constitutional processes at length and came to consensus on the general rules of the transition.

On the contrary, Egypt fell short of a political society that would enable a platform to reconcile the conflicting interests of political forces. In Egypt, in the absence of established CSOs that rallied people for democratic change, civic movements led by prominent activists such as Kefaya, April 6 Movement, and the NCA took the lead in mobilizing people for prodemocracy reforms in the years leading up to the 2011 uprisings. These prodemocracy movements were not formally established CSOs, instead, they were loosely structured networks free from the hierarchical structure typically found in a traditional civil society organization. Thus, they managed to reach out to people from diverse ideological background and affiliations, and rally people for mass protests. In the post-Mubarak era, they organized numerous protests and sit-ins to push the SCAF to submit power to a civilian authority and put an end to violations of rights and abuse of civilians. However, these pro-democracy movements failed to play a constructive role in the transition since they mainly coordinated their actions into street protests to oppose the policies of the interim government. They were not able to channel street activism into a united collective opposition force due to high level of fragmentation and weak internal cohesion within these movements. In addition, these groups remained aloof from party politics and didn't attempt to act as a mediator or arbiter between political parties. Their sole focus on street politics organizing demonstrations and protests led to their alienation and marginalization.

Civil society played a central role in moving the country toward democratic direction in Tunisia. Civil society played two critical roles during the transition: First, it acted as a watchdog keeping track of the performance of the interim government and the NCA on leading the transition and constitutional drafting, respectively. For instance, when religiously conservative articles that ran counter to gender equality were proposed in the new constitution, liberal and feminist organizations organized wide-scale protests in Tunis.[118] Second, civil society acted as a mediator and arbiter between the two opposing camps by facilitating dialogue and compromise among political actors when the course of transition bogged down in the midst of ideological confrontations.

In Tunisia, the political deadlock emerged mainly due to two reasons: First, there was a continuous delay in the adoption of the new constitution because of ideological clashes between Ennahda and other parties. Second, the troika government was severely criticized for its low-grade performance in the economic field and deteriorating security conditions due to rising acts of violence perpetrated by hardline religious groups and two high-profile political assassinations. Against this backdrop, Tunisian politics was characterized by continuous demonstrations and protests on the streets while the outlook for democracy was grim due to lack of trust and ideological division among the political elite. It was in this context that the UGTT stepped in and initiated the Tunisian National Dialogue Quartet in cooperation with other three key organizations; the UTICA, the LTDH, and the ONAT. Under the patronage of the UGTT, the national dialogue brought the political parties in the troika government on the table to discuss and agree on a plan that would lead the country out of the political impasse. The dialogue began in October 2013 and lasted for three months until political parties agreed on a roadmap that covered the governmental, constitutional, and electoral processes. Eventually, the unions' efforts paid off and the dialogue succeeded in the management of the political crisis and opened the way for a consensual constitution and the establishment of a technocratic government till the holding of the parliamentary elections.

In Tunisia, the success of the national dialogue is deeply rooted in the country's organized labor movement whose organizational weight and historical legitimacy have no parallel in the region. The UGTT, the national confederation of labor unions, was founded in 1946 following its break with the French CGT (General Confederation of Labor). The organization served as a cornerstone of the Tunisia's independence movement during the colonization period. Farhat Hached, the founder of the UGTT, learned union activism in the CGT, the French communist-leaning union where he had been a member for fifteen years before he founded the union in Tunisia. He resigned from the CGT due to its lack of support for Tunisians' struggle to gain independence from France indicating that the UGTT has been more than a labor union from its inception.[119] The union gained political legitimacy both nationally and internationally when Hached used the union to exert pressure on the French authorities for more social and political rights for Tunisia and casted a role for the union in the national liberalization struggle.

Once Tunisia gained its independence, the Tunisian president Habib Bourguiba attempted to mobilize the UGTT's prestige to consolidate his legitimacy and establish his own domination thereby creating a complex relationship between the labor union and the Tunisian state.[120] Unlike the other unions in the region which are entirely integrated into the state authority, the UGTT has enjoyed a considerable degree of autonomy from the ruling regime due to both its historical role and legitimacy gained through the independence struggle and its ambivalent relationship with the regime. The organization at times acted as a partner of the regime and other times as an opposition force mobilizing popular revolts against it. First, under Bourguiba, the union was integrated into the state machinery through several of its leading members appointed to important ministerial and bureaucratic positions in the state. Second, the union confronted the ruling regime during times of crisis and it supported various social movements structurally and politically. The UGTT was at the heart of the protest movements that created resistance to liberal economic reforms and massive privatization projects such as the general strike in 1978, the bread riots in 1984 and the protest movements demanding employment, better working conditions, and social justice in the Gafsa Mining Basin in 2008, the strikes in Ben Gardane in 2010, and Sidi Bouzid in 2011.

In a similar vein, one particular character of the Tunisian Revolution was that the protests originated in the offices of the UGTT where the union leaders opened their offices to the protestors and took a leading role in organizing rallies, marches and regional strikes. It was the UGTT activists who passed footage of Bouazizi's self-immolation to Aljazeera a day before organizing protests in Sidi Bouzid bringing the events of 2011 to the world attention.[121] After Ben Ali was removed from power, the UGTT continued to exert its influence over the interim government through the sit-ins, strikes, and protests it rallied. Therefore, during the climax of the political crisis, it came as no coincidence that the UGTT took on a mediating role between political actors and put pressure on them to accept its transitional roadmap to join the national dialogue.

In contrast, Egypt never had a strong labor union that existed independently from the regime. The Egyptian Trade Union Federation (ETUF), the leading labor union in Egypt was founded in 1957 by Gamal Abdel Nasser as a tool to bring labor activism under control. Under a state-controlled economy where several economic benefits and job security were provided to rank-and-file workers, there was no room left for the ETUF to play collective bargaining role or voice labor's demands to the regime. The union served as a state apparatus to maintain control over workers while mitigating economic benefits granted to workers under Nasser. During the last decade of Mubarak's rule, the ETUF's leadership became increasingly submissive to the regime and the regime interfered more heavily in the unions' elections.[122] Having been co-opted by the regime, the ETUF's executive board remained disconnected from rank-and-file workers, which forced labor activists to press for their demands outside the ETUF channels. The adverse effects of economic liberalization and massive privatization led Egyptian workers to stage unprecedented number of protests from 2004 to 2011. During the January 2011 uprisings, the ETUF leadership sided with the regime attempting to discourage workers from participating in the protests, however, labor activists mobilized workers and organized their own anti-regime protests independently from the union.[123] Despite the labor protests that contributed to the mass protests in 2011, the lack of leadership in the union and poor organizational structure undermined workers' power and precluded them from acting as a unified working class that would exert influence over transitional actors. In the post-Mubarak period, the successive governments attempted to take control of labor unions rather than negotiating with them for potential reforms.

In short, civil society mobilization was critical to the success of the uprisings in 2011 in both Tunisia and Egypt. However, in Tunisia civil society was central not only to the breakdown of the authoritarian regime but also to the maintenance of the democratic transition. CSOs and particularly labor unions acted as a catalyst in shaping the country's political transition along the desired outcomes. Egyptian civil society, on the other hand, was poorly organized and was not unified and strong enough to emerge as an arbiter or mediator. Therefore, transition in Egypt turned into a mere political game between two dominant actors: the Brotherhood and the military.

EXTERNAL INFLUENCE

Although most scholars in democratization field have concerned themselves with internal factors influencing democratic transitions, since the 1990s there has been an increasing scholarly interest in moving beyond internal factors when seeking to understand the specificities of political change. The end of the Cold War and the transition of several former communist states to democracy in a rather short period was indicative of the interplay between internal and external factors. External influence, whether it is military, economic or political, is central to explaining the authoritarian resistance in the Arab world which has long been subject to foreign influence beginning with the rise of colonialism, and continuing with the Cold War.

International influence on democratic transition often takes place in two ways: Leverage emerges when a state or a group of states use(s) political, economic, or military power to encourage or discourage a state in transition. Linkage exists when civil society actors, political movements, and institutions in a country are tied to those of democratic countries or Western led multilateral institutions.[124] There are several mechanisms of leverage such as diplomatic pressure, democratic conditionality, military intervention, and economic integration, among which conditionality comes to fore in pushing a state in transition toward democracy. Individual states or regional or international organizations could impose democratic conditionality to facilitate democratic transition of post-authoritarian states by offering it "carrots" to protect democracy such as financial support, free trade or market access, and membership in desirable organizations. On the other hand, this conditionality also includes "sticks" to a country in transition in the case of noncompliance to desired progress in building democratic institutions such as the threat of sanctions, terminating membership of international or regional organizations, and suspending financial aid.

In the context of the post-Arab Spring Middle East, the Arab countries swept by the uprisings of 2011 has poor linkage to the democratic countries of the West. Given the lack of an Arab democracy, they also had no model to aspire to in the region. Besides, Arab publics have been suspicious of the democracy promotion agenda of the United States in the region as they have witnessed its destructive impacts on countries such as Iraq, Afghanistan, Yemen, and Libya. The U.S. policies in the region have led to substantial anti-American sentiments and suffered from legitimacy in the eyes of Arab citizens. According to the Arab Barometer carried out soon after the uprisings, Egyptians and Tunisians mainly consider American influence on their countries negative and they see foreign influence as an obstacle to reform.[125]

On the other hand, in terms of leverage, international actors have been unwilling or unable to provide the kind of financial and political support that was so helpful in promoting or facilitating political and economic reforms implemented in Eastern and Central Europe. Western actors have been ambivalent about Arab transitions and combined with the effects of economic crises and internal challenges, they focused primarily on whether transitions in the region would serve their interests, thus, their suspicions and hesitancy tempered their response and prevented the mobilization of large-scale resources.[126] They failed to exert conditionality or diplomatic pressure to encourage democratic transitions in the region. Instead, Western support for the political change in the region has been defined by their strategic interests and security concerns.

From 2005 onwards, democratic elections held in the region meant the rise of Hezbollah in Lebanon, the victory of Hamas in the Palestinian elections, political Islamists in local elections in Saudi Arabia, and militias-backed Shiite Groups in the Iraqi parliament. These developments marked a significant turning point in the American democracy promotion and freedom agenda. The U.S. foreign policy in the Middle East confronted a democracy-stability dilemma, while the former was supposed to promote Western values and bring about more predictable governments with broad-public support, the latter was regarded as a more direct and likely outcome of supporting the existing military-backed autocrats in the region.

Western governments found their security interests in advancing their relationships with secular-minded autocrats aligned with the West due to their vested interests in the region such as ensuring the security of the oil supplies and energy corridors, containing Islamic fundamentalism, and protecting Israel's security. To this end, fearing of any Islamist takeover, the United States and the European Union gave precedence to relations with the ruling autocrats and avoided making reference to derailing human rights and civil liberties under Mubarak and Ben Ali regimes for decades. In a similar vein, they watched the course of events as they unfolded in Tunisia and Egypt, and they gave political support to the ouster of autocrats only after their removal from power became inevitable. Therefore, by 2011, it was certain that Arab countries in transition would have to depend on their internal dynamics for democratic change and would not enjoy political and financial aid for achieving democratic transition as was the case with the Eastern European States from 1990s onwards.

With respect to Egypt and Tunisia, external influence has played a divergent role. Foreign intervention has had stronger influence in Egypt when compared with Tunisia. Due to neighboring Israel, controlling the Rafah Gate and the Suez Canal and accommodating almost one-fourth of the population of the Arab world, Egypt is thought to be a pivotal country enjoying substantial geostrategic significance in the region and thus, it is considered to be a vital ally for the United States. Tunisia, on the other hand, is a small country having a population of only eleven million with very little oil and gas resources. It is geographically disconnected from the Israeli-Palestinian conflict and the politics of the Levant, which has made Tunisia a country of a less strategic influence in the region. On the other hand, Tunisia received much of its foreign funding from European countries both before and after the uprisings. In Egypt, economic and social development aid and civil society funds from the European countries and international institutions have been remarkable both prior and after of the uprisings, however, it was the U.S. aid, both military and economic, and the financial aid from the Gulf States that have considerably impacted the course of the transition serving to protect the status quo.

In pre-revolution Tunisia, political foreign assistance was an exception rather than the rule. Under Ben Ali, of around 9,000 associations operated throughout the country, most concentrated their activities on social and cultural issues. By law, associations were banned from working on themes related to human rights or other political fields. The legally restrictive framework forced the international donors to restrain from touching political subjects, and steered them toward working more on cultural and social issues. Besides, prior to the uprising, Tunisia had not been an attractive destination for international donors due to both its narrow strategic importance and low-impact potential arising from the repressive political environment. Before 2011, major international donors active in Tunisia mainly consisted of the EU Institutions including the European Commission and several EU member states such as France, Spain, Germany, Switzerland, and Italy. France has stood out as the most important aid donor providing almost 30 percent of the total financial assistance Tunisia received from international donors. This was to be expected as Tunisia remained in France's sphere of influence due its colonial heritage and the close bilateral relations between the two countries in cultural, social, and economic spheres. Besides, the European governmental and nongovernmental donors have enjoyed a great deal of reputation due to their contribution to Tunisian human rights defenders and civil society even before the revolution providing just below three-quarters of Tunisia's Official Development Assistance (ODA),[127] and the European presence in Tunisian civil society and other areas of development has expanded considerably after 2011.

Prior to 2011, the United States didn't provide significant financial assistance to Tunisia in the post-revolution era, and it didn't appear to be among the top ten donors that provided ODA to Tunisia in economy, social and civil society sectors according to the 2010–2011 data of OECD Aid statistics.[128] Besides, the U.S. assistance to Tunisia differs considerably from other countries in the region where majority of assistance is for military and security, yet military aid to Tunisia accounts for less than 15 percent of all U.S. assistance provided in 2011 and 2012.[129] In addition, prior to 2011, while 80 percent of the nonmilitary assistance is administered by USAID missions in the entire region, Tunisia didn't have a USAID mission and majority of assistance is received through U.S. programs such as the Middle East Response Fund (MERF), the Middle East Partnership Initiative (MEPI), The Overseas

Private Investment Corporation (OPIC), and the Millennium Challenge Corporation (MCC).[130] The relatively lower levels of U.S. development and military assistance to Tunisia largely explains the country's low geostrategic influence and importance to the U.S. political agenda in the region.

The postrevolutionary Tunisia has been open to foreign funding and international donors among which European countries and Japan came to the forefront, and they mainly concentrated their aid, loans, and technical assistance on preparing the grounds for elections, constitutional drafting process, policy development, capacity, and institution building. Since 2011, above three-quarters of the development assistance to Tunisia was received from the European Institutions and European countries including France, Germany, Italy, the UK, and Switzerland.[131] Furthermore, since 2011, the U.S. government has increased its funding and assistance for Tunisia considerably and in 2015, the Congress decided to increase the bilateral package to $141.9 million which was more than double the previous year's level of funding.[132] Behind the Congress decision to increase the financial aid to Tunisia lied the mounting economic and security challenges that has threatened Tunisia's political progress over the last few years. Nonetheless, the financial aid received by the Tunisian government from the United States was much lower compared to Egypt, Jordan, and Lebanon, and the U.S. administration didn't welcome the Tunisian government's request for an Memorandum of Understanding (MOU) that would commit the administration to provide an increased financial assistance at specific levels over several years (similar to the MOUs signed with major Middle East Allies) in 2017.[133]

On the other hand, foreign assistance had a much more decisive role for Egypt. Foreign donors to Egypt were active prior to the 2011 uprisings, and they continue to provide Egypt financial aid after Mubarak's fall. Based on the OECD Statistics 2015–2016 average, the top five ODA donors to Egypt include the UAE, EU Institutions, Germany, France, and Japan.[134] The EU's main donor is the European Commission which provided Egypt with €449.29 million from 2010 to 2013 to support the competitiveness of Egyptian economy, democratic reform, human rights, and good governance and to realize development goals with more society and environmentally friendly policies. The European Commission continued to support Egypt financially after the military coup, and by 2017, the overall EU financial assistance to Egypt amounted to over €1.3 billion in grants with 90 percent of the grants targeting economic and social development, renewable energy, waste management, and environment, while 10 percent was dedicated to support good governance, human rights, justice, and public administration.[135] The EU chose not to act on the conditionality clause within the framework of the association agreements of Euro-med Partnership Program that required the union to suspend the EU financial aid to Egypt in the face of the coup. By this move, the

EU indeed turned a blind eye to human rights violations under Sisi. Besides, the union legitimated the Sisi administration when the foreign policy chief of the EU, Catherine Ashton paid a visit to the country announcing the EU support for the June 30 roadmap.[136]

Egypt has been among the top recipients of the U.S. foreign aid in the world along with Afghanistan and Israel. As a part of the Camp David Accords commitment, Egypt has received $1.3 billion military aid and approximately $250 million Economic Support Funds (ESF) annually since 1983. Besides, the Egyptian government has been the largest recipient of the USAID assistance with approximately $250 million annually to support Egypt's economic development and infrastructure improvement.[137] After Mubarak's fall, the Obama Administration maintained the same level of funding while additional funds were channeled to assist Egypt's political transition. As of 2016, the portion of Egypt's bilateral aid dedicated to military and security assistance made up 90 percent of the U.S. foreign aid in Egypt.[138] The U.S. military and economic aid flew to Egypt interrupted even after the military coup in 2013 despite the fact that the Foreign Assistance Act passed in 1961 stated clearly that no government whose elected head is deposed by a military coup is eligible for the U.S. financial assistance.

For decades, the U.S. military and economic aid helped to maintain and expand the giant security apparatus and consolidated the successive military-backed governments in Egypt. The American economic and political support to the status quo aimed to ensure the cessation of hostilities against Israel and the American interests including access to Egyptian airspace and the prioritization of U.S. naval vessels through the Suez Canal.[139] To this end, in order to continue its financial aid to Egypt, the U.S. administration avoided defining the course of events during the violent removal of Morsi from power. On many occasions, the U.S. administration has undermined human rights abuses and even praised Sisi government for his so-called "democratic progress." They have pursued a business-as-usual approach with Sisi mainly stressing security, counterterrorism cooperation, maintaining peace with Israel and economic issues.

In 2014, the U.S. Congress legislated conditions to sustain financial assistance requiring Egypt to hold free and fair parliamentary and presidential elections, implement reforms to protect freedom of expression and association and take steps to govern democratically.[140] Egypt fulfilled none of these conditions, nonetheless, the U.S. administration only made some symbolic moves by expressing concerns about the death of civilians and ongoing violence in the country while remaining reluctant to suspend military and economic assistance to Egypt. What is worse, the U.S. officials described the current situation in Egypt as "the right path to democracy."[141] Sisi government remains fully confident that they will be able to protect their legitimacy and popular support in the international community notwithstanding the violent repression and various kinds of human rights abuses in the country.

On the other hand, most Egyptians consider the U.S. financial and military aid as a threat to achieving democracy in their country. The findings of a poll conducted by the Arab Forum for Alternatives in Cairo in 2012 found out that among Egyptians, European funding is perceived as the most positive (70 percent) followed by Japanese (63 percent), while two-thirds of respondents (66 percent) expressed that funding from the United States and the Gulf States played a negative role in Egypt's transition.[142]

Apart from the U.S. financial aid, the Gulf countries (with the exception of Qatar) worked fervently to maintain the status quo in Egypt. The Gulf States perceived the rise of the Brotherhood as a threat to their monarchies given that the Brotherhood enjoyed extensive organization with large popular support in those countries. Besides, the Brotherhood set a model that was perceived as a threat to the survival of Gulf Monarchies as they have reconciled Islam with democracy, which would ultimately challenge the Saudi Kingdom's claim to be sole protector of Islam. While the Mubarak regime was clearly in the Sunni coalition with the Gulf States backed by the United States, under Morsi, Egypt began to align itself to Iran and challenge the regional balance of power. In order to prevent the expansion of the Brotherhood's political model to the rest of the region and ensure its ideological interests, the Gulf States quickly moved to contain the spread of democracy and protect the regional balance of power by giving financial and political support to the military-backed regime. Saudi Arabia together with the UAE and Kuwait provided a combined aid package of $12 billion to the military regime immediately after the coup, which served to provide Sisi regime with much-needed political legitimacy and financial aid during Egypt's precarious transition.[143]

In conclusion, what was different in the case of Tunisia was the relative absence of external influence and its perceived lack of geopolitical importance including resource wealth. This enabled Tunisia to embark on a transition without any interference from foreign actors and forced divergent political forces to reconcile their differences. In contrast, the U.S. military aid and the aid package from the Gulf states reinforced the counterrevolutionary forces' hand vis-à-vis groups urging for a democratic change.

NOTES

1. According to the Freedom House Rating Scale 1= Most Free 7= Least Free. "Freedom in the World 2020-Country Reports: Tunisia," Freedom House, https://freedomhouse.org/country/tunisia/freedom-world/2020; "Freedom in the World

2020-Country Reports: Egypt," Freedom House, https://freedomhouse.org/country/egypt/freedom-world/2020

2. In Tunisia, it took protestors almost a month to oust Ben-Ali and similarly, the Egyptian uprisings lasted only eighteen days. In Egypt, 846 people were killed, and 338 people were killed in Tunisia during the uprisings. These figures indicate that regime change in two countries took place without significant violence compared to other Arab states.

3. Tunisia and Egypt, which belonged to the Ottoman Empire until 1881 and 1914, respectively, had a great deal of autonomy. Local rulers modeled on European states' governing institutions and modernized their militaries, infrastructure, and institutions based on those of European states. The French colonialization of Tunisia and British occupation of Egypt didn't reverse the trend of centralization and development which continued to the postindependence period in both states. Thus, the process of state building began far before gaining independence and the administrative continuity contributed to the strong statehood in both countries. James L. Gelwin, *The Arab Uprisings: What Everyone Needs to Know* (New York: Oxford University Press, 2015), 41–42.

4. Daniel Brumberg, "Democratization in the Arab World? The Trap of Liberalized Autocracy," *Journal of Democracy* 13, no. 4 (October 2002): 56.

5. Ellen Lust-Okar, "Divided They Rule the Management and Manipulation of Political Opposition," *Comparative Politics* 36, no. 2 (January 2004): 159–179.

6. Ibid., 57.

7. Khalil Al-Anani, "Liberal Autocracy in Egypt," *Brookings Institute*, June 24, 2008, https://www.brookings.edu/opinions/liberal-autocracy-in-egypt/

8. Sadiki, Bin Ali's "Tunisia: Democracy by Non-Democratic Means," 58.

9. Sadiki, "Political Liberalization in Bin Ali's Tunisia: Façade Democracy," 137.

10. "Arab Republic of Egypt: 2010 Article IV Consultation," *International Monetary Fund*, Country Report, no. 10/94 (April 2010), https://www.imf.org/external/pubs/ft/scr/2010/cr1094.pdf

11. "Tunisia: 2007 Article IV Consulting Mission, Preliminary Conclusions," *International Monetary Fund*, Country Report, no. 02/122 (May 2007), https://www.imf.org/en/News/Articles/2015/09/28/04/52/mcs062907

12. Patrick Bond, "Neoliberal Threats to North Africa," *Review of African Political Economy* 38, no. 129 (2011): 481–482.

13. Koenraad Bogaert, "Contextualizing the Arab Revolts: The Politics Behind Three Decades of Neoliberalism in the Arab World," *Middle East Critique Special Issue* 22, no. 3 (October 2013): 215.

14. "World Bank: Egypt's Middle Class Shrank in the Lead-up to the Arab Spring," *Mada Masr*, May 22, 2016, https://www.madamasr.com/en/2016/05/22/news/u/world-bank-egypts-middle-class-shrank-in-the-lead-up-to-arab-spring/; "Middle-Class Frustration Fueled the Arab Spring," *The World Bank*, October 21, 2015, http://www.worldbank.org/en/news/feature/2015/10/21/middle-class-frustration-that-fueled-the-arab-spring

15. "Most Improved in Doing Business 2008," *The World Bank*, http://www.doingbusiness.org/Reforms/Top-reformers-2008; Beinin, "The Working Class and the Popular Movement," 105.

16. Michael Koplow, "Why Tunisia's Revolution is Islamist Free," *Foreign Policy*, January 14, 2011.
17. Linz, and Stepan, *Problems of Democratic Transition and Consolidation*, 1.
18. Ibid.
19. The two turnover test, according to Huntington, reveals that a new democracy is consolidated satisfactorily if it survives two turnovers of power; that is, for an emerging democracy to be consolidated, free and fair elections must twice lead to the peaceful handover of power between the ruling part,y and its successful challenger in the election. See Huntington, *The Third Wave: Democratization in the Late Twentieth Century*, 267.
20. Linz, and Stepan, *Problems of Democratic Transition and Consolidation*, 1.
21. Lipset, "Some Social Requisites of Democracy," 69–105.
22. Huntington, *The Third Wave: Democratization*, 34–35.
23. Lipset, "Some Social Requisites of Democracy," 41.
24. Daniel Lerner, *The Passing of Traditional Society: Modernizing Middle East* (New York: Free Press of Glencoe, 1958), 4–24.
25. Ronald Inglehart, and Christian Welzel, "How Development Leads to Democracy," *Foreign Affairs*, March 1, 2009.
26. Lipset, "Some Social Requisites of Democracy," 84.
27. In 2010, GDP per capita in Egypt was 2616 US Dollars while GDP per capita in Tunisia was 4140 Dollars. "Country Profile: Egypt & Tunisia," *UNData*, http://data.un.org/CountryProfile.aspx?crName
28. Mohamed A. Chemingui, and Marco V. Sanchez, "Assessing Development Strategies to Achieve MDGs in the Republic of Tunisia," *United Nations Department for Social and Economic Affairs* (October 2011); Hai-Anh Dang, and Elena Ianchovichina, "Middle Class Dynamics and the Arab Spring," *Brookings Institute*, March 18, 2016, https://www.brookings.edu/blog/future-development/2016/03/18/middle-class-dynamics-and-the-arab-spring/
29. "Tunisia: Statistics," UNICEF (2012), https://www.unicef.org/infobycountry/Tunisia_statistics.html; "Egypt: Statistics," UNICEF (2012), https://www.unicef.org/infobycountry/egypt_statistics.html
30. Adult Literacy rate in Tunisia is 79 percent and 73.9 percent in Egypt (as of 2012). The secondary school participation in Tunisia is 69 percent among female and 77 percent among male, whereas in Egypt the difference is little with 69.5 percent among female and 70.5 percent among male. See "Egypt," "Tunisia," CIA World Factbook (2012), https://www.cia.gov/index.html
31. Eva Bellin, Explaining Democratic Divergence: Why Tunisia Succeeded and Egypt has failed," Workshop on The Arab Thermidor: The Resurgence of the Security State, October 10, 2014, https://pomeps.org/2014/12/10/explaining-democratic-divergence/
32. "GDP Growth Annual-Egypt, Arab Republic," *World Bank*, https://data.worldbank.org/indicator/NY.GDP.MKTP.KD.ZG?locations=EG; "GDP Growth Annual-Tunisia," World Bank, https://data.worldbank.org/indicator/NY.GDP.MKTP.KD.ZG?locations=TN
33. "Democratic Values in Egypt," *Pew Research Center*, May 22, 2014, http://www.pewglobal.org/2014/05/22/chapter-3-democratic-values-in-egypt/; Tunisian

Confidence in Democracy Wanes," *Pew Research Center*, October 15, 2014, http://www.pewglobal.org/2014/10/15/tunisian-confidence-in-democracy-wanes/

34. Ibid.

35. Ibid.

36. Adam Przeworski, Jose Antonio Cheibub, Michael E. Alvarez, and Fernando Limongi, *Democracy and Development: Political Institutions and Material Wellbeing in the World, 1950–1990* (Cambridge: Cambridge University Press, 2000).

37. Dankwart Rustow, "Transitions to Democracy: Towards a Dynamic Model," *Comparative Politics* 2, no. 3 (April 1970): 350.

38. Ibid.

39. Samuel P. Huntington, "Democracy's Third Wave," *Journal of Democracy* 2, no. 2 (Spring 1991): 33–34.

40. Ibid.

41. Giuseppe Di Palma, *To Craft Democracies: An Essay on Democratic Transitions* (Berkeley, Los Angeles, Oxford: University of California Press, 1990), 40–199.

42. Adam Przeworkski, "The Games of Transition," in *Issues in Democratic Consolidation: The New South American Democracies in Comparative Perspective*, ed. Scott Mainwaring, Guillermo O'Donnell, and J. Samuel Valenzuela (Notre Dame, IN: University of Notre Dame Press, 1992), 116.

43. In examining transitions from authoritarian regimes, O'Donnell and Schmitter analyze the relationships between "hard-liners" (duros) and "soft-liners" or reformers (blandos). Hard-liners are those who believe that the perpetuation of authoritarian rule is possible and desirable. These hard-liners are usually composed of several factions, but the main core of these hard-liners is "formed by those who reject viscerally the 'cancers' and 'disorders' of democracy and who believe that they have a mission to eliminate all traces of such pathologies from political life." With the beginning of transition, and even after democratic transition took place, those core hard-liners are likely to remain the stubborn source of attempted coups and conspiracies. The soft-liners can be distinguished from the hard-liners in that they are increasingly become aware that the regime they helped to implant, in which they usually occupy important positions, will have to make use, in the foreseeable future, of some degree or some form of electoral legitimation." To these soft-liners, the regime needs to reintroduce certain reforms acceptable to the moderate segments of the opposition and international public opinion. See Schmitter, and O'Donnell, *Transitions from Authoritarian Rule*, 16.

44. Przeworkski, "The Games of Transition," 124.

45. O'Donnell, Schmitter, *Transitions from Authoritarian Rule*, 42.

46. Ibid., 43–44.

47. Tarek Masoud, "Has the Door Closed on Arab Democracy," *Journal of Democracy* 26, no. 1 (January 2015): 81.

48. Jillian Schwedler, *Faith in Moderation: Islamist Parties in Jordan and Yemen* (New York: Cambridge University Press, 2006), 3.

49. Jillian Schwedler, "Can Islamists Become Moderates? Rethinking the Inclusion-Moderation Hypothesis," *World Politics* 63, no. 2 (April 2011): 352.

50. Ibid.

51. Carrie Rosefsky Wickham, "The Path to Moderation: Strategy and Learning in the Formation of Egypt's Wasat Party," *Comparative Politics* 36, no. 2 (January 2004): 206.
52. Linz, and Stepan, *Problems of Democratic Transition and Consolidation*, 1.
53. Stepan, "Tunisia's Transition and the Twin Tolerations," 92.
54. Lutfi Hajji, "The 18 October Coalition for Rights and Freedoms," *Arab Reform Initiative*, October 13, 2006. http://www.arab-reform.net/en/node/350
55. Stepan, and Linz, "Democratization Theory and the Arab Spring," 17.
56. Steve Coll, "The Casbah Coalition," *The New Yorkers*, April 4, 2011, https://www.newyorker.com/magazine/2011/04/04/the-casbah-coalition
57. Daniel Brumberg, "Could Tunisia's National Dialogue Model Ever Be Replicated?" *Washington Post*, October 12, 2015, https://www.washingtonpost.com/news/monkey-cage/wp/2015/10/12/could-tunisias-national-dialogue-model-ever-be-replicated/
58. Amel Boubekeur, "Islamists, Secularists and Old Regime Elites in Tunisia: Bargained Competition," *Mediterranean Politics* 21, no. 1 (2016): 119.
59. "Essebsi: Call of Tunisia Will Not Govern Alone Even If They Got a Majority," *Breaking News*, October 29, 2014, http://breakingnews.sy/en/article/48094.html
60. Nathan J. Brown, and Amr Hamzawy, "The Draft Political Platform of the Egyptian Muslim Brotherhood: Foray into Political Integration or Retreat into Old Positions," *Carnegie Papers Middle East Series*, no. 89 (January 2008): 1–6.
61. Rutherford, "Egypt: The Origins and Consequences of the January 25 Uprisings," 47–48.
62. Pioppi, "Playing with Fire. The Muslim Brotherhood," 60.
63. Nathan Brown, "Tracking the Arab Spring: Egypt's Failed Transition," *Journal of Democracy* 24, no. 4 (October 2013): 51.
64. Selim, "Egypt under SCAF and the Muslim Brotherhood," 185–186; Abdeslam Maghraoui, "Egypt's Failed Transition to Democracy?"
65. Brown, "Tracking the Arab Spring: Egypt's Failed Transition," 57.
66. "Tunisia's Elections: A Milestone on the Path to Democratic Transformation," *Doha Institute Arab Center for Research and Policy Studies Assessment Report* (October 2011), https://www.dohainstitute.org/en/PoliticalStudies/Pages/Tunisias_elections_A_milestone_on_the_path_to_democratic_transformation.aspx
67. Sarah J. Feuer, "From Political Islam to Muslim Democracy: Tunisia's Ennahda Changes Course," *Foreign Affairs*, June 8, 2016. https://www.foreignaffairs.com/articles/tunisia/2016-06-08/political-islam-muslim-democracy
68. Lin Noueihed, and Tom Perry. "Tunisian Islamists Show Strength at Chief's Return," *Reuters*, January 30, 2011. http://blogs.reuters.com/faithworld/2011/01/30/2011/01/30/tunisian-islamists-show-strength-at-chiefs-return/
69. David Hearst, "Rachid Ghannouchi Q&A: Thoughts on Democratic Islam," *Middle East Eye*, June 12, 2016. http://www.middleeasteye.net/news/rached-ghannouchi-interview-2016275498
70. Amin Saikal, and Amitav Acharya, *Democracy and Reform in the Middle East and Asia: Social Protest and Authoritarian Rule after the Arab Spring* (New York: I.B. Tauris, 2014), 33.

71. Ibid., 34.
72. Ibid.
73. Mara Revkin, "Egypt's Untouchable President," *Foreign Policy*, November 25, 2012, http://foreignpolicy.com/2012/11/25/egypts-untouchable-president/
74. Rutherford, *Egypt after Mubarak: Liberalism, Islam and Democracy* (Princeton, NJ: Princeton University Press, 2008), 18.
75. "The Muslim Brotherhood versus Ennahda," *Majalla*, December 26, 2013. http://eng.majalla.com/2013/12/ article55247739/the-muslim-brotherhood-versus-ennahda
76. Abdeslam Maghraoui, "Egypt's Failed Transition to Democracy: Was Political Culture a Major Factor?" *E-International Relations*, April 29, 2014, http://www.e-ir.info/2014/04/29/egypts-failed-transition-to-democracy-was-political-culture-a-major-factor/
77. Willow Wilson, "From Virginity Test to Power," *The Guardian*, September 3, 2012. https://www.theguardian.com/lifeandstyle/2012/sep/03/virginity-test-to-power
78. Pioppi Daniela, "Playing with Fire. The Muslim Brotherhood and the Egyptian Leviathan," *The International Spectator: Italian Journal of International Affairs* 48, no. 4 (December 2013): 60.
79. Walter Lippmann, "The Indispensable Opposition," *Atlantic Monthly*, CLXIV (1939): 234 as cited in Jason Brownlee, Tarek Masoud, and Andrew Reynolds, *The Arab Spring: Pathways of Repression and Reform* (Oxford and New York: Oxford University Press, 2015), 196.
80. Tarek Masoud, "Egyptian Democracy: Smothered in the Cradle, or Stillborn?" *The Brown Journal of World Affairs* 20, no. 2 (Spring/ Summer 2014): 13.
81. Ibid., 15.
82. Mustapha Kamel Al-Sayyid, "The Divergent Trajectories of Arab Dignity Revolts: Egypt and Tunisia," in *Re-envisaging West Asia: Looking Beyond the Arab Uprisings*, ed. Priya Singh (Delhi, India: Shipra Publications, 2016), 199.
83. National Election Authority, Egypt. https://www.elections.eg/en/
84. Ricardo Rene Laremont, *Revolution, Revolt and Reform in North Africa: The Arab Spring and Beyond* (New York: Routledge, 2014), 151.
85. Marina Ottoway, "Democratic Transitions and the Problem of Power," *Wilson Center Middle East Program Occasional Paper Series* (Spring 2014): 3–11.
86. Ibid.
87. Theda Skocpol, *States and Social Revolutions* (New York: Cambridge University Press, 1979), 32.
88. Eva Bellin, "The Robustness of Authoritarianism in the Middle East: Exceptionalism in Comparative Perspective," *Comparative Politics* 36, no. 2 (January 2004): 143.
89. Eva Bellin, "Reconsidering the Robustness of Authoritarianism in the Middle East: Lessons from the Arab Spring," *Comparative Politics* 44, no: 2 (January 2012): 127–149.
90. Steven Cook, *Ruling but not Governing: The Military and Political Development in Egypt, Algeria and Turkey* (Baltimore: John Hopkins University Press, 2007), 8.
91. Ibid.

92. Alfred Stepan, "Paths toward Redemocratization: Theoretical Comparative Considerations," in *Transitions from Authoritarian Rule: Prospects for Democracy*, ed. Guillermo O'Donnell, Philippe C. Schmitter, and Laurence Whitehead (Baltimore: Johns Hopkins University Press, 1896), 75–79.

93. Nikolay Marinov Hein Goemans, "Coups and Democracy," *British Journal of Political Science* 44, no. 4 (October 2014): 801.

94. Bellin, "The Robustness of Authoritarianism in the Middle East," 145.

95. Samuel P. Huntington, *The Soldier and the State: The Theory and Politics of Civil Military Relations* (Harvard University Press, 1957), 8–10.

96. Alfred Stepan, *Rethinking Military Politics: Brazil and the Southern Cone* (Princeton: Princeton University Press, 1988), 9.

97. Bellin, "The Robustness of Authoritarianism in the Middle East," 147–151.

98. Risa Brooks, "Subjecting the Military to the Rule of Law: The Tunisian Model," in *Building the Rule of Law in the Arab World: Tunisia Egypt and Beyond*, ed. Eva Bellin, and Heidi Lane (Boulder, CO: Lynne Rienner Publishers, 2016): 109–130.

99. William C. Taylor, *Military Responses to the Arab Uprisings and the Future of Civil-Military Relations in the Middle East* (New York: Palgrave Macmillan, 2014), 75.

100. Sherine Tadros, "Egypt Military's Economic Empire," *Aljazeera*, February 16, 2012. http://www.aljazeera.com/indepth/features/2012/02/2012215195912519142.html

101. Atef Said, "The Paradox of Transition to Democracy under Military Rule," *Social Research: An International Quarterly* 79, no. 2 (Summer 2012): 397.

102. Al-Sayyid, "The Divergent Trajectories of Arab Dignity Revolts: Egypt and Tunisia," 198.

103. Stepan, "Tunisia's Transition and the Twin Tolerations," 94.

104. Omar Ashour, "Collusion to Crackdown: Islamist-Military Relations in Egypt," *Brookings Doha Center Analysis Paper*, no. 14 (March 2015): 14.

105. Daniel Brumberg, "Reconsidering Theories of Transition," in *Reflections on the Arab Uprisings*, ed. Marc Lynch, POMEPS Studies 10, November 17, 2014, 11. https://pomeps.org/wp-content/uploads/2014/11/POMEPS_Studies_10_ Reflections _web1.pdf

106. Ibid.

107. Stepan, and Linz, "Democratization Theory and the Arab Spring," 21.

108. Larry Diamond, "Civil Society and the Development of Democracy," *Estudio*, Working Paper 1997/101 (June 1997): 25.

109. Gabriel Almond, and Sidney Verba, *The Civic Culture* (Princeton: Princeton University Press, 1963), 7–30.

110. Peter C. Weber, "Modernity, Civil Society and Sectarianism: The Egyptian Muslim Brotherhood and the Takfir Groups," *Voluntas* 24, no. 2 (June 2013): 513.

111. Vincent Durac, "A Flawed Nexus?: Civil Society and Democratization in the Middle East and North Africa," *Middle East Institute*, October 15, 2015, http://www.mei.edu/content/map/flawed-nexus-civil-society-and-democratization-middle-east-and-north-africa

112. Ibid.

113. Inmaculada Szmolka, "Exclusionary and Non-Consensual Transitions versus Inclusive and Consensual Democratizations: The Cases of Egypt and Tunisia," *Arab Studies Quarterly* 37, no. 1 (Winter 2015): 88.

114. Stepan, and Linz, "Democratization Theory and the Arab Spring," 23.

115. Stepan, "Tunisia's Transition and the Twin Tolerations," 94.

116. Ibid., 96.

117. Hajji, "The 18 October Coalition for Rights and Freedoms."

118. Bellin, "Explaining Democratic Divergence: Why Tunisia Succeeded."

119. Sarah Chayes, "How a Leftist Labor Union Helped Force Tunisia's Political Settlement," *Carnegie Endowment for International Peace*, March 27, 2014, https://carnegieendowment.org/2014/03/27/how-leftist-labor-union-helped-force-tunisia-s-political-settlement-pub-55143

120. Hela Yousfi, "The Tunisian Revolution: Narratives of the Tunisian General Labour Union," in *The Routledge Handbook of the Arab Spring*, ed. Larbi Sadiki (Milton Park: Routledge, 2015), 320.

121. Jeremy Bowen, *The Arab Uprisings: The People Want the Fall of the System* (London: Simon & Schuster, 2012), 38.

122. Dina Bishara, "Labor Movement in Tunisia and Egypt," *Stiftung Wissenschaft und Politik* (SWP). Comments 1 (January 2014): 2.

123. Dina Bishara, "The Power of Workers in Egypt's 2011 Uprising," in *Arab Spring in Egypt: Revolution and Beyond*, ed. Bahgat Korany, and Rabab El-Mahdi (Cairo and New York: The American University in Cairo Press, 2012), 84.

124. Steven Levitsky, and Lucan A. Way, "International Linkage and Democratization," *Journal of Democracy* 16, no. 3 (July 2005): 21–23.

125. Mathilde Dugit-Gros, "Foreign Influence in the Middle East: Changes in Perceptions and Expectations," *Arab Reform Initiative*, September 10, 2015, https://www.arab-reform.net/en/node/763

126. Ana Echagüe, "The Role of External Actors in Arab Transitions," *FRIDE Policy Brief*, no. 122 (April 2012): 1.

127. Kristina Kausch, "Foreign Funding in Post-Revolution Tunisia," *FRIDE Working Paper* (May 2013): 13.

128. Ibid.

129. Stephen McInerney, "The Federal Budget and Appropriations for Fiscal Year 2013: Democracy, Governance and Human Rights in the Middle East North Africa," *Project on Middle East Democracy* (July 2012): 26. https://pomed.org/wp-content/uploads/2012/07/FY2013-Budget-Report.pdf

130. Ibid.

131. "OECD-DAC Air Statistics, Recipients at a Glance: Tunisia, 2015–2016 Average," http://www.oecd.org/dac/stats/aid-at-a-glance.htm#recipients

132. Stephen McInerney, and Cole Bockenfeld, "The Federal Budget and Appropriations for Fiscal Year 2017: Democracy, Governance and Human Rights in the Middle East and North Africa," *Project on Middle East Democracy* (April 2016): 54. https://pomed.org/wp-content/uploads/2016/07/POMED_BudgetReport_FY17_Final-Web.pdf

133. Ibid., 55.

134. "OECD-DAC Air Statistics, Recipients at a Glance: Egypt, 2015–2016 Average," http://www.oecd.org/dac/financing-sustainable-development/development-finance-data/aid-at-a-glance.htm

135. "Report on EU-Egypt Relations in the Framework of the Revised ENP," *European Commission High Representative of the Union for Foreign Affairs and Security Policy*, July 13, 2017, 2. https://eeas.europa.eu/sites/eeas/files/2017_report_on_eu-egypt_relations_2015-2017.pdf

136. Alastair Sloan, "Is the EU legitimizing Sisi's Coup?" *Aljazeera*, April 20, 2014, https://www.aljazeera.com/indepth/opinion/2014/04/eu-legitimising-sisi-coup-egypt-20144161181767834.html

137. Mohamed Elagati, "Foreign Funding in Egypt after the Revolution," *Fride Working Paper* (2013): 14.

138. McInerney, and Bockenfeld, "The Federal Budget and Appropriations for Fiscal Year 2017," 26.

139. Farah Najjar, "Why US Aid to Egypt is Never under Threat," *Aljazeera*, October 3, 2017, https://www.aljazeera.com/news/2017/10/aid-egypt-threat-171002093316209.html

140. David Schenker, "A Moment of Decision on Egypt," *The Washington Institute Policy Analysis*, no. 2355, January 14, 2015, http://www.washingtoninstitute.org/policy-analysis/view/a-moment-of-decision-on-egypt

141. Michael R. Gordon, "Egyptians Following Right Path," *New York Times*, November 3, 2013, http://www.nytimes.com/2013/11/04/world/middleeast/kerry-egypt-visit.html

142. Elagati, "Foreign Funding in Egypt after the Revolution," 10.

143. David Hearst, "Why Saudi Arabia is Taking a Risk by backing the Egyptian Coup?" *The Guardian*, August 20, 2013, https://www.theguardian.com/commentisfree/2013/aug/20/saudi-arabia-coup-egypt

Conclusion

The outbreak of the popular protests in 2011 initially appeared to be an unstoppable course toward democratization. The popular protests raised many hopes for a new era of democratic regimes as they reflected Arab publics' demands for freedom, justice, and democracy. The magnitude of protest movements was great enough to generate pressure over authoritarian rulers to step down. However, these hopes were quickly dashed as the downfall of authoritarian rulers failed to deliver on expectations of a more representative government, supremacy of law, and better living standards Almost a decade after the uprisings broke out, protracted civil wars and chaos took precedence in the region while successful regime breakdowns failed to culminate in the establishment of democratic rule. In this gloomy political landscape, Tunisia emerged as a beacon of hope in the entire region as the sole Arab country that has successfully transitioned to democracy following the Arab Spring.

Though outside observers and analysts described the popular protests as "Arab Spring" with great expectations for democratic transitions, democratization prospects faded in all cases except one almost as speedy as they had appeared. In general, three lessons transpire from the wave of popular protests in the Arab world in 2011. The first lesson is that authoritarian collapse is not destined to end in democratization. Egypt's first democratically elected president and government were ousted in a military coup in mid-2013 and the country witnessed the reassertion of a new form of authoritarianism in which the military ruled at the helm rather than behind the curtain. The uprisings in Yemen, Libya, and Syria gave way to violent conflict that escalated into civil war and culminated in the breakdown of state institutions. In Tunisia, on the other hand, a functioning and relatively accountable political system was established, power was peacefully transferred from one political force to another through free and fair elections and a democratic constitution was drafted with the inclusion of diverse political and civil society groups.

Second, the unfolding of the events in the MENA region indicated that there is no single universally acceptable route to democratization. Even when the origins of the popular protests and the initial phase of the transition indicate remarkable similarities, two countries could take divergent transitional paths based on particular context-dependent factors.

Third, democratic transitions are assumed to be fulfilled when power is alternated peacefully between different political forces through free and fair elections, important steps are taken to ensure an independent judiciary and a democratic constitution is in place. However, it takes decades for a country that has transitioned from authoritarianism to democracy to consolidate its democratic governance while any country that is within the reach of democratic consolidation might fall into democratic regression and revert to authoritarianism. Therefore, it remains to be seen to what extent Tunisia will be able to shield its newly founded democracy from counterrevolutionary forces.

Whatever the domestic and international consequences of the Arab Spring protests are, the countries swept by the uprisings provide important cases to compare and test the widely accepted hypotheses in the field of comparative democratization. The downfall of the authoritarian rulers in both cases initiated transitions similar to those that took place in the third wave of democratization. Political groups previously suppressed by the regime, Islamist parties in the case of Tunisia and Egypt, moved into the centrum of political spectrum and were joined by dozens of newly formed opposition parties. Civil society organizations proliferated and interim governments led the transitional processes by organizing competitive multiparty elections and constitutional drafting processes. In both cases, constitutional drafting was marked by deep-seated ideological divisions as the main point of contention arose as regards to the adoption of *Sharia* as a source of legislation and thus, the future character of the state. Eventually, two years after the popular protests, both countries were plagued by political instability, insecurity, deepening economic crisis, and as a consequence, continuous street protests by civil society groups calling for the resignation of the incumbent governments and the holding of early elections.

Making use of the vast literature accumulated based on transition experiences of the former waves of democratization, this research first compared Tunisia and Egypt in terms of the structural factors such as wealth, GDP per capita, levels of literacy, the composition of the population, and the levels of popular support for democracy. Upon investigating those structural factors, this research came to the conclusion that there is no meaningful difference between the two countries as both of them fall into the category of lower-middle-class income developing countries and levels of support for democracy are alike. Therefore, the assumption of the structural approach that greater wealth, industrialization, higher literacy, and education levels would bring about democracy was inadequate to account for the divergence in the democratic outcome. While not eliminating the hypothesis that the level of development and wealth creates an environment that helps a country to maintain and consolidate its democracy, this research mainly indicates that democracy or reassertion of authoritarianism mainly depends on choices, behaviors and principal strategies of political agents.

On the other hand, historical and political structures largely determine decisions and political choices of agents, indicating that agents are deeply affected by structures while making certain choices. In this study, the level of elite consensus achieved in the two countries, the leadership styles of the transitional actors and their decisions seem to account for why Tunisia could achieve democratic transition but not Egypt. Nonetheless, in the context of post-2011 transitions in Tunisia and Egypt, decision-making processes and compromising or uncompromising attitudes of political agents are deeply affected by a number of structural constraints such as institutional endowment, the potential of civil society to make pressure on political elite, the distribution of power among divergent political forces, and the influence of external actors. Hence, those variables are also investigated in relation to their effect on why political actors took certain decisions, but not others, or they were more apt to compromise on critical issues in one country but in the other.

Democratic transitions succeed depending on how far rules of the game are set clearly, transparently, and with broad consensus of divergent political forces from the outset. The designing of the transition, that is, the sequencing and timing of the elections and constitutional drafting process was both opaque and troublesome in Egypt. A critical turning point emerged when transitional actors decided to hold elections before enacting a new constitution despite the outcry of civil society groups and secular political parties. This decision meant that a new system was built based on the old set of rules that has been designed to monopolize and consolidate power. It also meant that the political forces that would win electoral victory would become less eager to come to terms with other political groups on critical issues regarding the future of the state and society due to their majoritarian mindset in relation to democracy. In contrast, the transitional process in Tunisia gave precedence to the drafting of the constitution first, in other words, setting the rules of the game before giving a start signal to the match. This strategic choice enabled divergent political forces to come to compromise on key issues that would define the character of the future state and the relationship between religion and state affairs, in particular.

The designing of electoral and constitutional processes is of utmost significance to facilitate a democratic outcome. The constitutional process in Egypt was designed without clearly defined rules and procedures that would be outcome of negotiations and bargaining among transitional actors. The ambiguities and loopholes that emerged as a result of those unclear processes gridlocked the transition in Egypt from its outset. The electoral process in Egypt was designed in a manner that would strengthen the hands of political forces having better organizational strength and higher popular support while eliminating equal chances for smaller and less powerful political groups. On the contrary, the electoral law used in Tunisia was based on proportional representation with a 0-percent threshold, in other words, the electoral law was designed to promote pluralism and preclude one political party from gaining absolute majority. The electoral process was administered by an independent commission in Tunisia, and it was largely transparent. The initial decisions taken at the beginning of the transitional phase created more favorable conditions for Tunisia to become a democracy while generating numerous setbacks in the Egyptian case.

Second, the success of any democratic transition is largely determined by the constitutional process, to be more precise, both the manner in which constitution is drafted and its content. The Tunisian constitutional drafting process is a perfect example of a national reconciliation that could be achieved through consensus building. The Tunisian constitution came into being with the participation of civil society organizations and an elaborate process of political bargaining and negotiations between the secular and Islamist groups. On numerous points of contention such as the role of *Sharia* in state affairs, blasphemy, and the status of women, parties come to consensus through intense political dialogue and much of the credit could be attributed to the Ennahda party for compromising on its several standpoints. The outcome was a rather progressive constitution that guarantees fundamental freedoms and reflects the key tenets of democracy. On the other hand, in Egypt constitutional drafting was characterized by mistrust and ideological divisions. The constituent assembly tasked with the writing of the constitution was heavily dominated by Islamist members, which lead to distrust and suspicion among secular members. In terms of its content, both the 2012 and the 2013 constitutions of Egypt were revised versions of the constitution under Sadat and had nothing to do with the demands of the revolution. The single most important document for the new Egyptian state failed to gain political legitimacy.

In transitions from authoritarian regime to democracy, the political elite need to reach consensus on the key objectives of the transition and their future state and to achieve this, they need to compromise on their ideological stances and privilege establishing a democratic system over their pure partisan interests. The Tunisian political elite, Ennahda, secular political parties, and the chief labor union, acted on an understanding that monopolizing the political system was too heavy burden for one single group to carry and each of those political actors gave precedence to maintaining the country's political transition and moving it forward in line with the expectations of the larger society. Consensual politics became the new norm in Tunisia following the fall of the Ben Ali regime. First, the political elite came to sufficient agreement on the procedures to design a transitional roadmap. Besides, consensual politics was institutionalized in the form of the Higher Authority for the Realization of the Objectives of the Revolution, Political Reform, and the Democratic Transition including legal experts, civil society groups, intellectuals, and politicians. Third, Tunisian political elite reached an agreement on the character of the state, that is, the state would be a civic and democratic and its legitimacy would be drawn from popular sovereignty. This common understanding was achieved thanks to the ideological moderation by the Ennahda leadership who struggled hard to compromise the ideological stances of the hardliners within the party. Fourth, Ennahda leadership willingly stepped down and handed political power to a technocratic government in the face of mounting political unrest and instability. By doing so, they saved Tunisia from a never-ending political stalemate that had the risk of reverting the country to a new form of authoritarianism.

By contrast, Egypt experienced little political dialogue between ideological opponents. The whole transition process was perceived as a zero-sum game in which gains by one political force would definitely be a loss by another. Hence, transitional actors gave precedence to electoral politics rather than establishing a political platform to decide on the key issues surrounding the transitional process. The outcome of this perception was too many elections in rather short period of time with little common understanding and agreement on the future of the transition and thus, no meaningful outcome for a democratic transition.

Another important lesson that the divergence between the Tunisian and Egyptian transitional outcomes offered is how much the leadership styles of newly emerged political parties mattered to the democratic outcome of the transition. In both countries, political Islamists were faced with similar set of problems, yet how they approached those problems and their critical decisions made a difference in their transitional paths. Confident of their organizational strength and popular support, the Brotherhood leaders gave little weight to reaching out to opposition groups and embracing all fractions within the society. Their perception of democracy was based on a majoritarian mindset. Rather than unifying with the revolutionary groups and opposition parties against the old regime forces, the Brotherhood leaders chose to engage in a power-sharing agreement with the military in the belief that it would be to their advantage to act with the military rather than with the opposition groups against the old regime. By this fatal calculation, the Brotherhood alienated its potential allies and lost every single opportunity to build a coalition with revolutionary forces, which left them no ally to turn to when the military turned against them. Besides, Morsi's political discourse was polarizing, divisive, and ideological. He took a nonconciliatory stance and mobilized thousands of Brotherhood members to the streets in the face of escalating popular unrest and a deeply polarized society. The mounting polarization and street protests, in turn, played into the hands of the SCAF which could easily revert the transitional path to the old status quo.

On the contrary, the leadership of Ghannouichi helped Tunisia to soothe ideological polarization and bridge ideology-driven conflicts to achieve national reconciliation. Ghannouichi and other key leaders in the party were committed to the establishment of a secular democratic state. To this end, he advocated for an electoral formula which could serve the interests of smaller parties rather than allowing Ennahda to gain a landslide victory. During the times of political crisis, Ennahda leadership acted in a conciliatory manner that would in no way pave the way for escalation of the crisis and strengthen the hands of old regime supporters. Tunisia achieved consensual politics that is very rare in the region thanks to Ennahda's willingness to come to compromise at critical junctures.

In explaining the divergence in the democratic outcome between Tunisia and Egypt, perhaps the most important variable is the institutional endowment of the state, the institutional pillars on which the state is structured. The divergent role played by the militaries in Egypt and Tunisia is embedded in their historical legacy closely linked to the military's role in the country's struggle for independence. Since Egypt gained its independence, it was ruled by the generals from the army, and thus, the military establishment emerged as a privileged and autonomous institution in the state enjoying a wide range of political and economic interests. Indeed, the military in Egypt acted as a state within the state with its dominant role in the country's political life behind the curtain for several decades and its domination of almost two fifth of Egypt's economy. Therefore, immediately after the removal of Mubarak from power, to protect its institutional interests and even enhance them, the SCAF took over political affairs and remained rather reluctant to leave the political stage to a civilian force. The continuous intervention of the military in the political realm precluded the emergence of a civilian democracy from taking root. It also led the leftist and revolutionary opposition groups to turn to the military to intervene rather than confronting the Islamists in ballot boxes. In stark contrast, the Tunisian military has not been an institution of high concern. The army was poorly funded and equipped by Bourguiba and Ben Ali, and it was kept in the periphery to preclude any potential coup. Unlike the giant military apparatus in Egypt, the minimal role allocated to the military in Tunisia has been a blessing to the country's democratic transition in post-Arab Spring.

Another pivotal variable that facilitates or hinders democratic transition is the distribution of power among political forces. The former democratic transition experiences have indicated that democracy best flourishes in a country where there is relatively even distribution of political power and this makes it less likely for the dominant political force to be arbitrary and the opposition forces to be irreconcilable. Tunisia's transitional process took advantage of a relatively even distribution of power in the aftermath of the first elections in 2011. Ennahda party won a plurality rather than the majority of votes, which forced the party to seek allies from the secular camp and encouraged both secular and Islamist members of the assembly to compromise and negotiate during the constitutional drafting and its aftermath. In contrast, in the first parliamentary elections in Egypt, the Brotherhood together with the Salafist Al-Nour Party won almost two-thirds of the votes, which made the political Islamists more uncompromising in the belief that they didn't need to come to terms with the secular groups on the issues surrounding constitutional drafting and the transitional process. In addition, for power to be evenly distributed among divergent political forces, there should exist power vacuum after the breakdown of the authoritarian regime. In Egypt, the removal of Mubarak didn't generate a power vacuum that would be filled by a civilian political force as the military acted as the most powerful political force. Such a power vacuum emerged in Tunisia after Ben Ali's ouster due to the military's neutral stance and nonintervention in the political sphere.

This research has also revealed the centrality of civil society activism in both Tunisia and Egypt in the post-Arab Spring context. Similar to the transition experiences in democracy's third wave, civil society has loomed large in the deconstruction of authoritarianism in both Tunisia and Egypt. However, once the autocrats were ousted, civil society in the two countries played divergent roles. In Egypt, the role of civil society in the aftermath of the authoritarian breakdown was confined to street activism. They failed to channel street activism into a united opposition force in the political sphere. This was largely because civil society organizations had weak internal cohesion, and they were too fragmented to act as a collective force. Unlike Egypt, Tunisia had a vibrant civil society in which labor unions and secular civil society groups counterbalanced Islamist organizations. In Tunisia, civil society monitored the performance of the interim government and organized mass-scale protests when the transitional actors' roadmap ran counter to the demands of the revolution. Another critical role of the civil society in Tunisia was mediation and arbitration between opponent political forces and between society and transitional actors at large. When the political crisis was approaching its climax in 2013, the Tunisian General Labour Union with three other leading organizations stepped in to initiate a broad national dialogue and presented a transitional roadmap to the political actors declaring that they had to accept the roadmap to be involved in the national dialogue. It was this national dialogue that led Tunisia toward democracy.

Finally, the role of external actors has been decisive in the transition of the two countries. Egypt enjoys a great geopolitical power due to its strategic location neighboring Israel, controlling the Rafah Gate and the Suez Canal. The country has enjoyed substantial U.S. military aid for decades and it has been a beneficiary of financial aid from the Gulf monarchies. The financial aid provided to Egypt by external actors, be it economic and military, served to protect the old status quo and strengthen the economic and political status of the military, which in turn beclouded prospects for a civilian democratic rule in Egypt. To its advantage, Tunisia is detached from the quagmires of the Levant politics thanks to its distant location from the most conflict-ridden part of the Middle East. It doesn't share a border with Israel or control a geostrategic canal and bridge, nor is it an oil producer. Tunisia's perceived lack of geopolitical significance has been a blessing to the country allowing transitional actors to design a transitional roadmap free from any foreign influence. Unlike Egypt, U.S. military aid only constitutes a small portion of the total U.S. aid to the country. This also explains why the Tunisian military remained small and doesn't have political aspirations.

Consequently, the divergence in the transitional outcomes between Tunisia and Egypt manifested that there is no linear and predictable path to democracy. Transitioning to democracy is a complex and open-ended process that is not simply a matter of removing an autocrat from power, but rather a continuous process that develops a country's mindset, principles, and democratic values. The key variables underlined in this study indicate that the outcome of a transition from authoritarian regime to democracy first and foremost hinges on political actors, their commitment to democratic values and determination to move their country to democracy. The decision-making processes of political actors are also closely linked to a set of political and institutional structures such as civil society, institutional endowment, and external actors that encourage them to make compromise at critical points or lead them to become nonconciliatory in the face of political disagreements. Finally, the findings of this research provide important insights into the transitions from authoritarian rule by comparing two cases of regime changes, yet the end point of these transitions is still far from being certain. Tunisia has still a long way to go to consolidate its democracy. On the other hand, the restoration of authoritarianism in Egypt could end up with an autocracy with a democratic façade or the country could maintain its military dictatorship for some time to come.

Bibliography

Abdullah, Salma. "Tamarod Surpasses 22 Million Signatures." *Daily News Egypt*, June 29, 2013. https://dailynewsegypt.com/2013/06/29/tamarod-surpasses-22-million-signatures/

Aboulenein, Ahmed, and Eric Knecht. "Turnout Low in Egypt's Long-Awaited Parliamentary Election." *Reuters*, October 18, 2015. http://www.reuters.com/article/us-egypt-election-idUSKCN0SC07420151018

Abu Dhabi Gallup Center. "Egypt: The Arithmetic of the Revolution: An Empirical Analysis of Social and Economic Conditions in the Months before the January 25 Uprising." March 2011. http://www.gallup.com/poll/157043/egypt-arithmetic-revolution.aspx

Ahram Online. "Egypt Islamist Coalition Urges Opposition to Break from Mubarak Regime Figures." June 29, 2013. http://english.ahram.org.eg/NewsContent/1/64/75211/Egypt/Politics-/Egypt-Islamist-coalition-urges-opposition-to-break.aspx

Ahram Online. "Egypt Military Unveils Transitional Roadmap." July 3, 2013. http://english.ahram.org.eg/News/75531.aspx

Ahram Online. "Egypt's Army Ends Deadlock on Constituent Assembly." June 8, 2012. http://english.ahram.org.eg/NewsContentP/1/44212/Egypt/Egypts-army-endsdeadlock-on-constituent-assembly.aspx

Ahram Online. "Egypt's Presidency's Civil Society Bill 'Hostile to Freedom': NGOs." May 31, 2013. http://english.ahram.org.eg/NewsContent/1/64/72807/Egypt/Politics-/Egypt-presidencys-civil-society-bill-hostile-to-fr.aspx

Ahram Online. "Full Translation of Egypt's New-Protest Law." November 25, 2013. http://english.ahram.org.eg/News/87375.aspx

Ahram Online. "High Constitutional Court withdraws from constituent assembly." June 12, 2012. http://english.ahram.org.eg/NewsContent/1/64/44669/Egypt/Politics/High-Constitutional-Court-withdraws-from-constitue.aspx

Ahram Online. "In Sunday statement SCAF Hits back at Brotherhood Criticisms." March 25, 2012. http://english.ahram.org.eg/NewsContent/1/0/37691/Egypt/0/In-Sunday-statement,-SCAF-hits-back-at-Brotherhood.aspx

Ahram Online. "Political Forces Reach Uneasy Agreement on Egypt's Constituent Assembly." June 7, 2012. http://english.ahram.org.eg/NewsContent/1/64/44134/ Egypt/Politics-/Political-forces-reach-uneasy-agreement-on-Egypts-.aspx

Ahram Online. "SCAF, Political Parties Agree to 6 criteria for Forming Constituent Assembly." April 28, 2012. http://english.ahram.org.eg/News/40374.aspx

Ahram Online. "Tens of Thousands Attend 'Save the Revolution' Day." April 1, 2011. http://english.ahram.org.eg/NewsContent/1/64/9055/Egypt/Politics-/Tens-of-Thousands-attend-Save-the-Revolution-day.aspx

Aknur, Muge, and Irem Askar Karakır. "The Reversal of Political Liberalization in Egypt." *Ege Academic Review* 7, no. 1 (2001): 311–333.

Al-Ahram. "Dialogue Dashed." November 7, 2013. http://weekly.ahram.org.eg/News/4574/-/-.aspx

Al Ahram. "Downtown Showdown." no. 154, August 4–10, 2005. http://weekly.ahram.org.eg/Archive/2005/754/eg7.html

Al Akhbar. "Mubarak Sons Stand Trial for Corruption." July 9, 2012. http://english.alakhbar.com/content/mubarak-sons-stand-trial-corruption

Al-Ali, Zaid. "The New Egyptian Constitution: An Initial Assessment of Its Merits and Flaws." *OpenDemocracy*, December 26, 2012. https://www.opendemocracy.net/zaid-al-ali/new-egyptian-constitution-initial-assessment-of-its-merits-and-flaws

Al-Anani, Khalil. "Liberal Autocracy in Egypt." *Brookings Institute*, June 24, 2008. https://www.brookings.edu/opinions/liberal-autocracy-in-egypt/

Albrecht, Holger. "Egypt's 2012 Constitution: Devil in the Details, Not in Religion." *United States Institute of Peace*, PeaceBrief 139, January 25, 2013. https://www.usip.org/sites/default/ files/PB139-Egypt%E2%80%99s%202012%20Constitution. pdf

Alexander, Christopher. "Authoritarianism and Civil Society in Tunisia." *Middle East Report*, 205, Vol. 27 (Winter 1997).

Alexander, Christopher. "Tunisia's Protest Wave: Where it Comes from and What it Means." *Foreign Policy*, January 3, 2011. https://foreignpolicy.com/2011/01/03/tunisias-protest-wave-where-it-comes-from-and-what-it-means/

Alexander, Christopher. *Tunisia: Stability and Reform in the Modern Maghreb*. New York: Routledge, 2010.

Aleya-Sghaier, Amira. "The Tunisian Revolution: The Revolution of Dignity." *The Journal of the Middle East and Africa* 3, no. 1 (2012): 18–45.

Al-Hilali, Amal. "Ennahda Members Make Conflicting Statements about Women's Rights in Tunisia." *Al-Arabiya News*, November 13, 2011. https://www.alarabiya.net/articles/2011/11/13/176916.html

Alianak, Sonia L. *Middle Eastern Leaders and Islam: A Precarious Equilibrium*. New York: Peter Lang, 2007.

Alianak, Sonia L. *Transition Towards Revolution and Reform: The Arab Spring Realised?* Edinburg: Edinburg University Press, 2014.

AliRiza, Fadıl. "Old Political Habits in Tunisia." *Carnegie Endowment for International Peace*, June 16, 2015. http://carnegieendowment.org/sada/60406#comments

AliRiza, Fadıl. "Why Counterterrorism could be the Death of Tunisian Democracy." *Foreign Policy*, December 30, 2015. https://foreignpolicy.com/2015/12/30/why-counterterrorism-could-be-the-death-of-tunisian-democracy/

Aljazeera. "Egypt Constitution Approved by 98.1 percent." January 24, 2014. http://www.aljazeera.com/news/middleeast/2014/01/egypt-constitution-approved-981-percent201411816326470532.html

Aljazeera. "Egypt Court Orders Dissolving of Parliament." June 14, 2012. http://www.aljazeera.com/news/middleeast/2012/06/201261412453853275̃8.html

Aljazeera. "Egypt Dissolves the Former Ruling Party." April 16, 2011. http://www.aljazeera.com/news/middleeast/2011/04/2011416125051889315.html

Aljazeera. "Egypt's Sisi Approves Controversial NGO Law." May 29, 2017. http://www.aljazeera.com/news/2017/05/egypt-sisi-approves-controversial-ngo-law-170529182 720099.html

Aljazeera. "Essebsi Wins Tunisia Presidential Vote." December 23, 2014. https://www.aljazeera.com/news /middleeast/ 2014/12/essebsi-declared-tunisia-presidential-winner-2014122212464510622.html

Aljazeera. "Timeline: Egypt's Revolution." February 14, 2011. https://www.aljazeera.com/news/middleeast/2011/01/201112515334871490.html

Aljazeera. "Tunisia Protesters Urge Government to Resign." October 24, 2013. http://www.aljazeera.com/news/africa/2013/10/tunisia-protests-urge-government-resignation-2013 10237 2524 126573.html

Aljazeera. "Tunisia Signs New Constitution Into Law." January 27, 2014. https://www.aljazeera.com/news/%20africa/2014/01/tunisia-assembly-approves-new-constitution-201412622480531861.html

Aljazeera. "Tunisia's Youssef Chahed Names New Cabinet." September 6, 2017. https://www.aljazeera.com/news/2017/09/tunisia-youssef-chahed-names-cabinet-170906173 802326.html

Allahoum, Ramy. "Will Tunisia's Municipal Elections Change Anything?" *Aljaazera*, April 16, 2018. https://www.aljazeera.com/indepth/features/tunisia-municipal-elections-change-180416155940797.html

Allani, Alaya. "The Islamists in Tunisia Between Confrontation and Participation 1980–2008." *The Journal of North African Studies* 14, no. 2 (June 2009): 257–272.

Almond, Gabriel, and Sidney Verba. *The Civic Culture*. Princeton: Princeton University Press, 1963.

Al-Sayyid, Mustapha Kamel. "The Divergent Trajectories of Arab Dignity Revolts: Egypt and Tunisia." In *Re-envisaging West Asia: Looking Beyond the Arab Uprisings*, edited by Priya Singh, 187–202. Delhi, India: Shipra Publications, 2016.

Amara, Tarek. "Tunisia Approves Illegal Enrichment Law to Strengthen Anti-Corruption Fight." *Reuters*, July 18, 2018. https://www.reuters.com/article/us-tunisia-corruption-law/tunisia-approves-illegal-enrichment-law-to-strengthen-anti-corruption-fight-idUSKBN1K72QJ

Amara, Tarek. "Two Dead as Protestors Attack U.S. Embassy in Tunisia." *Reuters*, September 14, 2012. http://www.reuters.com/article/us-protests-tunisia-school-id USBRE88D18020120914

Amnesty International. "Egypt: Amnesty International Report 2008. Human Rights in the Arab Republic of Egypt." May 28, 2008. http://www.refworld.org/docid/483e2788c.html

Amnesty International. "Egypt: Continuing Arrests of Critics and Opponents "Chill" Prospects for Reform." May 27, 2005.

Amnesty International. "Egypt Rises: Killings, Detentions and Torture in the 25 January Revolution." May 19, 2011. https://www.amnesty.org/en/documents/mde12/027/2011/en/

Amnesty International. "Tunisia: Abuses in the Name of Security Threatening Reforms." February 10, 2017. https://www.amnesty.org/en/latest/news/2017/02/tunisia-abuses-in-the-name-of-security-threatening-reforms/

Amnesty International Press Release. "Egypt: Proposed Constitutional Amendments Greatest Erosion of Human Rights in 26 Years." March 18, 2007. https://www.amnesty.org/en/documents/mde12/008/2007/en/

Amnesty International Public Statement. "Egypt: Continuing Crackdown on Muslim Brotherhood." August 30, 2007. https://www.amnesty.org/download/Documents/64000/ mde120282007en.pdf

Anderson, Lisa. "Politics in the Middle East: Opportunities and Limits in the Quest for Theory." In *Area Studies and Social Science: Strategies for Understanding Middle East Politics*, edited by Mark Tessler, Jodi Nachtwey, and Anna Banda, 1–10. Bloomington, IN: Indiana University Press, 1999.

Ashour, Omar. "Collusion to Crackdown: Islamist-Military Relations in Egypt." *Brookings Doha Center Analysis Paper*, no. 14 (March 2015): 1–43.

Atallah, Samer. "Egypt's New Constitution: Repeating Mistakes." *Aljazeera*, January 14, 2014. http://www.aljazeera.com/indepth/opinion/2014/01/egypt-new-constitution-repeating-mistakes-201411255328300488.html

Auf, Yussef. "Egypt's New Parliament: What Do the Results Mean?" *Atlantic Council*, January 7, 2016. http://www.atlanticcouncil.org/blogs/menasource/egypt-s-new-parliament-what-do-the-results-mean

Ayadi, Mohamed, and Wided Mattoussi. "Scoping of the Tunisian Economy." *WIDER Working Paper*, 074 (2014): 1–16.

Aydoğan, Abdullah, and Kadir Yildirim. "The Economic and Political Dissatisfaction behind Tunisia's Protests." *Carnegie Endowment for International Peace*, January 23, 2018. http://carnegieendowment.org/sada/75334

Ayubi, Nazih N. *Overstating the Arab State: Politics and Society in the Middle East*. London: I. B. Tauris, 2009.

Aziz, Sahar F. "Military Electoral Authoritarianism in Egypt." *Election Law Journal* 16, no. 2, 2017.

Baram, Marcus. "How the Mubarak Family Made Its Billion." *Huffington Post*, November 2, 2011. http://www.huffingtonpost.com/2011/02/11/how-the-mubarak-family-made-its-billions_n_821757.html

Bassiouni, M. Cherif. *Chronicles of the Egyptian Revolution and Its Aftermath: 2011–2016*. Cambridge: Cambridge University Press, 2016.

Bayat, Asaf. *Life as Politics: How Ordinary People Change the Middle East*. Stanford: Stanford University Press, 2009.

BBC News. "Egypt President-Elect Mohammed Morsi Hails Tahrir Crowds." June 29, 2012. http://www.bbc.com/news/world-middle-east-18648399

BBC News. "Profile: Egypt's Tamarod Protest Movement." July 1, 2013. http://www.bbc.com/news/world-middle-east-23131953

BBC News. "Protest Camp: Raba'a Al-Adawiya." July 18, 2013. http://www.bbc.com/news/world-middle-east-23356339

BBC News. "Tunisian Politician Mohammed Brahmi Assassinated." July 25, 2013. http://www.bbc.com/news /world-africa-23452979

Beinin, Joel. "The Working Class and the Popular Movement." In *The Journey to Tahrir*, edited by Jeannie Sowers, and Chris Toensing, 92–106. New York: Verso, 2012.

Bellin, Eva, "Explaining Democratic Divergence: Why Tunisia Succeeded and Egypt has failed." Workshop on the Arab Thermidor: The Resurgence of the Security State, October 10, 2014. https://pomeps.org/2014/12/10/explaining-democratic-divergence/

Bellin, Eva. "Reconsidering the Robustness of Authoritarianism in the Middle East: Lessons from the Arab Spring." *Comparative Politics* 44, no. 2 (January 2012): 127–149.

Bellin, Eva. "The Robustness of Authoritarianism in the Middle East: Exceptionalism in Comparative Perspective." *Comparative Politics* 36, no. 2 (January 2004): 139–157.

Bellin, Eva. "Tunisian Industrialists and the State." *World Development* 22, no. 3 (1994): 427–436.

Bishara, Dina. "Labor Movement in Tunisia and Egypt." *Stiftung Wissenschaft und Politik* (SWP). Comments 1 (January 2014): 1–8.

Bishara, Dina. "The Power of Workers in Egypt's 2011 Uprising." In *Arab Spring in Egypt: Revolution and Beyond*, edited by Bahgat Korany, and Rabab El-Mahdi, 83–104. Cairo and New York: The American University in Cairo Press, 2012.

Black, Ian. "Mohammed Morsi: The Egyptian Opposition Charge Sheet." *The Guardian*, July 3, 2013. https://www.theguardian.com/world/2013/jul/03/mohamed-morsi-egypt-president opposition

Bogaert, Koenraad. "Contextualizing the Arab Revolts: The Politics behind Three Decades of Neoliberalism in the Arab World." *Middle East Critique Special Issue* 22, no. 3 (October 2013): 213–234.

Bond, Patrick. "Neoliberal Threats to North Africa." *Review of African Political Economy* 38, no. 129 (2011): 481–495.

Borger, Julia, Angelique Chrisafis, and Chris Stephen. "Tunisian National Dialogue Quartet Wins 2015 Nobel Peace Prize." *The Guardian*, October 9, 2015. https://www.theguardian.com/world/ 2015/oct/09/tunisian-national-dialogue-quartet-wins-2015-nobel-peace-prize

Boubekeur, Amel. "Islamists, Secularists and Old Regime Elites in Tunisia: Bargained Competition." *Mediterranean Politics* 21, no. 1 (2016): 107–127.

Bowen, Jeremy. *The Arab Uprisings: The People Want the Fall of the System*. London: Simon & Schuster, 2012.

Breaking News. "Essebsi: Call of Tunisia Will Not Govern Alone Even if They Got a Majority." October 29, 2014. http://breakingnews.sy/en/article/43094.html

Bremmer, Ian. "The Top 5 Countries Where ISIS Gets Its Foreign Recruits." *TIME Magazine*, April 14, 2017. http://time.com/4739488/isis-iraq-syria-tunisia-saudi-arabia-russia/

Brooks, Risa. "Subjecting the Military to the Rule of Law: The Tunisian Model." In *Building the Rule of Law in the Arab World: Tunisia, Egypt and Beyond*, edited by Eva Bellin, and Heidi Lane, 109–130. Boulder, CO: Lynne Rienner Publishers, 2016.

Brown, Nathan J., and Amr Hamzawy. "The Draft Political Platform of the Egyptian Muslim Brotherhood: Foray into Political Integration or Retreat into Old Positions." *Carnegie Papers Middle East Series*, no. 89 (January 2008): 1–24.

Brown, Nathan J., Michele Dunne, and Amr Hamzawy. "Egypt's Controversial Constitutional Amendments." *Carnegie Endowment for International Peace*, March 23, 2007. https://carnegieendowment.org/files/egypt_ constitution_web-commentary01.pdf

Brownlee, Jason. "A New Generation of Autocracy in Egypt." *The Brown Journal of World Affairs* 14, no. 1 (Fall/Winter 2007): 72–85.

Brumberg, Daniel. "Could Tunisia's National Dialogue Model Ever Be Replicated?" *Washington Post*, October 12, 2015. https://www.washingtonpost.com/news/monkey-cage/wp/2015/10/12/ could-tunisias-national-dialogue-model-ever-be-replicated/

Brumberg, Daniel. "Democratization in the Arab World? The Trap of Liberalized Autocracy." *Journal of Democracy* 13, no. 4 (October 2002): 56–68.

Brumberg, Daniel. "Reconsidering Theories of Transition." In *Reflections on the Arab Uprisings*, edited by Marc Lynch. POMEPS Studies 10, November 17, 2014. https://pomeps.org/wp-content/ uploads/2014/11/POMEPS _ Studies_10_ Reflections_web1.pdf

Cairo Institute for Human Rights Studies. "One Year into Mohammed Morsi's Term Manifold Abuses and the Systematic Undermining of the Rule of Law." June 26, 2013. http://www.cihrs.org/?p=6849&lang=en

Carlstrom, Gregg. "Explainer: Inside Egypt's Recent Elections." *Aljazeera*, November 15, 2011. http://www.aljazeera.com/indepth/spotlight/egypt/2011/11/201111138837156949.html

Carlstrom, Gregg, and Evan Hill. "Scorecard: Egypt since the Revolution." *Aljazeera*, January 24, 2012. http://www.aljazeera.com/indepth/interactive/2012/01/20121227117613598.html?xif=;Protests

Carnegie Endowment for International Peace. "Results of Shura Council Elections." February 29, 2012. http://egyptelections.carnegieendowment.org/2012/02/29/results-of-shura-council-elections

Carnegie Endowment for International Peace. "Tunisia's Municipal Elections." May 10, 2018. http://carnegieendowment.org/sada/76299

Chayes, Sarah. "How a Leftist Labor Union Helped Force Tunisia's Political Settlement." *Carnegie Endowment for International Peace*, March 27, 2014. https://carnegieendowment.org/ 2014/03/27/how-leftist-labor-union-helped-force-tunisia-s-political-settlement-pub-55143

Chemingui, Mohamed A., and Marco V. Sanchez. "Assessing Development Strategies to Achieve MDGs in the Republic of Tunisia." *United Nations Department for Social and Economic Affairs* (October 2011): 1–46.

Churchill, Erik. "The Call for Tunisia." *Foreign Policy*, June 27, 2012. http://foreignpolicy.com/2012/06/27 /the-call-for-tunisia/

CIA World Factbook. "Egypt", "Tunisia". 2012. https://www.cia.gov/index.html

Clancy-Smith, Julia. "From Sidi Bou Zid to Sidi Bou Said: A Longue Duree Approach to the Tunisian Revolutions." In *The Arab Spring: Change and Resistance in the Middle East*, edited by Mark L. Haas, and David W. Lesch. Boulder, 13–34. CO: Westview Press, 2013.

CNN. "Protestors Say Egypt Elections Rigged." December 12, 2005. http://edition.cnn.com/ 2005/WORLD/africa/12/12/egypt.election.protest/index.html?iref= allsearch

Coll, Steve. "The Casbah Coalition." *The New Yorkers*, April 4, 2011. https://www.newyorker.com/magazine/2011/04/04/the-casbah-coalition

Constitutional Declaration of Egypt. March 30, 2011. http://www.wipo.int/edocs/lexdocs/laws/en/eg/eg04 6en.pdf

Constitution of the Arab Republic of Egypt. Unofficial Translation, 2014. http://www.sis.gov.eg/Newvr/Dustor-en001.pdf

Cook, Steven. *Ruling but not Governing: The Military and Political Development in Egypt, Algeria and Turkey*. Baltimore: John Hopkins University Press, 2007.

Cook, Steven. "Tunisia: First Impression." *Council on Foreign Relations*, November 12, 2014. https://www.cfr.org/blog/tunisia-first-impressions

Cordall, Simon Speakman. "Amnesty of the Corrupt: Tunisia's Move to Heal Old Wounds Branded A Sham." *The Guardian*, October 27, 2017. https://www.theguardian.com/global-development/2017/oct/27/tunisia-recnciliation-act-dismissed-amnesty-of-the-corrupt

Crumley, Bruce. "Tunisia Pushes Out Its Strongman: Could Other Arab Countries Follow?" *Time Online*, January 14, 2011. http://content.time.com/time/world/article/0,8599,2042541,00.html

Dahl, Robert. *Polyarchy: Participation and Opposition*. New Haven: Yale University Press, 1971.

Dang, Hai-Anh, and Elena Ianchovichina. "Middle Class Dynamics and the Arab Spring." *Brookings Institute*, March 18, 2016. https://www.brookings.edu/blog/future-development/ 2016/03/18/middle-class-dynamics-and-the-arab-spring/

Davies, James C. "Toward a Theory of Revolution." *American Sociological Review* 27, no. 1 (February 1962): 5–19.

Deutsche Welle. "Tunisia Protests: Is there a Trade-off between a Strong Economy and Democracy?" January 9, 2018. https://www.dw.com/en/tunisia-protests-is-there-a-trade-off-between-a-strong-economy-and-democracy/a-42037864

Diamond, Larry. "Civil Society and the Development of Democracy." *Estudio*, Working Paper 1997/101 (June 1997): 1–71.

Diamond, Larry. "Why Are There No Arab Democracies?" *Journal of Democracy* 21, no. 1 (January 2010): 93–104.

Di Palma, Giuseppe. *To Craft Democracies: An Essay on Democratic Transitions*. Berkeley, Los Angeles, Oxford: University of California Press, 1990.

Doha Institute Arab Center for Research and Policy Studies. "Tunisia's Elections: A Milestone on the Path to Democratic Transformation." *Assessment Report* (October 2011) https://www.dohainstitute.org/en/Political Studies/Pages/Tunisias_elections_ A_milestone_ on_the_path_to_democratic_transformation.aspx

Downs, George W., and Bruce Bueno de Mesquita. "Development and Democracy." *Foreign Affairs* 84, no. 5 (Sep.–Oct. 2005): 77–86.

Dreisbach, Tristan, and Robert Joyce. "Revealing Tunisia's Corruption under Ben Ali." *Aljaazera*, March 27, 2014. https://www.aljazeera.com/indepth/features/2014/03/revealing-tunisia-corruption-under-ben-ali-201432785 825560542.html

Dugit-Gros, Mathilde. "Foreign Influence in the Middle East: Changes in Perceptions and Expectations." *Arab Reform Initiative*, September 10, 2015. https://www.arab-reform.net/en/ node/763

Durac, Vincent. "A Flawed Nexus?: Civil Society and Democratization in the Middle East and North Africa." *Middle East Institute*, October 15, 2015. http://www.mei.edu/content/map/flawed-nexus-civil-society-and-democratization-middle-east-and-north-africa

Echagüe, Ana. "The Role of External Actors in Arab Transitions." *FRIDE Policy Brief*, no. 122 (April 2012): 1–6.

Egypt Independent. "Brotherhood Leader: Proposed Constitutional Amendments Mostly Reasonable." February 27, 2011. http://www.egyptindependent.com/brotherhood-leader-proposed-constitutional-amendments-mostly-reasonable/

Egypt Independent. "Egypt Army Topples Morsy." July 3, 2012. http://www.egyptindependent.com/egypt-army-topples-morsy/

Egypt Independent. "Egypt's Brotherhood Wins 47% of Parliament Seats." January 21, 2012. http://www.egyptindependent.com/egypts-brotherhood-wins-47-parliament-seats/

Egypt Independent. "Judges Club Lashes Out at Morsy's Decisions." November 22, 2012. http://www.egyptindependent.com/judges-club-lashes-out-morsy-s-decisions/

Egypt Independent. "Morsi Issues New Constitutional Declaration." November 22, 2012. http://www.egyptindependent.com/morsy-issues-new-constitutional-declaration/

Egypt Independent. "SCAF Expands Its Power with Constitutional Amendments." June 17, 2012. http://www.egyptindependent.com/scaf-expands-its-power-constitutional-amendments/

Egypt Independent. "Secular Figures Withdraw from Constituent Assembly, Call Draft Egypt's Downfall." November 18, 2012. http://www.egyptindependent.com/secular-figures-withdraw-constituent-assembly-call-draft-egypt-s-downfall/

Elagati, Mohamed. "Foreign Funding in Egypt after the Revolution." *Fride Working Paper* (2013): 1–20.

El-Din, Gamal Essam. "Islamists Dominate Egypt's Constituent Assembly." *Ahram Online*, March 25, 2012. http://english.ahram.org.eg/NewsContent/1/0/37606/Egypt/0/Islamists-dominate-Egypts-constituent-assembly.aspx

El-Din, Gamal Essam. "Tightening the Grip." *Al-Ahram Weekly*, no. 1053, June 23–29, 2011. http://weekly.ahram.org.eg/Archive/2011/1053/eg5.html

El-Ghobashy, Mona. "Egypt Looks Ahead to Portentous Year." *Middle East Research*, February 2, 2005. http://www.merip.org/mero/mero020205

El-Hennawy, Noha. "Controversy Heightens over Proposed Constitutional Amendments." *Egypt Independent*, March 3, 2011. http://www.egyptindependent.com/controversy-heightens-over-proposed-constitutional-amendments/

El-Masri, Samar. "Tunisian Women at a Crossroads: Cooptation or Autonomy?" *Middle East Policy Council* 22, no. 2 (Summer 2015). https://www.mepc org/tunisian-women-crossroads-cooptation-or-autonomy

El Nadeem Center for Rehabilitation of Victims of Violence. "Torture in Egypt during a Year of Muslim Brotherhood Rule." June 26, 2013. https://alnadeem.org/en/content/torture-egypt-during-year-muslim-brotherhood-rule

El-Sherif, Ashraf. "Egypt's Post-Mubarak Predicament." *Carnegie Endowment for International Peace*, January 29, 2014. https://carnegieendowment.org/2014/01/29/egypt-s-post-mubarak-predicament-pub-54328

Epatko, Larisa. "Mubarak in 1993: Egypt Keen on Democracy, But It Will Take Time." *PBS Newshour*, February 4, 2011. http://www.pbs.org/newshour/rundown/mubarak-on-democracy

Eskandar, Wael. "Year of the SCAF A Time-line of Mounting Repression." *Ahram Online*, February 11, 2012. http://english.ahram.org.eg/NewsContent/1/64/34046/Egypt/Politics-/Year-of-the-SCAF-a-timeline-of-mounting-repression.aspx

Esposito, John L., Tamara Sonn, and John Obert Voll. *Islam and Democracy after the Arab Spring*. Oxford: Oxford University Press, 2016.

European Commission High Representative of the Union for Foreign Affairs and Security Policy. "Report on EU-Egypt Relations in the Framework of the Revised ENP." July 13, 2017. https://eeas.europa.eu/sites/eeas/files/2017_report_on_eu-egypt_relations_2015-2017.pdf

Fahim, Kareem. "In Upheaval for Egypt, Morsi Forces out Military Chiefs." *New York Times*, August 12, 2012. https://www.nytimes.com/2012/08/13/world/middleeast/egyptian-leader-ousts-military-chiefs.

Fahim, Kareem, and Mayy El Sheikh. "New Egyptian Cabinet Includes Many Holdovers." *New York Times*, August 2, 2012. http://www.nytimes.com/2012/08/03/world/middleeast/new-egyptian-cabinet.html?mcubz=0

Feuer, Sarah J. "From Political Islam to Muslim Democracy: Tunisia's Ennahda Changes Course." *Foreign Affairs*, June 8, 2016. https://www.foreignaffairs.com/articles/tunisia/2016-06-08/political-islam-muslim-democracy

Feuer, Sarah J. "Islam and Democracy in Practice: Tunisia's Ennahda Nine Months In." *Middle East Brief* 66 (September 2012): 1–8.

Feuer, Sarah. "Tunisia, A Success Story? The Troubles Rattling Its Fragile Democracy." *Foreign Affairs*, July 6, 2017. https://www.foreignaffairs.com/articles/tunisia/2017-07-06/tunisia-success-story

Financial Times. "Tunisia in Turmoil, Interview Transcript: Rachid Ghannouchi." January 18, 2011. https://www.ft.com/content/24d710a6-22ee-11e0-ad0b-00144feab49a

Fitouri, Samia. "Tunisia Still Undecided Over Form of Government for New Democracy." *Tunisia Live*, February 10, 2012. http://www.tunisia-live.net/2012/02/10/tunisia-still-undecided-over-form-of-government-for-new-democracy/

Freedom House. "Freedom in the World 2015: Tunisia." https://www.refworld.org/publisher,FREEHOU,,TUN,5502f33b9,0.html

Freedom House. "Freedom in the World 2016: Tunisia." https://freedomhouse.org/sites/default/files/FH_FITW_Report_2016.pdf

Freedom House. "Freedom in the World 2018-Country Reports: Tunisia." https://freedomhouse.org/report/freedom-world/2018/tunisia

Freedom House. "Freedom in the World 2020-Country Reports: Egypt." https://freedomhouse.org/country/egypt/freedom-world/2020

Freedom House. "Freedom in the World 2020-Country Reports: Tunisia." https://freedomhouse.org/country/tunisia/freedom-world/2020

Freedom House. "Middle East and North Africa." https://freedomhouse.org/regions/middle-east-and-north-africa

Fukuyama, Francis. *The End of History and the Last Man*. New York: The Free Press, 1992.

Gall, Carlotta. "The Return of Thousands of Young Jihadists." *The New York Times*, February 25, 2017. https://www.nytimes.com/2017/02/25/world/europe/isis-tunisia.html

Gana, Nouri. *The Making of the Tunisian Revolution: Contexts, Architects, Prospects*. Edinburgh: Edinburgh University Press, 2013.

Gelwin, James L. *The Arab Uprisings: What Everyone Needs to Know*. New York: Oxford University Press, 2015.

Ghabian, Najib. *Democratization and Islamist Challenge*. Boulder, CO: Westview Press, 1997.

Ghabra, Shafeeq. "The Egyptian Revolution: Causes and Dynamics." In *Routledge Handbook of the Arab Spring: Rethinking Democratization*, edited by Larbi Sadiki, 199–214. London and New York: Routledge.

Ghafar, Adel Abdel. *Egyptians in Revolt: The Political Economy of Labor and Student Mobilizations 1919–2011*. New York: Routledge, 2017.

Ghannam, Angy. "Islamists in Egypt's tourist spots win surprise support." *BBC News*, December 28, 2011. http://www.bbc.com/news/world-middle-east-16348229

Gluck, Jason. "Constitutional Reform in Transitional States: Challenges and Opportunities Facing Egypt and Tunisia." *United States Institute of Peace*, Peacebrief *92*, April 29, 2011. https://www.usip.org/sites/default/files/PB92.pdf

Gobe, Eric. "The Gafsa Mining Basin between Riots and a Social Movement: Meaning and Significance of a Protest Movement in Ben Ali's Tunisia." *HAL Working Paper*, 2010. https://halshs.archives-ouvertes.fr/halshs-00557826

Gordon, Michael R. "Egyptians Following Right Path." *New York Times*, November 3, 2013. http://www.nytimes.com/2013/11/04/world/middleeast/kerry-egypt-visit.html

Grugel, Jean. *Democratization: A Critical Introduction*. Houndmills, NY: Palgrave Macmillan, 2000.

Guazzone, Laura. "Ennahda Islamists and the Test of Government in Tunisia." *The International Spectator* 48, no. 4 (December 2013): 30–50.

Guo, Sujian. "Democratic Transition: A Critical Overview." *Issues & Studies* 35, no. 4 (July/August 1999): 133–148.

Hajji, Lutfi. "The 18 October Coalition for Rights and Freedoms." *Arab Reform Initiative*, October 13, 2006. http://www.arab-reform.net/en/node/350

Halabi, Yakub. *US Foreign Policy in the Middle East: From Crises to Change*. New York: Routledge, 2016.

Hamad, Mahmoud. "The Constitutional Challenges in Post-Mubarak Egypt." *Insight Turkey* 14, no. 1 (2012): 51–69.

Hamzawy, Amr. "Egypt: Evaluating Proposed Constitutional Amendments." *Los Angeles Times*, March 7, 2011. http://carnegieendowment.org/2011/03/07/egypt-evaluating-proposed-constitutional-amendments-pub-42923

Hamzawy, Amr. "Egypt's Parliament Opens Doors for More Repression." *Washington Post*, September 22, 2016. https://www.washingtonpost.com/news/global-opinions/wp/2016/09/22/ egypts-parliament-opens-the-door-for-more-repression/?utm_term=.4694e755e641

Hamzawy, Amr. "The Tragedy of Egypt's Stolen Revolution." *Aljazeera*, January 25, 2017. http://www.aljazeera.com/indepth/features/2017/01/tragedy-egypt-stolen-revolution-170125062306232.html

Handy, Howard, and staff team. *Egypt: Beyond Stabilization, Toward a Dynamic Market Economy*. Washington, DC: International Monetary Fund, 1998.

Hearst, David. "Why Saudi Arabia is Taking a Risk by backing the Egyptian Coup?" *The Guardian*, August 20, 2013. https://www.theguardian.com/commentisfree/2013/aug/20/saudi-arabia-coup-egypt

Hermassi, Abdelbaki. "Socio-economic Change and Political Implications." In *Democracy Without Democrats? The Renewal of Politics in the Muslim World*, edited by Ghassan Salame. London, New York: I.B. Tauris, 1994.

Heydemann, Steve. "Upgrading Authoritarianism in the Arab World." *Saban Centre for Middle East Policy Analysis Paper*, no. 13 (October 2007): 1–38.

Hibou, Béatrice. "Domination & Control in Tunisia: Economic Levers for the Exercise of Authoritarian Power." *Review of African Political Economy* 33, no. 108 (June 2006): 185–206.

Hill, Evan. "Election Day in Mansoura." *Aljazeera*, November 29, 2010. http://archive.is/20120708001856/blogs.aljazeera.com/blog/middle-east/election-day-mansoura

Hinnebusch, Raymond. "Authoritarian Persistence, Democratization Theory and the Middle East: An Overview and Critique." *Democratization* 13, no. 3 (June 2006): 373–395.

Hubbard, Ben, and David Kirkpatrick. "Sudden Improvements in Egypt Suggest a Campaign to Undermine Morsi." *New York Times*, July 10, 2013. http://www.nytimes.com/2013/07/11/world/ middleeast/improvements-in-egypt-suggest-a-campaign-that-undermined-morsi.html

Hulsman, Cornelis, Diana Serodio, and Jayson Casper. "The Development of Egypt's Constitution: Analysis, Assessment and Sorting through the Rhetoric." *Arab-West Report* (May 2013): 8–95.

Human Rights Watch. "Egypt: New Law Keeps Military Trials of Civilians." May 7, 2012. https://www.hrw.org/news/2012/05/07/egypt-new-law-keeps-military-trials-civilians

Human Rights Watch. "Egypt: New Parliament Should Fix Abusive Laws." January 12, 2016. https://www.hrw.org/news/2016/01/12/egypt-new-parliament-should-fix-abusive-laws

Human Rights Watch. "Egypt: Rab'a Killings Likely Crimes against Humanity." August 12, 2014. https://www.hrw.org/news/2014/08/12/egypt-raba-killings-likely-crimes-against-humanity

Human Rights Watch. "Egypt: Year of Abuses under Al-Sisi." June 8, 2015. https://www.hrw.org/news/2015/06/08/egypt-year-abuses-under-al-sisi

Human Rights Watch. "New Constitution Mixed on Support of Rights." November 30, 2012. https://www.hrw.org/news/2012/11/30/egypt-new-constitution-mixed-support-rights

Human Rights Watch. "No Joy in Egypt." January 25, 2012. https://www.hrw.org/news/2012/01/25/no-joy-egypt

Human Rights Watch. "World Report 2010: Egypt." https://www.hrw.org/world-report/2010/ countrychapters/egypt

Human Rights Watch. "World Report 2018: Tunisia." https://www.hrw.org/world-report/2018/country-chapters/tunisia

Huntington, Samuel P. "Democracy's Third Wave." *Journal of Democracy* 2, no. 2 (Spring 1991): 12–34.

Huntington, Samuel. *The Soldier and the State: The Theory and Politics of Civil Military Relations*. New York: Belknap Press, 1957.

Huntington, Samuel. *The Third Wave: Democratization in the Late Twentieth Century*. Norman: University of Oklahoma Press, 1991.

Hurriyet Daily News. "Judge Orders Mubarak Sons Detained in New Case." August 2, 2012. http://www.hurriyetdailynews.com/judge-orders-mubarak-sons-detained-in-new-case--26930

Hussein, Abdel-Rahman. "Egypt: Mohamed Morsi Cancels Decree that Gave him Sweeping Powers." *The Guardian*, December 9, 2012. https://www.theguardian.com/world/2012/dec/09/egypt-mohamed-morsi-cancels-decree

Hussein, Walaa. "Egypt's Tamarod Outlives Its Purpose." *Al-Monitor*, May 8, 2015. http://www.al-monitor.com/pulse/originals/2015/05/egypt-tamarod-movement-political-campaign-mubarak-sisi.html

Ibrahim, Ekram. "6th of April 2008: A Workers' Strike Which Fired the Egyptian Revolution." *Ahram Online*, April 6, 2012. http://english.ahram.org.eg/NewsContent/1/64/38580/Egypt/ Politics-/th-of-April--A-workers-strike-which-fired-the-Egyp.aspx

Ikram, Khalid. *The Egyptian Economy, 1952–2000: Performance, Policies and Issues*. New York: Routledge, 2006.

Inglehart, Ronald, and Christian Welzel. "How Development Leads to Democracy." *Foreign Affairs*, March 1, 2009.

Inman, Philip. "Mubarak Family Fortune Could Reach 70 Billion Dollars." *The Guardian*, February 4, 2011. https://www.theguardian.com/world/2011/feb/04/hosni-mubarak-family-fortune

International Monetary Fund. "Arab Republic of Egypt: 2010 Article IV Consultation." *Country Report*, no. 10/94 (April 2010). https://www.imf.org/external/pubs/ft/scr/2010/cr1094.pdf

International Monetary Fund. "Tunisia: 2007 Article IV Consulting Mission, Preliminary Conclusions." *Country Report*, no. 02/122 (May 2007). https://www.imf.org/en/News/Articles/2015/09/28/04/52/mcs062907

International Republican Institute. "Public Opinion Survey of Tunisians November 23 to December 2017." January 10, 2018. http://www.iri.org/sites/default/files/2018-01-10_tunisia_poll_presentation.pdf

International Republican Institute. "Survey of Tunisian Public Opinion." February 2014. http://www.iri.org/sites/default/files/2014%20April%2023%20Survey%20of%20Tunisian%20Public%20Opinion,%20February%2012-22,%202014.pdf

International Republican Institute Center for Insights. "Tunisia Poll: Underperforming Economy and Corruption Continue to Drive Intense Satisfaction." September 26, 2017. https://www.iri.org/resource/tunisia-poll-underperforming-economy-and-corruption-continue-drive-intense-dissatisfaction

Irshad, Ghazala. "Egypt's Political Transition: A Timeline of Egypt's Political Transition." *The Cairo Review of Global Affairs* (Summer 2012). https://www.thecairoreview.com/timelines/timelines-egypts-political-transition/

Isbell, Thomas. "Separate or Compatible? Islam and Democracy in Five North African Countries." *Afrobarometer Dispatch* 188, February 14, 2018. https://afrobarometer.org/publications/ad188-separate-and-compatible-islam-and-democracy-five-north-african-countries

Ismael, Tareq Y., Jacqueline S. Ismael, and Glenn E. Perry. *Government and Politics of the Contemporary Middle East. Continuity and Change*. New York: Routledge, 2016.

Jamal, Amaney, and Mark Tessler. "The Democracy Barometers: Attitudes in the Arab World." *Journal of Democracy* 19, no. 1 (January 2008): 97–110.

Kaldor, Mary and Ivan Vejvoda. "Democratization in Eastern and Central European Countries." *International Affairs* 73, no. 1 (January 1997): 59–82.

Kassem, Maye. *Egyptian Politics: The Dynamics of Authoritarian Rule*. Boulder, CO and London: Lynne Rienner Publishers, 2004.

Kausch, Kristina. "Foreign Funding in Post-Revolution Tunisia." *FRIDE Working Paper* (May 2013): 1–19.

Keane, John. *The Life and Death of Democracy*. UK: Simon & Schuster, 2009.

Khalifa, Sherif. *Egypt's Lost Spring: Causes and Consequences*. Santa Barbara, CA: Praeger Publishers, 2015.

Kienle, Eberhard. "More Than a Response to Islamism: The Political Deliberalization of Egypt in the 1990s." *Middle East Journal* 52, no. 2 (Spring 1998): 219–235.

Kingsley, Patrick. "Abdal Fatah Al-Sisi Won 96.1% of Vote in Egypt Presidential Election, Say Officials." *The Guardian*, June 3, 2014. https://www.theguardian.com/world/2014/jun/03/abdel-fatah-al-sisi-presidential-election-vote-egypt

Kingsley, Patrick. "Egyptian Judge Sentences 720 Men to Death." *The Guardian*, April 28, 2014. https://www.theguardian.com/world/2014/apr/28/egyptian-judge-sentences-720-men-death

Kirkpatrick, David D., and Karem Fahim. "Egypt Race Pits Aide to Mubarak against Islamist." *New York Times*, May 25, 2012. http://www.nytimes.com/2012/05/26/world/middleeast/egypt-presidential-election-runoff.html?mcubz=0

Kirkpatrick, David D., Kareem Fahim, and Ben Hubbard. "By the Millions, Egyptians Seek Morsi's Ouster." *New York Times*, June 30, 2013. http://www.nytimes.com/2013/07/01/world/middleeast/egypt.html

Kitschelt, Herbert. "Political Regime Change: Structure and Process-Driven Explanations?" *American Political Science Review* 86, no. 4 (December 1992): 1028–1034.

Koplow, Michael. "Why Tunisia's Revolution is Islamist Free." *Foreign Policy*, January 14, 2011.

Lerner, Daniel. *The Passing of Traditional Society: Modernizing Middle East*. New York: Free Press of Glencoe, 1958.

Levitsky, Steven, and Lucan A. Way. "International Linkage and Democratization." *Journal of Democracy* 16, no. 3 (July 2005): 20–34.

Levitsky, Steven, and Lucan Way. "The Rise of Competitive Authoritarianism." *Journal of Democracy* 13, no. 2 (April 2002): 20–34.

Linz, Juan. *The Breakdown of Democratic Regimes: Crisis, Breakdown and Reequilibration*. Baltimore: John Hopkins University Press, 1978.

Linz, Juan J., and Alfred Stepan. "Towards Consolidated Democracies." *Journal of Democracy* 7, no. 2 (April 1996): 14–33.

Linz, Juan, and Alfred Stepan. *Problems of Democratic Transition and Consolidation: Southern Europe, South America and Post-Communist Europe*. Baltimore: John Hopkins University Press, 1996.

Lippmann, Walter. "The Indispensable Opposition." *Atlantic Monthly*, CLXIV (1939): 234 as cited in *The Arab Spring: Pathways of Repression and Reform*, edited by Jason Brownlee, Tarek Masoud, and Andrew Reynolds. Oxford and New York: Oxford University Press, 2015.

Lipset, Seymour M. "Some Social Requisites of Democracy: Economic Development and Political Legitimacy." *American Political Science Review* 53, no. 1 (March 1959): 69–105.

Lust-Okar, Ellen. "Divided They Rule the Management and Manipulation of Political Opposition." *Comparative Politics* 36, no. 2 (January 2004): 159–179.

Mada Masr. "World Bank: Egypt's Middle Class Shrank in the Lead-up to the Arab Spring." May 22, 2016. https://www.madamasr.com/en/2016/05/22/news/u/world-bank-egypts-middle-class-shrank-in-the-lead-up-to-arab-spring/

Maghraoui, Abdeslam. "Egypt's Failed Transition to Democracy: Was Political Culture a Major Factor?" *E-International Relations*, April 29, 2014. http://www.e-ir.info/2014/04/29/egypts-failed-transition-to-democracy-was-political-culture-a-major-factor/

Mainwaring, Scott. "Transitions to Democracy and Democracy and Democratic Consolidation: Theoretical and Comparative Issues." *Kellogg Institute*, Working Paper 130 (November 1998): 1–43.

Mainwaring, Scott, Guillermo O.'Donnell, and J. Samuel Valenzuela. *Issues in Democratic Consolidation: The New South American Democracies in Comparative Perspective*. Notre Dame: University of Notre Dame Press, 1992.

Majalla. "The Muslim Brotherhood versus Ennahda." December 26, 2013. http://eng.majalla.com/2013/12/article55247739/the-muslim-brotherhood-versus-ennahda

Mansour, Sherif. "Enough is Not Enough: Achievements and Shortcomings of Kefaya, the Egyptian Movement for Change." In *Civilian Jihad: Nonviolent Struggle, Democratization and Governance in the Middle East*, edited by Maria J. Stephan, 205–218. New York: Palgrave Macmillan, 2009.

Mansour, Sherif. "On the Divide: Press Freedom at Risk in Egypt." *A Report by the Committee to Protect Journalists* (CPJ), August 14, 2013. https://cpj.org/reports/2013/08/on-divide-egypt-press-freedom-morsi.php

Maria Cristina Paciello, "Tunisia: Changes and Challenges of Political Transition," *MEDPRO Technical Report* 3 (May 2011).

Marinov, Nikolay, and Hein Goemans. "Coups and Democracy." *British Journal of Political Science* 44, no. 4 (October 2014): 799–825.

Marks, Monica. "Tunisia Opts for an Inclusive New Government." *The Washington Post*, February 3, 2015. https://www.washingtonpost.com/news/monkey-cage/wp/2015/02/03/ tunisia-opts-for-an-inclusive-new-government/?utm_term=.307df1b7184e

Masoud, Tarek. "Egyptian Democracy: Smothered in the Cradle, or Stillborn?" *The Brown Journal of World Affairs* 20, no. 2 (Spring/ Summer 2014): 3–19.

Masoud, Tarek. "Has the Door Closed on Arab Democracy." *Journal of Democracy* 26, no. 1 (January 2015): 74–87.

McInerney, Stephen. "SCAF's Assault on Egypt's Civil Society." *Foreign Policy*, September 28, 2011.

McInerney, Stephen. "The Federal Budget and Appropriations for Fiscal Year 2013: Democracy, Governance and Human Rights in the Middle East North Africa." *Project on Middle East Democracy* (July 2012): 2–35. https://pomed.org/wp-content/uploads/2012/07/ FY2013-Budget-Report.pdf

McInerney, Stephen and Cole Bockenfeld. "The Federal Budget and Appropriations for Fiscal Year 2017: Democracy, Governance and Human Rights in the Middle East and North Africa." *Project on Middle East Democracy* (April 2016): 1–75. https://pomed.org/wp-content/ uploads/ 2016/07/POMED_BudgetReport _FY17 _Final-Web.pdf

Mckenna, Amy. *The History of Northern Africa*. New York: Britannica Educational Publishing, 2010.

Mersch, Sarah. "Tunisia's Compromise Constitution." *Carnegie Endowment for International Peace*, January 21, 2014. http://carnegieendowment.org/sada/?fa=54260

Miller, Laurel E., Jeffrey Martini, F. Stephen Larrabee, Angel Rabasa, Stephanie Pezard, Julie E. Taylor, and Tewodaj Mengistu. *Democratization in the Arab World: Prospects and Lessons from Around the Globe*. Santa Monica, CA: RAND Corporation, 2012.

Mitchell, Timothy. "Dreamland: The Neoliberalism of Your Desires." *Middle East Research 210*, no. 29, Spring 1999. https://www.merip.org/mer/mer210/dreamland-neoliberalism-your-desires?em_x=22

Momani, Bessma. "In Egypt, 'Deep State' vs. 'Brotherhoodization'." *The Brookings Institution*, August 21, 2013. https://www.brookings.edu/opinions/in-egypt-deep-state-vs-brotherhoodization/

Moore, Barrington. *Injustice: The Social Bases of Obedience and Revolt*. New York: White Plains, 1967.

Murphy, Emma C. *Economic and Political Change in Tunisia: From Bourguiba to Ben Ali*. New York: St. Martin's Press, 1999.

Nagarajan, Karatholuvu Viswanatha. "Egypt's Political Economy and the Downfall of the Mubarak Regime." *International Journal of Humanities and Social Science* 3, no. 10 (May 2013): 22–39.

Najjar, Farah. "Why US Aid to Egypt is Never under Threat." *Aljazeera*, October 3, 2017. https://www.aljazeera.com/news/2017/10/aid-egypt-threat-171002093316209.html

National Democratic Institute. "Final Report on the 2014 Legislative and Presidential Elections in Tunisia." https://www.ndi.org/sites/default/files/Tunisia%20Election%20Report%202014_EN_SOFT%20(1).pdf

National Democratic Institute. "Final Report on the Tunisian National Constituent Assembly Elections." October 23, 2011. https://www.ndi.org/files/tunisia-final-election-report-021712_v2.pdf

National Election Authority, Egypt. https://www.elections.eg/en/

New York Times. "Egypt Supreme Council of the Armed Forces: Statements and Key Leaders." February 14, 2011. http://www.nytimes.com/interactive/2011/02/10/world/middleeast/20110210egypt-supreme-council.html?mcubz=0

New York Times. "Egypt's Imitation Election." September 11, 2005. http://query.nytimes.com/gst/fullpage.html?res=9E07E5D61331F932A2575AC0A9639C8B63

Noueihed, Lin, and Tom Perry. "Tunisian Islamists Show Strength at Chief's Return." *Reuters*, January 30, 2011. http://blogs.reuters.com/faithworld/2011/01/30/2011/01/30/tunisian-islamists-show-strength-at-chiefs-return/

NPR. Interview with David Kirkpatrick "Morsi's Ouster in Egypt: A "Bookend" for the Arab Spring." July 22, 2013. http://www.npr.org/2013/07/22/203616418/morsis-ouster-in-egypt-a-bookend-for-the-arab-spring

O'Donnell, Guillermo. *Modernization and Bureaucratic Authoritarianism: Studies in South American Politics*. Berkeley, CA: University of California Press, 1973.

O'Donnell, Guillermo, Philippe Schmitter, and Laurence Whitehead. *Transitions from Authoritarian Rule: Prospects for Democracy*. Baltimore: Johns Hopkins University Press, 1986.

OECD. "OECD-DAC Air Statistics, Recipients at a Glance: Egypt, 2015–2016 Average." http://www.oecd.org/dac/financing-sustainable-development/development-finance-data/aid-at-a-glance.htm

OECD. "OECD-DAC Air Statistics, Recipients at a Glance: Tunisia, 2015–2016 Average." http://www.oecd.org/dac/stats/aid-at-a-glance.htm#recipients

Omri, Mohamed Salah. "Tunisian Constitution: The Process and the Outcome." *Jadaliyya*, February 12, 2014. http://www.jadaliyya.com/Details/30221/The-Tunisian-Constitution-The-Process-and-the-Outcome

Osman, Magued. "The President's Approval Rating after 11 Months in Office." *Egyptian Center for Public Opinion Research* (Baseera), May 29–30, 2013. http://baseera.com.eg/EN/PressPoll-Ar/24_En.pdf

Ottoway, Marina, and Julia Choucair-Vizoso. *Beyond Façade: Political Reform in the Arab World*. Washington: Carnegie Endowment, 2008.

Paciello, Maria Cristina. "Egypt: Changes and Challenges of Political Transition." *Mediterranean Prospects Technical Report*, no. 4 (May 2011): 1–31.

Perkins, Kenneth J. *A History of Modern Tunisia*. Cambridge: Cambridge University Press, 2004.

Pew Research Center. "Democratic Values in Egypt." May 22, 2014. http://www.pewglobal.org/2014/05/22/chapter-3-democratic-values-in-egypt/

Pew Research Center. "Egyptians Increasingly Glum." *Global Attitudes Project*, May 16, 2013. http://www.pewglobal.org/2013/05/16/egyptians-increasingly-glum/

Pew Research Center. "Tunisian Confidence in Democracy Wanes." October 15, 2014. http://www.pewglobal.org/2014/10/15/tunisian-confidence-in-democracy-wanes/

Pew Research Center. "US Wins No Friends, End of Treaty with Israel Sought; Egyptians Embrace Revolt Leaders, Religious Parties and Military, As Well." April 25, 2011. http://www.pewglobal.org/files/2011/04/Pew-Global-Attitudes-Egypt-Report-FINAL-April-25-2011.pdf

Pickard, Duncan. "Identity, Islam and Women in the Tunisian Constitution." *Atlantic Council*, January 24, 2014. http://www.atlanticcouncil.org/blogs/menasource/identity-islam-and-women-in-the-tunisian-constitution

Pickard, Duncan. "The Current Status of Constitution Making in Tunisia." *Carnegie Endowment for International Peace*, April 19, 2012.

Pioppi, Daniela. "Playing with Fire. The Muslim Brotherhood and the Egyptian Leviathan." *The International Spectator: Italian Journal of International Affairs* 48, no. 4 (December 2013): 51–68.

Prashad, Vijay. *The Death of the Nation and the Future of the Arab Revolutions*. California: California University Press, 2016.

Pratt, Nicola. *Democracy & Authoritarianism in the Arab World*. Boulder, CO: Lynne Reinner Publishers, 2007.

Pridham, Geoffrey. *The Dynamics of Democratization. A Comparative Approach*. London and New York: Continuum, 2000.

Project on Middle East Democracy. A Conversation with Dr. Ashraf El Sherif "A Dangerous Deterioration: Egypt under Al-Sisi." June 2017. http://pomed.org/pomed-publications/a-dangerous-deterioration-egypt-under-al-sisi-a-conversation-with-dr-ashraf-el-sherif/

Przeworski, Adam, and Fernando Limongi. "Modernization: Theories and Facts." *World Politics* 49, no. 2 (January 1997): 155–183.

Przeworski, Adam, Jose Antonio Cheibub, Michael E. Alvarez, and Fernando Limongi. *Democracy and Development: Political Institutions and Material Well-being in the World, 1950–1990*. Cambridge: Cambridge University Press, 2000.

Rahman, Natalya. "Democracy in the Middle East and North Africa: Five Years After the Arab Uprisings." Arab Barometer-Wave IV (October 2018).

Reuters. "Tunisian Constitution Will Make No Place for Faith." November 4, 2011. https://af.reuters.com/article/commoditiesNews/idAFL6E7M42ND20111104

Revkin, Mara. "Egypt's Untouchable President." *Foreign Policy*, November 25, 2012. http://foreignpolicy.com/2012/11/25/egypts-untouchable-president/

Revkin, Mara, and Yussef Auf. "Beyond the Ballot Box: Egypt's Constitutional Challenge." *Atlantic Council Issue Brief* (June 2012). https://www.files.ethz.ch/isn/145484/94969_ACUS_Egypt_Challenge_final-rev.pdf

Revkin, Mara, and Yusuf Auf. "Egypt's Constitutional Chaos." *Foreign Policy*, June 14, 2012.

Rifai, Ryan. "Timeline: Tunisia's Uprising." *Aljazeera*, January 23, 2011. http://www.aljazeera.com/indepth/spotlight/tunisia/2011/01/201114142223827361.html

Ross, Michael L. "Does Oil Hinder Democracy?" *World Politics* 53, no. 3 (April 2001): 325–361.

Rupert, James. "Tunisians Riot Over Bread Price Rise." *Washington Post*, January 4, 1984. https://www.washingtonpost.com/archive/politics/1984/01/04/tunisians-riot-over-bread-price-rise/a5aa4a75-9651-4a30-919e-9c297b3fdb38/?utm_term=.8923cf5026cc

Rustow, Dankwart. "Transitions to Democracy: Towards a Dynamic Model." *Comparative Politics* 2, no. 3 (April 1970): 337–363.

Rutherford, Bruce. *Egypt after Mubarak: Liberalism, Islam and Democracy*. Princeton, NJ: Princeton University Press, 2008.

Rutherford, Bruce K. "Egypt: The Origins and Consequences of the January 25 Uprisings." In *The Arab Spring: Change and Resistance in the Middle East*, edited by Mark L. Haas, and David W. Lesch, 35–63. Boulder, CO: Westview Press, 2013.

Ryan, Yasmine. "Who Killed Tunisia's Chokri Belaid?" *Aljazeera*, September 12, 2013. http://www.aljazeera.com/indepth/%20features/2013/09/201394183325728267.html

Sadiki, Larbi. "Bin Ali's Tunisia: Democracy by Non-democratic Means." *British Journal of Middle Eastern Studies* 29, no. 1 (2002): 57–78.

Sadiki, Larbi. "Engendering Citizenship in Tunisia: Prioritizing Unity over Democracy." In *North Africa: Politics, Region, and the Limits of Transformation*, edited by Yahia Zoubir, and Haizam Amirah-Fernandez. London: Routledge, 2008.

Sadiki, Larbi. "Political Liberalization in Bin Ali's Tunisia: Façade Democracy." *Democratization* 9, no. 4 (Winter 2002): 122–141.

Said, Atef. "The Paradox of Transition to Democracy under Military Rule." *Social Research: An International Quarterly* 79, no. 2 (Summer 2012): 397–434.

Salloukh, Bassel F. "The Arab Uprisings and the Geopolitics of the Middle East." *The International Spectator: Italian Journal of International Affairs* 48, no. 2 (June 2013): 32–46.

Sartori, Giovanni. *The Theory of Democracy Revisited*. Chatnam, NJ: Chatham House Publishers, 1987.

Schafer, Isabel. "The Tunisian Tradition: Torn Between Democratic Consolidation and Neo-Conservatism in an Insecure Regional Context." *European Institute of the Mediterranean*, no. 25 (August 2015): 7–50.

Schenker, David. "A Moment of Decision on Egypt." *The Washington Institute Policy Analysis*, no. 2355, January 14, 2015. http://www.washingtoninstitute.org/policy-analysis/view/a-moment-of-decision-on-egypt

Schmitter, Philippe. "Transitology: The Science or the Art of Democratization." In *The Consolidation of Democracy in Latin America*, edited by Joseph S. Tulchin, and Bernice Romero, 11–44. Boulder, CO: Lynne Rienner Publishers, 1995.

Schmitter, Philippe C., and Guillermo O'Donnell. *Transitions from Authoritarian Rule: Tentative Conclusions About Uncertain Democracies*. Baltimore: John Hopkins University Press, 1996.

Schmitz, Hans Peter, and Susan K. Sell. "International Factors in Processes of Political Democratization: Towards a Theoretical Integration." In *Democracy without Borders: Transnationalization and Conditionality in New Democracies*, edited by Jean Grugel, 23–41. London: Routledge, 1999.

Schumpeter, Joseph. *Capitalism, Socialism and Democracy*. 2nd Ed. New York: Harper & Brothers, 1947.

Schwedler, Jillian. "Can Islamists Become Moderates? Rethinking the Inclusion-Moderation Hypothesis." *World Politics* 63, no. 2 (April 2011): 347–76.

Schwedler, Jillian. *Faith in Moderation: Islamist Parties in Jordan and Yemen*. New York: Cambridge University Press, 2006.

Selim, Gamal. "Egypt under SCAF and the Muslim Brotherhood: The Triangle of Counter Revolution." *Arab Studies Quarterly* 37, no. 2 (Spring 2015): 177–199.

Selim, Gamal. *The International Dimensions of Democratization in Egypt*. Switzerland: Springer International Publishing, 2015.

Serodio, Diana. "Internal Dynamics of the Second Constituent Assembly." In *Development of Egypt's Constitution: Analysis, Assessment and Sorting through the Rhetoric*, edited by Cornelis Hulsman, Diana Serodio, and Jayson Casper, 45–47. Cairo: Arab-West Report, May 2013.

Shadid, Anthony, and David D. Kirkpatrick. "Promise of Arab Uprisings is Threatened by Divisions." *The New York Times*, May 21, 2011. https://www.nytimes.com/2011/05/22/world/middleeast/22arab.html

Shirayanagi, Kouichi. "Ennahda Spokeswoman Souad Abderrahim: Single Mothers are a Disgrace to Tunisia." *Tunisia Live*, November 9, 2011. http://allafrica.com/stories/201111281676.html

Skocpol, Theda. *States and Social Revolutions*. New York: Cambridge University Press, 1979.

Slachman, Michael. "Egyptian Political Dissident, Imprisoned for Years, is Suddenly Released." *The New York Times*, February 18, 2009. http://www.nytimes.com/2009/02/19/world/middleeast/19egypt.html

Sloan, Alastair. "Is the EU legitimizing Sisi's Coup?" *Aljazeera*, April 20, 2014. https://www.aljazeera.com/indepth/opinion/2014/04/eu-legitimising-sisi-coup-egypt-20144161181767834.html

Stacher, Joshua. "Egypt: The Anatomy of Succession." *Review of African Political Economy* 35, no. 116 (June 2008): 301–314.

Stepan, Alfred. *Rethinking Military Politics: Brazil and the Southern Cone*. Princeton: Princeton University Press, 1988.

Stepan, Alfred. "Tunisia's Transition and the Twin Tolerations." *Journal of Democracy* 23, no. 2 (April 2012): 89–103.

Stepan, Alfred, and Juan J. Linz. "Democratization Theory and the Arab Spring." *Journal of Democracy* 24, no. 2 (April 2003): 15–30.

Subramanian, Arvind. "Egypt: Poised for Sustained Growth?" *Finance and Development* 34, no. 4 (December 1997): 44–45.

Sullivan, Denis. "Will Egypt's Muslim Brotherhood Run in 2010." *Carnegie Middle East Center*, May 5, 2009. http://carnegie-mec.org/sada/23057

Szmolka, Inmaculada. "Exclusionary and Non-Consensual Transitions versus Inclusive and Consensual Democratizations: The Cases of Egypt and Tunisia." *Arab Studies Quarterly* 37, no. 1 (Winter 2015): 73–95.

Tadros, Sherine. "Egypt Military's Economic Empire." *Aljazeera*, February 16, 2012. http://www.aljazeera.com/indepth/features/2012/02/2012215195912519142.html

Tajine, Synda. "Will Tunisian Women Become 'Complimentary' to Men by Law?" *Al-Monitor*, August 14, 2012. http://www.al-monitor.com/pulse/politics/2012/08/tunisia-are-womens-rights-fading.html

Tavana, Daniel, and Alex Russell. "Previewing Tunisia's Parliamentary and Presidential Elections." *Project on Middle East Democracy*, October 2014. https://pomed.org/wp-content/uploads/2014/10/Tunisia-Election-Guide-2014.pdf

Tavana, Daniel, and Alex Russell. "Tunisia's Parliamentary and Presidential Elections." *Project on Middle East Democracy*, October 2014. http://pomed.org/wpcontent/uploads/2014/10/Tunisia-Election-Guide-2014.pdf

Taylor, William C. *Military Responses to the Arab Uprisings and the Future of Civil-Military Relations in the Middle East.* New York: Palgrave Macmillan, 2014.

Teorell, Jan. *Determinants of Democratization: Explaining Regime Change in the World 1972–2006.* Cambridge: Cambridge University Press, 2010.

The Constitution of Tunisia, 1959. http://www.wipo.int/edocs/lexdocs/laws/en/tn/tn028en.pdf

The Constitution of the Tunisian Republic, Translated by UNDP and International IDEA. January 26, 2014. http://www.constitutionnet.org/files/2014.01.26_-_final_constitution_english _idea_ final.pdf

The Economist. "The Islamist Conundrum." October 22, 2011. http://www.economist.com/node/21533411

The Guardian. "Anger as Tunisia Grants Amnesty to Officials Accused of Corruption." September 15, 2017. https://www.theguardian.com/world/2017/sep/15/anger-as-tunisia-grants-amnesty-to-officials-accused-of-corruption

The Guardian. "Egypt Set for Mass Protest as Army Rules out Force." January 31, 2011. https://www.theguardian.com/world/2011/jan/31/egyptian-army-pledges-no-force

The Guardian. "Hosni Mubarak's Speech." February 2, 2011. https://www.theguardian.com/world/2011/feb/02/president-hosni-mubarak-egypt-speech

The Guardian. "Morsi's Supporters Clash with Protestors outside Presidential Palace in Cairo." December 5, 2012. https://www.theguardian.com/world/2012/dec/05/morsi-supporters-protest-presidential-palace-cairo

The Guardian. "Tunisian Prime Minister, Mohammed Ghannouichi Resigns amid Unrest." February 27, 2011. https://www.theguardian.com/world/2011/feb/27/tunisian-prime-minister-ghannouchi-resigns

The Guardian. "US Embassy Cables: Finding a Successor to Ben Ali in Tunisia." January 17, 2011. https://www.theguardian.com/world/us-embassy-cables-documents/49401

The Guardian. "US Embassy Cables: Tunisia-a U.S. Foreign Policy Conundrum." December 7, 2010. https://www.theguardian.com/world/us-embassy-cables-documents/217138

The International Bank for Reconstruction and Development/World Bank. *Unlocking the Employment Potential in the Middle East and North Africa: Toward a New Social Contract*. Washington, DC, 2004.

The New Arab. "A Timeline for Tunisia's Revolution." January 13, 2015. https://www.alaraby.co.uk/english/blog/2015/1/13/a-timeline-for-tunisias-revolution

The New Constitution of the Arab Republic of Egypt. 2012. http://www.constitutionnet. org/sites/ default/files/final_constitution_30_nov_2012_-english-_-idea .pdf

The New York Times. "Egyptian Voters Approve Constitutional Changes." March 20, 2011. http://www.nytimes.com/2011/03/21/world/middleeast/21egypt.html?mcubz=0

The Tahrir Institute for Middle East Policy. "Battle of the Camel " February 2, 2011. https://timep.org/timeline/feb2-11

The World Bank. "Middle-Class Frustration Fueled the Arab Spring." October 21, 2015. http://www.worldbank.org/en/news/feature/2015/10/21/middle-class-frustration-that-fueled-the-arab-spring

The World Bank. "Most Improved in Doing Business 2008." http://www.doingbusiness.org/Reforms/Top-reformers-2008

UNData. "Country Profile: Egypt & Tunisia." http://data.un.org/CountryProfile.aspx?crName

UNICEF. "Egypt: Statistics." 2012. https://www.unicef.org/infobycountry/egypt_statistics.html

UNICEF. "Tunisia: Statistics." 2012. https://www.unicef.org/infobycountry/Tunisia_statistics.html

United Nations Development Program. "Egypt Human Development Report." 2008.

Valenzuela, J. Samuel. "Democratic Consolidation in Post-Transitional Settings: Notion, Process and Facilitating Conditions." *Kellogg Institute*, Working Paper 150 (December 1990): 1–38.

Waterbury, John. *The Egypt of Nasser and Sadat: The Political Economy of Two Regimes*. Princeton, NJ: Princeton University Press, 1983.

Way, Lucan. "Comparing the Arab Revolts: The Lessons of 1989." *Journal of Democracy* 22, no. 4 (October 2011): 13–23.

Weaver, Matthew, Paul Owen, and Tom McCarthy. "Egypt Protests: Army Issues 48-Hour Ultimatum-As it Happened." *The Guardian*, July 1, 2013. https://www.theguardian.com/world/middle-east-live/2013/jul/01/egypt-stanoff-millions-protest

Weber, Peter C. "Modernity, Civil Society and Sectarianism: The Egyptian Muslim Brotherhood and the Takfir Groups." *Voluntas* 24, no. 2 (June 2013): 509–527.

Werr, Patrick, and Andrew Torchia. "Analysis: New Egypt Government May Promote Welfare, Not Economic Reform." *Reuters*, July 17, 2013. https://www.reuters.com/article/us-egypt-economy-policy-analysis /analysis-new-egypt-government-may-promote-welfare-not-economic-reform-idUSBRE96G0IP20130717

Whitehead, Laurence. *Democratization: Theory and Experience*. Oxford: Oxford University Press, 2002.

Wickham, Carrie Rosefsky. "The Path to Moderation: Strategy and Learning in the Formation of Egypt's Wasat Party." *Comparative Politics* 36, no. 2 (January 2004): 205–28.

Williams, Daniel. "Egypt Extends 25-Year-Old Emergency Law." *Washington Post*, May 1, 2006. http://www.washingtonpost.com/wp-dyn/content/article/2006/04/30/AR200604300 1039 .html

Williamson, Scott, and Nathan J. Brown. "Egypt's New Law for Parliamentary Elections Sets up a Weak Legislature." *Atlantic Council*, June 24, 2014. http://www.atlanticcouncil.org/blogs/mena source/egypt-s-new-law-for-parliamentary-elections-sets-up-a-weak-legislature

Willis, Michael. "Political Parties in the Maghrib: The Illusion of Significance?" *The Journal of North African Studies* 7, no. 2 (2002): 1–22.

Wilson, Willow. "From Virginity Test to Power." *The Guardian*, September 3, 2012. https://www.theguardian.com/lifeandstyle/2012/sep/03/virginity-test-to-power

World Bank. "GDP Growth Annual-Egypt, Arab Republic." https://data.worldbank.org/indicator/NY.GDP.MKTP.KD.ZG?locations=EG

World Bank. "GDP Growth Annual-Tunisia." https://data.worldbank.org/indicator/NY.GDP.MKTP.KD.ZG?locations=TN

Yousfi, Hela. "The Tunisian Revolution: Narratives of the Tunisian General Labour Union." In *The Routledge Handbook of the Arab Spring*, edited by Larbi Sadiki, 319–330. Milton Park: Routledge, 2015.

Zogby Research Services. "After Tahrir: Egyptians Assess Their Government, Their Institutions and Their Future." June 2013. https://static1.squarespace.com/static/52750dd3e4b08c252c 723404/t/52928b8de4b070ad 8eec181e/1385335693242/Egypt+June+2013+FINAL.pdf

Index

9/11, 48

activism, street, 173, 196, 221; civil society, 193, 221; grassroots, 177; Islamist, 195; labor, 199; union, 198
Afek Tounes, 66
African Union, 30
Afrobarometer, 28
agency-centered approach, 6, 22
Al-Adly, Habib, 98
Al-Azhar, 120, 123, 129, 130, 132
Al-Nour Party, 113, 119, 120, 184, 221
Al-Qaeda, 48, 71, 74
Al-Selmi document, 110, 176, 179, 190
Al-Sisi, Abdel Fattah, 116, 191; authoritarianism, 135–38; counterrevolution, 139, 140, 204; coup, 130; financial aid to, 205; the new election system, 134; the political roadmap under, 131–33; the US, 204
amnesty, of 1989 under Ben Ali, 44; to Ben Ali era officials under Essebsi, 70; Essebsi's proposal of, 71; to political prisoners after Ben Ali's fall, 53, 73
Amnesty International, 58, 101, 102, 104, 147
ancien regime, 84, 135, 191
Ansar Al-Sharia Tunisia (AST), 71

anti-terrorism law, of 1992 under Mubarak, 96
April 6 movement, 102, 104, 115, 129, 130, 139, 196
Arab Barometer, 29, 33, 200
Arab Forum for Alternatives, 205
Arab-Israeli conflict, 31
Arab-Israeli war, 86, 92
Arab League, 31, 93
Arab nationalism, 92, 141
Arab Opinion Index, 67
Arab socialism, 37, 83, 92
Arab Socialist Union (ASU), 93
army, Tunisian, 52, 184, 188, 189; the 2013 constitution of Egypt, 131; 2015 elections, 134; coup, 4, 136, 137; during popular protests in Egypt, 105, 106; Egyptian, 92, 189, 220; Egyptian transition, 116, 127; the new NGO law in Egypt, 139; support for protests, 188
Assembly of the Representatives of the People (ARP), 66
Associations Law, 96, 193
austerity measures, 37–39, 70, 160
authoritarianism, 4, 16, 19, 21, 166, 167, 182, 191; the 2012 constitution in Egypt, 122; Arab Spring, 155; Ben Ali's rule, 44, 45, 49; break with, 62, 67, 83, 91, 92, 126; civil society,

195, 221; Ghannouichi government, 53; Morsi, 117, 127; rentier effect, 29; reversion to, 62, 67, 73, 74, 216, 217, 219; Sisi, 131, 134, 135, 162, 215, 222; Tunisian constitution of 1957, 54
authoritarian upgrading, 91, 193

Bahrain, 2, 32, 155
balance of power, 31, 168, 183, 205
Bardo National Museum attack, 71
Bayat, Asaf, 35
Belaid, Chokri, 60–62, 181
beltagaya, 128
Ben Achour, Yadh, 52, 55
Ben Achour Commission, 55, 161, 196
Ben Ali, Zine el-Abidine, 2, 6, 16, 28, 41; civil society, 194–96, 198; corruption, 39, 46, 50, 61, 69, 70; during Tunisian protests, 50–53; economic liberalization, 39, 45, 159; following the fall of, 56, 57, 62, 63, 161, 171, 173, 177, 184, 219, 221; military, 188, 189, 220; Nidaa Tounes, 67, 68, 73; opposition to, 49; police state, 71, 72; political Islam, 48, 160; political liberalization, 38, 43, 45, 48, 158; RCD, 55, 61; Tunisian economy, 38; Tunisian politics, 41, 43–47, 158; Tunisian revolution, 35, 36; the West, 201, 202; women rights, 58
Ben Gardane strikes, 198
blasphemy, 58, 124, 127, 132, 218
Bouazizi, Mohammed, 2, 36, 39, 50, 103, 198
Bourguiba, Habib, 36; army, 188, 189, 220; authoritarianism, 47, 48; the National Pact, 44; Nidaa Tounes, 67, 72; political, social and economic reforms under, 41, 42; secular state, 41, 160; social crisis, 43; Tunisian economy, 37–38; UGTT, 198; women rights, 58

Bourguibaism, 41, 61
Brahmi, Mohammed, 62
Bread, freedom, social justice, 3, 90
Bread Riots, 37, 40, 160, 198

A Call from Tunis, 195
Camp David Accords, 93, 96, 204
casualties, during the Tunisian uprisings, 53; during the Egyptian uprisings, 104
censorship, 16, 72, 96
civil society, 3, 6, 156, 158, 167, 168, 192; Arab world, 193; democratic divergence between Tunisia and Egypt, 217–19, 221, 222; in Egypt, 91, 95, 99; Egyptian transition, 108, 110, 112, 124, 126, 162, 175, 180; international influence, 200, 202; the Quartet, 63; in Tunisia, 43, 44, 46, 184; Tunisia and Egypt, 194–99; Tunisian transition, 52–55, 62, 70, 74, 161, 162, 171; under Sisi, 135, 136, 139, 191
Civil Society Organization (CSO), 193, 194, 196, 199
civil wars, 2, 140, 155, 215
Cold War, 1, 192, 200
colonialism, 3, 200
Confédération Générale du Travail (CGT), 197, 198
Congrès pour la République (CPR), 56, 57, 66, 172, 195
consensual politics, 68, 171, 219, 220
constitutional drafting, 6, 216; in Egypt, 84, 118, 120, 121, 125, 180, 217; in Tunisia, 73, 160, 161, 203, 218, 221
Coptic, Christians, 32, 128, 147, 184; churches, 112, 120, 121, 129, 130
counterrevolution, 129, 131, 135, 139
counterrevolutionary forces, 155, 205, 216
counterterrorism law of 2015, Egypt, 138; Tunisia, 71
coup d'état. *See* military coup

debts, 87; credit card, 40; external, 37, 38, 88, 89, 140; public, 70
Declaration of the Fundamental Principles of the New Egyptian State. *See* Al-Selmi document
deep state, in Egypt, 128, 129, 131, 137, 179, 183–85
democratic consolidation, 5, 14, 15; Tunisia, 69, 162, 186, 216
Democratic Patriots Movement, 60
democratic reforms, 95, 104, 155, 203
democratic transition, 1, 4, 5, 13–15, 18, 20, 22, 23, 215, 216; in the Arab Middle East, 27, 30–32; civil society, 192–94, 196, 199; Egypt's failed, 135, 155; external influence, 200, 201; institutional endowment, 185–87, 190, 191; Tunisia, 36, 52, 55, 74; Tunisia and Egypt, 161–63, 165–74, 181, 217–19, 221
Destourians, 61
Diamond, Larry, 29, 192
domino effect, 35

economic development, 3, 5, 6; democracy, 17, 20, 21; democratization, 12, 163, 164, 166, 167; military in Egypt, 187; in Tunisia under Ben Ali, 40, 43, 44; USAID assistance to Egypt's, 204
economic liberalization, Ben Ali, 39, 45, 159; Mubarak, 91, 159, 199
Egyptian military, 112, 131, 189
Egyptian Trade Union Federation (ETUF), 199
El-Baradei, Mohamed, 144
electoral authoritarianism, 19, 131, 135
electoral fraud, under Mubarak's rule, 96, 101
electoral law, drafted by Ben Achour Commission in Tunisia, 55, 218; of 1984 under Mubarak, 94, 95; of 2014 in Tunisia, 66; amendments to (under the SCAF), 109, 112, 162; Quartet

63; the Supreme Constitutional Court, 190; under Sisi, 133, 134, 152
elite consensus, 6, 168, 175, 217
emergency law, imposed by Sadat, 91; petition against, 98; Sisi, 191; Tunisia, 72; under Mubarak, 96
Ennahda, 4; 2011 elections, 56, 160, 172, 183; 2014 elections, 66–68, 174; assassination of Belaid, 61; assassination of Brahmi, 62; crackdown on, 45, 53; criticism to Essebsi government, 72; national dialogue, 181; the new constitution, 54, 57–60; opposition to, 63; political consensus, 64, 65; political Islam, 28, 44, 177–79, 183, 218; *Sharia*, 57, 65, 180; Tunisian transition, 73, 173, 174, 176, 184, 195, 197, 219–21
Essebsi, Beji Caid, 53, 61, 67, 68, 70–73, 174
Essebsi, Hafedh Caid, 68
Ettakatol, 56, 57, 172, 195
European Union (EU), 201–4
exceptionalism, Arab, 1; cultural, 27, 29; Tunisian, 42
external factors, 156, 200
external influence, 168, 200, 201, 205

Finance Act of 2018, 70
financial aid, 30, 189, 200–205, 222
financial crisis, 87, 159
First-Past-the-Post (FPTP), 55
food prices, 40, 85, 88
foreign aid, 30; Mubarak, 87, 91; Sadat, 86; the US, 204
France, 41, 172, 195, 198, 202, 203
Freedom and Justice Party (FJP), electoral victory, 113–14; Ennahda, 160, 180, 183–84; the new Constituent Assembly, 119; the new constitution, 121, 126; opposition to, 128; in presidential elections, 114; prosecution of, 136; public support

of, 126; rift with the Egyptian
military, 114
Freedom House, 19, 27, 35, 68
freedom of association, 11; Mubarak,
96; Sisi, 137, 138; under the new
Tunisian constitution, 65
freedom of expression, 11; the 2012
constitution of Egypt, 124; Ben Ali,
44, 48, 72; Mubarak, 96; Sadat, 93;
under Sisi, 138, 204
Free Officers Coup, 83, 92, 189
fulool, 128
fundamentalist, threat, 47, 48; Jihadist
groups, 62

Gafsa riots, 40, 198
Gama'a al-Islamiyya, 94, 95, 129
GDP growth, in Tunisia, 38, 165; in
Egypt, 88, 90, 128, 165
GDP per capita, Tunisian, 38, 50;
Egyptian, 165
Ghannouichi, Mohammed, 52;
government, 53
Ghannouichi, Rachid, the new Tunisian
constitution, 54, 57; leadership, 177–
79, 181, 220; National Constituent
Assembly, 56
Guidance Bureau, 177
Gulf Cooperation Council, 30
Gulf States, 21, 87, 91, 93, 165, 202,
205

Hached, Farhat, 198
Hamas, 201
Hammami, Hamma, 62
Hezbollah, 201
Higher Authority for the Realization
of the Objectives of Revolution,
Political Reform, and Democratic
Transition, 52, 171, 172, 219
human rights, 14, 194, 201; abuses
under Sisi regime, 139, 191, 204,
205; activists, 102, 127, 138;
derogation under the SCAF's rule,
111, 112; Morsi, 127; organizations

in Tunisia, 41, 42, 58, 63; under
Ben Ali's rule, 43, 44, 48, 196, 202;
violations under Mubarak's rule, 98,
99, 101, 126, 195, 203
Human Rights Watch, 102, 111, 136
hybrid regimes, 19, 166, 192

ideological moderation, 219
imprisonment, of Islamists in Tunisia,
44, 71; of Ayman Nour, 101; of
Hamadi Jabali, 78; of journalists and
human rights activists in Tunisia, 49;
of journalists during Mubarak era, 96
Independent Commission for Election
Review (ICER), 95
inequality, 20, 70, 85, 87, 160
infitah policy, 37
inflation, 38, 70, 85, 86, 88, 90, 140,
166
instability, 3, 37, 63, 128, 135, 140, 155,
166, 181, 216, 219
Instance Supérieure Indépendante pour
les Elections (ISIE), 66, 172
institutional endowment, 168, 175, 217,
220, 222
institutionalism, 14; military, 187
International Monetary Fund (IMF), 38,
87, 88, 90, 94, 140, 159
International Republican Institute (IRI),
70, 112, 147
Iran, 3, 23, 31, 32, 205
Iraq, 32, 71, 200, 201
Islamic Alliance, 94
Islamic fundamentalism, 201
Islamic Jihad, 94
Islamic State of Iraq and Syria (ISIS),
71, 74
Islam is the solution, 94, 177
Israel, 90, 92–94, 116, 188, 201, 204,
222
Israeli-Palestinian conflict, 189, 201
Israeli security, 83, 201

Jabali, Hamadi, 56, 60, 61, 78, 172
jihadist group(s), 62, 71, 72, 191

Jomaa, Mehdi, 63, 68
June 17 Supplementary Constitutional Declaration, 115, 116

Kasserine, attacks in, 71
Kefaya movement, 98–100, 104, 129, 196
Kemalist revolution, 35
Kuwait, 140, 205

labor unions, 43, 157, 175, 182, 183, 192, 194, 195, 197, 199, 221
Larayedh, Ali, 60
Law on Access to Information and the Law on Reporting Corruption cases and Protecting Whistleblowers, 69
League of Arab States, 30
Leagues for the Protection of the Revolution, 60
liberal autocracy under Mubarak, 131
Libya, 2, 32, 36, 39, 40, 71
Ligue Tunisienne de Droits de l'Homme (LTDH)-Tunisian Human Rights League, 42, 63, 197
Lippman, Walter, 182
Lipset, Seymour Martin, 20, 21, 163, 164
l'Union Tunisienne de l'Industrie, du Commerce et de l'Artisanat (UTICA), 61, 63, 197

Mansour, Adly, 130, 132, 133, 137
March 30 Constitutional Declaration, 107–9, 114, 118, 119, 182
Marzouki, Moncef, 56, 57, 172
media, 11; in Egypt, 95–99, 102, 104, 105, 107, 126–30, 135, 136, 138; social, 157, 158; in Tunisia, 45, 48, 49, 51, 60, 72, 74, 79
middle class, 21, 164; cooptation of, 160; democratic divergence, 165; Egypt, 87, 165; in Tunisia, 40, 163, 165
Middle East and North Africa (MENA), 1; civil society in, 193; democratic deficit in, 27, 32, 35; democratic transition in, 216; Egyptian economy in, 88; elite consensus in, 170; foreign aid to, 30; institutional endowment in, 185; political liberalization in, 45; support for democracy in, 28, 29; Tunisian economy in, 38–39
Middle East Partnership Initiative (MEPI), 202
Middle East Response Fund (MERF), 202
military aid, 30; to Egypt, 204; to Tunisia, 202; the US, 83, 205
military authoritarianism, 155, 162
military coup, 2; in Egypt, 84, 125, 131, 133, 136, 155, 175, 180, 183, 186–88, 191, 203, 204, 215
military trials, during Mubarak's rule, 111; of civilians in the 2012 constitution, 121, 126, 191
Millennium Challenge Corporation (MCC), 203
minorities, 10, 16, 28, 170; in 2012 constitution in Egypt, 124; in 2013 constitution in Egypt, 132, 133; in Tunisia, 178
modernization theory, 6, 20, 21, 163–66
Morsi, Mohammed, presidential election, 114, 115; 2012 constitution, 132; deep state, 184; following the fall of, 133, 136; foreign policy, 205; leadership, 177, 179, 180–82, 220; military coup, 130, 131, 191; November Decree, 117, 118, 121, 125, 180; opposition to, 125–29, 135, 176; rise to power, 116; the US, 204
Mouvement de la Tendance Islamique (MTI), 43, 44
Mubarak, Gamal, 89, 90, 98, 105, 159
Mubarak, Hosni, 2, 4, 6, 16, 28, 32, 83; 1971 constitution, 108; 2007 constitutional amendment, 109; civil society and labor unions, 194–96, 199; corruption charges against, 90;

during the popular protests, 104–6;
Egypt's economy, 88, 89, 159;
following the ouster of, 112–15,
117, 121, 125–31, 133–35, 137,
139, 140, 162, 175, 176, 179, 183,
184, 190, 191, 203, 204, 220, 221;
the Gulf States, 205; Islamists, 91,
94–96, 160, 177; open-door policy,
87; opposition to, 99–102; ouster of,
112; political legitimacy, 84, 85, 103;
political liberalization, 91, 93, 94,
158, 160; political repression, 97, 98;
popular protests against, 101, 102;
resignation of, 107; trial of, 110, 111

mukhabarat state, 47, 91, 142

Muslim Brotherhood (MB), 4, 28,
32, 83; association with Islamic
extremism, 95; constitutional
amendments under Mubarak, 101,
103; constitutional declaration under
the SCAF, 107, 109; constitutional
drafting in post-Mubarak era,
116, 118–20; during the Egyptian
uprisings, 105; elections under
Mubarak, 94, 97, 100; Ennahda, 160,
163, 174, 176, 185; military coup,
136, 139; opposition to, 126–28, 130;
post-Mubarak elections, 112, 114,
115; public opinion polls about, 125;
services provided by, 94; suppression
of, 91, 96, 102

Nasser, Gamal Abdel, 83; Arab
socialism, 37; authoritarianism, 92;
economy policies, 86, 87; labor
unions, 199; nationalization, 85, 92,
189; pan Arabism, 31, 92; political
legitimacy, 93, 160

National Association for Change
(NAC), 104

National Authority for the Regulation
of Nongovernmental Foreign
Organizations, 96

National Coalition for Supporting
Legitimacy, 130

National Constituent Assembly (NCA),
2011 elections, 55–56; democratic
transition, 161, 196, 197; the
new constitution, 64–65; political
crisis in, 62, 63; rifts over the new
constitution in, 57–59

National Democratic Party (NDP), 84,
89, 93–100, 103, 105, 107, 110, 111,
158, 183

national dialogue, 6, 63, 68, 73, 108,
118, 130, 162, 173, 174, 181, 197,
198, 222

nationalism, Bourguiba, 41; Arab, 92,
141; Egypt, 83

nationalization, 85, 92

National Pact, under Bourguiba, 44

National Salvation Front (NSF),
formation of, 62, 117; anti-Morsi
mobilization, 129, 130, 180, 194

national unity, 3, 31; 2012 constitution
of Egypt, 117; balance of power,
182; government in Tunisia, 69, 70;
political tensions, 161

Nidaa Tounes, 61, 62, 66–68, 73, 74,
174, 176

Nobel Peace Prize, 64, 144

Nongovernmental Associations Law,
under Mubarak, 96; ratified by Sisi,
138, 139

Non-governmental Organization (NGO),
57, 58, 96, 112, 126, 138, 139, 158,
195

Nour, Ayman, 101

November Decree, 116–18, 121, 125,
126, 180

October 18 Coalition, 174, 196

O'Donnell, Guillermo, and Schmitter,
Philippe, 10, 16, 17, 23, 170, 208

Official Development Assistance
(ODA), 202–3

oil curse, 29

oil rents, 30

Okba Ibn Nafaa, 71

opinion polls, 28, 125, 138, 190

Ordre National des Avocats de Tunisie (ONAT), 63, 197
Organization for Economic Cooperation and Development (OECD), 202–3
Overseas Private Investment Corporation (OPIC), 203

pact-making, 170, 173, 191
pan-Arabism, 31, 92
Parti Socialiste Destourien (PSD), 44
personal status law, under Bourguiba, 42
Pew Research Center, 85, 125, 128, 141, 165, 166
police state, 48, 61, 71, 72, 98, 114, 139
political crisis, Tunisia, 43, 60, 61, 181, 197, 198, 220, 221; Egypt, 100, 118, 191
political Islam, 31; Ben Ali, 48; elections in the Levant, 201; Ghannouichi, 178, 183; movements, 6, 28, 29, 57; Muslim Brotherhood, 136; Tunisia and Egypt, 219
political legitimacy, 17, 38, 84, 160, 161, 205, 218
political liberalization, 16, 23, 158; Ben Ali, 38, 43, 45, 48, 158; Mubarak, 91, 93, 158, 160
political society, 195, 196
political stability, 40, 49, 71, 74, 166
Popular Front for the Realization of the Objectives of the Revolution, 62, 80
popular protests, 2–4, 6, 27, 156, 157, 185, 215, 216
power equilibrium, 6, 156, 182, 183
press law, Ben Ali, 43; Mubarak, 96
privatization, 38, 39, 49, 87–89, 102, 159, 198, 199
procedural democracy, 10
Progressive Democratic Party (PDP), 56, 195
proportional representation (PR), 55–56, 112, 134
Przeworski, Adam, 18, 22

public sector, 37, 39, 85–89, 92, 97, 102, 128, 159

Qatar, 130, 205
Quartet, 63, 64, 181, 197

Raba'a Al-Adawiya, massacre, 136, 137
radical Islamism, 30, 98
radicalism, 71, 114
Rassemblement Constitutionnel Démocratique (RCD), 46, 47, 51–53, 55, 61, 72, 73, 173
Reconciliation Law, 70
regional disparity, 40
religious freedom, 42, 72
rentier state, 29, 91
repression, 16, 17, 30, 36, 158, 167, 187, 205; Egypt, 83, 91; of Ennahda, 45; of media under Ben Ali's rule, 49; of the Muslim Brotherhood, 102; of the opposition under Ben Ali's rule, 50, 72; under Mubarak's rule, 95, 98, 100, 101, 104, 160; under Sisi regime, 137; of the unions in Tunisia, 43
resistance, Ennahda, 52, 160; against Morsi's policies, 117, 128, 179; against the Muslim Brotherhood, 160; authoritarian, 200; to change, 167; to dictatorship, 195; fighters led by Bourguiba, 188; from old guards in Tunisia, 162; of militaries, 187; UGTT, 198
revenue streams, 30, 91
reversion, to authoritarianism, 162, 167; *ancien* regime, 191; old regime, 168
Revolutionary Command Council (RCC), 92
Rustow, Dankwart, 31, 166

Sadat, Anwar, 83, 131, 218; assassination of, 93, 96; economic liberalization, 87, 92; foreign policy, 92; Islamists, 91, 94; open-door

policy, 86, 159; treaty of peace with Israel, 93
Salafists, Tunisia, 57, 67, 72; Egypt, 111, 113, 120, 131, 180, 184, 221
Saudi Arabia, 3, 32, 51, 130, 140, 201, 205
sectarianization, 32
secularism, 164
secularists, Tunisia, 56, 59, 60; Egypt, 113, 132, 176; Nidaa Tounes, 61
seculars, 4, 67, 114, 157, 161, 171–73, 179, 183
secular state, 48, 62, 65
security forces, 11–30; in Egypt, 84, 98, 102–4, 127–30, 136, 137, 175; in Tunisia, 68, 71, 72, 188, 194
self-immolation, 2, 36, 39, 50, 198
Shafiq, Ahmed, 90, 114, 115, 145
Sharia, 28, 216, 218; Egyptian constitution, 123, 132, 160, 174, 177, 181; Tunisian constitution, 57, 65, 180
Shia, Egyptian, 124, 157
Shura, 28, 44
Shura Council, 95, 108, 113, 117–20, 122, 133
single mothers, the new Tunisian constitution, 58
socioeconomic development, 5, 163, 166
Soviet Union, 1, 19, 46, 86, 92
state of emergency, Ben Ali, 51, 72; 2012 constitution of Egypt, 122; Essebsi, 71; Mubarak, 87, 91, 96, 98, 99, 102, 103; under the SCAF, 107, 110, 111
Stepan, Alfred, 172, 190, 191, 195; Linz, Juan, 13, 15, 17, 171
strategic approach, 20, 22, 24, 26
strikes, 3, 38, 49, 50, 72, 104, 106, 112, 160, 198
Structural Adjustment Program (SAP), 38, 87
structural approach, 20, 21, 156, 163, 217

subsidies, 37, 43, 85–89, 93, 109, 128, 160
substantive democracy, 11, 12
Suez Canal, 85, 87, 91–93, 130, 201, 204, 222
Suleiman, Omar, 104–6
Sunni, doctrine, 83, 123; Arabs, 157; coalition, 205
Supreme Administrative Court (SAC), 111
Supreme Constitutional Court (SCC), 114–16, 118, 121–22, 128, 130
Supreme Court of the Armed Forces (SCAF), 84–106; alliance with the Muslim Brotherhood, 175, 176, 182; constitutional drafting, 119, 121, 122, 124, 128, 132; overthrow of the Egyptian revolution, 184, 188–91, 194, 196, 220; takeover of power, 107–16
Supreme Judicial Council, Egypt, 65
surveillance, 47, 48, 60, 72, 91, 142, 183
Syria, 2, 32, 36, 71, 92, 93, 98, 140, 155, 157, 193, 215

Tamarod, 129, 130, 183, 194
Tantawi, Hussein, 106, 107, 115, 116
terrorist attacks, democracy, 15; in Tunisia, 61, 67, 71, 74, 82; under the SCAF's rule, 112, 140, 147, 182, 194
timeline, of the key events during the Tunisian revolution, 51, 52; of the key events during the Egyptian revolution, 105, 106, 108, 117
Trabelsi, family, 39, 49, 159; Leila, 49, 50
trade unions, 54, 96, 164, 173, 194
transition theory, 22, 156, 168
troika, 56, 57, 62, 67, 73, 172, 173, 197
Tunisian military, 188, 189, 220, 222
Turkey, 29, 35

tutelage, 161, 172, 196; military, 162, 176, 186
tutelary democracy, 16
twin tolerations, 173

unemployment, 37, 39, 48, 49, 51, 60, 62, 69, 70, 90, 126, 166
Union for Tunisia, 62, 80
Union Générale Tunisienne du Travail (UGTT), *infitah* policy, 37; during the Tunisian revolution, 53, 54. Gafsa riots, 40, 41; historical role and legitimacy, 198 national dialogue, 181, 184, 197; the new constitution, 58; political crisis, 61–63
Union Patriotique Libre (UPL), 66, 174

United Arab Emirates (UAE), 3, 130, 140, 203, 205
United Arab Republic, 92
United States (US), 30, 32, 48, 60, 83, 87, 91, 93, 94, 101, 112, 189, 200–205, 222
United States Agency for International Development (USAID), 202, 204

War on terror, 48
Wikileaks, 48

Yemen, 2, 3, 32, 36, 140, 155, 157, 200, 215
Yom Kippur War, 93

Zogby Research Services, 126

About the Author

Ayfer Erdogan is Dr. Lecturer of modern languages at Yildiz Technical University, Istanbul. She holds an MA degree in politics and international studies with specialization in Eurasian studies from Uppsala University, and a PhD in international relations and political science from Yildiz Technical University. She has published widely on Middle Eastern politics, democratic transitions, political Islam, and civil society.

www.ingramcontent.com/pod-product-compliance
Lightning Source LLC
Chambersburg PA
CBHW020113010526
44115CB00008B/816